# Risk Quantitation and Regulatory Policy

*Row 1:* J. Peto; M. Corn, R.E. Albert, B.D. Goldstein.
*Row 2:* P.W. Preuss; R.A. Merrill; F.P. Perera; M.C. Pike.
*Row 3:* I.F.H. Purchase; I.B. Weinstein, R. Wilson; J. Van Ryzin; R.H. Reitz.
*Row 4:* P.J. Landrigan; L.B. Lave; J.A. Swenberg; M.F. Lyon, J.V. Neel.

# Risk Quantitation and Regulatory Policy

Edited by

**DAVID G. HOEL**
National Institute of Environmental Health Sciences

**RICHARD A. MERRILL**
School of Law
University of Virginia

**FREDERICA P. PERERA**
School of Public Health
Columbia University

COLD SPRING HARBOR LABORATORY
1985

## BANBURY REPORT SERIES

Printed in the United States of America
Cover and book design by Emily Harste

**Library of Congress Cataloging in Publication Data**
Main entry under title:

Risk quantitation and regulatory policy.

(Banbury Report, ISSN 0198-0068 ; 19)
Bibliography: p.
Includes index.
1. Toxicology–Mathematical models–Congresses.
2. Risk management–Mathematical models–Congresses.
3. Epidemiology–Mathematical models–Congresses.
4. Environmental health–Government policy–United
States–Decision making–Congresses.   I. Hoel, David G.
II. Merrill, Richard A.   III. Perera, Frederica P.
IV. Series.
RA1199.R57    1985      363.1'79      85-3803
ISBN 0-87969-219-7

# Participants

**Roy E. Albert,** Institute of Environmental Medicine, New York University Medical Center

**Murray Steven Cohn,** Directorate for Health Sciences, Consumer Product Safety Commission

**Morton Corn,** School of Hygiene and Public Health, The Johns Hopkins University

**Robert L. Dedrick,** Biomedical Engineering and Instrumentation Branch, Division of Research Services, National Institutes of Health

**James R. Gillette,** National Heart, Lung, and Blood Institute, National Institutes of Health

**Bernard D. Goldstein,** Environmental Protection Agency

**Michael D. Hogan,** National Institute of Environmental Health Sciences

**Peter Barton Hutt,** Covington & Burling, Washington, D.C.

**John Kaldor,** International Agency for Research on Cancer, Lyon, France

**Richard A. Kimerle,** Monsanto Company

**Philip J. Landrigan,** National Institute for Occupational Safety and Health

**Lester B. Lave,** Graduate School of Industrial Administration, Carnegie-Mellon University

**Mary F. Lyon,** MRC Radiobiology Unit, Harwell, Didcot, Oxon, England

**Richard A. Merrill,** School of Law, University of Virginia

**James V. Neel,** Department of Genetics, University of Michigan Medical School

**Frederica P. Perera,** Division of Environmental Sciences, School of Public Health, Columbia University

**Julian Peto,** Section of Epidemiology, Institute of Cancer Research, Sutton, England

**Malcolm C. Pike,** Imperial Cancer Research Fund, University of Oxford, Radcliffe Infirmary, Oxford, England

**Peter W. Preuss,** Directorate for Health Sciences, Consumer Product Safety Commission

**Iain F.H. Purchase,** Imperial Chemical Industries PLC, Cheshire, England

**Richard H. Reitz,** Toxicology Research Laboratory, Dow Chemical Company

**James A. Swenberg,** Chemical Industry Institute of Toxicology

**Michael R. Taylor,** King & Spalding, Washington, D.C.

**John Van Ryzin,** Division of Biostatistics, Columbia University

**I. Bernard Weinstein,** Division of Environmental Sciences of the School of Public Health and the Cancer Center, Columbia University

**James D. Wilson,** Monsanto Company

**Richard Wilson,** Department of Physics and Energy and Environmental Policy Center, Harvard University

# Preface

*Perhaps they have been so successful because they worry?*

Humans are very likely the only animals that worry. The well developed ability of using past experience to project present conditions into future consequences is almost a characteristic of our species. While we have been habitually engaging in such exercises, probably for millenia, there is little evidence that we, as a species, have been becoming progressively better at it. What we have clearly become much better at, however, is the ability to create ever more complex and direly portentous conditions which form the starting points for such analyses.

Over the past several decades the realization has grown that one major area deserving of worry on a very large scale is the impact of widening technological developments upon human health. The desirability of an institutional basis for health risk assessment and for subsequent action based upon such analysis has been codified in a broad range of empowering federal statutes. Risk assessment and risk management are becoming recognized as legitimate partners in the rational development of our massive technological potential. Worry on this sort of scale, however, with its extensive legal underpinnings and its broad social and economic ramifications, must be done in a commensurately compelling and reliable manner.

A physicist once observed that it was necessary to use mathematics because it was the only way in which he could convince himself that he had really thought about a problem. In the realm of risk assessment, this has almost been raised to a legal principle. Risk quantitation has become intrinsic to the regulatory process. However, as the emphasis has shifted from such things as acutely toxic chemicals, to concerns regarding chronic low-level exposure to possible teratogenic or carcinogenic substances or processes, the procedures for quantitating risk have become greatly complicated and, often, highly controversial. The statutory requirement for such quantitative evidence as part of the regulatory process, in combination with the very real impediments currently inherent in the derivation of such numbers, has been the frequent source both of public consternation and of institutional conflict.

The May, 1984 Banbury Center conference on Risk Quantitation and Regulatory Policy brought together legal, regulatory, and research representatives to consider the most efficacious ways in which the science of risk assessment might be made accessible and amenable to incorporation into regulatory policy formulations. Under consideration was the use of risk quantitation in regulatory decisionmaking, the currently available methods for identifying and quantifying human health risks, applications of the procedures involved in specific case instances, and the mechanisms for most appropriately incorporating such analyses into regulatory policy. The papers and discussions of this conference comprise the substance of this present volume.

I wish to take this opportunity to extend my thanks to Dean Richard Merrill of the University of Virginia School of Law and to Dr. David Hoel, Director of the Biometry and Risk Assessment Program of the National Institute of Environmental Health Sciences for their participation in the formulation of the conference program as well as for their efforts in joining with Dr. Frederica Perera of the Columbia University School of Public Health in the preparation of this book. I am also once again greatly indebted to the dedication and unstinting efforts of Judith Blum, the Banbury Center editor, and Bea Toliver, Banbury Center administrative assistant, for the indispensable roles played by each of them, respectively, in the production of this book and in the organization and holding of the original conference upon which it is based. It is also with pleasure that I acknowledge the great help of the U.S. Department of Energy, the Monsanto Company, and the National Distillers and Chemical Corporation for their support of this project.

**Michael Shodell**
**Director**
**Banbury Center**

# Contents

# Session 1:
# Regulatory Programs Utilizing Risk Assessment

# The Role of Quantitative Risk Assessment in Environmental Regulations

**LESTER B. LAVE**
Graduate School of Industrial Administration
Carnegie-Mellon University
Pittsburgh, Pennsylvania 15213

In one view of the world, environmental hazards are akin to smoking guns—there is a dead or wounded victim, an obvious cause, and an obvious solution. In this 1960s view, solving environmental problems is only a matter of will.

Congress embodied this simple view in the Clean Air Act, Clean Water Act, and other environmental legislation. When this caricature was obviously inapplicable, as with pesticides, Congress mandated a balancing of risk and benefit, but still saw the problem as a straightforward, somewhat simple one. Unfortunately, environmental legislation, even including the Federal Insecticide, Fungicide, and Rodenticide Act (FIFRA), embodies notions that are dysfunctional in attempting to manage complicated environmental problems.

## THE RISK MANAGEMENT PROCESS

One attempt to characterize the process for managing risks is shown in Figure 1. The crucial steps in the process are: (1) screening the tens of thousands of possible threats to find which are most important; (2) quantitative risk assessment to find the magnitude of the problem associated with alternative actions, from doing nothing to banning the offending substance; (3) economic analysis to estimate the social costs associated with implementing each alternative; and (4) formulating goals to decide which solution is preferred, given the remaining risk and the social costs of each. This paper is focused on the second, but I want to discuss the others briefly.

## Screening

There are approximately 60,000 chemicals in common use, with about 1000 new ones introduced each year (National Academy of Sciences 1984). To be useful, a screening program would have to be capable of handling all of the new chemicals and also be capable of addressing the existing chemicals within a span of 5–10 years. Furthermore, the screen would have to provide data on how long each chemical will persist in the environment and what will be the reaction products; on whether it is reconcentrated biologically or through some other mechanism; and on such biological properties as carcinogenesis, mutagenesis, teratogenesis, and the chemical's ability to cause acute or chronic disease or to produce subtle effects on

3

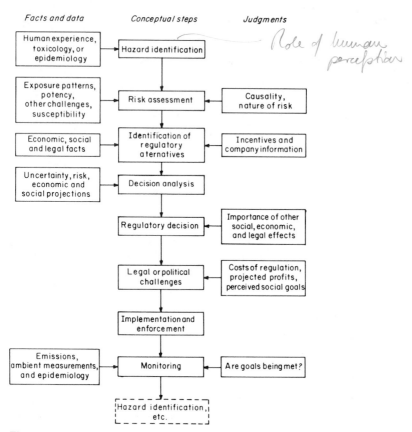

**Figure 1**
Hazard management. Reprinted, with permission, from Lave (1982).

development, learning, or libido. These data would have to be provided in no more than several weeks and at a cost of no more than perhaps $10,000 per chemical.

Long-term bioassays provide little of this information and are too time-consuming and costly to be an attractive screening tool. There are short-term tests that appear to predict carcinogenicity well. A battery of these tests appears to screen problem carcinogens with 90% accuracy and to have a cost of perhaps $5000 per chemical (L.B. Lave et al., unpubl.). Attention to this problem is warranted and is predicted to have a high payoff.

## Economic Analysis

The estimation of the social resources required to implement control is inherently uncertain. Analyses can only use currently available technologies (or perhaps those that are about to become available). However, when regulations are implemented, there is enormous incentive for research and development to find cheaper solutions. Another difficulty is that virtually all of the required data are in the hands of those to be regulated. Not only are there potential problems with how forthcoming the potential regulatees might be, but there is no easy way to check the data to ensure completeness and accuracy.

Most of these problems are inherent and little can be done. However, environmental regulation has tended to operate in an adversarial framework, with each side preparing for litigation. Even if the company should lose at influencing the regulation and then at challenging it in court, it can still control and disclose data in such a way as to minimize the necessity to comply with the regulation. Given these difficulties, it is surprising that companies ever cooperate with regulatory agencies. Such cooperation might be traced either to the public spirit of executives or perhaps to the desire of companies to use the regulatory process to protect themselves from competition.

This is one area where a less adversarial approach has much to offer. Sharing the possibilities and uncertainties would inform all sides and help to lead to better decisions. In other countries, this negotiated approach seems to work better. In Germany, in particular, committees of management, workers, and government regulators negotiate solutions to problems where there is a carcinogenic chemical that cannot be eliminated from the workplace (Delong 1983).

## FORMULATING RISK GOALS

Setting risk goals is one of my favorite topics (Lave 1981). Without some notion of goals and the desirable tradeoffs between risk reduction and social expenditures, the rest of the process is useless. Congress has addressed risk goals with the platitude of "no risk is acceptable," contradictory requirements that risks be eliminated but that the requirements be practicable, or statements about process (for example, Congress sets out a decision framework for an agency, but does not specify a risk goal). By specifying process, Congress manages to disguise the implied risk goal sufficiently to shield itself from attack, while giving the agency sufficient information that it knows, vaguely, what Congress desires. For example, Congress wrote in the Clean Air Act that the Environmental Protection Agency (EPA) was to set primary air quality standards that "protect the most sensitive group in the population with an ample margin of safety." Congress has instructed EPA in various statutes that it is to choose the "best practical control technology," the "best available control technology," or the "least achievable emission rate." In FIFRA, Congress instructed EPA to balance the risk of a pesticide against its benefit. While these risk goals are not quantitative, they certainly indicate to EPA how stringent the risk goals should be for each type of environmental problem.

Recently, three agencies took the risk of announcing quantitative risk goals. The Food and Drug Administration (FDA) announced that it would not consider a substance to be a carcinogen if it caused less than one cancer in each 1,000,000 lifetimes of those exposed. EPA put the number at one in 100,000 to one in

1,000,000. The Nuclear Regulatory Commission (NRC) announced that nuclear power should not increase the cancer death rate by 0.1%, or one additional cancer death in 1000. It is interesting that the EPA goal is less stringent than the FDA goal, and the NRC goal is a factor of 200 less stringent than the FDA goal. These goals have proven controversial; one of the NRC commissioners denounced their proposed safety goal (U.S. Nuclear Regulatory Commission 1982).

## QUANTITATIVE RISK ASSESSMENT

Happily, the subject of this volume is quantitative risk assessment, the easiest of the four major steps (U.S. Office of Technology Assessment 1981; Lave 1982; Marcus 1983). Many scientists discourse at length on the tentative theories, lack of data, and arbitrary assumptions (Interagency Regulatory Liaison Group 1980). Although these difficulties are acknowledged, the problems are small compared with the difficulties associated with the other three steps. This is a nice, tractable problem that we already have reasonable answers to, and the quality of the answers is getting better every year.

I don't want to be too cavalier in dismissing the objections of skeptics. The reasonable range of answers produced by quantitative risk assessment (QRA) is often so large that it is not helpful. The primary argument in favor of QRA is that it is a systematic, scientific approach to the problem of estimating risks. Stating the problem in scientific terms assures that critics will have a field day turning over every rock that hides an assumption or flaw. It assures that scientists will challenge every theory and propose alternatives and that scientists will challenge existing data and go out to collect their own data to test other theories. In short, treating risk estimation as a scientific venture will result in a ferment of theoretical and laboratory activity leading to advances in knowledge that will make risk estimation less uncertain over time.

I also have to admit that I speak as an academician. If I were in a sea of crises with several nipping at tender parts of my flesh, I might be tempted to rely more on accumulated years of wisdom. However, I hope I would understand why my less harassed colleagues took a longer range view.

Several years ago there were many hopes and concerns about QRA. The first was that it would solve all problems by providing the crucial information needed. By now it is evident that no one piece of information is sufficient, as Figure 1 shows. An ancillary concern was that QRA would act as a steamroller, pushing aside other concerns. Clearly, QRA has not been so important, although it does tend to highlight some risks as extremely large and others as quite small.

I remember what seemed a novel objection from a toxicologist: QRA would give too much emphasis to toxicological data and would therefore lead risk decisions astray. Although this toxicologist knows his methods and their execution better than I, there is no alternative to being arbitrary. Another concern was that QRA would be proindustry and antienvironmental. This objection always gave me pause, since it seemed to imply that using data and analysis would hurt the environmental cause. If I believed that, I would want to change my affiliation.

Instead, the real problem has been that QRA has the same problems as all scientific analysis. It is often done quickly, with too little attention to the details. Thus the result is sloppiness that might result in a bias toward over or underregulation. When that sloppiness is deliberate, as in an attempt to achieve some political objective, there are problems. More often, the problems stem from the normal human failings of trying to do too much too quickly. The end of the world is more likely to come from inattention than from malevolence.

Quantitative risk assessment is deceptively simple. All that is needed is an estimate of how much disease will occur as a result of various levels of exposure and then an estimate of current and alternative future levels of exposure. The latter can come from epidemiology, toxicology, or years of experience. The former can come from detailed field surveys or rough guesses.

Much of the squabbling has resulted from naivete about how accurately the dose-response relationship can be estimated. Even when epidemiological studies are available, there are inevitable problems with the studies. Furthermore, one is always having to extrapolate from high levels of exposure to much lower doses. More generally, the extrapolation is from a single long-term bioassay. The twin extrapolations from high to low doses and from rodents to humans are fraught with difficulties. In the absence of theory that would give a better answer, the assumptions are always made that a rat carcinogen is a human carcinogen and that response is proportional to dose (with no threshold). Neither of these assumptions is of the sort that makes one rest easy. However, both are conservative in the sense that they do not underestimate the risk to humans. Until better theories are confirmed by data, these assumptions will be used because they will not underestimate the risks to humans, although they can prove misleading in assigning priorities based on the possible harm from each substance.

The last point is worth a bit of elaboration. The standard assumptions used in QRA are meant to produce such conservative estimates of risk that it would be extraordinarily unlikely that the estimate would understate the actual risk. However, when these estimates are used for a different purpose, such as setting priorities, the results can be misleading. The assumptions could result in overestimating the risks associated with chemical A by a factor of 10,000 whereas they accurately estimate the risks of chemical B. This result could, to our regret, easily lead to the focusing on A and the neglect of B.

If the goal is setting priorities based on risk, the best approach would be to use procedures that scientists believe will estimate those risks best, rather than procedures that have greater internal validity. For example, toxicological data might suggest that a one-hit model is a good description of the risks for B, but that there seems to be a threshold for A. If so, it is foolish to disregard this information and treat both chemicals as if the linear, no threshold model were the appropriate one. More extreme cases arise when the group doing a QRA of chemical B make extreme assumptions about the route of exposure or other aspects that raise the possible risks of this chemical, relative to those of chemical A. Unfortunately, the lesson is that if risk priorities are the goal, one uses risk estimates developed for other purposes at one's peril.

## IMPROVING QRA

QRA is a relatively new tool that has not been widely used. Some people have expected it to solve all problems, as if one estimate that the risk was x would be dispositive in regulatory decisions. In fact, even if one knew the risk with certainty, other aspects of the decision, including implications for control costs and for equity, would be important. Indeed, perhaps the greatest usefulness of QRA is in responding to the Supreme Court in *Benzene* (Industrial Union Department 1980) that an agency had to find a significant risk before it could regulate (and presumably have its regulation reduce that risk). In providing an estimate of the risk level, QRA is the first necessary step in estimating whether there is a significant risk, and whether the proposed regulation lowers that risk. Furthermore, QRA allows a quantitative comparison of the residual risks among alternative proposals. Thus, it is a necessary datum in formulating regulations that are cost-effective.

At this time, there is a great deal of uncertainty associated with quantitative risk estimates. The National Academy of Sciences Saccharin Committee asserted that there was a seven orders of magnitude range between the high and low estimates of the bladder cancer risk from saccharin.

To narrow the uncertainty range in the near future requires better data. For each issue, a better estimate is needed of the dose-response relationship and individual exposures. More generally, what is needed is a better understanding of the mechanisms producing the harm. Only with such understanding can one understand whether the dose-response relationship really is linear, whether the route of exposure matters, and whether reaction products have to be considered.

In the near future, there is no substitute for better, more complete laboratory, epidemiology, and exposure data. However, these data will not sharpen the theory concerning the proper way to extrapolate to humans at low doses. Doing that requires basic science understanding of the physiological mechanisms. Although the hope of the present is better, more careful collection of data, the long-term hope is for better basic science that will sharpen data collection and allow a more powerful interpretation of what will always be too limited data. However, this is not a plea for more basic science funding to study whatever might seem interesting; rather it is a plea to have the basic researchers understand what is required and work with the risk assessors to target their efforts.

## CONCLUSION

If risk regulation is to be other than arbitrary and capricious, QRA is essential. However, decision makers have to learn more about the limitations and strengths of QRA to use the estimates properly. The approach will increase controversy in the short term, since alternative models, data interpretation, and alternative data sets will be used to derive very different risk estimates. However, the result will sharpen the modeling and data collection, leading to better risk estimation and hence better regulation.

## ACKNOWLEDGMENTS

This work was supported by a National Science Foundation grant.

## REFERENCES

Delong, J.V. 1983. A Contrast Between USA and FRG Regulation. Working Paper, Carnegie-Mellon University.

Industrial Union Department. 1980. *AFL-CIO v. American Petroleum Institute and Others.* 448 U.S. 607.

Interagency Regulatory Liaison Group. 1980. Scientific Bases for Identification of Potential Carcinogens and Estimation of Risks. In *Annual review of public health* (ed. L. Breslow et al.), vol. 1. Annual Reviews, Palo Alto, California. **1:** 345.

Lave, L. 1981. *The strategy of social regulation.* Brookings Institution, Washington, D.C.

_____. 1982. *Quantitative risk assessment in regulation.* Brookings Institution, Washington, D.C.

Marcus, G. *A review of risk assessment methodologies,* Committee on Science and Technology, 98 Congress, First Session, Serial B, U.S. G.P.O., Washington, D.C.

National Academy of Sciences. Steering Committee on Identification of Toxic and Potentially Toxic Chemicals for Consideration by the National Toxicology Program. 1984. *Toxicity testing: Strategies to determine needs and priorities.* National Academy Press, Washington, D.C.

U.S. Nuclear Regulatory Commission. 1983. *Safety goals for nuclear power plants: A discussion paper.* NUREG-0880. Washington, D.C.

U.S. Office of Technology Assessment. 1981. *Assessment of technologies of determining cancer risks from the environment.* Washington, D.C.

## COMMENTS

**PERERA:** EPA has regulated some substances on the basis of estimated lifetime cancer risks of one in one million; furthermore, the agency issues guidance to states for drinking water standards that covers risks from one in 100,000 to one in ten million. Therefore, if EPA is in fact now viewing estimated risks of one per 100,000 and greater as a prerequisite for action, this is a major policy change.

**LAVE:** EPA has different programs and statutory mandates. The statutory mandates, for example, for TSCA and FIFRA are very different from the statutory mandates for drinking water. Betty Anderson is the one who describes $10^{-5}$ or $10^{-6}$ as being the sort of criterion EPA uses to judge whether a risk is negligible. I infer that she is really talking about TSCA and FIFRA rather than about drinking water.

**PREUSS:** I have not heard $10^{-5}$ mentioned as a risk trigger before. One study, done 2 or 3 years ago, looked at FIFRA and, as I recall, found that decisions were made on pesticides at risks ranging anywhere from $10^{-4}$ to $10^{-9}$; so even in implementing that single statute, there was a tremendous inconsistency. I'm sure that throughout the program at EPA, there is not a single number, but a variety of risk factors that are used.

**LAVE:** Yes. I think there has been some attempt at attaining convergence on a single target. So far, little convergence has occurred.

**PURCHASE:** In a recent paper in *Fundamental and Applied Toxicology,* the past presidents of the Society of Toxicology pleaded that risk assessment procedures should aim towards risks which were actually measurable or close to being measurable. The figures that you have described here are inconceivable to the average person who has absolutely no concept of what a "risk of $10^{-6}$" is in his lifetime. The general public, I believe, would think it was meaningless.

**LAVE:** When I talk with less knowledgeable groups, one of the questions I ask them is what sort of safety goals they think the federal regulatory agencies are striving for. What are the risks of Love Canal or Three Mile Island? People have the impression that risk levels are on the order of one cancer in two lifetimes or one cancer in ten lifetimes. When I provide the figures for the kinds of risks that we're talking about, they almost always react in disbelief, saying, "That couldn't be right. It couldn't be that safe." Yet, if FDA and EPA set less stringent risk goals, they might face intense criticism from consumerists. The Nuclear Regulatory Commission announced a goal of an increase of no more than 0.1% in cancers due to nuclear power, i.e., one additional cancer for every 1000 current cancers. Critics claimed this goal wasn't sufficiently stringent. Even one of the NRC Commissioners attacked the proposal, saying that the proposals would condone thousands of deaths from nuclear reactors over the next 10 years.

**PURCHASE:** I'm afraid that in the whole area of safety, if you start changing goals by increasing the numerical estimate of risk, everyone immediately reacts adversely because they think that somehow they're being put at a greater risk. But by changing the risk goal from $10^{-6}$ to $10^{-4}$, there's no difference for practical purposes.

**WEINSTEIN:** Could you translate that into the number of additional deaths per year?

**LAVE:** Approximately two million people die in the United States each year, and about 18% of them die of cancer. So we have on the order of 360,000 people who die each year of cancer. If you had a risk of $10^{-6}$ per lifetime, then that would be an increase of one cancer in a million deaths; instead of having 360,000 cancer deaths each year, the U.S. would have 360,002.

**PURCHASE:** That is if the whole population of the U.S. were exposed constantly for the whole of their lifetime?

**LAVE:** Assuming the whole population were uniformly exposed over their lifetimes and assuming a uniform age distribution.

**PETO:** A risk of $10^{-6}$ is one or two deaths a year in the whole U.S. They're ridiculously low risks.

**PIKE:** They're not ridiculously low risks because they refer to only one chemical, and, moreover, what one is often hoping to achieve when regulating one compound is, in fact, to regulate through this compound a whole class of compounds, all of which might have risks associated with them. We also ought to be clear about the proper definition of time risk. The best definition is the risk of being diagnosed with the cancer by some fixed age (usually taken as 70 for man), from exposure to the compound at a fixed daily dose, in the absence of all other causes of death. This definition avoids the problem that arises, when one attempts to take into account general mortality, of the risk from the compound apparently being higher for healthier people.

**LAVE:** But there are all sorts of close approximations.

**PIKE:** Unfortunately, they are not all that close. The EPA, for example, in discussing the risk of asbestos in drinking water, where they used the sort of definition you were talking about of relating the risk to other deaths, gave an answer that is off by a factor of 100.

**GILLETTE:** Another major problem, though, is to determine whether the calculated figure is meaningful in the first place. How can you confirm that the toxicant caused one death out of two million people from this calculation when the incidence of the disease caused by all sources is much greater?

**LAVE:** No, you certainly can't. But, look, let's be a little careful. If you were setting your criteria on what is a statistically significant increase, that would be a very different standard. If you were talking about rare causes of death, such as leukemia or mesothelioma, then a few cases would constitute a significant increase in incidence. If you were talking about much more routine causes of death, lung cancer or perhaps heart disease, then you'd need huge increases in cases in order to have a significant increase.

**GILLETTE:** That's precisely the problem. One of the problems is the specificity and accuracy of the diagnosis. If someone has a very rare disease that is very obvious, a physician is likely to detect it. If someone has a disease that is not very easily diagnosed and not easily separated from other causes, the physician is not likely to detect it and thus that person is not counted. The fact is, there is no way of validating the risk assessment in the human population in these situations.

**WEINSTEIN:** However, one could do it by extrapolation. Must everything be verified on the basis of human data?

**J. WILSON:** Eventually it has to be.

**LAVE:** What you have is an estimate. The question is how close that estimate is to any kind of reality. The more you know about a mechanism, so that you're not doing a "black box" extrapolation, then the more confident you can be in your estimate. Consider analyses of nuclear or chemical plants. These often end up with probabilities of large problems on the order of $10^{-8}$. Are such calculations meaningful? The problem is not the small size of the probabilities so much as their standard errors. That is, if you estimate a risk to be one in 100,000, that estimate is not very useful if it could be as large as one in 1000 or as small as zero. I don't think the problem is that inherently a number like one in 100,000 doesn't mean anything. The problem is what are the error bars about that number.

**CORN:** I'd like to clarify the current policy of EPA; I can't speak to FDA or NRC policies. Your presentation suggests that these numbers are a trigger point for regulation. On the contrary, the EPA Administrator has asked only that all of the organizational components of the Agency provide a risk assessment as one of the components of their health hazard assessments. The Cancer Assessment Group has presented their assessments, and the Science Advisory Board has required that they put boundaries on the calculated estimates. The boundaries are very, very wide. There can be many reasons why the Agency would regulate a lesser risk. For example, intervention may be very easy, or it may be inexpensive. So these are not triggering numbers. In fact, I don't think any decision in EPA has been made on the basis of the calculation of a risk; but it's a very good additional input to the decision makers, even though it may have error bounds of $10^4$ or $10^5$. Some components of the Agency are performing quantitative risk assessments; some are not. The Administrator is asking that they all do it. At this time, there is no indication of how it will factor into any given decision.

**LAVE:** Let me say a last word. The argument for quantitative risk assessment is that in the absence of risk numbers, you are making decisions on a completely arbitrary basis. You don't have enough information to set priorities; you don't have enough information to decide that one risk is very important. The real issue is whether the current calculations mean anything. If they're the best numbers you have and they mean even a little bit, then they're the best information for regulatory decisions. They shouldn't be dispositive, but they should be used. However, it is essential to get more accurate estimates. We must tighten the error bars. That's not going to come from getting larger samples for epidemiology, or doing yet more long-term bioassays, or having more animals in the group. It's really going to come from more information about mechanisms.

# Use of Quantitative Risk Assessment in Regulatory Decisionmaking under Federal Health and Safety Statutes

**PETER BARTON HUTT**
Covington & Burling
Washington, D.C. 20044

Risk assessment and risk management are relatively new terms in the field of government regulation of health and safety. These concepts, however, have their origins in antiquity. Indeed, government regulation to protect the public health and safety represents one of the oldest forms of government control of commercial enterprise.

## FOOD AND DRUG REGULATION IN THE ANCIENT WORLD

The earliest recorded regulation of health and safety occurred to protect the public health against unsafe food. These controls, in the form of the dietary laws of Moses, were a direct reflection of judgment based upon human experience. They prohibited, for example, the use of pork or the meat of any diseased animal, undoubtedly as a result of the observation that consumption of these products frequently led to human disease.

Roman civil law included a broad edict against any form of commercial fraud. Under this law, adulteration of food or drugs constituted a civil offense, subject to government prosecution, and resulted in such punishment as condemnation to the mines or temporary exile.

It is not surprising that early laws were designed to protect against food and drug adulteration. Pliny the Elder, writing in the 1st century A.D., documented numerous examples of widespread adulteration of the food and drug supply. Pliny deplored the "avarice and luxury" of the merchants, who "spoil everything with fraudulent adulterations":

> "So many poisons are employed to force wine to suit our taste—and we are surprised that it is not wholesome!"

Other authors in ancient Greece and Rome reported similar problems.

## FOOD AND DRUG REGULATION IN ENGLAND

Early English statutes were directed primarily at assuring that a given quantity of food would be sold at a given price. Very quickly, however, it became apparent that the price of food could not be controlled without adequate regulation of food quality. Accordingly, as early as 1266, Parliament enacted the Assize of Bread, which prohibited the sale of any staple food product "that is not wholesome for Man's Body." That statute remained the law of England until 1844. It is apparent, moreover, that the more modern statutes subsequently enacted in England and later in the United States have not found better or more explicit language to convey the legislative directive to prohibit unsafe food.

Throughout the history of the Assize of Bread, however, enforcement remained subject to human experience and judgment—the same inexact factors on which the dietary laws of Moses were based. Risk assessment at that time depended solely on trial and error on humans.

## THE DAWN OF ENVIRONMENTAL EPIDEMIOLOGY

The effect of the environment on public health was the subject of one of the works of the school of Hippocrates, *Air, Water, and Places*. Other writers in ancient Greece and Rome also observed the importance of environmental factors in human health.

Although the scientific basis for the relationship of sanitation to health was not yet understood, the public water supply and sewage systems in Rome demonstrated a sound appreciation that pure water is essential to good health. English medieval laws were also designed to protect against environmental pollution.

## THE DAWN OF TOXICOLOGY

Hippocrates is credited as the founder of medicine because he related all health and disease to natural, rather than supernatural, causes. Many of the writers in ancient Greece and Rome recognized that the same substance has different effects at different levels of consumption. But it was Paracelsus, an enigmatic alchemist writing in the first half of the 16th century, who first clearly articulated the concept of a dose-response curve:

> "All substances are poison; there is none which is not a poison. The right dose differentiates a poison and a remedy."

For all its insight, however, this did not advance risk assessment or regulatory decisionmaking at all. Paracelsus correctly pointed out that there is a line that divides a safe and an unsafe dose, but he offered no criteria for determining how or where to draw the line. Thus, he merely restated the problem that existed from the time of Moses. It took almost another four centuries before the dose-response curve assumed its present importance in risk assessment.

## THE DAWN OF OCCUPATIONAL EPIDEMIOLOGY

The effect of occupation upon health was the subject of observations by writers in early Greece and Rome. The first study of occupational health, however, was the work by Paracelsus entitled *On the Miners' Sickness and Other Diseases of Miners.* A number of studies on other occupations followed, culminating in the comprehensive *Diseases of Workers* by Ramazzini in 1700, which covered 42 categories of workers (subsequently expanded to 54 categories in the second edition of 1713). In 1775, Pott ascribed cancer of the scrotum in chimney sweeps to the soot they encountered in their daily work, the first direct linkage of human cancer to a specific occupational cause through epidemiological observation.

## THE DAWN OF CHEMISTRY

Although even Pliny and his contemporaries could find gross adulteration of food and drugs, it was another 15 centuries before chemical techniques began to be developed to analyze for the presence of adulterants. Led by the landmark work of Robert Boyle in the second half of the 17th century, new tests were developed for food and drug adulteration. As the field of chemistry developed, detection of adulteration advanced beyond individual opinion—based upon such uncertain tests as burning, sight, taste, and smell—and relied instead upon objective and reproducible criteria.

These new chemical tests, in turn, led to increased public concern about the safety of the food supply. A 1760 pamphlet warned about the "destructive ingredients . . . to health" used in "eatables and drinkables." This concern culminated in the publication, in 1820, of Frederick Accum's *Treatise on Adulterations of Food and Culinary Poisons.* In that treatise, Accum described, in detail and at length, the numerous kinds of adulteration practiced on both food and drugs, and the various methods available to detect them. He documented widespread problems throughout the food and drug supply, many of which were "highly deleterious" to the public health. His treatise was an immediate and worldwide success, and galvanized scientists into further studies and legislators into the enactment of more modern laws to protect the public health and safety.

## THE RISE OF PUBLIC HEALTH LAWS

Chadwick, working in England in 1842, documented the importance of sanitation in protecting the public health. Following that lead, Shattuck issued his monumental *Report of the Sanitary Commission of Massachusetts* in 1850, documenting the decrease in average life expectancy at birth in America's large urban centers because of insanitation. Shattuck recommended enactment of statutes to control the food and drug supply as part of a broad public health approach. Following that report, boards of health were established throughout the country and regulatory controls were strengthened at the state and local level.

## EARLY AMERICAN REGULATORY STATUTES

The American colonies imported the same laws to protect the public health and safety that existed in England. After the American Revolution, moreover, these laws were reenacted and made permanent. Throughout the 19th century, protection of public health and safety was considered largely a state and local matter, and thus each jurisdiction had its own specific enactments.

As early as 1813, however, Congress enacted the first federal regulatory statute to protect the public against unsafe and ineffective smallpox vaccine. The statute lasted only until 1822 when it was repealed in an early wave of regulatory reform. In 1848, Congress enacted a new law to protect against the importation of unsafe or ineffective drug products, a law that lasted until it was superseded in 1926; and in the late 1800s Congress passed a series of laws designed to protect against the spread of illness through diseased livestock. In 1902, following the death of 11 children in St. Louis from a contaminated vaccine, Congress enacted yet another statute to require the premarketing testing and approval of all biological products, a statute that remains in force to this day.

## THE FOOD AND DRUGS ACT OF 1906

From 1879 to 1906, Congress investigated the safety of the food and drug supply and debated at length whether broad federal controls should be enacted to regulate it. In order to dramatize problems with the food supply, Dr. Harvey W. Wiley, then Director of the Bureau of Chemistry (which later became the Food and Drug Administration), established a "poison squad" of 12 young male employees of the Bureau. During 1902–1904, feeding experiments were conducted on these 12 young men using the following five preservatives that were then found in the American food supply: boric acid and borax, salicylic acid and salicylates, sulfurous acid and sulfites, benzoic acid and benzoates, and formaldehyde. Detailed records were kept on all of the subjects. The results, published in five parts during 1904–1908, provoked widespread interest throughout the country and unquestionably contributed greatly to the enactment of the 1906 law.

It is important to understand the significance of the 1902–1904 human feeding experiments on these five classes of food preservatives. As far back as the ancient world of Greece and Rome, animal experimentation was commonly practiced. Indeed, numerous erroneous theories about human anatomy were perpetrated for centuries as a result of reliance upon animal experimentation without confirmation based on human observation. Through the end of the 1800s, however, animal experimentation remained essentially an ad hoc matter. Physicians and scientists, who had now become aware of the differences in anatomy between animals and humans, distrusted animal testing as a model for judgment about human safety. There were, moreover, no uniform animal colonies on which to conduct experiments, and the concept of untreated controls and statistical evaluation had not yet been advanced. Thus, although some individual scientists stressed the use of animal testing for safety evaluation in the late 1800s, virtually all risk assessment relied on human feeding studies. When Boylston demonstrated the safety of smallpox innoculation in 1721 and Waterhouse demonstrated the safety of smallpox vaccination in 1799–1802, for example, they did their work by human experimentation.

Because of the controversies about whether the use of those preservatives tested by Wiley as well as other food ingredients violated the safety provisions of the 1906 Act, President Roosevelt appointed a five-man Referee Board of Consulting Scientific Experts in February 1908, chaired by president Ira Remsen of Johns Hopkins University, to rule on these issues. This was the first scientific regulatory advisory committee in history.

Faced with the single human feeding study on sodium benzoate, the Referee Board promptly determined that additional scientific studies were needed. Rather than turn to animal experiments, however, three of the members of the Referee Board returned to their academic institutions and proceeded to conduct three additional human feeding studies on the students at Columbia, Northwestern, and Yale. Following these additional studies, they reconvened and determined that the existing levels of sodium benzoate used in the food supply were safe.

In the *Lexington Mill* decision in 1914, the Supreme Court construed the food safety provisions of the 1906 Act in a practical and common sense way. The Court held that the Food and Drug Administration (FDA) was not required to prove that an added substance was in fact harmful, but only that there was a reasonable possibility of harm. It also held that the FDA must consider the actual conditions of use of the substance in determining whether there exists a reasonable possibility of injury to consumer health, because a small amount of an otherwise deleterious ingredient may not be harmful. This remarkable decision, reflecting a sound balance between strong consumer protection and an understanding of the dose-response curve, was explicitly retained by Congress as the controlling precedent under the 1938 Act and remains with undiluted force to this day. The holding in *Lexington Mill*, indeed, is virtually indistinguishable from the more recent decision of the Court in the Occupational Safety and Health Administration (OSHA) *Benzene* case in 1980.

## THE DEVELOPMENT OF ANIMAL TOXICITY TESTING

From Moses to Wiley, as we have seen, safety determinations were made on the basis of direct human observation. This human epidemiology included everything from random observations of daily experience, to studies of particular issues, to actual experimentation on human subjects. Not until the work of Chadwick and Shattuck in the 19th century were even crude statistical analyses attempted. Although some testing was conducted on animals, it was regarded as unreliable and insufficient for any final human safety determination.

At the same time that Wiley was conducting his human feeding experiments, however, the foundation was being laid for modern animal toxicity testing. Following the rediscovery of Mendel's principles of genetics, American scientists began during the 1910s to develop colonies of pure inbred strains of rodents, on which an enormous body of toxicological knowledge was obtained. As the Wistar, Sprague-Dawley, Osborne-Mendel, and other rat strains became available, large scale animal toxicity testing became feasible for the first time. Although the history of the development and acceptance of these colonies has not yet been written, it is apparent that the reproducibility of results on these animal colonies, and thus the ability of physicians and scientists to compare these results with human experience, ultimately overcame the earlier scientific distrust of the use of animals as models for human toxicity. Within a very short period of time, animal testing became an accepted part of toxicology. Throughout the 1930s, animal toxicity testing was common.

## THE USE OF SAFETY FACTORS

As long as safety evaluation remained primarily based upon direct observation of human experience, safety determinations were almost completely judgmental in nature. There could be no attempt at quantification of risk. One searches in vain, for example, for any analytical evaluation, or even discussion, of the elements that went into the consideration given by Wiley and the Referee Board to the determinations they made about the safety of sodium benzoate during 1904–1909.

With the advent of controlled animal experimentation, however, operational definitions of safety were for the first time feasible. The insight of Paracelsus—that the toxic response is a function of the dose—could at long last serve as the basis for regulatory decisions.

During the 1940s, FDA toxicologists and pharmacologists, led by Dr. Arnold Lehman, developed an informal safety factor for regulatory purposes. Based upon the work of colleagues in England and America, FDA concluded that there was potentially a tenfold greater sensitivity of humans than test animals, and potentially a tenfold difference in susceptibility among members of the human population, providing a safety factor of 100. A safe level for humans (now called the acceptable daily intake or ADI) was determined by dividing the lowest "no effect level" (now called the no observed effect level or NOEL) by this safety factor of 100.

The 100:1 safety factor was undoubtedly more intuitive than scientific when it was first suggested. Indeed, the FDA scientists emphasized during the 1950s, even after they had been using it for some time, that human safety determinations could not be made solely on the basis of a safety factor but must include scientific judgment as well. Since then, some have sought to demonstrate that the 100:1 safety factor has a relatively strong basis in the biological sciences, and this factor has been codified in FDA regulations and remains in widespread use throughout the world for all toxic effects which have been shown to have a threshold effect level.

## THE SPECIAL PROBLEM OF CARCINOGENS

Animal toxicity testing for carcinogenicity occurred throughout the 1930s, and as early as 1945 Berenblum pointed out that "it is frequently necessary to evaluate carcinogenic potency and neoplastic response on a quantitative basis." Even at that early date, however, knowledge about the uncertainty of a threshold for carcinogens caused the FDA to impose more stringent safety factors. The Agency initially adopted a 2000:1 and then a 5000:1 safety factor for carcinogens. By 1950, however, FDA concluded that no safety factor could be justified for a carcinogen because there was no scientific proof of a threshold effect level for carcinogens, and it imposed a zero tolerance for any carcinogen in the food supply. In that year, FDA banned two nonnutritive sweeteners (dulcin and P-4000) from the food supply on the basis of animal feeding studies demonstrating carcinogenicity. When this policy of zero tolerance for carcinogens was codified into statutory law as part of the Food Additive Amendments of 1958, in the famous Delaney Clause, FDA acquiesced on the ground that a specific anticancer provision merely reflected existing Agency policy and thus made no change in the law.

As a practical matter, a zero tolerance on carcinogens in the food supply meant that no carcinogen could purposely be added, and that no carcinogenic contaminant could be present at the level of the sensitivity of the detection methodology available at that time. At the beginning of the 1950s, detection methodology was generally sensitive in the range of 20–50 ppm. By the end of the 1960s, detection methodology was sensitive in the very low ppb range.

## REGULATION OF CARCINOGENIC ANIMAL DRUGS

Prior to 1958, FDA had approved the use of diethylstilbestrol (DES) as a growth promotant in livestock and poultry, under conditions which the Agency determined would not result in residues in human food based upon the most sensitive detection methodology then available. When FDA discovered residues of DES in poultry in the late 1950s, the Agency withdrew approval for use of this drug in poultry but continued its use in livestock. This action was taken on the broad ground that the residues were not proved to be safe and was upheld upon court challenge.

Following enactment of the Delaney Clause, the Agency refused to grant new approvals of DES, although it was precluded by the law from revoking the old approvals. Congress therefore enacted the "DES proviso" in 1962 explicitly to require FDA to continue to approve DES for use in food-producing human food under detection methodology specified by FDA. FDA adopted an official analytical method sensitive to 2 ppb for purposes of enforcing this provision.

In 1972, however, radioactive tracer studies found residues of DES in livestock even after substantial periods of withdrawal of the drug. FDA promptly withdrew approval of DES.

It was immediately apparent to the Agency, moreover, that the ramifications of the DES crisis went far beyond the specific substance involved. If DES could be found in livestock, at low levels, after a lengthy period of withdrawal, it was apparent that any other carcinogenic animal drug, or indeed any other carcinogenic feed ingredient or contaminant, could also be found if the detection methodology were sufficiently sensitive. Thus, over a weekend, the entire basis on which FDA had been regulating carcinogenic substances in the diet of animals was destroyed. FDA no longer had any rational basis for setting the level of sensitivity for an acceptable detection methodology for carcinogenic substances in livestock because it was now certain that those substances would be present at some finite level even if they could not be detected. Since the Agency believed that no level of a carcinogen could be regarded as safe, its only option was to ban all carcinogenic substances from animal feed and animal drugs—an impractical, if not impossible, result.

## FDA ADOPTION OF LOW-DOSE EXTRAPOLATION FOR QUANTITATIVE RISK ASSESSMENT IN 1972

The concept of quantifying human risk from carcinogenic substances, on the basis of mathematical extrapolation from animal feeding studies, had already been explored by scientists for some 25 years. During this time, however, it had remained an entirely academic inquiry, unrelated to regulatory decisionmaking.

In 1945, for example, Berenblum published a system for grading carcinogenic potency of chemicals. Iversen and Arley developed a model beginning in 1950 based on a one-hit theory of carcinogenicity. Fisher and Holloman advanced a multicellular concept in 1951. Nordling and Stocks proposed multistage theories in 1953, which were modified by Armitage and Doll in 1954.

In 1961, Mantel and Bryan not only advanced their own log-profit mathematical model for determining carcinogenic risk through low-dose extrapolation, but urged that a risk of $10^{-8}$ (one in 100 million) be regarded as a "virtually safe dose" for purposes of human exposure. In 1970, indeed, Gross and Mantel published a paper applying the Mantel-Bryan model to the regulation of methyl salicylate, which involved apparent reproductive rather than carcinogenic effects.

Thus, by 1972 there was a substantial body of theoretical literature on low-dose extrapolation from animal toxicity studies for purposes of determining human risk from carcinogens. Within days after FDA withdrew approval of DES in 1972, Dr. Richard Lehman of the FDA Bureau of Veterinary Medicine walked into the office of the FDA Chief Counsel, described the Mantel-Bryan method, and suggested it might be useful in handling problems like DES in the future. The applicability of this concept to regulating carcinogenic animal drugs was immediately apparent, particularly because no other method of regulation remained feasible. The task of preparing an appropriate regulation incorporating the concept was begun promptly, but the complexity of the regulatory and scientific issues, and the need for broad consensus within the Agency, resulted in a delay of almost a year before a proposed regulation was actually published in the Federal Register. The July 1973 proposed regulation represented the first regulatory use of low-dose extrapolation for purposes of quantifying human risk from a carcinogen and establishing a "safe" level of human exposure.

FDA proposed to require use of the mathematical model advanced by Mantel and Bryan in 1961 to determine the level at which a carcinogenic residue in human food would present no more than a one in 100 million lifetime cancer risk to the exposed individual. (The one in 100 million risk level was later determined to be too stringent, and was reduced to one in one million.) The manufacturer of any carcinogenic animal drug was required to develop an analytical model sufficiently sensitive to determine a residue of the drug in food at the level which represented that risk. (This approach is therefore commonly referred to as the sensitivity of the method or SOM concept.) If a residue could not be detected in food at that level, use of the carcinogenic animal drug would be approved. Thus, through this approach, FDA directly defined the concept of a "significant" carcinogenic risk using quantitative risk assessment based upon low-dose extrapolation.

After extensive public comment, FDA revised the proposed regulation and promulgated it in final form in February 1977. The final regulation adopted one in one million as an insignificant risk level and substituted the "improved" Mantel-Bryan mathematical model published by Mantel in 1975. That final order was overturned in the courts on the procedural ground that no opportunity had been given to the public for comment on the 1975 Mantel-Bryan mathematical model. The entire regulation was reproposed in March 1979 with additional changes. A final regulation, with additional changes, is presently awaiting final promulgation. Since 1972, however, the regulation of carcinogenic animal drugs has proceeded using the basic concept of low-dose extrapolation to determine an insignificant level of human risk of cancer.

## THE PROLIFERATION AND REFINEMENT OF MATHEMATICAL MODELS

If it achieved nothing else, the July 1973 proposal published by FDA galvanized biological scientists into considering still further refinement of mathematical models for low-dose extrapolation to reflect the most recent knowledge and hypotheses about the carcinogenic process. A vast body of literature has developed on this subject. Indeed, it has become a scientific subspecialty of its own. Because of the great improvement in the methodology, and the realization that further insights are likely to come rapidly in the future, FDA has now concluded that it should not specify any mathematical model or quantitative risk assessment methodology by regulation, but must instead leave such details for constantly changing administrative guidelines.

## THE SIGNIFICANCE OF THE RISK LEVELS OBTAINED THROUGH QUANTITATIVE RISK ASSESSMENT

Throughout its consideration of this approach, FDA has been careful to state that the concept of low-dose extrapolation is designed to produce an upper bound risk level under worst case assumptions, not an actual projection of the expected risk. FDA has stated that "the agency is now confident that it possesses the capacity, through the use of extrapolation procedures, to assess adequately the upper level of risk presented by . . . a carcinogenic chemical." In the preambles to its animal drug SOM regulations, FDA has stated that a level of a carcinogenic substance that represents a negligible individual lifetime risk of cancer "can properly be considered of insignificant public health concern" and "represents no significant carcinogenic burden in the total diet of man." The Agency has stated that, as a practical matter, an insignificant risk of that nature over a lifetime "imposes no additional risk of cancer to the public." FDA has recently characterized this level of risk as an "extremely small, perhaps nonexistent, theoretical risk" that "represents a calculated statistical upper bound estimate of a conservative model" and "does not represent a documented experience or a real expectation."

## USE OF LOW-DOSE EXTRAPOLATION BY EPA BEGINNING IN 1976

EPA was created by an Executive Order issued in 1970 to consolidate regulation of environmental safety, including pesticides. During the first half of the 1970s, EPA proposed to take action against three important pesticides that had been found to be carcinogenic in test animals: DDT, aldrin/dieldrin, and chlordane/heptachlor. The administrative proceedings, which consumed several years, presented the same difficult questions of regulating carcinogens that FDA had already faced in the area of animal drugs. In an attempt to codify its developing policy for carcinogens, EPA published general cancer principles in May 1976, which included the use of low-dose extrapolation to assess the level of human risk through quantitative risk assessment.

Unlike the FDA proposal of 1972, the EPA principles of 1976 did not adopt either a specific mathematical method or a specific level of acceptable human risk. Beginning in 1976, however, the EPA Carcinogen Assessment Group (CAG) has undertaken quantitative risk assessments on a wide variety of chemicals, including pesticides and air and water pollutants. As one example, EPA used this approach in 1980 to establish an acceptable level of 1 ppm of $N$-nitroso contaminants in pesticide products, which it calculated to represent less than one in one million individual lifetime risk of human cancer. More recently, EPA has applied the FDA SOM policy to approve a pesticide which is added to animal feed and produces a carcinogenic metabolite in poultry thus making it subject to the Delaney Clause.

## OTHER USES OF QUANTITATIVE RISK ASSESSMENT BY FDA IN REGULATORY DECISIONS

In addition to the use of quantitative risk assessment to regulate carcinogenic animal drugs beginning in 1972, FDA gradually realized that the large number of carcinogens throughout the food, drug, and cosmetic supply required application of quantitative risk assessment whenever the regulation of a carcinogenic substance was involved. This realization has not come easily or quickly, but has progressed gradually over the past decade.

The driving force behind this change in approach has not been any change in FDA dedication to public protection in general or food safety in particular, but simply the practical need to reflect new scientific information about the nature of the food, drug, and cosmetic supply, obtained during the 1970s. When FDA entered the 1970s, the Agency believed that it was feasible to eliminate virtually all carcinogens from the food supply. By the end of the 1970s, the Agency had indisputable proof that this is impossible. Thus, it became essential to adjust regulatory policy to accommodate this new scientific information.

First, the DES crisis taught FDA that low levels of previously undetected levels of carcinogens would soon be detected throughout the food supply, as the sensitivity of detection methodology improved. It was simply a matter of time. As the decade progressed, more and more carcinogenic contaminants were in fact discovered. Second, EPA announced that the entire water supply contained more than ten known carcinogens. Since virtually all food is processed or made with water, there would be little food that is not subject to this source of carcinogenic contamination. Third, the National Cancer Institute began a series of animal bioassays on common chemicals (now carried on under the National Toxicology Program), about half of which have been shown to be carcinogenic. Academic and industrial testing has similarly shown the carcinogenicity of a number of chemicals. Some of these chemicals are found as contaminants in food and some are natural constituents of important raw agricultural commodities. Fourth, even the form of cooking used to prepare food was shown to produce carcinogenic contamination. Charcoal broiling and any type of pyrolysis is sufficient to produce carcinogens in the food. As a result, FDA was forced in 1979 to admit, in a preamble printed in the Federal Register, that:

"A requirement for warnings on all food that may contain an inherent carcinogenic ingredient or a carcinogenic constituent (in contrast to a deliberately added carcinogenic substance) would apply to many, perhaps most, foods in a supermarket."

Since then, it has become clear that one could not survive on a diet that was entirely free of carcinogenic substances.

Faced with this developing information, FDA has taken a number of steps to refine its regulatory policy to avoid making the law and the Agency look foolish.

In 1974, FDA submitted a report on the Delaney Clause to Congress. In this report, the Agency described its interpretation of the law. First, FDA stated that only an oral feeding study automatically triggers the Delaney Clause prohibition. Any other type of testing—such as gavage (intubation), injection, or implantation—requires an additional finding that the test is appropriate. Second, FDA stated that a secondary carcinogen is not subject to the Delaney Clause. The Agency explained that the Delaney Clause does not apply where a substance causes a pathologic change at a particular level. It is that pathologic change rather than the substance that leads to cancer, and there is an adequate margin of safety below the threshold at which the pathologic change occurs. FDA had, on the basis of this interpretation, earlier approved the essential nutrient, selenium, in spite of evidence that it is a secondary carcinogen, and had explained that it would not ban alcoholic beverages in spite of overwhelming evidence that it is a secondary carcinogen in humans. Third, FDA related its SOM interpretation, already described above. Fourth, FDA stated that the Delaney Clause does not apply to carcinogenic contaminants naturally present in food or added in the course of food manufacture or processing. Only if the food itself, containing those contaminants, were tested and found carcinogenic would the Delaney Clause become applicable. This interpretation has subsequently been formalized and applied as the "constituents policy." Fifth, FDA stated that carcinogenic environmental contaminants may be permitted in the food supply as "unavoidable" under the exception authorized by Section 406 of the Federal Food, Drug, and Cosmetic (FD&C) Act. Later that year, FDA utilized this interpretation to set tolerances, confirming earlier informal action levels, for the potent carcinogenic mycotoxin, aflatoxin, in peanuts and for carcinogenic PCBs in food packaging.

Nonetheless, FDA did not proceed to interpret the Delaney Clause out of existence or to diminish its efforts to reduce consumer exposure to carcinogens where that was feasible. In 1974, the Agency banned the sale of natural sassafras bark for use in making sassafras tea because its principal flavor constituent is safrole, a carcinogen that FDA banned in 1960. The Agency did not, however, ban nutmeg, which contains safrole at a lower level. In 1976, the Agency proposed to ban saccharin for use in food, but Congress intervened to grant a statutory moratorium. FDA also summarily banned a number of color additives during the 1970s by deleting them from the Agency's provisional list. FDA's action was strongly upheld in the courts in the only litigated case.

Based upon findings of carcinogenicity, FDA banned acrylonitrile for use in beverage containers in 1977. Following a court decision in 1979 holding that FDA could ignore insignificant levels of risk, however, the Agency has now begun to determine acceptable risk levels for acrylonitrile, polyvinyl chloride, 2-nitropropane, and other food packaging additives that pose extremely small levels of human risk as a result of their intended uses.

In 1978, based upon a finding of carcinogenicity, FDA proposed to require a cancer warning on the labels of all hair dye products containing the substance 2,4-DAA (4-MMPD). In the face of a quantitative risk assessment showing an individual lifetime cancer risk of less than one in one million, FDA nonetheless persisted and promulgated a final regulation requiring a more stringent warning than Congress has required for cigarettes. Upon confronting a challenge brought by the cosmetic industry in the courts, however, FDA signed a consent order staying the regulation, remanding it for reconsideration, and stipulating that any further rulemaking would utilize "scientifically accepted procedures of risk assessment" to determine whether the substance presents "a generally recognized level of insignificant risk to human health." Since then, FDA has not proceeded further on this matter.

In 1980, FDA approved the use of a carcinogenic hair dye, lead acetate, which had been shown to present a less than one in one million individual lifetime cancer risk. When consumer advocates objected to this action, the Agency reiterated its decision in 1981. No court action was brought to challenge the final decision.

The regulation of color additives has been plagued, throughout this time, by the detection of carcinogenic contaminants in many of the pure dyes. FDA disapproved a number of color additives on this ground, and in 1978 proposed to disapprove one that it had already approved when it discovered that the substance was contaminated with β-naphthalamine. Industry objected to this action on the ground that the risk presented by this contaminant was less than one in one million individual lifetime cancer risk. No further action has been taken by FDA on this proposal.

In 1982, indeed, the Agency implemented one of the interpretations of the 1974 report to Congress, by publishing an advance notice of proposed rulemaking setting out a "constituents policy" to handle these matters. Under this approach, any non-functional constituent in products regulated by the Agency would not be subject to the absolute prohibition of the Delaney Clause, and would be regarded as "safe" under the general safety provisions of the law if it posed only an insignificant risk of cancer utilizing scientifically acceptable procedures for quantitative risk assessment. Based on that policy, FDA has subsequently approved a number of color additives and food additives containing nonfunctional carcinogenic contaminants. The policy itself has now been upheld in a decision in the United States Court of Appeals for the Sixth Circuit, which held that the Delaney Clause does not apply to nonfunctional substances and that a cancer risk of between one in 30 million and one in 300 million can properly be regarded by FDA as "safe." Following this approach, EPA has used the FDA constituents policy to approve pesticides.

## USE OF QUANTITATIVE RISK ASSESSMENT BY CPSC AND OSHA

For policy and philosophical reasons unrelated to their statutory authority, CPSC and OSHA were initially reluctant to incorporate any form of quantitative risk assessment in their regulatory decisions. In the *Aqua Slide "N" Dive* case in 1978, however, the court rejected a warning required by CPSC on swimming pool slides, on the ground that the risk involved was less than the risk an average person has of being killed by lightning. In the *Benzene* decision in 1980, the Supreme Court interpreted the Occupational Safety and Health Act to apply only to significant risks to human health. Since then, both agencies have begun to incorporate quantitative risk assessment into their regulatory decisions. In its 1983 proposal to regulate ethylene oxide, for example, OSHA relied heavily upon a quantitative risk assessment.

The courts, however, have pushed both CPSC and OSHA to improve their risk assessment methodology. In the *Gulf South Insulation* case, the United States Court of Appeals for the Fifth Circuit in 1983 overturned the CPSC ban on ureaformaldehyde foam insulation because of an inadequate assessment of the cancer risk. In the *Asbestos Information Association* case, the same court in 1984 overturned the OSHA emergency temporary standard for worker exposure to asbestos because the risk assessment on which OSHA relied was not adequately supported by the administrative record. In both cases, the court was careful to support the use of risk assessment methodology but to be insistent, nonetheless, that it be substantiated rather than speculative.

## THE STRENGTHS AND WEAKNESSES OF QUANTITATIVE RISK ASSESSMENT

It is thus clear, from the developments during the past 12 years, that quantitative risk assessment represents the principal focus of regulatory decisionmaking for carcinogens for the foreseeable future. Like all regulatory tools, however, it must be recognized that this approach has both strengths and weaknesses.

The major strength of quantitative risk assessment is that it permits regulatory agencies to base their decisions on an evaluation of the potential human risk involved. Prior approaches, such as safety factors or the level of detection of the available analytical methodology, relied instead upon the artificial concept that substances are either safe or unsafe.

The need for evaluation and comparison of the level of risk presented by carcinogens has become more important as regulatory agencies have begun to recognize that it is impossible to eliminate all carcinogens from the environment. It is increasingly apparent, indeed, that everything we consume modifies the carcinogenic process in one way or another. It is likely, in fact, that particular substances may act differently under varying circumstances, either to promote or to retard cancer. Under these complex circumstances, which are not yet understood, a simplistic distinction between safe and unsafe substances is impossible.

Quantitative risk assessment permits regulators to differentiate between significant and insignificant risk, and thus better to tailor regulatory decisions to the goal that has existed throughout the centuries—protection of the public health and safety. Thus, its appeal to regulatory agencies is overwhelming.

At the same time, the obstacles to quantitative risk assessment remain formidable. Use of this technique depends, for example, upon the availability of adequate and reliable animal data and human exposure information. Uncertainty about the process of carcinogenesis in humans has led to the development of mathematical models that are extraordinarily conservative. Conservative assumption is piled upon conservative assumption, with the result that the upper bound risk that is usually calculated vastly overstates any realistic risk potential. Use of different mathematical models or different scaling or exposure assumptions can result in large differences in the calculated risk and make risk comparisons impossible. Any calculated risks, moreover, are easily misunderstood as hard numbers by the general public. Quantitative risk assessment is also frequently misapplied to secondary carcinogens as well as to primary carcinogens, largely because of the extreme difficulty at this time in distinguishing between the two.

Quantitative risk assessment in itself, moreover, does not predetermine the outcome of any regulatory decision. As the National Academy of Sciences has recently emphasized, risk management (i.e., a regulatory decision) is entirely separate and distinct from risk assessment (i.e., an evaluation of the level of risk presented by a particular substance). Numerous policy and practical judgments are required to convert a risk assessment into a regulatory decision.

In spite of these weaknesses and drawbacks, however, quantitative risk assessment remains the best way currently available to organize and analyze toxicity data for purposes of making difficult regulatory decisions for carcinogens. Although this is not yet a mature science, enormous progress has been made since FDA initiated the process in 1972; and it can be anticipated that substantially greater progress will be forthcoming in the future as more scientific information becomes available about the process of carcinogenesis itself.

## CONCLUSION

The future of all health and safety regulation is inseparable from the future of quantitative risk assessment. Since we now understand that it is impossible to have a risk-free environment, the only realistic approach for government regulatory agencies necessarily includes an assessment of existing risks and the reduction in those risks that is feasible through alternative regulatory actions.

Perhaps the most difficult task facing government and industry today is to reeducate the American public to understand that no element of our environment, including the food supply, can ever be expected to be entirely safe. Everything we consume or touch represents some degree of risk. Far from promising regulatory action that guarantees safety, regulatory agencies can promise only to reduce risks to the lowest level feasible or, in any event, to a level that is acceptably small.

It will take some years before this new understanding permeates our society. In the interim, severe misunderstandings and dislocations have occurred and will continue to occur. Unrealistic expectations about public protection cannot easily or quickly subside. This educational process, on which the success of quantitative risk assessment and future regulatory approaches depends, is thus the single most important objective for the future.

## EDITOR'S NOTE

For comments on P.B. Hutt's paper, see comment section of the following paper by M.R. Taylor.

# The Inevitability of Risk Quantitation and Its Potential Contribution to Food Safety Regulation

MICHAEL R. TAYLOR
King & Spalding
Washington, D.C.

## INTRODUCTION

Except as an academic matter, the debate about whether quantitative risk assessment has a role in public health decisionmaking is over. Quantitative risk assessment is being used daily by all the federal health and safety regulatory agencies as they attempt to deal with potential carcinogenic hazards. Thus, the important question now is not whether risk assessment should be used but how. How can risk quantitation best contribute to the rather complex scientific, administrative, legal, and political processes through which regulatory decisions are made? How can its contribution be improved in the future?

This paper approaches these questions by considering the use of risk assessment in the field of food safety regulation. It begins by suggesting reasons why some role for quantitative risk assessment is inevitable and then makes several observations about the present and future role of this analytical tool in food safety regulation.

## THE INEVITABILITY OF QUANTITATIVE RISK ASSESSMENT

There are two basic reasons why quantitative risk assessment is inevitable: (1) Simply because it is in fact available, and (2) because it is useful.

Certain nonscientific features of the health and safety regulatory process compel the use of risk quantitation simply because the methodology is there. The regulatory process is, for better or worse, open and participatory. It involves not just the regulators and the regulated, but also consumers, legislators, the scientific community, and the media, all of whom are asking the same question: How great is the risk? And most of whom are looking for simple answers. When methods exist that seem capable of providing such answers, they will inevitably be used. Disclaimers may be provided concerning the uncertainties and imprecision in any quantitative assessment of risk, and it may be asserted that the numbers are only a part of the basis on which decisions are made; but, when the public debate begins on a specific issue, the pressure to quantify the potential risk is virtually irresistible.

The Food and Drug Administration's (FDA's) effort in 1977 to explain its proposed ban of saccharin provides a nice illustration of this phenomenon.[1] Quan-

---

[1] Food and Drug Administration, *Saccharin and Its Salts, Proposed Rule and Hearing,* 42 Fed. Reg. 19,996, 20,000–02 (April 15, 1977).

titative estimates of risk were presented then not because they were important to the decision, but because they were thought necessary to explain and justify the decision to the public.

Risk quantitation is also made inevitable, however, by the fact that it is useful. Whatever its imperfections, quantitative risk assessment provides a basis for distinguishing among carcinogens of widely varying potencies and for illustrating how, for a particular substance, risk is expected to decline with dose.

These capabilities were what led to one of FDA's earliest uses of quantitative risk assessment in considering a tolerance for aflatoxin in peanuts and peanut products.[2] The law required that a tolerance for this potent carcinogen be set at the level "necessary for the protection of public health" but taking into account the "unavoidability" of the substance, which really means the amount of food that would have to be disposed of to achieve a certain tolerance.[3] One option for FDA was to avoid quantification of the risk and simply set the tolerance at the lowest level that could be reliably detected for enforcement purposes. This option would have provided the maximum feasible health protection, but it also would have had an unacceptably large impact on the food supply. Thus, some means had to be found for determining how much above the threshold of detectability the tolerance should be set. The only rational basis for doing this, FDA decided, was to assess the risks associated with a range of possible tolerances and compare those risks with the varying amounts of food loss expected at each tolerance. Thus, in the aflatoxin case, FDA found risk quantitation useful both to illustrate the need for a tolerance and to help determine what the tolerance should be.

Other examples could be provided to illustrate the inevitability of quantitative risk assessment, but the point has already been made. The methods are available and they have been found useful. It is simply unimaginable that their use will do anything but expand.

## RISK QUANTITATION IN FOOD SAFETY REGULATION

Given that risk quantitation is inevitable, how can and should it be used in formulating public policy concerning the management of health risks? This topic is too broad to address systematically in a brief paper, but one can begin to approach it by making some observations about the nature of the role risk assessment currently plays in one area of regulation, i.e., food safety, and considering how that role might evolve in the future. Food safety regulation is itself a broad topic, encompassing numerous kinds of safety issues and falling within the jurisdiction of at least three federal regulatory agencies: the Food and Drug Administration, the

---

[2] Food and Drug Administration, *Aflatoxin in Shelled Peanuts and Peanut Products Used as Human Foods, Proposed Tolerance*, 39 Fed. Reg. 42748 (December 6, 1974); Food and Drug Administration, *Assessment of Estimated Risk Resulting from Aflatoxins in Consumer Peanut Products and Other Food Commodities, Notice of Availability*, 43 Fed. Reg. 88081 (March 3, 1978).

[3] 21 U.S.C. § 346. *See, e.g.,* 39 Fed. Reg. at 42750-51.

Environmental Protection Agency, and the U.S. Department of Agriculture. For brevity, this paper will focus on issues of carcinogenicity and the activities of the Food and Drug Administration.

## The Legal Framework Is Receptive to Risk Quantitation

Most debates about current uses of risk quantitation include some discussion of whether the law allows the use of risk assessment for carcinogens. The short answer is that even the most stringent regulatory statutes—those governing food and color additives, with their Delaney Clause[4]—provide ample opportunity for the use of risk assessment.

Under some statutes, the legal availability of risk assessment as a decision tool is obvious. For example, statutes that establish a standard of "unreasonable risk" or that call for a balancing of risks and benefits clearly accommodate the use of quantitative risk assessment.[5]

Food and color additives, however, are subject to a requirement that they be shown to be "safe" and to the Delaney Clause, which provides that an additive shall be deemed "unsafe" if it has been found to "induce cancer" in animals.[6] Even under those seemingly inflexible provisions, however, FDA has found substantial opportunity for the use of quantitative risk assessment in evaluating animal carcinogens.

For example, FDA has interpreted the Delaney Clause as applying only to the "additive as a whole" and not to each of its individual constituents.[7] Under this legal interpretation, FDA is able to avoid applying the Delaney Clause in cases where individual constituents of an additive, but not the additive as a whole, have been found to induce cancer. The additive, including its carcinogenic constituent, is then evaluated under the so-called general safety standard. Quantitative risk assessment is used as part of the basis for determining whether that safety standard, expressed as a "reasonable certainty of no harm," has been met. This interpretation of the Delaney Clause and the use of quantitative risk assessment to determine whether a small amount of a carcinogen can be approved as "safe" constitute an outright reversal of FDA's traditional approaches. The new approaches nevertheless were upheld recently by the U.S. Court of Appeals in a case involving their ap-

---

[4] There actually are three Delaney Clauses, covering food additives, 21 U.S.C. § 348(c)(3)(A); color additives, 21 U.S.C. § 376(b)(5)(B), and animal drugs, 21 U.S.C. § 360b(d)(1)(H). Although differences exist among them, the basic language of the "food additive" Delaney Clause is illustrative for present purposes:

*Provided,* That no additive shall be deemed to be safe if it is found to induce cancer when ingested by man or animal, or if it is found, after tests which are appropriate for the evaluation of the safety of food additives, to induce cancer in man or animal, . . .

[5] Consumer Product Safety Act, 15 U.S.C. § 2051 ("unreasonable risk"); Federal Insecticide, Fungicide, and Rodenticide Act, 7 U.S.C §§ 136(bb), 136a(c)(5)(D) ("unreasonable risk to man or the environment taking into account the economic, social, and environmental risks and benefits . . .").

[6] See note 4, *supra.*

[7] 47 Fed. Reg. 14464 (April 2, 1982).

plication to the color additive, D&C Green No. 5, which is known to contain the carcinogen p-toluidine.[8]

FDA's successful experience with its so-called constituents policy graphically illustrates the flexibility inherent in the law to accommodate new scientific methods for evaluating the safety of substances.[9] It also makes an important point about the nature of safety decisions and the role risk quantitation can play in making them. Safety decisions involve the exercise of scientific and policy judgment. There are no bright lines between "safe" and "unsafe" and thus no clear-cut, objective standards for deciding what is safe. For this reason, in the Green No. 5 case, neither FDA nor the court adopted any quantitative risk level as the benchmark for determining safety. They both simply concluded that the risk estimates considered by FDA (indicating a maximum lifetime risk of one in 30 million) supported the judgment that Green No. 5 is safe. As discussed further below, this suggests that the challenge for risk assessment is not merely to produce more refined numerical estimates of risk but to contribute as much useful information as possible to the judgment about safety.

## Current Methods Are Adequate for Protecting Public Health

Although it seems clear that the law is ready for risk assessment, some observers question whether current methods of risk quantitation are ready to be used as tools for protecting the public health. The question is whether the methods are sufficiently sound scientifically and reliable in actual use to serve as the basis for good public health decisions.

Current methods of quantitative risk assessment are sometimes criticized as crude, imprecise, and lacking in a complete scientific foundation. In a certain sense, all these criticisms are correct. Current methods of quantitative risk assessment rely heavily on assumptions and inferences concerning the quantitative relationship between observable high-dose responses and unobservable low-dose responses in animals, as well as the relationship between animal and human response. They also rely on generally sketchy information concerning the nature and extent of human exposure to the substance in question. The degree of uncertainty that persists on these matters means that as a scientific tool quantitative risk assessment needs maturing. This does not mean, however, that current methods of quantitative risk assessment are not fully adequate for making public health decisions.

In the first place, it is important to remember what is claimed for current methods of risk quantitation. No one claims that they are able to produce accurate predictions of true human risk. Instead, the methods are claimed to provide estimates of the likely upper limit on human risk. They do this by systematically making the assumption, or drawing the inference at each point in the decision process where uncertainty remains, that will be most likely to avoid understating the predicted

---

[8] *Scott v. Food and Drug Administration*, 728 F.2d 322 (6th Cir. 1984).

[9] M.R. Taylor, 1984. Interpreting the safety standard — A collaborative model. *J. Am. Coll. Toxicol.* **3:** 103.

human risk.[10] For example, the results obtained in the most sensitive animal species are generally used; dose-response is assumed to be linear in the observed range; and conservative assumptions are made about the quantitative relationship between animal and human doses. These and other assumptions have the cumulative effect of tending strongly to overstate true risk, sometimes by substantial amounts.

Thus, it is not the accuracy of quantitative risk assessment that has persuaded regulators of its usefulness. It is rather the consistent tendency of current methods to overstate risk, coupled with the judgmental nature of safety decisions. Regulators can use risk assessment to support judgments about safety, confident that the true human risk will almost certainly not exceed the estimated risk and, in all likelihood, will be substantially smaller. Thus, although greater precision in risk quantitation would be desirable for many reasons, precision simply is not a prerequisite to its usefulness in food safety decisionmaking. It is enough that current methods can distinguish reliably between substances that are likely to pose a risk worth worrying about and those likely to be of no genuine concern.

## Challenge for the Future

To date, the primary uses of risk quantitation have been to help demonstrate that a substance poses a clearly insignificant risk (as in the case of some trace carcinogenic constituents) or to compare the risks posed at various exposure levels by substances recognized to pose significant risks (such as aflatoxin).

The challenge for the future, however, is to incorporate quantitative risk assessment into a more sophisticated, broad-based approach to evaluating the potential human health effects of animal carcinogens and making judgments about their safety. Current approaches tend to be limited to a quantitative analysis of a limited subset of the available animal data. Quantitative extrapolations are made from high dose to low dose and then to humans. The resulting number, imprecise as it is, is then used as the basis for making a regulatory decision. This method disregards, however, the vast amount of information that is available (or at least potentially available) about the biological and biochemical properties of the substance under study; information that should properly influence the ultimate judgment about a substance's potential human health effects.

Thus, risk assessment can make its most meaningful contribution to food safety decisions by transcending the merely quantitative approach. When available, information should be considered on such matters as the strength of the evidence underlying the basic finding of carcinogenicity; the human relevance of the animal results, based on comparative metabolism and other information; the mechanism of action because that might affect the dose-response relationship and the possibility of a threshold; and the true nature of human exposure as affected, for example, by man's metabolic handling of the substance.

---

[10] J.V. Rodricks and M.R. Taylor, Application of risk assessment to food safety decision making. *Regul. Toxicol. Pharmacol.* **3:** 275 (1983).

One reason risk assessment has been limited in the past to simple quantitative extrapolations is that the information needed to do more has been lacking. Indeed, even the theoretical basis for using the kind of information just described needs improvement in some respects. For some substances, however, enough information may already have been generated to permit a broader approach to risk assessment; and recent developments in FDA's approach to carcinogens have created the incentive to expand the data base even further.

FDA now seems prepared at least to listen to scientifically based arguments concerning the human safety of animal carcinogens that go beyond current quantitative extrapolations. The challenge is to consider in a rigorous way what effect the other available information has on the estimate of risk, up or down. It would be ideal if this effect could be expressed in quantitative terms, and that may someday be possible. The fundamental goal of risk assessment, however, must be to express as fully as possible what is known about the potential human risk posed by a substance, whether that is done quantitatively or qualitatively.

This is the only approach that does justice to the judgmental character of safety decisions, and it will help ensure that science makes its maximum contribution to the process.

## COMMENTS

**R. WILSON:** I have about four thoughts that have come to my mind, mostly from Peter Hutt's comments. He referred to the early FDA safety factor of 100:1 as the standard safety factor. If you apply that 100:1 safety factor in air pollution problems, such as "Should we breathe the air out here?", the answer is "You certainly should not," because if you go 100 times above the present level of particulates, you certainly find adverse effects on humans, such as in London in 1953. So, there is absolutely no question that if you try to apply 100:1 consistently in all the governmental decisions, you will just get into grave trouble.

**PETO:** But you only use a large safety factor in the absence of human data. If you have human data showing a risk of 1% or 2%, you assume that the risk will be about 100 times lower when you reduce exposure 100-fold.

**HUTT:** The FDA has applied the 100:1 safety factor with a great deal of discretion over the years. It has varied it up and down, depending upon the quality of the data, the uniqueness of the situation, and the practicalities involved.

**R. WILSON:** You said something I completely disagree with, something like, "If you couldn't find an effect, you couldn't worry about it." Historically that is not what has happened in protection of public health. In the last century, some of the great improvements of public health have occurred because we've done things even though we have just suspected an effect, without our actually finding it. For example, water was purified long before one really found a specific effect of impure water.

**HUTT:** Obviously, what I meant was not understood. What I said was that if one could not detect a substance in the food, FDA could not ban it because the Agency did not know, and thus could not prove, it was there. The way the law was written in 1962 is what I call the "hide and go seek" theory of food safety. Congress amended the statute in 1962 to add the DES Proviso, explicitly to say that the Agency had to approve DES and any other carcinogenic animal drug unless, under methods specified by the Secretary, a residue was found. So if FDA found no residue using the most sensitive method, the Agency had to continue to approve DES.

**R. WILSON:** You could demand a more sensitive method or find a procedure to use anecdotal, indirect evidence suggesting that a risk is there.

**HUTT:** That is exactly what FDA did with quantitative risk assessment in 1972. The Agency demanded more sensitive methods than were feasible at that time, and therefore said it would not approve any carcinogenic animal drugs until such methods were developed.

**R. WILSON:** My third comment is that when FDA first suggested this limit of one in $10^6$ per life—which is close to one in $10^8$ per year—it suggested this be calculated using the Mantel-Bryan model. The difference between going from an annual risk level of one in $10^6$ to one in $10^8$ using the Mantel-Bryan model is usually about a factor of three. However, we have now switched to the linear proportional model, and thus it becomes much more important whether you use one in $10^6$ or one in $10^8$ annual risk because that represents a 100-fold difference in dose. I think one in $10^6$ per life becomes an almost impossible goal in many ways.

**HUTT:** It is impossible to achieve $10^{-6}$ for any important carcinogenic direct food additive; but it can be achieved by dozens of contaminants, residues, and minor substances.

**R. WILSON:** My fourth comment comes from your suggestion that risk assessment is used to explain rather than reach regulatory decisions. This is inevitable because the first time you use a risk assessment you want to try it out for size and see if your purpose is really achieved.

**HUTT:** I was curious about Michael's [Taylor] characterization, because the FDA's first use of quantitative risk assessment was as a decisionmaking tool. It had nothing to do with mere explanation. We had a crisis and we had to figure out how to regulate these products.

**TAYLOR:** Let's look at that another way. It seems to me that one reason it recommended itself was because it was a system; it was a rational basis for making and explaining these decisions. Those gut judgments about where safety lies could have been made without quantifying the risk. But the notion of going out to the public and saying, "We have decided that this level of analytical sensitivity is safe and this one isn't," surely had no appeal.

**HUTT:** I do not think we could have set a single level on the basis of gut reaction, without actually going through the risk assessment itself. Maybe now that risk assessment has become better understood and more refined, one can have those kinds of gut reactions. But when it started, nobody had the vaguest idea what the endpoint of the calculation would be.

**PURCHASE:** It was mentioned earlier that there had been discussions between regulatory scientists from America and the Federal Republic of Germany about the way in which these judgments were made. Your argument here is that it's inevitable that we have to do risk assessments in this way. I wonder if the Germans have found it as inevitable as you have.

**LAVE:** The two bilateral conferences came about because the West German Ministry of Science and Technology was trying to impose a quantitative risk requirement on the chemical industry and the German chemical industry was resisting. The first of these conferences took place in Bonn and brought American experts to convince the Germans. The second one was held in the U.S. The Germans basically were saying that they didn't want and didn't need quantification, that good engineering judgment was really all that was required. Their American counterparts were saying, "You really do need to look at these risks in detail and you need to quantify them. There will be many uncertainties, but the discipline of going through that is well worthwhile." An interesting suggestion about managing risk came from the second conference. The Germans have a different approach to toxic substances that cannot be removed from the workplace. Where they can't take them out, they have committees consisting of workers, employers, and regulators, who collectively decide what will be the tolerable level. They don't presume to have the government speak "from on high" as to what a tolerable level is. The company might say, "If the standard is that stringent, we may have to close the plant." The workers might say, "This other risk level is too high." The groups work out some solution. Is it the best one? I don't know. But, by definition, it turns out to be one that's acceptable to the various parties in the negotiation, which seems to be a better system than ours.

**WEINSTEIN:** Why is it better? Do you know that it's creating a safer work environment?

**LAVE:** Not necessarily a safer work environment. I think it's creating a work environment which the two principal parties agree to and which a neutral third party, namely the government, accepts.

**WEINSTEIN:** But is that the goal?

**LAVE:** That depends on whether you have a specific safety goal in mind or whether you are trying to find a solution that is broadly acceptable. When the risk levels are smaller than $10^{-3}$, I believe the more important issue is finding something that all parties think is acceptable.

**LANDRIGAN:**   Those overall risk figures, though, of $10^{-3}$ and $10^{-6}$ seldom apply to the workplace. Exposures are already several orders of magnitude higher there. Therefore, a regulator is in a better position in the occupational setting than in a general environmental setting to actually define risk. The point is that real disease is considerably more likely to result from workplace exposures.

**LAVE:**   Sure. But, again, the point was to get the parties to agree on a risk level. The neutral third party makes sure that neither one side nor the other is being stampeded.

**NEEL:**   Peter, you expressed some interest in the history of inbred animal strains. Much of the credit, I think, should go to C.C. Little and the group in Bar Harbor at the Jackson Lab; and George Snell and Elizabeth Russell could tell you quite a bit. But a point that should accompany this history is the extent to which we are now realizing the very large differences from one inbred line to another in endpoints. The use of inbred lines was great for the experimenters—they didn't have to maintain so many animals—but one strain may give a rather different view of risk than another strain. This is now coming on very strong. I was impressed this morning that nobody had said a word about ALARA (as low as reasonably achievable). Certainly in the field of radiation, which is my field, this approach is coming on at least as strong as efforts of risk assessment. I have just been part of an EPA committee reviewing the plans to return high-level radioactive waste to the ground from which it sprang. The EPA estimated that disposal of these wastes would not result in more than 1000 excess deaths over a 10,000-year period. The extrapolations involved in arriving at that would just blow your mind. But, as we tried to understand how EPA had arrived at this position, it did look a bit as if they had set a risk level that they felt the public would accept and then worked backwards from that. This risk, incidentally, is less than if the uranium ore had never been mined, because the waste is going back into much safer places than it came out of. So, this is a new use of the word "risk." A committee of responsible citizens said "You know, this is too much," and we recommended that they ease up by at least a factor of 10 because the cost of achieving this is not inconsiderable. Each of these depositories is going to cost $8 or $10 billion and we're going to need 10 or 12 of them.

**HUTT:**   We were talking about quantifying the risk. We did not talk about the next question, namely, once you quantify the risk, what can you do about it? Sometimes you can and sometimes you cannot do anything about it. FDA quantified the risk on saccharin and said "We are going to ban it," but Congress said "You are not going to ban it." In the aflatoxin situation, FDA conducted a quantified risk assessment, using Mantel-Bryan rather than straight-line extrapolation, and found that they had just accounted for a major portion of all the liver cancer in the United States coming just from aflatoxin in peanuts.

Therefore, the Agency had to throw out the whole calculation as not being very helpful, and it went back to epidemiology and based the risk assessment on that. Then it encountered the other problem: If you reduce aflatoxin to a certain level in peanuts, you can still have 80% of the peanuts in the country; but if you reduce it just a little bit further, you have eliminated 80% of the peanuts. The FDA decided for that reason that the higher level was acceptable.

**SWENBERG:** It would seem that a problem in the German mediation example suggests that much depends on the socioeconomics of that particular area and plant. If you're in a depressed area where there's no other employment, these employees may be willing to assume a much greater risk than if you're in an area where they can get a job easily. How do you control for that?

**LAVE:** That's why you have the government regulator as part of the negotiations, to make sure there's not that kind of stampeding. Alternatively, a powerful union could stampede the employer. We see such a situation with arsenic at the ASARCO plant in Tacoma. Apparently the workers get such high exposure to arsenic that their perspiration is actually green. Yet, these workers are reported to oppose more stringent regulation.

**PERERA:** In the smelter case, EPA went to the community and essentially asked: "What levels of cancer risk are you willing to accept, given the fact that you may be losing your jobs if we set standards too stringently?" This approach has been variously characterized as "your money or your life" and "health versus jobs." The mayor of Tacoma testified that it was unfair to put the question to the workers and the community in this either/or way, and that, in fact, one could achieve both health protection and economic viability.

# Legal Impediments to the Use of Risk Assessment by Regulatory Agencies

RICHARD A. MERRILL
Dean and Daniel Caplin Professor of Law
University of Virginia
Charlottesville, Virginia 22901

## OVERVIEW

The previous papers have succeeded in generating interest and perhaps igniting concern, particularly among scientists, about the use of quantitative risk assessment in the evaluation of environmental hazards to health. As a law professor should, I want to write about cases—actual court decisions—to suggest that perhaps the fresh enthusiasm for quantitative risk assessment, whether in ranking risks, explaining decisions, or actually setting allowable exposure limits should be tempered by the early judicial responses to this technique. My lawyer colleagues may take issue with my cautionary message, but it is worth conveying nonetheless, and indeed may reassure some in the scientific community who fear that we are going too far, too fast.

My subject is the possible legal impediments to the use of risk assessment in regulatory decisionmaking. I write about three quite recent cases, two of which involved people present at this conference, who may have a different window on the judicial decisions that emerged.

Michael Taylor and Peter Hutt have alluded to the several uses that quantitative risk assessment now enjoys in the regulatory community. These include not only sorting (i.e., priority setting), but fixing assay criteria (e.g., for animal drugs) (Chemical Compounds 1979), determining the threshold of risk significance (a function for which the technique is now used by OSHA) (Ethylene Dibromide 1983; Ethylene Oxide 1983), comparing regulatory strategies (to which Lester Lave has previously alluded) (OSHA Asbestos ETS 1983), and, indeed, for balancing the costs and benefits of alternative control strategies (Aflatoxins 1978; Polychlorinated Biphenyls 1979).

The utility of risk quantification depends on three factors: One is the relative ease of analysis and its expense, i.e., the extent to which risk estimation in support of regulatory decisions escapes excessive data requirements. Second is the accuracy of the estimates that are produced, something about which we may not have clear guidance for a long time. And, third, are possible legal impediments to its use. I focus on the last point for two reasons. For many years it was vigorously asserted, especially by people at OSHA, that quantitative risk assessment was precluded or at least discouraged by the language of certain regulatory laws (OSHA Brief 1980; Carcinogen Policy 1980). More important, we now have some judicial rulings that may require regulatory agencies to reassess their approach to this tool.

**41**

## INTRODUCTION

Let me turn first to the possible statutory impediments to agency performance of quantitative risk assessment. I embrace the conclusion that I have heard my colleague, Peter Hutt, often assert: No regulatory agency faces serious statutory impediments to the doing of quantitative risk assessment. Initially, I stress "doing" and not "relying upon." One is hard pressed to find any statute governing a federal regulatory program that expresses or, I would argue, implies that the administering agency may not legitimately attempt to quantify the risks it is concerned about. This is true, I believe, at all stages of the decisionmaking process—whether the agency is sorting candidates for regulation or attempting, at least for internal purposes, to estimate the risks of specific hazards that it has chosen to regulate.

Legally mandated time limits for decisionmaking may occasionally impede rigorous quantification. Some agencies are by statute directed to act within a short period of time (OSHA 1982; TSCA 1982); and if an agency is determined to follow those directions, or if it is under a court order to act within a specified time, performance of a quantitative risk assessment may be difficult to accomplish, particularly if it requires generation of new exposure data. This, however, is a resource constraint, not a legal barrier.

Budgetary limits may also impede performance of sophisticated risk assessments, particularly those that depend upon gathering new exposure information. Agency resources may not support the kind of studies that members of the scientific community, even those working for the agency, believe should be done before risks can be quantified. But, once again, the statutes do not say you may not quantify.

Some statutes may make quantification an ostensibly academic exercise. Michael Taylor has related that when FDA in 1977 attempted to ban saccharin, based in part on the Delaney Clause's prohibition against direct food additives that cause cancer, it nonetheless performed a quantitative risk estimate and published this estimate in the course of explaining why it thought the risk posed was serious enough to regulate (Saccharin 1977). But the agency's estimate was not formally a basis for the regulatory decision. One may find congressional hints in other regulatory laws that reliance upon a quantitative risk assessment as a ground for decision would be impermissible. A possible example is section 112 of the Clean Air Act, which requires the EPA to establish standards for hazardous air pollutants that will provide "an ample margin of safety."[1]

The notion, however, that there are any statutory impediments to the doing, or serious impediments to reliance on, quantitative risk assessments is overblown. The questions for regulators, therefore, are as follows: What kinds of assessments? When should they be performed? How should they be used? And, what difficulties are decisions based on risk assessments likely to encounter in court?

---

[1] Clean Air Act, 42 U.S.C. § 7412(b)(1)(B) (1982).

## ADMINISTRATIVE LAW CONSTRAINTS

There are some other legal constraints on the use of quantitative risk assessment, which are not found in statutory criteria for exposure control decisions. They are found in the general principles of administrative law, either codified in statute or emerging from court decisions. One is the general obligation of an agency to adhere to precedent—its own precedent—unless it provides a satisfactory explanation for change in policy (Davis 1977). This constraint is not, as a practical matter, likely to prove an important one in this context.

More important constraints are the procedural requirements for the adoption of general rules by regulatory agencies. Peter Hutt has reported that it was in 1973 that FDA first proposed criteria for regulating animal drug residues that incorporated quantitative risk assessment. (Acceptability of Assay Methods 1973). In 1977 the agency issued final regulations, which were overturned in court later the same year (Animal Health Institute 1977; Chemical Compounds 1977). A new proposal was published in 1979 (Chemical Compounds 1979). As yet there has been no final rule embodying the policy that was advanced by FDA in 1973. Peter Hutt will be quick to say that the agency is nonetheless following that policy; but the FDA has no formal rule authorizing the use of quantitative risk assessment and is on soft legal ground if it were challenged in court. Thus, agencies may be impeded in adopting quantitative risk assessment or, more accurately, in changing their current approaches because they appreciate the difficulties and delays associated with public rulemaking.

Finally, administrative law doctrine holds that a regulatory agency, in making general rules about control strategies or resolving specific disputes, must justify its actions not only in terms of its governing statute but based on facts in the administrative record (*Industrial Union* 1980; APA 1982; *State Farm* 1983). An agency must persuade a reviewing court that its decision is not arbitrary or capricious or, in some cases, is supported by substantial evidence (*Gulf South* 1983). These legal formulae don't reveal much about judicial behavior, but they do remind regulators that they must be able to convince at least one third party—a court—that reliance on quantitative risk assessment makes sense.

## CASE LAW

Any scientist who ventured theories about judicial reactions to the use of quantitative risk assessment on the basis of the sample size available to me would be drummed out of the profession. I will discuss only five cases, only three of which involve review of agency risk estimates; and in only two of these three cases was the agency's risk assessment disputed. We are surely going to see more such cases, however, and the opinions in these cases may help us anticipate judicial attitudes in the future.

In a word, the courts are schizophrenic. Both the Supreme Court—in the decision involving OSHA's benzene standard (*Industrial Union* 1980)—and the D.C. Circuit Court of Appeals appear to have encouraged OSHA and FDA to quantify the risks of compounds that they attempt to regulate. In the benzene case, the Supreme Court was quite explicit. The D.C. Circuit, in a case challenging FDA's attempt to regulate beverage containers made of acrylonitrile (*Monsanto* 1979) was more oblique. But the message of the two cases is that a prudent regulator should attempt to quantify— to determine whether the risk posed by a chemical is worth worrying about.

In three other cases, all decided in the last year and one-half, courts have been called upon to review agency risk assessments for particular products. Let me begin with a case related to Michael Taylor's discussion of FDA's use of quantitative risk assessment (*Scott v. Food and Drug Administration* 1984). The case involved a consumer challenge to FDA's reapproval—actually its failure to ban—the color additive Green No. 5, which contains *p*-toluidine as a contaminant (D&C Green No. 5 1982).

*P*-toluidine is, I understand, a recognized animal carcinogen. The petitioner argued that FDA's failure to ban the color containing this carcinogen was incompatible with the Delaney Clause and with the general safety standard for color (and food) additives. The FDA, for its part, explained that the contaminant is present in such tiny amounts that the risk posed for human beings exposed to Green No. 5 is very small—somewhere between one case in 30,000,000 lifetimes and one in 300,000,000 lifetimes, according to two different estimates. This risk is indeed so small, FDA continued, that Green No. 5 can be viewed as safe and thus approvable under the Federal Food, Drug, and Cosmetic Act. The petitioner did not contest FDA's risk estimate; rather, he challenged the agency's use of risk assessment to justify the approval of a color additive containing a carcinogen.

This challenge failed. The Sixth Circuit upheld FDA's legal theory that a quantitatively trivial risk associated with a trace carcinogen in a color (or presumably a food) additive is not subject to the Delaney Clause. It may be noteworthy that the court upheld FDA's use of quantitative risk assessment to justify nonregulation. The agency was not seeking to curtail use of a commercial compound. It is also worth noting that the plaintiff did not take serious issue with FDA's exposure estimates or with the extrapolation model on which it relied. In the other two cases, both decided in the Fifth Circuit Court, petitioners attacked both the agencies' exposure estimates and the assumptions underlying their methods for estimating the risks of low doses of toxic agents.

The first of these cases involved the Consumer Product Safety Commission. *Gulf South Insulation Co. v. CPSC* (1983) was an industry challenge to the Commission's ban of urea formaldehyde foam insulation—a ban against future installations of UF foam insulation in residences, most particularly mobile homes, and in commercial buildings. The agency had found that formaldehyde leaking from this kind of insulation posed an unreasonable health risk to purchasers and occupants. With the aid of an inter-agency group of scientists assembled by the National Toxicology Program, the agency had performed a quantitative assessment that estimated the lifetime cancer risk to residents of insulated homes at from 0 to 37 or from 0 to 51 additional cancers per million persons exposed. The different upper bound estimates reflected different exposure estimates. One set of exposure estimates was derived from a study of homes in which the insulation had actually been installed. Another set of estimates was derived by measuring leaking formaldehyde from test wall panels made by homebuilders and home installers. The differences between the two exposure estimates were not wide (Ashford et al. 1983).

The risk estimate, based on laboratory studies of insulated wall panels held under simulated home conditions, ranged between 0 and 37 per million. The risk estimate based on in-home measurements of some 1100 homes ranged between 0 and 51 per million.

The insulation industry sharply attacked the CPSC's reliance upon these estimates. The court agreed that the agency's exposure data were seriously flawed because it had relied in substantial part on homes that were identified by residents who had complained about unpleasant odors and various acute irritations (Ashford et al. 1983). Local public health officials measured the levels of formaldehyde in these homes. Roughly two-thirds of the homes in the sample of 1164 were so-called "complaint homes"; but the formaldehyde levels measured in some 350 other randomly selected homes were similar to those in the "complaint homes" (Ashford et al. 1983; Petition for Rehearing 1983).

The CPSC was sharply criticized for relying essentially on a single bioassay—the CIIT study on formaldehyde. The agency had not relied squarely on the later NYU study, which was reported after the rulemaking proceeding had concluded, so that it was not technically part of the administrative record. The court also faulted the Commission for assertedly failing to take account of the several negative epidemiological studies of formaldehyde's carcinogenicity—some nine or ten in all (*Gulf South* 1983).

In addition, the court's original opinion contains a footnote that appears to jeopardize other underpinnings of the quantitative risk assessment methodology used by the Commission and other regulatory agencies. The court questioned the agency's implicit assumption of dose comparability between animals and man, i.e., its assumption that formaldehyde displays the same dose-response relationship in humans that is observed in test animals. Finally, the court asserted that the agency was on thin ice in making the assumption that there is no threshold, or safe, dose for formaldehyde:

> n.19 At least two of the assumptions are of questionable validity. The Commission assumed that at identical exposure levels the effective dose for rats is the same as that for humans. The industry points out that the effective dose for mice is much less than that for rats and argues that it is far more sensible to assume that rats equal mice than that rats equal humans.

Probably the most controversial assumption incorporated into Global 79 is that the risk of cancer from formaldehyde is linear at low dose—in other words that there is no threshold below which formaldehyde poses no risk of cancer.

As the Commission acknowledges, this assumption leads inescapably to the conclusion that ambient air is carcinogenic, albeit to a lesser extent than UFFI.[2]

In response to a petition for a rehearing filed by the government, the court reiterated its judgment that the CPSC's quantitative risk assessment was not a sufficient justification for regulation because, to quote the court, "[t]o make precise estimates, precise data are needed."[3]

The final case I want to bring to your attention, also from the Fifth Circuit, is *Asbestos Information Ass'n v. OSHA* (1984), decided March 7, 1984. This was a challenge by manufacturers and users to OSHA's emergency temporary standard for employee exposure to asbestos. The emergency standard would have reduced permitted exposure from the current limit of 0.2 particles per cubic meter of air to 0.05 particles—a 75% reduction. Under its statute OSHA may summarily issue an emergency rule requiring immediate reduction in exposure levels for workplace substances that are perceived to pose a "grave danger" to workers (OSHA 1982). It was such an emergency rule that the agency issued for asbestos. By law an emergency standard may remain in effect for only 6 months, during which time OSHA is supposed to complete the rulemaking process to establish a permanent standard, conceivably at the same level (OSHA 1982). But it is almost a practical impossibility for the agency to meet such a timetable. Thus, there usually is a hiatus between the expiration of an emergency standard at the end of 6 months and the time a final standard becomes effective—potentially quite a lengthy hiatus.

This statutory framework is important for the court's analysis of OSHA's emergency standard for asbestos and, specifically, for the risk estimate that the agency offered as part of its justification for issuing the standard. The court explained that the issue before it was whether the agency's estimate of the number of lives saved by reducing asbestos exposure for 6 months was supported by "substantial evidence" and, if so, whether that estimate demonstrated that current exposure levels constituted a "grave danger" (*Asbestos* 1984).

By one calculation, OSHA had estimated that as many as 210 lives could be saved by the 6-month reduction in exposure among the entire group of employees exposed to asbestos. In this estimate the agency assumed that many were in fact experiencing higher levels than the current standard allowed (*Asbestos* 1984). Assuming that no employees were currently being exposed to higher levels than the current standard permitted, OSHA estimated that as many as 80 lives could be saved (*Asbestos* 1984). The industry sharply attacked these risk estimates, stressing their substantial uncertainty, questioning the reliability of OSHA's estimates of the number of workers exposed to asbestos, and disputing the agency's initial assumption that many workers are in fact exposed at levels much higher than the prevailing standard. The court seemed concerned about all of these issues but, perhaps more

---

[2] *Gulf South Insulation v. United States Consumer Product Safety Commission,* 701 F.2d 1137, 1147 n.19 (5th Cir. 1983).

[3] *Gulf South Insulation v. United States Consumer Product Safety Commission,* 701 F.2d 1137, 1146 (5th Cir. 1983).

importantly, it was also troubled by the procedural posture of the case. Under the law, an emergency standard can be issued without any opportunity for public comment; public rulemaking only commences with publication of the emergency rule. Thus the risk estimates on which OSHA relied had not previously been exposed to scrutiny outside the agency (*Asbestos* 1984). In short, nobody who objected to OSHA's emergency standard or its underlying risk assessment had had an opportunity to be heard by the agency before the case got into court.

The Fifth Circuit's opinion in the asbestos case paints with a broader brush, by contrast with the *Gulf South* opinion which treated the different elements of quantitative risk assessment in some detail. The court also touched upon several other grounds of invalidity of the standard. But the court's language parallels *Gulf South* in displaying skepticism about the agency's methodology for quantifying the health consequences of regulation.

## CONCLUSION

Let me suggest some common threads in the latter two cases. In each, the regulatory agency relied on quantitative risk assessment to justify new controls on exposure; by contrast, in the Green No. 5 the FDA invoked risk assessment to justify non-intervention. Second, and probably more important, in both cases which set aside the regulation and the agency's risk estimate is questioned, the opposing parties vigorously contested the agency's methodology, its data, and the appearance of precision attached to the derived numbers. Finally, as I have noted, it is significant that both cases arose in the Fifth Circuit.

I do not defend these decisions, either in terms of the applicable statutes or in terms of the facts presented. I offer them as possibly illustrative of judicial attitudes toward the exercise (i.e., quantitative risk estimation) whose scientific underpinnings are discussed in this volume.

## REFERENCES
### Cases

*Animal Health Institute v. FDA,* [1977-1978 Transfer Binder] Food Drug Cosm. L. Rep. (CCH) ¶ 38,154 (D.D.C. February 8, 1978).

*Asbestos Information Ass'n v. OSHA,* 727 F.2d 415 (5th Cir. 1984).

*Gulf South Insulation v. United States Consumer Product Safety Commission,* 701 F.2d 1137 (5th Cir. 1983).

*Industrial Union Dept. v. American Petroleum Institute,* 448 U.S. 607 (1980).

*Monsanto Co. v. Kennedy,* 613 F.2d 947(D.C. Cir. 1979).

*Motor Vehicles Mfrs. Ass'n v. State Farm Mut. Automobile Ins. Co.,* 103 S. Ct. 2856 (1983).

*Scott v. Food and Drug Administration,* 728 F.2d 322 (6th Cir. 1984).

Petition for Rehearing (Respondent), *Gulf South Insulation v. United States Consumer Product Safety Commission,* 701 F.2d 1137 (5th Cir. 1983).

## Statutes and Regulations

Administrative Procedure Act, 5 U.S.C. §§ 553, 556–57 (1982).

Aflatoxins in Shelled Peanuts and Peanut Products Used as Human Foods, 43 Fed. Reg. 8808 (1978) (to be codified at 21 C.F.R. pt. 109) (proposed March 3, 1978).

Chemical Compounds in Food-Producing Animals: Criteria and Procedures for Evaluating Assays for Carcinogenic Residues, in Edible Products of Animals, 42 Fed. Reg. 10412 (1977) (to be codified at 21 C.F.R. pts. 8, 500, 514, and 571).

Chemical Compounds in Food-Producing Animals: Criteria and Procedures for Evaluating Assays for Carcinogenic Residues, 44 Fed. Reg. 17070 (1979) (to be codified at 21 C.F.R. pts. 70, 500, 514 and 571) (proposed March 20, 1979).

Clean Air Act, 42 U.S.C. § 7412(b)(1)(B) (1982).

Compounds Used in Food-Producing Animals: Procedures for Determining Acceptability of Assay Methods Used for Assuring the Absence of Residues in Edible Products of Such Animals, 38 Fed. Reg. 19226 (1973) (to be codified at 21 C.F.R. pt. 135) (proposed July 19, 1973).

D&C Green No. 5; Listing as a Color Additive in Drugs & Cosmetics, 47 Fed. Reg. 49629 (1982) (to be codified at 21 C.F.R. pts. 74, 81 and 82).

Identification, Classification and Regulation of Potential Occupational Carcinogens, 45 Fed. Reg. 5001 (1980) (to be codified at 29 C.F.R. pt. 1990).

Occupational Exposure to Ethylene Dibromide, 48 Fed. Reg. 45956 (1983) (to be codified at 29 C.F.R. pt. 1910) (proposed October 7, 1983).

Occupational Exposure to Ethylene Oxide, 48 Fed. Reg. 17284 (1983) (to be codified at 29 C.F.R. pt. 1910) (proposed April 21, 1983).

Occupational Safety and Health Act, 29 U.S.C. § 655(c) (1982).

OSHA ETS for Occupational Exposure to Asbestos, 48 Fed. Reg. 51,086 (1983) (to be codified at 29 C.F.R. pt. 1910).

Polychlorinated Biphenyls (PCB's); Reduction of Tolerances, 44 Fed. Reg. 38330 (1979) (to be codified at 29 C.F.R. pt. 109).

Saccharin and Its Salts, 42 Fed. Reg. 19996 (1977) (to be codified at 21 C.F.R. pts. 145, 150, 172, 180, 189, 310, 430, 510, 589, and 700) (proposed April 15, 1977).

Toxic Substances Control Act, 15 U.S.C. § 2603(f) (1982).

## Articles and Books

Ashford, N.A., C.W. Ryan, and C.C. Caldart. 1983. A hard look at federal regulation of formaldehyde: A departure from reasoned decisionmaking. *Harv. Envtl. L. Rev.* 7: 297.

Brief for the Federal Parties, *Industrial Union Dept. v. American Petroleum Institute,* 448 U.S. 607 (1980).

Davis, K.C. 1977. *Administrative law: Cases-text-problems,* 6th ed. West Publishing Co., St. Paul, Minnesota.

## COMMENTS

**ALBERT:** Does the court have a scientist as an amicus curiae?

**MERRILL:** There's no evidence, in the report of the record in either case, that the court has access to the advice of independent scientists. Indeed, there are real impediments to courts' seeking such advice. Occasionally, a court happens upon such expertise by chance. I am familiar with one case involving EPA water pollution standards for the paper pulp industry, about which the author of the opinion later confirmed that the court was aided enormously in evaluating the EPA record by a law clerk who happened to have prior training as an engineer before going to law school. In general, however, courts are not permitted to go beyond the information the parties provide. So what we may see in these cases are the results of skillful argumentation by one side that convinces the judges that an agency may well be wrong. It is hard to know what to make of the cases. I don't present them as the wave of the future. All we know is they are the crest of the present.

**CORN:** Many who have dealt with the Fifth Circuit Court of Appeals suggest that the asbestos Emergency Temporary Standard (ETS) was a good opportunity for the court to cast aspersions on quantitative risk assessment. No ETS would have gotten through that court. The court is so constitutionally opposed to the idea of an ETS that, regardless of the standard's defensibility, the burden of proof could not be met. An ETS bypasses "due process."

**MERRILL:** That is quite plausible. An ETS is an extreme regulatory action. OSHA has previously had difficulty getting emergency standards upheld by other circuits. Your speculation, however, leads one to ask why the court would spend time on a gratuitous discussion of OSHA's quantitative risk assessment.

**R. WILSON:** I think OSHA missed out both in asbestos and in the previous (1977) case of benzene, where it also proposed an Emergency Temporary Standard. Both compounds have been in use for a very long time at a higher level. To suddenly come up with an emergency sounds a little peculiar unless there's some brand new piece of data which everybody is agreed upon. I think there is a common sense point in there.

**MERRILL:** I couldn't agree with you more. In the asbestos case, however, the court goes out of its way to say it is permissible for OSHA to issue an emergency standard for a familiar workplace hazard if it has new information— and that new information can consist solely of improved analysis of old information—which suggests that the hazard is greater than it previously believed. But, I do not discount the theory that it is the unusual procedural posture of the case, coupled with the facts that asbestos has been around for a long time and that exposure limits are already pretty low, which leads the Fifth Circuit to question OSHA's risk assessment.

**TAYLOR:** Another way to try to make sense of those cases, though—and this may be more pessimistic, if one hopes that agencies will use risk assessment more—is that the decision may be explainable by the very nature of quantitative risk assessment, which, of course, is only putting upper limits on risk and is having to acknowledge that the risk may well be zero. Because, if the Agency has to demonstrate affirmatively, as in the asbestos and formaldehyde cases, that there is a risk that justifies action, one can imagine why a court, given the inherent limitations of risk assessment, would say, "You haven't made the showing." But in the *Scott* case, the question is, "Has the Agency, exercising its expert judgment, plausibly ruled out the possibility of a risk worth worrying about?" Then, the fact that the risk is somewhere between zero and some upper limit is not of concern to the court.

**MERRILL:** Dr. Albert's question earlier suggests that education of the judiciary is an important prerequisite to the successful use of this technique. However, understanding is not only a function of what happens in the courtroom when litigants present their cases. It can also be aided by organized involvement of scientific groups in administrative and judicial proceedings. I spent a week last summer teaching a group of appellate judges about quantitative risk assessment. One of them was a member of the Fifth Circuit Court of Appeals— though not, I hasten to add, a member of the panel that decided the *Gulf South* case.

**COHN:** I didn't feel the range of 0–51 was really of much concern to the court. I saw them attacking the underlying data, saying that the data from the CIIT study were too variable and the exposure data were too variable. Even if the range had been 50–51, the result would have been the same.

**R. WILSON:** The formaldehyde case is much more serious than the asbestos case. We were not debating temporary 6-month standards. We're not going to have great catastrophes in this world. But if we can't control insulation when the scientific evidence suggests one should, then it's a far more serious situation. I'm not worried about the 6 months' additional exposure to asbestos; it's 30 years from now that I'm concerned with.

**WEINSTEIN:** I'd like to hear from the lawyers and policymakers. How are decisions made in other areas of risk extrapolation? We're talking about chemical risks, but this problem is not unique. What about physical hazards, risks associated with medical diagnostic techniques and drug treatment, low-level radiation or the risks of nuclear warfare? Are there principles or lessons to be learned from these areas that can be applied to risk extrapolations related to chemical hazards?

**MERRILL:** I'll venture a speculation. I would put aside nuclear war risk because I don't know anything about governmental decisionmaking with respect to that; and I dare say it would not be very illuminating. In regulating air safety, for example, where we have a fair amount of epidemiology and long experience, quantification is routinely used for estimating the effects of different air traffic control safeguards that might be implemented. It was, as Lester

[Lave] well knows, one of the areas in which cost/benefit analysis was first used in determining whether or not certain investments in length of runways, or radar, or lighting systems were worthwhile.

**LAVE:** It is routinely used all the time. The FAA has explicit criteria about the value of preventing a premature death.

**WEINSTEIN:** What sorts of rules of thumb are used, or what's acceptable?

**LAVE:** The figure they were using up until recently was $300,000 per premature death. I did a detailed look at an analysis of "frangible lighting standards for airports." These are light poles that easily break so that they wouldn't cause an airliner to crash. The FAA estimated the number of crashes that would be prevented by these frangible standards and then estimated the accidental deaths that would be averted. Each averted death was valued at $300,000. For big airports with lots of activity, frangible lighting standards had benefits greater than costs. For airports that had a small number of operations, costs exceeded benefits, and the FAA recommended against replacing the existing standards.

**WEINSTEIN:** How many deaths are you allowed?

**LAVE:** It isn't how many deaths. The question is whether the cost of replacing light poles with frangible lighting standards is less than or more than the dollar benefits of averting crashes, where a value of $300,000 is put on each premature death.

**PERERA:** How did they pick that number?

**LAVE:** The number came from a "human capital" approach, in which the FAA tried to estimate how much earnings would be lost if an air traveler died. The number was derived in the 1960s when air travelers had relatively high incomes. For some strange reason, that number has not escalated with inflation. I don't believe that number can now be supported.

**R. WILSON:** The National Highway Transportation Safety Administration (NHTSA) has been using about $175,000 as a suggested amount to spend to save a life by installing guard rails, lighting, and all those things. But, when the Ford Motor Company executives used this number of $175,000 to calculate whether to install a better gas tank on the back of the Pinto and did not destroy the piece of paper, they got into trouble.

**LAVE:** The important point is that both NHTSA and FAA go through quantitative risk assessment. They are not criticized for this. The FAA goes through a full-blown benefit/cost analysis, putting a dollar value on deaths averted. NHTSA does a cost-effectiveness kind of analysis. They start with preventing the crashes that cost the least to prevent per life saved. Crashes may be easier to analyze and the estimates may seem more certain than the risks of chemical carcinogens. However, analyses of chemical plant or nuclear catastrophes have probabilities of $10^{-8}$ or $10^{-12}$. The real probability for a disaster could range from $0-10^{-5}$, rather than the $10^{-9}$ estimated. These numbers appear to be as uncertain as carcinogenic risks.

# Session 2: Epidemiology in Risk Estimation

# Epidemiology and Risk Assessment: Estimation of GI Cancer Risk from Asbestos in Drinking Water and Lung Cancer Risk from PAHs in Air

**MALCOLM C. PIKE**
Imperial Cancer Research Fund's
Cancer Epidemiology & Clinical Trials Unit
University of Oxford
Radcliffe Infirmary
Oxford OX2 6HE, United Kingdom

## INTRODUCTION

Epidemiological studies, animal carcinogenesis experiments, in vitro mutagenesis and transformation assays, and knowledge of basic biological and chemical processes, may all provide information relevant to the assessment of human cancer risk from exposure to a particular compound. Risk estimates based on epidemiological data are, however, likely to be much superior to estimates derived from other information. No interspecies extrapolation is involved, only extrapolation from a high to a low dose; and the high doses are often not too different from the low levels at which regulations may be envisaged. Risk estimation from epidemiological data is, however, not necessarily straightforward, and in this paper, I will illustrate by two examples—asbestos in drinking water and polycyclic aromatic hydrocarbons (PAHs) in air—the principles on which I believe it should be based.

## GENERAL PRINCIPLES

The epidemiologic data that has been of most use for risk assessment purposes has come from studies of occupational groups. Epidemiological correlation studies, which relate cancer rates to general exposures, e.g., cancer of the bladder to the average level of trihalomethanes in the drinking water in different geographic areas of the U.S. (Safe Drinking Water Committee 1980), have also been used; but these studies are seldom particularly convincing, because the differences in cancer rates in the different areas and the exposure differences are not large enough for one to be able to comfortably ignore the possibility that other (unmeasured) differences between the areas (i.e., confounding factors) could explain any correlations found. Studies of occupational groups, exposed to high levels of the compound being studied, essentially avoid this problem of confounding, since it can usually be convincingly argued that confounding factors are unlikely to be able to explain any but a small fraction of the observed occupational risk.

Occupational studies do, however, pose special problems of their own when it comes to interpreting their relevance to population exposures. For example, when

**55**

discussing asbestos exposure, one has to ask how the fiber size difference between insulation worker exposure and child in classroom exposure should be taken into account when estimating risk to the latter from data on the former. An even more difficult problem is that of multiple exposures—occupational groups are seldom exposed to only a single noxious substance, and separating the effects of the different compounds may not be easy.

In the simplest terms an occupational study has an exposed group (E) and an unexposed group (U), and their cancer rates at the site being studied are $r_E$ and $r_U$. The cancer burden from the exposure can be expressed either as a ratio of rates, or relative risk, i.e., $RR = r_E/r_U$, or as a difference of rates, i.e., $DR = r_E - r_U$. Both RR and DR are valid measures of the risk to the occupational group, but they implicitly make very different assumptions about the risks to individuals with different underlying cancer risks. The multiplicative index, RR, implicitly assumes that the risk of cancer is increased in proportion to the individual's underlying risk; whereas the additive index, DR, implicitly assumes that the increased cancer risk is independent of the individual's underlying risk. Occupational studies unfortunately rarely provide enough data to enable one to distinguish between possible models (i.e., the multiplicative or additive models, or something intermediate, or some completely different model). Selection of a model is nevertheless critical in risk assessment and a choice cannot be avoided. In the absence of evidence to the contrary, the additive model is usually chosen (Safe Drinking Water Committee 1977).

Whatever model is chosen, the cancer burden has then to be connected with some measure of the occupational exposure so that extrapolation down to population exposure levels may be made. The standard linear dose-effect models are $RR = 1 + a \cdot dose$ and $DR = b \cdot dose$, where a and b are constants to be estimated. Dose may be measured in a variety of ways: it is commonly taken to be cumulative exposure. It is not self-evident that linearity of cancer burden is a sensible assumption, but there is seldom sufficient data available to enable any other reasonable assumption to be made. Cumulative exposure appears at first to be the self-evidently correct measure of dose; it has, however, been clearly shown that equal doses measured in this way can have very different effects (e.g., cigarette smoking measured as pack-years does not have a fixed effect on lung cancer incidence but has a much greater effect at a low intensity for a long time—a person aged 60 who smoked 15 cigarettes per day from age 20 to age 60 (30 pack-years total) has more than ten times the lung cancer incidence rate of a person aged 60 who smoked 30 cigarettes per day from age 20 to age 40 and then stopped smoking (also 30 pack-years total) (Committee on Pyrenes and Selected Analogues 1983).

A rough, but very important, check on a risk estimate calculated from occupational studies can often be made by comparing the results observed in other epidemiological studies (usually correlational) to the results which would be predicted on the basis of the occupational studies derived risks. Such comparisons will, in particular, guard one against accepting falsely inflated risks (e.g., because of unrecognized multiple exposures) calculated from occupational studies.

Having quantitated the carcinogenic risk from exposure in RR or DR terms, it is then most helpful if the result is expressed in a standard format. The notion of cancer risk assessment, and its attendant implied notion of comparing risks from exposure to different compounds, essentially assumes the existence of a commonly agreed scale of measure of cancer risk. The measure adopted by the Safe Drinking Water Committee of the National Research Council (Safe Drinking Water Committee 1977) is the "lifetime risk," i.e., the probability of being diagnosed with the cancer by age 70, a "lifetime," in the absence of other causes of death, from exposure to the compound at a given uniform chronic dose. This measure has been found particularly useful in comparing human data and experimental animal data and forms the basis of the current methods of extrapolating animal data to man (Santodonato et al. 1981). It is clear that this measure does not satisfactorily express all aspects of risk, since it takes no account of the seriousness of the induced cancers, but all risk assessments made should at least be expressed in this form, as well as any others that individual authors may feel appropriate, so that some simple comparisons can be made between compounds. The "lifetime risk" is virtually identical with the cumulative incidence rate to age 70 used by the International Agency for Research on Cancer (Stukonis 1978).

## GI CANCER AND ASBESTOS IN DRINKING WATER

An excess of GI cancers has been found in workers exposed to asbestos through inhalation. This effect is presumed to be due to the asbestos fibers these workers swallow. The possible effect of population exposure to swallowed asbestos became a matter of some public concern in the U.S. when the public water supply of Duluth, Minnesota, obtained from Lake Superior, was found to be heavily contaminated with such fibers. A subsequent survey of U.S. drinking water supplies counting fibers by transmission electron microscopy (TEM) showed that some 20% were contaminated by more than one million fibers per liter ($10^6$ TEMFPL). (Note: asbestos concentrations in water have also been reported in terms of mass per liter, but this measurement is not considered useful in the evaluation of possible carcinogenic effects.)

Some doubt exists about whether the excess of GI cancers in asbestos workers is real or is an artifact of misdiagnosed mesotheliomas that arise directly from the inhaled asbestos. Since this is a methods volume, not a substance volume, I will not discuss the issue here, but simply assume that the GI cancer risk is real and due to the asbestos actually swallowed (see Safe Drinking Water Committee [1983] for details of the following analysis).

For asbestos, there is some evidence suggesting that the multiplicative model is the model of choice: in particular, the multiplicative model is generally regarded as providing a reasonable description of the extensive data on lung cancer and asbestos exposure. There is also some evidence suggesting that one should adopt the linear dose-effect model for RR (i.e., RR $= 1 + a \cdot$dose) with dose being taken as cumulative exposure. For GI cancers, too few data exist to establish or refute linearity, but such a relationship has been clearly shown for lung cancer and asbestos exposure. Measuring dose as cumulative exposure is generally accepted as fitting the data on asbestos-induced cancer reasonably well.

From a series of occupational studies, a best value for the RR for GI cancer for a person who has swallowed $h.10^{12}$ TEMF was estimated as

$$RR = 1 + 0.05h. \tag{1}$$

A man who has been drinking 2 liters of water per day (standard man water consumption) containing $d.10^6$ TEMFPL for n years has consumed $h.10^{12}$ TEMFs, where $h = n(365.25)2d.10^{-6}$. His RR of GI cancer in this nth year of exposure will be

$$\begin{aligned} RR &= 1 + 0.05h \\ &= 1 + n(365.25)d.10^{-7}. \end{aligned} \tag{2}$$

This will also be the RR at age n for a man who has consumed such water throughout life, e.g., for a man aged 57.5 years, the RR will be

$$\begin{aligned} RR &= 1 + 57.5(365.25)d.10^{-7} \\ &= 1 + 0.0021d. \end{aligned}$$

Table 1 shows the results of calculations based on this equation, indicating the consequences in terms of GI cancer for U.S. white males who drink 2 liters of water containing $d.10^6$ TEMFPL per day throughout life. The additional risk of GI cancer for our 57.5-year-old man above is $0.0021d(131.1/10^5) = 0.2754d/10^5$. Summing these additional risks to age 70 gives us a lifetime risk of $9.1d/10^5$ or $(1/9.1)10^6 = 0.11(10^6)$ TEMFPL is estimated as leading to one GI cancer case per 100,000 men exposed over a 70-year lifespan.

## Comparisons with Results of Other Epidemiological Studies

For the situation we are considering here, checking the quantitative risk estimates we arrived at above on the basis of occupational studies means checking against the results of studies that looked directly at GI cancer rates in cities with different levels of asbestos in their water supply.

For obvious reasons, one of the first areas to be studied was Duluth. Levy et al. (1976) studied GI cancer rates in Duluth in 1970 and concluded that "there was no consistent pattern of statistically significant differences." The risk estimates we derived above would predict just such a result.

The Duluth water supply may be estimated as containing no more than an average of some $8.10^6$ TEMFPL from 1955 when contamination began to 1970, so that our equation 2 would predict the RR for GI cancer in 1970 as

$$RR = 1 + 15(365.25)8.10^{-7} = 1.004.$$

RRs of this magnitude are far too small for any epidemiological study to detect. This is a fine illustration of the fact that negative epidemiological results can be

**Table 1**
Calculation of Additional Risk of Gastrointestinal Cancer Incidence in U.S. White Males from Swallowing 2d million TEM Fibers Daily Throughout Life.[a] Additional Relative Risk per $10^{12}$ TEM Fibers Swallowed Assumed to be 0.05.

| Age group (years) | Underlying incidence rate per 100,000/year | Asbestos swallowed ($10^9$ TEM fibers) | Additional relative risk (RR) | Additional incidence rate |
|---|---|---|---|---|
| 10–14 | 0.1 | 9.13d | 0.00046d | 0.0000d |
| 15–19 | 0.9 | 12.78d | 0.00064d | 0.0006d |
| 20–24 | 1.2 | 16.44d | 0.00082d | 0.0009d |
| 25–29 | 2.5 | 20.09d | 0.00100d | 0.0025d |
| 30–34 | 5.0 | 23.74d | 0.00118d | 0.0058d |
| 35–39 | 8.5 | 27.39d | 0.00136d | 0.0116d |
| 40–44 | 20.2 | 31.05d | 0.00156d | 0.0313d |
| 45–49 | 43.1 | 34.70d | 0.00174d | 0.0748d |
| 50–54 | 79.1 | 38.35d | 0.00192d | 0.1517d |
| 55–59 | 131.1 | 42.00d | 0.00210d | 0.2754d |
| 60–64 | 209.1 | 45.66d | 0.00228d | 0.4774d |
| 65–69 | 320.1 | 49.31d | 0.00246d | 0.7892d |
| Total | 4,104.5 | | | 9.1060d |

[a]Underlying GI cancer incidence rates taken from Cutler and Young (1975) for the combined sites of esophagus, stomach, small and large intestine, and rectum

considered as providing important evidence against a compound's being carcinogenic only after the dose-effect relationship has been considered in detail.

Similar comparisons with the results of studies in other areas showed no serious disagreement with the occupational studies derived risk estimate (Safe Drinking Water Committee 1983).

The above is what I would consider a proper standard approach to risk estimation from epidemiological data, the novel feature being that, because of the risk model adopted, the estimate of risk depended on the background rate of the disease.

This is not the approach adopted by the Environmental Protection Agency (EPA) in their Ambient Water Quality Criteria Document. This document measures the relevant lifetime cancer risk as (number of excess deaths from GI cancer)/(total expected number of deaths from all causes).This measure has the attractive property of considering excess deaths as more important if the population is otherwise very healthy; but it is a confusing, very imprecisely defined measure and its use should be discouraged.

## LUNG CANCER AND PAHs IN AIR

Various PAHs, notably benzo[a]pyrene (B[a]P), are known animal carcinogens, and their presence in city air has been a cause of concern for many years. However, the general level of PAHs declined dramatically from the late 1950s to the late 1970s with the introduction of controls on the burning of fossil fuels, notably coal, and on automobile exhaust emissions; and interest in their effects naturally waned somewhat. The rapid increase in popularity of diesel cars with their dirty emissions in the late 1970s rekindled interest in estimating the cancer risk from inhaling PAHs; and recent reports of two National Research Council Committees (Diesel Impacts Study Committee 1981; Committee on Pyrene and Selected Analogues 1983) have fully discussed the issues involved. In this section of my paper I will discuss the approach I took in my report for the Committee on Pyrene and Selected Analogues to estimating the lung cancer risk from PAHs in air.

The two sources of epidemiological data on human exposure to PAHs on which reliance may be placed are work around coke ovens and cigarette smoking. Although cigarette smoking is of overwhelming importance as a cause of lung cancer, it is still far from established that the PAH content of cigarette smoke is the major factor responsible for lung cancer development in cigarette smokers. Risk estimation for PAHs in air is much more likely to be better estimated from the exposure of coke oven workers. The data on lung cancer in coke oven workers are, however, much less precise than the data on lung cancer and cigarette smoking. The lung cancer risks of coke oven workers have, in fact, always been measured in relation to lung cancer rates in the nonexposed; and cigarette smoking has been responsible for some 90% of the lung cancers in these nonexposed. To measure the lung cancer risk associated with coke oven exposure, and hence to estimate lung cancer risk from general PAH exposure, it is thus essential to understand the risk from cigarette smoking.

Much of what has been learned about the quantitative relationship between cigarette smoking and lung cancer may be summarized by the statement, "The excess lung cancer incidence of a smoker, compared with a nonsmoker, is proportional to the number of cigarettes smoked per day and to the duration of smoking raised to the power 4.5." If we write the excess incidence of a smoker aged t years who started smoking at age w years and who smokes c cigarettes per day as $I_c(t,w)$, this statement may be expressed mathematically as

$$I_c(t,w) = ac(t - w)^{4.5} \tag{3}$$

where the constant a is approximately $10^{-11}$ for U.K. smokers. We may express the lung cancer risks from cigarettes in terms of lifetime risk by first using equation 3 with exposure starting at birth, so that the lung cancer rate at age t from c cigarettes per day will be

$$I_c(t,0) = act^{4.5} \tag{4}$$

and the lifetime risk can then be shown to be

$$CI_c(T) = 1 - \exp[- ac(70^{5.5}/5.5)]. \tag{5}$$

The lifetime lung cancer risk associated with one U.K. cigarette per day is 2.52%.

The lung cancer risk associated with cigarette smoking depends strongly on age at which smoking started, i.e., on the duration of exposure. For a smoker at age 60, starting to smoke at age 15 (compared to starting at age 20) will increase the extra lung cancer rate by 70%. To make valid comparisons between groups of persons exposed to different concentrations of PAH-containing mixtures (e.g., different occupational groups), we must therefore know their comparative smoking habits, not only in terms of number of cigarettes smoked per day, but also in terms of age at starting (and stopping) smoking.

If a person aged 60 who has smoked 30 cigarettes per day from age 20 to age 40 (30 pack-years in total) is compared with a person at the same age (60) who has smoked 15 cigarettes per day from age 20 to age 60 (also 30 pack-years in total), then calculations based on equation 3 show that the latter person will have more than 10 times the lung cancer rate of the former. This strongly suggests that to understand quantitatively the effect of exposure to any PAH-containing mixture, one must know not only the total cumulative exposure, but also the time over which it is accumulated.

With this background information on the relationships of lung cancer with cigarette smoking, we can proceed to look at the studies of occupational groups exposed to PAH-containing mixtures. No occupational study has been conducted in such a way as to provide sufficient data to establish the correct risk model. Studies comparing urban and rural lung cancer rates (or rates in heavily polluted and lightly polluted areas) in persons with different smoking habits do provide relevant data, but the studies generally have few deaths and do not clearly identify the correct model. Data from the studies of Stocks (1957) and Hitosugi (1968) illustrate the point; in both studies, the data from the smokers are in good agreement with an additive model for the effect of air pollution, and these data provide no evidence for a multiplicative model. The data from nonsmokers, however, confuse the picture. In Stock's study, the effect of air pollution is smaller in the nonsmokers; in Hitosugi's study, there is no effect in nonsmokers. The problem may simply result from basing the rates on such small numbers of deaths in nonsmokers or from misclassifying the smoking habits of a few persons who died of lung cancer. Because the additive model provides such a good fit to the data on smokers, it appears most sensible to assume this model for lung cancer risk from occupational exposure to PAH-containing mixtures.

Further analysis shows that to use the occupational studies for risk assessment purposes, one should assume that occupational exposures can be expressed as cigarette equivalents, i.e., assume that the form of equations 3–5 will hold for the excess lung cancer from such exposure. We saw when discussing lung cancer and cigarette smoking that dose (number of cigarettes per day) and duration (number of years smoked) of exposure are critical in determining lung cancer risk. To be useful for risk estimation purposes, an occupational study must, therefore, at a minimum, provide a quantitative estimate of the occupational group's exposure to PAH-containing mixtures (i.e., provide estimates of intensity of exposure and number of years exposed). With this information and comparative information on the smoking habits of the exposed and nonexposed workers, we can estimate the absolute risk from such exposure. Unfortunately, only one occupational study (Doll et al. 1972) of groups with high exposure to a PAH-containing mixture supplied even this minimal information.

Doll et al. (1972) followed a cohort of carbonization workers in British gasworks. The intensity of carbonization workers' exposure to PAHs was measured by noting the B[$a$]P content of the air: they were exposed to B[$a$]P at an estimated average air concentration of 3000 ng/m$^3$ during an 8-hour shift (some 100 times background B[$a$]P air pollution). The carbonization workers experienced a 142% increase in lung cancer mortality, compared with their nonexposed workmates. Although the smoking habits of only some 10% of the cohort were noted, the exposed and nonexposed workers appear to have had very similar smoking habits, with an average current consumption of approximately ten cigarettes per day. It is reasonable, therefore, to assign the excess lung cancer in the exposed group to their working conditions, specifically to the air to which they were exposed.

From the data given by Doll et al. (1972), it is possible, making rough adjustments for such factors as job changes away from the carbonization process, to estimate, expressing the gasworkers' exposure in constant-exposure terms, i.e., as though the men had breathed such air throughout the day every day, that the average B[$a$]P-carbonization pollution to which they were exposed was roughly 750 ng/m$^3$. This led to a 142% increase in the rate of lung cancer over background, roughly 90% of which was caused by the men's smoking habits. Thus, if we assume that the men started work and started to smoke regularly at roughly the same age, we may write (in lung cancer terms) 10 cigarettes per day = 0.9 and B[$a$]P-carbonization at 750 ng/m$^3$ = 1.42.

These two equations permit us to express B[a]P-carbonization in terms of U.K. cigarettes as B[a]P-carbonization at 47 ng/m$^3$ = 1 cigarette.

Making allowance for the different breathing habits of manual workers and standard man, we finally arrive at a figure of B[$a$]P-carbonization at 60 ng/m$^3$ = 1 cigarette.

Using equation 5, this translates into a lifetime lung cancer risk associated with exposure to B[$a$]P-carbonization at 1 ng/m$^3$ of 43/100,000.

To complete this risk assessment, one, of course, needs to measure the relative carcinogenicities of PAH-air pollution (as measured by B[$a$]P concentration). This is discussed in the report of the Committee on Pyrene and Selected Analogues (1983).

## Comparisons with Results of Other Epidemiological Studies

The above calculations based on the British gasworkers studies can be checked, at least for rough agreement, against the results of a variety of other epidemiological data.

Coke oven workers in the U.S. have been found in an epidemiological cohort study to have experienced a substantial excess risk of lung cancer (Redmond et al. 1972). This study did not, however, give any data on the smoking habits of the workers, on length of employment, on age, or on level of PAH exposure. Assuming that exposed and nonexposed workers had the same cigarette smoking habits, that the unexposed worker lung cancer rate was the U.S. average, and that the B[a]P concentrations were the same as at other coke ovens in the U.S., one finds that the U.S. results are in close agreement with the U.K. gasworkers' experience.

Detailed study of reports of the lung cancer experience of other occupationally exposed groups revealed that no other groups had very high exposure to PAHs. In particular, the study of London Transport Authority diesel bus garage workers concluded that "the indications are that the overall exposure of garage workers to benzo[a]pyrene during their working lives would not differ much from those of the general population" (Waller 1980). Studies of these groups is noninformative.

Although urban-rural comparisons of lung cancer rates are, for a variety of reasons, generally uninformative, the comparison undertaken by Stocks (1957) of Liverpool to parts of North Wales is uniquely useful. He not only measured air pollution, but also addressed the issue of long-term smoking habits. His data suggest a risk assessment figure for B[a]P coal-burning air pollution only 20% higher than the risk we derived above from Doll's (1972) study of British coke oven workers.

Correlation studies of different states in the U.S. in relation to cigarette sales and average air pollution were shown to give nonsense answers.

Finally the lung cancer rates of nonsmokers can be analyzed in relation to the average air pollution they will have been subject to during their lives. Such analysis suggests that if all their lung cancers were due to air pollution, then the estimate of risk for B[a]P air-pollution would be about one-third higher than the British coke oven workers derived figure.

The analysis of the epidemiologic data on the carbonization workers is again a proper standard approach, which attempts to take into account the knowledge of cigarette smoking-induced lung cancer that has been obtained over the last 30 years. It is not the approach adopted by the Diesel Impacts Study Committee who, in my opinion, adopted the wrong model in their analysis and used uninformative data on persons exposed to diesel fumes at too low levels to enable sensible estimates of risk to be derived.

## CONCLUSION

These two case studies have shown that even epidemiological studies seldom provide simple clear-cut answers to the risk assessment question. The studies themselves all too often suffer from various inadequacies, such as imprecise dose measurements and poor recording of confounding factors; and the assumptions made in the analysis, for example, about the dose-effect relationship, can often not be based on a firm foundation. It is still true, however, that epidemiological evidence-based risk assessment is likely to be much superior to other estimates, and if attention is given to using as much as possible of the relevant epidemiological information available, serious errors in risk estimates are unlikely.

## REFERENCES

Committee on Pyrene and Selected Analogues. 1983. *Polycyclic aromatic hydrocarbons: Evaluation of sources and effects.* Board on Toxicology and Environmental Health Hazards, Commission on Life Sciences, National Research Council, National Academy Press, Washington, D.C.

Cutler, S.J. and Y.L. Young (eds.). 1975. *Third national cancer survey: Incidence data.* National Cancer Institute Monograph 41. DHEW Publ. No. (NIH) 75–787, Bethesda, Maryland.

Diesel Impacts Study Committee. 1981. *Health effects of exposure to diesel exhaust.* The Report of the Health Effects Panel. National Research Council, National Academy Press, Washington, D.C.

Doll, R., M.P. Vessey, R.W.R. Beasley, A.R. Buckley, E.C. Fear, R.E.W. Fisher, E.J. Gammon, W. Gunn, G.O. Hughes, K. Lee, and B. Norman-Smith. 1972. Mortality of gasworkers—Final report of a prospective study. *Br. J. Ind. Med.* **29:** 394.

Hitosugi, M. 1968. Epidemiologic study of lung cancer with special reference to the effect of air pollution and smoking habits. *Inst. Publ. Health Bull.* **17:** 237.

Levy, B.S., E. Sigurdson, J. Mandel, E. London, and J. Pearson. 1976. Investigating possible effects of asbestos in city water: Surveillance of gastrointestinal cancer incidence in Duluth, Minnesota. *Am. J. Epidemiol.* **103:** 362.

Redmond, C.K., A. Ciocco, J.W. Lloyd, and H.W. Rush. 1972. Long-term mortality study of steelworkers. VI. Mortality from malignant neoplasms among coke oven workers. *J. Occup. Med.* **14:** 621.

Safe Drinking Water Committee. 1977. *Drinking water and health.* Board on Toxicology and Environmental Health Hazards, Commission on Life Sciences, National Research Council, Washington, D.C.

_____.1980. *Drinking water and health,* vol. 3. Board on Toxicology and Environmental Health Hazards, Commission on Life Sciences, National Research Council, National Academy Press, Washington, D.C.

_____. 1983. *Drinking water and health,* vol. 5. Board on Toxicology and Environmental Health Hazards, Commission on Life Sciences, National Research Council, National Academy Press, Washington, D.C.

Santodonato, J., P. Howard, and D. Basu. 1981. Health and ecological assessment of polynuclear aromatic hydrocarbons. *J. Environ. Pathol. Toxicol.* **5:** 1.

Stocks, P. 1957. *Cancer in North Wales and Liverpool regions.* Supplement to British Empire Cancer Campaign Annual Report, 1957.

Stukonis, M.K. 1978. *Cancer incidence cumulative rates.* IARC Internal Technical Reports No. 78/002. International Agency for Research on Cancer, Lyon, France.

Waller, R. 1980. Trends in lung cancer in London in relation to exposure to diesel fumes. In *Health effects of diesel engine emissions: Proceedings of an international symposium.* EPA-600/9-80-057b. U.S. Environmental Protection Agency Office of Research and Development, Cincinnati, Ohio.

## EDITOR'S NOTE

For comments on M.C. Pike's paper, see comment section of the following paper by P.J. Landrigan et al.

# Approaches to the Estimation of Exposure in Occupational Epidemiology

PHILIP J. LANDRIGAN, JAMES M. MELIUS, ROBERT A. RINSKY, AND
MICHAEL J. THUN
Division of Surveillance, Hazard Evaluations, and Field Studies
National Institute for Occupational Safety and Health
4676 Columbia Parkway
Cincinnati, Ohio 45226

## OVERVIEW

Quantification of exposure is an essential prerequisite to quantitative risk assessment but is a frustratingly difficult endeavor in occupational epidemiology. Approaches to the estimation of exposure in retrospective epidemiologic studies include (1) use of surrogate measures of exposure such as duration of employment or job category; (2) construction of additive exposure models from work history files and past industrial hygiene measurements; and (3) direct calculation of exposure from personal monitoring data. With careful application, exposure estimates derived from each of these sources can serve as a basis for the derivation of exposure-effect relationships and thence for quantitative estimation of risk.

## INTRODUCTION

Accurate quantification of exposure is a prerequisite to the determination of exposure-effect relationships in occupational epidemiology (Nordberg 1976). The accurate measurement of exposure is therefore fundamental to the quantitative assessment of risk.

Measurement of exposure is, however, never easy, and it is particularly difficult in the retrospective analyses of mortality that constitute the type of study most commonly undertaken in occupational epidemiology. Among the factors that may contribute to the difficulties of exposure assessment in occupational studies are incompleteness of work history files, inadequate information on potentially confounding exposures, variations over time-in-measurement techniques, and the frequently sporadic nature of past environmental and biological sampling. Seldom do these difficulties lead to incorrect imputation of exposure-effect relationships where, in fact, none exist. Not infrequently, however, they produce misclassification, and this misclassification can, in turn, distort exposure-effect relationships. Such distortion may, in the first instance, produce an underestimation of the range of exposures and hence result in an apparent minimization of the exposure-effect relationship for those members of a population who have incurred the highest levels of exposure. Misclassification of exposure data tends also to produce a blurring of relationships at lower levels of exposure, such that the exposure-effect relationship becomes lost in background variation and its shape in the low-dose range cannot accurately be determined (Land 1980).

To reduce inaccuracy in the quantification of exposure, occupational epidemiologists have had to learn to collaborate closely with industrial hygienists and analytical chemists. From this collaboration have emerged a number of strategies for the quantitative reconstruction of past exposures. These approaches range from the use of such surrogate measures of exposure as duration of employment or job category to complex summation models in which formulae are developed for the interpolation of exposures between known points and for the translation of area-based industrial hygiene measurements to measurements of individual exposure. This paper will review some of these approaches.

## Duration of Employment as a Measure of Exposure

The simplest approach to the estimation of exposure in cohort mortality studies is the use of analysis by duration of employment. This approach assumes that longer duration of employment reflects increased exposure.

The main advantage of this approach is the ease with which it can be applied. It provides a straightforward mechanism for the analysis of complex, multi-year work histories. Several major assumptions are, however, inherent in this approach and must be recognized. First, this approach, unless it is appropriately weighted, will not account for variations in exposure that may occur over time. Also, it overlooks the possible influence of variations in rate of exposure on disease occurrence. If, for example, the biologically significant exposure of a population to a toxin is characterized principally by a series of short-term peaks, duration of employment may not accurately reflect this biologically significant dose. Third, although observation of increasing risk with increasing duration of exposure argues for the existence of an exposure-effect relationship, such a finding is not sufficient by itself to quantify the risk relationship.

A study of mortality from leukemia in a population of rubber workers exposed to benzene used duration of employment as a surrogate measure of exposure in an initial analysis of the data (Rinsky et al. 1981). This analysis found that seven leukemia deaths had occurred in the population, as compared to 1.25 such deaths expected on the basis of the mortality experience of the general population of the United States (standard mortality ratio [SMR] = 560; $p < 0.001$). When these observed leukemia deaths were examined by duration of employment, it was found that workers with less than 5 years of employment had two deaths versus 1.0 expected (SMR = 2.0). By contrast, workers with 5 or more years of employment had five leukemia deaths versus 0.23 expected (SMR = 2100) (Table 1). The result supports the notion that there is an increased risk of death from leukemia with increasing cumulative exposure to benzene. By themselves, however, these data provide no information on risk of leukemia at specific levels of benzene exposure.

A similar example is provided by a recently updated retrospective analysis of the mortality experience of workers engaged in the production of cadmium (Thun

## Table 1
### Observed and Expected Leukemia Deaths Among 748 White Males Exposed to Benzene[a]

| Group | Observed deaths | Expected deaths | SMR |
|---|---|---|---|
| Less than 5 years' exposure | 2 | 1.0 | 200 |
| More than 5 years' exposure | 5 | 0.23 | 2100 |
| All workers | 7 | 1.25 | 560 |

[a]Modified from Rinksy et al. (1981).

et al. (1984). This study evaluated 602 white male workers with at least 6 months of production work in a cadmium plant between 1940–1969, and it followed the vital status of this population through 1978. Analysis of these data found that overall mortality from respiratory cancer was significantly greater among these cadmium workers than in the general population of the United States (16 respiratory cancer deaths observed versus 10.87 expected, SMR = 147).

In an initial quantitative analysis of these data, mortality was evaluated in relation to duration of employment (Table 2). That analysis found that workers with less than 2 years' employment in cadmium production had no excess in respiratory cancer mortality. By contrast, workers with 2–9 years' employment had an approximate doubling over expectation in deaths from respiratory cancer (standardized rate ratio [SRR] = 220). Inexplicably, however, no further increases in mortality from respiratory cancer were observed in workers employed for longer than 9 years.

These findings provide at least some support for the notion that an exposure-effect relationship exists between cadmium exposure and death from respiratory cancer. However, these data by themselves provide no information on the degree of risk which may exist at any given level of cadmium exposure. Further, the paradoxical plateauing of risk observed beyond 9 years of exposure beclouds somewhat the conclusion that there exists an exposure-effect relationship. Resolution of

## Table 2
### Lung Cancer Mortality by Duration of Employment in Cadmium Plant[a]

| Duration of employment | No. of deaths | Mortality rate[b] | SRR[c] |
|---|---|---|---|
| 6–23 months | 0 | 0 | — |
| 2–9 years | 9 | 15.73 | 2.2 |
| 10–19 years | 3 | 14.28 | 2.0 |
| 20 + years | 4 | 16.28 | 2.2 |

[a]Modified from Thun et al. (1984).
[b]Rate × 10,000 person-years, directly standardized for age and calendar time to the person-years distribution of the overall cadmium cohort
[c]Standardized rate ratio (SRR) = directly standardized mortality rate of subgroup/summary rate for U.S. white males

these issues requires the development of additional, more sophisticated exposure modeling.

## Job Category as a Measure of Exposure; Additive Exposure Models

One more highly sophisticated approach to exposure definition has been to use information on job assignment as a surrogate indicator of exposure and to combine that information with data on either airborne concentrations of contaminants or on personal (breathing zone) levels. This juxtaposition of data from personnel and exposure files permits the development of additive models for estimation of cumulative exposure (A. Smith et al. 1980). Such techniques permit a considerable gain in flexibility in exposure modeling. Also this approach is well able to reflect changes in exposure over time. However, it must be noted that this approach rests on the assumption that external exposure equates with biologically significant dose. This equation rests on the caveats (1) that inhalation rates are equal in all jobs studied and (2) that fractional deposition of airborne particles in the lungs is the same at all levels of exposure (Smith et al. 1984). Also, it must be noted that this approach depends absolutely on the quality of past personnel and exposure records. In facilities with multiple chemical exposures, personnel records may not permit differentiation among job classifications and may therefore not provide an accurate basis for estimates of individual dose. Multiple work assignments in a given exposure area, use of personal protective equipment, and changes in industrial processes over time also may lead to inaccuracies in estimation of exposure.

A time-integrated approach to exposure modeling was employed in a study of the mortality of workers exposed to chrysotile asbestos in textile manufacture (Dement et al. 1983). Cumulative fiber exposure for each worker was calculated by integration of job history data with industrial hygiene sampling data. This approach permitted the calculation of an average airborne fiber concentration for each job in the facility. Changes in these exposures over time were taken into account.

Analysis of the overall mortality experience of the population showed excess deaths in several categories, particularly for lung cancer (SMR = 135) and for nonmalignant respiratory disease (SMR = 294). For both of those causes of death, risk increased with increases in estimated exposure. For lung cancer, in workers with less than 1000 cumulative exposure-days (fiber/cc times days), five deaths were observed versus 3.58 expected (SMR = $140, p > 0.05$) (Table 3). By contrast, for those workers with greater than 100,000 cumulative exposure-days, two deaths were observed, against only 0.11 expected (SMR = $1818, p < 0.05$). A plot of standardized mortality ratios (SMRs) for lung cancer in workers with greater than 15 years' latency versus cumulative exposure demonstrates a linear relationship. Deaths from nonmalignant respiratory disease demonstrate a similar pattern.

Another recent study used a similar approach to evaluate the relationship between cumulative dust exposure and mortality from respiratory disease among underground miners (Brown et al. 1983). Cumulative dust days of exposure for each worker were calculated by integration of data on duration of employment in each job (from

**Table 3**
Exposure-response Relationship for Lung Cancer Among
Male Chrysolite Asbestos Textile Workers Achieving 15 or More
Years Latency[a]

| Cumulative exposure (fiber/cc × days) | Observed | Expected | SMR |
|---|---|---|---|
| < 1000 | 5 | 3.58 | 140 |
| 1000–10,000 | 9 | 3.23 | 279[b] |
| 10,000–40,000 | 7 | 1.99 | 352[b] |
| 40,000–100,000 | 10 | 0.91 | 1099[b] |
| > 100,000 | 2 | 0.11 | 1818[b] |
| Total | 33 | 9.82 | 336[b] |

[a]Modified from Dement et al. (1983).
[b]$p < 0.05$

personnel records) with data on average dust exposure for each job category (based on exposure data for each year).

In the analysis, 53 deaths from nonmalignant respiratory disease (NMRD) were observed as compared with only 19.00 such deaths expected (SMR = 279, $p < 0.01$). An increasing risk of death from NMRD was found with increasing cumulative exposure to dust. Workers with over 20 years' latency but with less than 40,000 dust days showed no increased risk, whereas those with similar latency and over 640,000 cumulative dust days demonstrated an eightfold increase in risk of death from NMRD (Table 4).

An additive exposure model has been employed recently by Rinsky and colleagues to undertake a quantitative examination of exposure-effect relationships in their aforementioned study of leukemia mortality in workers exposed to benzene (1981). In this extended analysis, Rinsky et al. constructed a summation model in which

**Table 4**
Nonmalignant Respiratory Disease Mortality Among Underground
Miners with Greater than 20 Years' Latency: Exposure-Response
Relationship[a]

| Cumulative dust days | Observed deaths | Expected deaths | SMR |
|---|---|---|---|
| < 20,000 | 0 | 0.17 | — |
| 20,000–40,000 | 0 | 0.67 | — |
| 40,000–80,000 | 2 | 1.45 | 138 |
| 80,000–160,000 | 7 | 2.10 | 333 |
| 160,000–320,000 | 5 | 3.92 | 128 |
| 320,000–640,000 | 21 | 6.55 | 321 |
| > 640,000 | 16 | 1.82 | 879 |

[a]Modified from Brown et al. (1983).

## Table 5
## Lung Cancer Among Cadmium Production Workers by Cumulative Exposure to Cadmium[a]

| Cumulative exposure (mg-days/m³) | TWA equivalent[b] | Deaths | SMR | SRR[c] |
|---|---|---|---|---|
| < 584 | < 40 μg/m³ | 2 | 53 | 0.48 |
| 585–2920 | 41–200 μg/m³ | 7 | 152 | 1.55 |
| > 2921 | > 200 μg/m³ | 7 | 280 | 3.45 |

[a]Modified from Thun et al. (1984).
[b]Represents the TWA that over a 40-year working lifetime would result in this exposure
[c]SRR = Directly standardized rate ratio

they reconstructed data on individual exposure for each member of the population through the juxtaposition of job history files with industrial hygiene measurements. Initial examination of these data suggests that the slope of the exposure-effect relationship may actually be steeper than that seen in the original model; this finding suggests that the original analysis, based solely on duration of employment, may have tended to foreshorten the range of exposures and thus minimized apparent risk at high levels of exposure. Additionally, the data from the new model appear to indicate that the risk of excess mortality from exposure to benzene extends downward to exposure levels at least as low as 1 ppm.

An additive exposure model has also been used to undertake a further examination of exposure-effect relationships in the cohort of cadmium production workers described above (Thun et al. 1984). In this extension of the analysis, area industrial hygiene data on airborne concentrations of cadmium in 11 work areas for various time periods were combined with information on job history from each worker's personnel file to estimate each worker's cumulative exposure to airborne cadmium (expressed as mg-days/m³) (T.J. Smith et al. 1980).

In the subsequent reexamination of exposure-effect relationships, a statistically significant association was found between increases in risk of death from respiratory cancer and increasing cumulative exposure to cadmium (Table 5). The apparent leveling off of risk which had been observed in the previous analysis after 9 years' employment was no longer observed. The paradoxical plateauing of risk was apparently explained by the fact that heaviest exposure to cadmium was experienced by most workers during their first few years of employment when they were assigned to undesirable, high-exposure, entry-level jobs. Most workers who stayed longer than a few years moved into cleaner jobs with less exposure to cadmium; this migration accounted for the apparent plateau effect. However, for those relatively few workers who remained in high-exposure jobs, risk continued to increase directly in proportion to their cumulative exposure.

Comparison of this exposure-effect relationship with current occupational exposure criteria for cadmium indicates that a statistically significant excess risk of

**Table 6**
Deaths for All Malignant Neoplasms by Cumulative Radiation
Exposure Among Shipyard Workers[a]

| Cumulative radiation dose | Observed | Expected | SMR |
|---|---|---|---|
| 0.001–0.029 | 29 | 33.2 | 87.4 |
| 0.030–0.099 | 32 | 37.1 | 86.3 |
| 0.100–0.499 | 46 | 56.8 | 81.0 |
| 0.500–0.999 | 26 | 23.5 | 111 |
| 1.00–4.99 | 45 | 42.8 | 105 |
| 5.00–14.99 | 17 | 18.0 | 94.4 |
| 15.000 and over | 6 | 7.2 | 83.3 |
| Total | 201 | 218.5 | 92.0 |

[a]Modified from Rinsky et al. (1984).

lung cancer is evident in workers whose mean lifetime exposure equates with 40 years' exposure to cadmium at concentrations above the current OSHA standard of 200 $\mu$g/$M^3$ (SRR = 3.45). No excess of lung cancer is found in these workers whose mean lifetime exposure equates with 40 years' exposure at concentrations below the current NIOSH-recommended standard level of 40 $\mu$g/$M^3$.

## Use of Personal Exposure Data

A still more accurate estimate of past exposure may be obtained when personal exposure monitoring data are available. Those data may be used alone or in conjunction with other estimates of exposure.

Personal monitoring data were used to assess radiation exposure in a study of cancer mortality among workers at a naval shipyard in New Hampshire (Rinsky et al. 1980). This study was stimulated by concern that excess cancer deaths had occurred among the shipyard workers as a result of exposure to ionizing radiation. A historical prospective mortality study was conducted using information on job history and mortality combined with data from the extensive radiation exposure monitoring program (using film badges) at the shipyard (Waxweiler et al. 1983). Based on these data, it was possible to divide the cohort into three subgroups: (1) 7615 individuals who had a recorded lifetime cumulative radiation exposure of at least 0.001 rem; (2) 15,585 individuals who were never monitored (considered to be nonexposed); and (3) 1345 individuals who were monitored for radiation, but whose total lifetime cumulative dose was 0.000 rem.

Neither the overall population nor any of the three subgroups showed any statistically significant excesses in mortality from any specific cause. Also, no consistent patterns of excess mortality due to malignant neoplasms were observed when analyses were conducted in relation to various levels of cumulative radiation exposure (Table 6).

Further analyses, which incorporated more detailed evaluations of exposure,

## Table 7
Lung Cancer Case Control Study of Exposures to Asbestos, Welding, and Radiation Among Shipyard Workers—Univariate Analysis[a]

| Exposure | Odds ratio (OR) | Confidence interval |
|---|---|---|
| Radiation | 1.23 | 0.91–1.67 |
| Radiation over 1 rem | 1.60 | 1.02–2.52 |
| Asbestos | 1.24 | 0.92–1.60 |
| Welding | 1.13 | 0.76–1.68 |
| Asbestos and/or welding | 1.43 | 1.12–1.81 |

[a]Modified from Rinsky et al. (1984).

were then conducted for deaths due to lung cancer (Rinsky et al. 1984). These analyses were conducted using a nested case-control approach, a technique that provides an efficient mechanism for the estimation of past exposures for workers exposed to multiple occupational toxins. For 405 men who died of lung cancer and for 1215 matched controls, work histories were examined to evaluate individual exposures to asbestos and to welding fumes, as well as to radiation. Exposures to asbestos and welding fumes in each job were assessed by review of industrial hygiene records for that job category, and then were classified as nonexistent, possible, or probable. This semiquantitative categorization is obviously crude in comparison to the more sophisticated data which were available for assessment of radiation exposure.

The standardized mortality ratio for death from lung cancer was found to be significantly elevated in this analysis for those workers who had a cumulative radiation exposure of 1.00 rem or greater (SMR = 1.60; confidence interval [CI] 1.02-2.52) (Table 7). Mortality was also elevated in workers with exposure to asbestos and welding fumes (SMR = 1.43; CI 1.12-1.81). To determine if the elevated risk observed in the radiation workers was attributable to radiation itself, to either asbestos or welding fumes, or to an interaction, the data were analyzed further using a conditional logistic regression model. No statistically significant interaction was found between radiation exposure and exposure to either asbestos or welding. Further, this analysis found that the significance of the excess risk observed in relation to radiation disappeared when the data were controled for the effects of exposures to asbestos and to welding (Table 8). However, in the reverse analysis, the association between lung cancer and exposure to asbestos and welding fumes was found to be statistically significant, even with radiation exposure included in the model (odds ratio [OR] 1.41; CI 1.09–1.81). These results indicate that the observed excess mortality from lung cancer could not be ascribed to radiation, but rather was influenced by exposure to either asbestos or to welding fumes.

When they are available, personal exposure data are easy to use in cohort mortality analyses; they allow stratification by cumulative dose categories. Also, rate of exposure can be factored into these analyses. However, personal sampling data may not always accurately reflect personal exposures. The use of personal protective

**Table 8**
Lung Cancer Case Control Study of Exposures to Asbestos, Welding, and Radiation Among Shipyard Workers—Conditional Logistical Regression Analyses[a]

| Exposure | Odds ratio (OR) | Confidence interval |
|---|---|---|
| Radiation | 1.18 | 0.86–1.62 |
| Radiation 0.001–0.999 rem | 1.05 | 0.74–1.51 |
| Radiation greater than 1 rem | 1.47 | 0.93–2.34 |
| Asbestos and/or welding | 1.41 | 1.09–1.81 |

[a]Modified from Rinsky et al. (1984).

equipment, extensive dermal exposure, and short-term, high-level exposures may not be reflected in personal sampling data. The use of biological monitoring data may, in the future, overcome some of these deficiencies, but at present such information is rarely available.

## CONCLUSION

Occupational epidemiology has historically been concerned with the establishment of qualitative relationships between exposure and disease. The demonstration of such categorical relationships is, however, not sufficient for the quantitative assessment of risk. Quantitative risk estimation requires increasingly sophisticated approaches to quantitative estimation of exposure. Data obtained from biological monitoring programs, and particularly data obtained from programs of genotoxic monitoring, may in the future prove extremely useful as a basis for the quantitative assessment of exposure.

## REFERENCES

Brown, D., S.D. Kaplan, R.D. Zumwalde, and V.E. Archer. 1985. *Retrospective cohort mortality study of underground gold mine workers.* In *Silica and cancer: Controversy in occupational medicine* (ed. D.F. Goldsmith, D.M. Winn, and C.M. Shy). Praeger, Philadelphia, Pennsylvania. (In press).

Dement, J.M., R.L. Harris, M.J. Symons, and C.M. Shy. 1983. Exposures and mortality among chrysotile asbestos workers. Part II: Mortality. *Am. J. Ind. Med.* **4:** 421.

Land, C. 1980. Estimating cancer risks form low doses of ionizing radiation. *Science* **209:** 1197.

Nordberg, G.F. 1976. Dose. In *Effects and dose-response relationships of toxic metals* (ed. G.F. Nordberg). Elsevier Scientific Publishing, Amsterdam, The Netherlands.

Rinsky, R.A., R.J. Young, and A.B. Smith. 1981. Leukemia in benzene workers. *Am. J. Ind. Med.* **2:** 217.

Rinsky, R.A., R.D. Zumwalde, R.J. Waxweiler, W.E. Murray, P.J. Bierbaum, P.J. Landrigan, M. Terpilak, and C. Cox. 1981. Cancer mortality of a naval nuclear shipyard. *Lancet* **1:** 231.

Rinsky, R.A., J.M. Melius, R.W. Hornung, R.D. Zumwalde, R.J. Waxweiler, P.J. Landrigan, P.J. Bierbaum, and W.E. Murray. 1985. *Case control study of lung cancer in civilian employees at the Portsmouth Naval Shipyard.* National Institute for Occupational Safety and Health Report.

Smith, A., R.J. Waxweiler, and H.A. Tyroler. 1980. Epidemiologic investigation of occupational carcinogenesis using serially additive expected dose model. *Am. J. Epidemiol.* **112:** 787.

Smith, T.J., R.J. Anderson, and J.C. Reading. 1980. Chronic cadmium exposures associated with kidney function effects. *Am. J. Ind. Med.* **1:** 319.

Smith, T.J., S.K. Hammond, F. Laidlaw, and S. Fine. 1984. Respiratory exposures associated with silicon carbide production: Estimation of cumulative exposures for an epidemiological study. *Br. J. Ind. Med.* **41:** 100.

Thun, M., T.M. Schnorr, A.B. Smith, W.E. Halperin, and R.A. Lemen. 1985. *Mortality among a cohort of U.S. cadmium production workers—An update.* J. Nat'l. Cancer Inst. (in press).

Waxweiler, R.J., J.J. Beaumont, J.A. Henry, D.P. Brown, C.F. Robinson, G.O. Ness, J.K. Wagoner, and R.A. Lemen. 1983. A modified life-table analysis system for cohort studies. *J. Occup. Med.* **25(2):** 115.

## COMMENTS

**REITZ:**   Is there any way you can incorporate data on latency periods, time since first exposure, or time since last exposure, into your system?

**LANDRIGAN:**   Yes. In the NIOSH life-table program, which we used as the basis for all of our mortality calculations, we are able to consider both duration of exposure and latency. For example, in the data from Portsmouth Navy Shipyard, we performed cross-tabulations in which for each cause of death, such as leukemia, we examined mortality by cumulative radiation dose along one axis and by latency along the other. Although the number of cases was small, in the case of leukemia we did not see any significant trends along either axis.

**CORN:**   What are your comparison populations in those studies? Are you using people from the plants, or are you using the general population for comparison groups?

**LANDRIGAN:**   We compared the mortality experience of the workers exposed to radiation with that of the general U.S. population and also with that of workers in the shipyard who were not exposed to radiation.

**ALBERT:**   There is a large amount of both positive and negative epidemiologic data which is lost to the world of quantitative risk assessment for the lack of exposure data. Would it be possible, given certain job descriptions and certain kinds of operations during certain periods of time, to characterize the level of exposure for these particular instances with an acceptable range of uncertainty?

**LANDRIGAN:** I think that although such an exercise can be undertaken within a single plant, it can be done only with difficulty across all plants. Each plant is different.

**J. WILSON:** Each plant differs in time, too.

**LANDRIGAN:** Yes. Furthermore, a worker who is called a drum roller at one plant does not perform the same function or have the same exposures as a worker who is employed as a drum roller at another plant.

**PURCHASE:** I know that in the case of vinyl chloride, if you use the term "autoclave operator" in the United Kingdom it is a totally different job from the "autoclave operator" in the U.S., and, therefore, any comparison must take that into account. I have another question about the SAED (Serial Additive Expected Dose) system that Waxweiler has developed. It seems to me that it takes no account of the features that Dr. Pike was mentioning in the cigarette example, in that it just multiplies the dose in each fraction of time and then adds them up. If you did that for the cigarette example, you'd get the wrong answer since it is likely that the exposures which occurred immediately preceding the development of the cancer are less important in the development of the cancer than earlier exposures.

**LANDRIGAN:** Your point is well taken. At present, unfortunately, our life-table program does not have sufficient flexibility to permit differential weighting of exposures or lagging of exposures.

**PIKE:** What you need to do is to take whatever biology you already know and see whether the data are compatible, rather than ask the question the other way around. We do know quite a bit, and I think we should build that information into the model.

**PURCHASE:** In most instances, the incidence of the cancer, at least in experimental systems, is proportional to the dose and time to the third or fourth power. If this SAED model were altered to take that into account, it might then be more useful.

**PIKE:** We don't really know that this relationship holds for cigarette smoking. There is some evidence suggesting that the number of cigarettes should be raised to a power higher than one, maybe as high as two. Latency, however, is a tricky issue. The formula that describes smokers' lung cancer incidence so well (i.e., incidence is proportional to $a \cdot t^{4.5}$ [$a$ = number of cigarettes per day; $t$ = duration of smoking]), involves no latent period, certainly no 20-year delay before the first cancer occurs. The reason cancer incidence data often appears to show a long latent period is because it takes a long time (duration of exposure) before the incidence is high enough to be recognized—especially if it has to be recognized against a significant background rate.

**R. WILSON:** Isn't it right to say that the age distribution of cancer results from both the duration of exposure and the latency?

**PETO:** The more carcinogens you look at, the wider the range of time and age patterns. Data on mesothelioma and lung cancer show totally different age and time relationships in asbestos workers; and nasal cancer and lung cancer show totally different relationships in nickel refiners. It's hardly an exaggeration to say that there are as many different age and time patterns as there are carcinogens for which there are data to study. There are one or two that look vaguely like each other; radiation for lung cancer looks a bit like asbestos, for example. But such similarities seem to be the exception rather than the rule.

**PIKE:** But don't you have to take the best model that you can find?

**PETO:** If you haven't any direct evidence on the right model for a particular cancer, your chance of choosing the right one is about one in ten if you limit the choice to the patterns that have been observed so far, or one in 50 if you assume there are another 40 that we haven't yet studied.

**LAVE:** But you said the question is "What is the chance of choosing the right one?" That's not the right question. The issue you want to put is "What's the best you can do?"

**PETO:** The only way to approach that is by trying to assess how model-dependent the prediction is.

**R. WILSON:** But some of those models can be tested in animals—although the relationship between animal data and man is, of course, uncertain. You would expect some relationship between incidence and age and duration of exposure to show up in animal data. There have been extraordinarily few examinations of animal data from that point of view. We have collected all the benzo[a]pyrene data in one package; and whereas the data have often been said to be inconsistent, they can be shown to be consistent using a reasonable version of the Doll-Armitage model.

**WEINSTEIN:** Dose and time relationships can also be organ-specific. For example, breast cancer induction is highly age-dependent both in experimental animals and humans. There are so many variables that we cannot assume that a simple relationship between dose, time, and incidence applies to all carcinogenic agents, tissues, and species.

**PETO:** The remarkable thing about abestos and nickel is that they cause two cancers and, in each case, the two cancers they cause show totally different age and time relationships. So these depend both on the agent and the organ. Furthermore, you can get the same organ with totally different patterns for different agents.

**LAVE:**   Malcolm [Pike] made a different point. Epidemiological data are scarce and there are only a small number of data points. At the same time, you have a rich array of models and hypotheses. It is easy to overfit any data set. The issue is not whether the data ought to speak—the data always will say something vague. You must narrow the number of hypotheses and models that you're willing to put to the data. You must use whatever biology you can. Will you know enough from biology to specify exactly the power of t? The answer is "Certainly not." But, at least, you can start trying to fit models that have biological plausibility, rather than trying to fit the most general class of models and hope the data will eliminate all possibilities save one. That could never happen.

**PIKE:**   If you have a new substance which you know truly nothing about, then it is difficult to do anything truly sensible. But if there have been animal experiments or the chemists can relate it to other more understood compounds or they can give you some idea on how it may act, then you should use that information.

**CORN:**   Going back to the exposure question, we have done a good deal of "retrospective industrial hygiene." You can't just say the person is a bagger and worked with a powder, because the cohesivity of the specific material, the particle size, etc., involve enormous ranges of dustiness. We have tried to bracket the exposure. We have simulated the previous practices and measured the airborne dust. We have done that by interviewing the older employees who told us the way things were 30 and 40 years ago. People remembered the dustiest part of the plant. We asked them: "What went on there? How did you do it?" Then we simulated those procedures and obtained the needed measurement. This approach yields the epidemiologists the exposure point they're most interested in, that is the upper limit of exposure or the worst situation.

**PETO:**   But that would give you the lowest estimated risk, not the highest. The dustier it is, the less risky it is per unit dose. Anecdotes about past exposure always suggest that conditions were appalling; but the evidence, at least in terms of changes in excess risk, often suggests that they are exaggerated. The risk per unit dose is the observed excess divided by the estimated dose; so if you overestimate the dose you underestimate the risk.

**CORN:**   But the workmen have a good memory of where they didn't want to work in the plant. They'll tell you that the feeder operation was the worst; they didn't like the feeder operation because they couldn't breathe. Then you'll say, "Now, tell us some other places." They'll tell you a place and you ask, "Was it worse than the feeder?" What the epidemiologist wanted was a couple of rankings to get four points along this curve. You, the person interested in the environment, can help them get those points. That is what we try to do. It has worked for a few industries that have wanted to go back 30–50 years.

**PURCHASE:** There's one further pitfall that you have to keep your eye on in the SAED method and that is that if you do a retrospective construction of exposure levels and you're dealing with more than one chemical, then the comparison between the chemicals may be very difficult. So, for example, if you were dealing with sulphur dioxide, which because of its irritancy has an immediate impact on the individual (who smells it), and you were comparing that with vinyl chloride, which has no immediate effect at much higher levels, the actual levels they were exposed to might be very different from their recollection of levels of exposure. That comparison has to be done very carefully.

**CORN:** It's really a big jigsaw puzzle. It's best done across an industry if you can get the necessary cooperation. The epidemiologist tallies their numbers and workforce, and the environmental specialist gets plants at different stages of development—the industry has very old plants, new plants, and plants in between. For example, you can make measurements in an old plant in order to obtain estimates of past exposure because that process is quite similar to what you learned from interviews that the old plant employing the worker was like.

**J. WILSON:** I think your point is, and I agree with it completely, that you're much better off putting the effort into a thorough study of a few cases rather than trying to put together a dictionary of what all the terms mean so they can be applied broadly.

**CORN:** Yes.

**LANDRIGAN:** Another point, too, which is essential in these studies, is that there must be collaboration among industrial hygienists, chemists, and epidemiologists. Epidemiologists cannot possibly hope to influence the process of quantitative risk assessment when they undertake analyses of mortality without benefit of data on exposures.

# The Use of Epidemiological Data for the Assessment of Human Cancer Risk

JOHN KALDOR and NICHOLAS DAY
International Agency for Research on Cancer
150 Cours Albert Thomas
69372 Lyon-Cedex 08, France

## OVERVIEW

Epidemiological data can only rarely provide the basis for quantification of the carcinogenic risk posed by a chemical to which humans are exposed. It is, nevertheless, important to have an understanding of the capabilities and limitations of epidemiological data in the estimation of risk, both in order to evaluate available epidemiological results and to define their role in the setting of regulatory policy. In this paper, we examine some of these limitations from a statistical point of view. The level of relative risk detectable by a cohort study is presented, as well as the precision available for low-dose interpolation under a quadratic dose-response. Two examples are given to illustrate some of the problems associated with model-fitting and low-dose interpolation from epidemiological data.

## INTRODUCTION

Epidemiological data must play a central role in the quantitative evaluation of the carcinogenic risk posed by an agent to which humans are exposed. Its most direct application occurs when risk assessment can be made from an epidemiological study in which the cancer rate has been accurately measured at all exposure levels of interest, as is the case, for example, with the classic studies of lung cancer following cigarette smoking. This situation, although ideal from the point of view of carcinogenic risk assessment, obtains infrequently in practice, either because of the lack of populations exposed sufficiently long ago for an elevated risk to become apparent or of sufficient size to enable the detection of risk, or because the appropriate studies on such populations have not been carried out.

A more common situation is the one in which a population which has been exposed to the agent under investigation is available for study, but the relationship between exposure level and carcinogenic risk is not clearly defined at exposure levels below those observed to have carcinogenic effect. In this case, estimation of the risk at these lower exposure levels must rely on interpolation using a mathematical model of risk. For example, the permissible level for benzene exposure in the United States has been defined in this way.

There can obviously be no direct role of epidemiological information in determining the potential risk to populations exposed to chemicals on which there is no epidemiological data. However, the validation of animal cancer bioassays and short-term tests as predictors of carcinogenic risk must ultimately be made against epidemiological data. It is, therefore, essential from this more general point of view to understand the capabilities and limitations of such data in the measurement of risk.

This paper is concerned with examining some of these limitations, in the context of the epidemiological cohort study. Thus we specifically consider a study design in which the number of cancer cases observed among exposed individuals is to be compared to the number of cases expected on the basis of rates obtained from a large external comparison population. Using standard statistical theory, we calculate the maximum relative risk that might realistically be excluded by such results for an exposure which is noncarcinogenic. We then consider low-dose interpolation from cohort study data. Expected lower limits on estimated "safe" doses are calculated when a linear interpolation term is estimated for a chemical which in fact produces a purely quadratic relative risk function. Finally, we review some examples of data from the epidemiological literature, for which reasonable exposure and risk estimates are available, from the point of view of the goodness of fit of various models for relative risk and the implications for low-dose interpolation.

## RESULTS

### Limits of Risk Detectable

Table 1 reports the expected 95% confidence limits for the relative risk, estimated from a single exposed group of individuals when the exposure in fact produces no increase in risk. These limits are based on the approximation for calculating confidence limits on a standardized mortality ratio (Rothman and Boice 1979). The upper limit represents the smallest level of risk that one can reasonably expect to exclude for the sample sizes given. Conversely, it may be viewed as the lowest true risk that stands a high probability of being detected. Cohort studies would rarely record more than a few hundred cases of the event of interest (such as deaths from the relevant cancer). Moreover, when individuals are classified by level of exposure, the number of cases in each group may be considerably fewer. For

**Table 1**
Expected Confidence Limits for a Standardized Mortality Ratio from a Cohort Study Estimated Using an External Comparison Group, When the True Relative Risk is 1

| Number of Cases | Lower limit | Upper limit |
| --- | --- | --- |
| 50 | 0.758 | 1.319 |
| 100 | 0.801 | 1.216 |
| 250 | 0.883 | 1.132 |
| 1000 | 0.939 | 1.064 |

example, in the British doctors' study of smoking and mortality, lung cancer was recorded as the underlying cause of death in about 215 men who had constant smoking habits; and only 14 cases occurred in men who reported regularly smoking between one and nine cigarettes per day (Doll and Peto 1978). The most extensive study of asbestos exposure yielded about 500 cases of lung cancer (Selikoff et al. 1980), and that for nickel workers about 140 (Doll et al. 1970). It is clear from Table 1 that even the largest cohort study could not effectively differentiate relative risks less than about 1.05 from unity.

## Limits of Extrapolation Accuracy

An increased risk even of the minimum magnitude detectable by an epidemiological study is far in excess of what might be considered as an "acceptable" relative risk. For example, an exposure with a relative risk of 1.05 for lung cancer would raise the background lifetime incidence of lung cancer in the United States from about 5% to 5.25%, resulting in approximately 250 excess cases over the lifetime of 100,000 exposed individuals. In order to estimate dose levels associated with lower levels of risk, interpolation models must be used.

Although many different models have been suggested for this purpose (Whittemore and Keller 1978), including a number having a reasonable biological basis, none has been clearly demonstrated to be superior to the others in terms of its ability to fit observed data. However, it is generally agreed that the possibility of a linear effect of dose at risk levels below those detectable by epidemiological means must be allowed for (Crump et al. 1976). The use of linear interpolation is conservative from the point of view of risk estimation, by comparison with most other suggested dose-response models. If a linear term is present but rather small in the function relating risk to exposure level, it will not necessarily be apparent in the range of observation; but it will dominate the function at low levels of risk. Linear interpolation also appears to be justified by epidemiological data on most known human carcinogens for which reasonable dose-response data are available (Day 1984) and certainly has never been clearly invalidated. In order to determine the effect of linearity on low-dose interpolation, we calculated the expected lower bounds of the 95% confidence limit for the dose required to produce specified relative risks, when the relative risk is in fact a purely quadratic function of dose. The bounds $d_Q^*$, the lower bound using purely quadratic interpolation, and $d_L^*$, the lower bound allowing for the possibility of a linear term, were calculated by supposing that the maximum likelihood estimates of the parameters a and b in the relationship

$$R_d = 1 + ad + bd^2$$

where $R_d$ is the relative risk at dose d, are distributed normally with expected value a and b respectively, and variance-covariance matrix given by the inverse of the expected information matrix (Cox and Hinkley 1974). For the calculation of $d_Q^*$, it was assumed that $a = 0$, so that the only parameter to be estimated was b. The observed number of cancer cases at exposure level d was assumed to be a Poisson random variable, with mean $R_d E_d$, where $E_d$ is the expected number of cases at level d based on rates in the external comparison population. The relative risk (RR) at the highest dose level is 5. Table 2 presents values of $d_L^*$, $d_Q^*$ and the ratio $d_L^*/d_Q^*$, for studies with various total number of expected cases, and equal allocation of this total among three equally spaced non-zero dose levels. As we would expect, the ratio decreases rapidly with the level of risk. When the dose required to produce an excess relative risk of $10^{-4}$ is to be estimated, and 1000 cases are expected overall, the lower limit of the 95% confidence limit of the dose is about 25 times lower under linear interpolation than under purely quadratic interpolation. If the excess of interest is $10^{-5}$, the factor is about 100. Another way to express the latter result is that even when there is no linear term, we cannot expect to exclude the possibility of a linear term whose effect is to reduce 100-fold the estimated $d_Q^*$ for excess relative risks of $10^{-5}$. These results show how conservative linear extrapolation can be in this limiting situation where the relative risk might be well approximated by a threshold model.

It is interesting to note that the ratios are rather constant over different allocations of expected cases to the dose levels (results not shown) and even over different total number of cases. Of course, the size of the actual confidence intervals for $d_L^*$ and $d_Q^*$ decreases with increasing total numbers of events.

## Fitting Dose-response Models to Data

As indicated earlier, there are very few examples of epidemiological studies in which reliable dose measurements have been made. Day (1984) has summarized many of the results from the larger studies available. We have chosen two cases from the literature to illustrate the process of fitting different relative risk models to observed data. The first of these is the effect of short duration exposure to ionizing radiation on the risk of stomach cancer. The information on this relationship comes

## Table 2
Expected Lower Confidence Limits for the Dose to Produce Specified Risk Levels, Estimated from a Cohort Study with Four Equally Spaced Dose Groups, and Equal Expected Numbers in Each

| Size of excess relative risk | Total number of expected events | $d_L^*$ | $d_Q^*$ | Ratio $d_L^*/d_Q^*$ |
|---|---|---|---|---|
| $10^{-3}$ | 50 | $3.7 \times 10^{-4}$ | $1.4 \times 10^{-2}$ | 0.03 |
| | 100 | $5.2 \times 10^{-4}$ | $1.5 \times 10^{-2}$ | 0.04 |
| | 1000 | $1.6 \times 10^{-3}$ | $1.5 \times 10^{-2}$ | 0.11 |
| $10^{-4}$ | 50 | $3.7 \times 10^{-5}$ | $4.4 \times 10^{-3}$ | 0.008 |
| | 100 | $5.2 \times 10^{-5}$ | $4.6 \times 10^{-3}$ | 0.01 |
| | 1000 | $5.6 \times 10^{-4}$ | $4.8 \times 10^{-3}$ | 0.03 |
| $10^{-5}$ | 50 | $3.7 \times 10^{-6}$ | $1.4 \times 10^{-3}$ | 0.003 |
| | 100 | $5.2 \times 10^{-6}$ | $1.5 \times 10^{-3}$ | 0.004 |
| | 1000 | $1.6 \times 10^{-5}$ | $1.5 \times 10^{-3}$ | 0.01 |

**Table 3**
Stomach Cancer and Ionizing Radiation: Relative Risks Observed
in Three Different Studies[a]

| Dose (rads) | A-bomb survivors[b] | Ankylosing[c] spondylitis series | Irradiated cervical[d] cancer patients |
|---|---|---|---|
| 0 | 0.99 (708) | — | — |
| 1–9 | 0.98 (473) | — | — |
| 10–49 | 1.02 (340) | — | — |
| 50–99 | 0.95 ( 91) | — | — |
| 100–199 | 0.96 ( 64) | — | 1.0 (86) |
| 200–299 | 1.20 ( 32) | 1.55 (31) | — |
| 300–399 | 1.39 ( 17) | — | — |
| 400+ | 1.65 ( 29) | — | — |

[a] Number of cases in parentheses
[b] Kato and Schull (1982)
[c] Smith and Doll (1982). The dose estimate of 250 rads comes from Smith (p.c.).
[d] Day and Boice (1984)

from three major sources. These are the studies on A-bomb survivors (Kato and Schull 1982), patients irradiated during the treatment of ankylosing spondylitis (Smith and Doll 1982), and women given radiation treatment for cervical cancer (Day and Boice 1984). Table 3 gives the relative risks for stomach cancer observed in these studies. Although only the relative risk at the highest dose level is significantly different from unity, there is a general impression of increasing relative risk over the higher portion of the dose range. We used the statistical program GLIM (Baker and Nelder 1978) to fit three simple curves to the A-bomb survivor data. The purely quadratic relative risk model fits slightly better than the purely linear model, but the difference is not great, and neither fit is significantly worse than the mixed linear-quadratic model (Fig. 1). On the other hand, the results of low-dose interpolation from these models obviously differ greatly, with the lower 95% confidence limit on the estimated dose to produce an excess relative risk of $10^{-4}$ being about 50-fold lower in the linear case than the quadratic. When the data from the other two studies are also used to fit the curves, the difference in fit between the linear and quadratic models becomes more marked, since the confidence limits about the response at the crucial intermediate doses are reduced and the dose-response becomes more clearly quadratic. However, they still cannot be distinguished by simple statistical criteria.

The second example we consider is the data reported by Doll and Peto (1978). They examined the dose-response relationship between number of cigarettes smoked per day and the incidence of lung cancer among men who started smoking between the ages of 16–25, smoked 40 cigarettes or less per day, and who reported no change in their smoking habits. They can therefore be thought of as exposed to a constant dose from roughly the same age. The estimated relative risk differs significantly from one at all non-zero levels, and Doll and Peto concluded that the

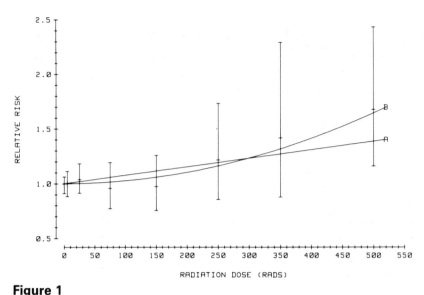

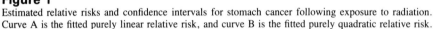

**Figure 1**

Estimated relative risks and confidence intervals for stomach cancer following exposure to radiation. Curve A is the fitted purely linear relative risk, and curve B is the fitted purely quadratic relative risk.

incidence data were best described using a quadratic relative risk function. We once again used GLIM, this time to fit three two-parameter families of relative risk functions, which are specified in the legend to Figure 2. As can be seen from this figure, all three resulting curves essentially fit equally well. At low excess relative risks, the first two are dominated by a linear term in dose, whose estimated coefficient is roughly equal for the two models (0.45 and 0.37 respectively). However, the third family is dominated by a term approximately equal to the square root of dose, so that interpolation from this model would produce very different results from the other two. Although this third family may be somewhat artificial, in the sense that it would be hard to justify from the point of view of current theories of carcinogenesis, it certainly cannot be empirically demonstrated to be inferior to the first two.

These two examples provide a strong contrast in observed relative risk. The relative risk of stomach cancer following exposure to ionizing radiation is comparable to levels observed in many studies of cancer following occupational exposure from which conclusions with regard to carcinogenicity have had to be drawn. The data on the smoking and lung cancer relationship, on the other hand, probably represent the strongest dose-response result in cancer epidemiology. Nevertheless, although certain statements can be made definitively about the relative risk in the observed range, there are clearly problems of interpretation when interpolation is attempted, even in this case.

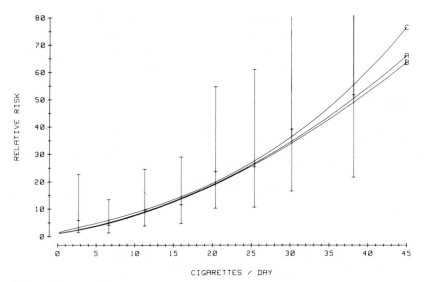

**Figure 2**
Estimated relative risks and confidence intervals for lung cancer among smokers aged 40–79 with regular smoking habits (Doll and Peto 1978). (Curve A: $1 + Ud + Vd^2$); (curve B: $[1 + Ud]^V$); (curve C: $\exp [Ud^V]$; where d is cigarettes per day.

## DISCUSSION

In this paper, we have examined some of the statistical limitations on risk estimation and low-dose interpolation from epidemiological cohort studies. In general, cohort studies with an internal comparison group and case-control studies would be somewhat less precise than external comparison cohort studies with the same number of events; so the calculations reported represent the upper limit of epidemiological precision. Moreover, we have not considered the effect of controlling for confounding factors, which would also weaken the precision of a study. Another simplification we have made is to ignore the role of time variables, such as age at exposure, time since exposure, and duration of exposure, on the estimation of risk. In practice, the effect of these variables must be accounted for in the analyses of epidemiological studies.

The initial impression gained from the results presented in this paper is somewhat discouraging. The risks of a magnitude which concern us cannot be detected by epidemiological means and there is a large amount of uncertainty associated with interpolation below the range of response observable in an epidemiological study. However, the results may be viewed from another perspective. Although it would be too extreme to suggest that only epidemiologically demonstrable risks should be of concern, it is also clear that epidemiological results will never be able to provide a definitive basis for a risk assessment of the kind that has been advocated, or even mandated, by various governmental agencies (Montesano and Tomatis 1977). A reasonable compromise, therefore, may be attainable by choosing as a goal for regulation a level of risk below the level of epidemiological detectability, but still within a region where the required interpolation methods may be credible in the sense that estimation of the corresponding exposure level can be made in a manner that is robust to the misspecification of the model used to interpolate.

## REFERENCES

Baker, R.J. and J.A. Nelder. 1978. *The GLIM system,* Release 3. Oxford, Numerical and Logarithms Group.

Cox, D.R. and D. Hinkley. 1974. *Theoretical statistics.* Chapman and Hall, London, England.

Crump, K.G.S., D.G. Hoel, C.H. Langley, and R. Peto. 1976. Fundamental carcinogenic processes and their implications for low dose risk assessment. *Cancer Res.* **36:** 2973.

Day, N.E. 1984. Epidemiological methods for the assessment of human cancer risk. (in press).

Day, N.E. and J.D. Boice, Jr., eds. 1984. *Second cancer in relation to radiation treatment for cervical cancer. Results of a cancer registry collaboration.* International Agency for Research on Cancer (IARC Scientific Publications No. 52), Lyon, France.

Doll, R. and R. Peto. 1978. Cigarette-smoking and bronchial carcinoma: Dose and time relationships among regular smokers and life-long non-smokers. *J. Epidemiol. Community Health* **32:** 303.

Doll, R., L.G. Morgan, and F.E. Speizer. 1970. Cancers of the lung and nose in nickel workers. *Br. J. Cancer* **24:** 623.

Kato, H. and W.J. Schull. 1982. Studies of the mortality of A-bomb survivors. 7. Mortality, 1950-1978: Part I. Cancer mortality. *Radiat. Res.* **90:** 395.

Montesano, R. and L. Tomatis. 1977. Legislation concerning chemical carcinogens in several industrialised countries. *Cancer Res.* **37:** 310.

Rothman, K.J. and J.D. Boice, Jr. 1979. *Epidemiological analysis with a programmable calculator.* U.S. Department of Health, Education and Welfare. Washington, D.C.

Selikoff, I.J., E.C. Hammond, and H. Seidman. 1980. Latency of asbestos disease among insulation workers in the United States and Canada. *Cancer* **46:** 2736.

Smith, P. and R. Doll. 1982. Mortality among patients with ankylosing spondylitis after a single treatment course with x-rays. *Br. Med. J.* **284:** 449.

Whittemore, A.S. and J.B. Keller. 1978. Quantitative theories of carcinogenesis. *SIAM Rev.* **20:** 1.

## COMMENTS

**WEINSTEIN:** Are you saying in Table 1 that it wouldn't matter if you calculated this for a rare tumor or a common tumor? If you were looking at lung cancer versus angiosarcomas, would the figures be the same?

**KALDOR:** Yes. They are based only on the expected number of cases in the population.

**WEINSTEIN:** It would seem to me that a common tumor is more likely to have multiple causes than a rare tumor. Therefore, with common tumors there would be a greater error in ascribing a particular case to a specific causative factor.

**KALDOR:** The calculations presented are only intended to indicate the size of relative risk detectable in an epidemiological cohort study. If an excess is detected, other factors must come into consideration in ascribing its cause. Certainly, significance tests are only a part of the whole process of evaluating an epidemiological study.

**CORN:** You said you used a 95% confidence interval. I protest the procedure of epidemiologists' using that one value and not giving anyone the option of thinking about the confidence limit with the interpretation of the individual study. In other words: ($p > x$). I'd like to know for lesser $p$ values.

**KALDOR:** I agree that a $p$ value should always be presented, rather than an upper bound for the $p$ value, but in this instance I am simply talking about expected confidence limits for the relative risk.

**CORN:** With 95% confidence between the lower and the upper limit?

**KALDOR:** Yes.

**CORN:** I'm saying let's not take 95%.

**PETO:** In fact, you should take more than 95%. So many epidemiological studies are done that many isolated excess risks will turn up by chance. For example, nobody has reported an excess of bladder cancer in nickel workers, but we found three compared with 0.6 expected in one subgroup, which is significant at the 5% level. However, I don't believe that nickel refining causes bladder cancer. It hasn't turned up in any other study, and we did dozens of significance tests on different cancers and different groups. You need to apply a more stringent test when you're producing a new hypothesis than when you're testing an established one.

**CORN:** But when you get the small numbers, the statistical trap, which you haven't mentioned yet, is that if I suddenly see three cases in a nickel factory, then I would immediately begin to do a study. If I include those three cases in the study which brought my attention to it in the first place, I have a tautological situation.

**KALDOR:** Certainly. There are many possible biases. I'd like to emphasize that I have considered a somewhat idealized situation.

**CORN:** My point is that with this simplistic model I could narrow those limits by lowering the confidence to, let's say, 90%. That may be a very meaningful thing to do.

**KALDOR:** The table I presented was intended to illustrate what can be done with 95% confidence, but I could have done the same thing for 90% or for 20%.

# Problems in Dose-response and Risk Assessment: The Example of Asbestos

JULIAN PETO
Section of Epidemiology
Institute of Cancer Research
Sutton, Surrey, SM2 5PX,
United Kingdom

## INTRODUCTION

The selection of an inappropriate model of carcinogenesis can lead to gross errors in the predicted effects of exposure to a carcinogen. For example, the increase in lung cancer incidence caused by cigarette smoking is approximately proportional to the product of the dose (number of cigarettes smoked per day) and the fourth or fifth power of duration of smoking (Doll 1978; Doll and Peto 1978) (in fact, the dose-dependence may include linear and quadratic terms). It is, therefore, impossible to base useful predictions on the cumulative dose (total number of cigarettes smoked), as the eventual risk caused by smoking ten cigarettes/day for 40 years may be 50 times greater than that caused by smoking 40 cigarettes/day for 10 years. The term "dose" should thus be used only to describe the dose-rate of exposure to a carcinogen (cigarettes per day or fibers/ml of asbestos), and the effects of temporal variables (age, time since first exposure, duration of exposure) should be examined separately. There is no useful general formula that describes the effects of all carcinogens. Asbestos appears to act as an initiator (early stage carcinogen) in mesothelioma induction, but as a promoter (late stage carcinogen) for lung cancer (Peto et al. 1982); cigarette smoking seems to both initiate and promote lung cancer induction; and ionizing radiation probably acts primarily at one or more intermediate or late stages in the induction of most or all carcinomas (Doll 1978). These different effects may lead to very different predictions of lifelong risk, although they can all be explained within the framework of a simple multistage model of carcinogenesis (Day and Brown 1980).

## CANCER INCIDENCE IN ASBESTOS WORKERS

### Assumption of Linear Dose-response, Fiber Type Differences, and Measures of Exposure

The dependence of lung cancer and mesothelioma incidence rates on age, duration of asbestos exposure, and smoking are reasonably well established. Four further assumptions are required for low-dose extrapolation from observations on heavily exposed industrial cohorts, however, and all are open to serious doubt:

(1) Linear dose-response is assumed in the following models, but existing exposure

data, although consistent with this assumption, are not accurate enough to exclude other models, particularly at low doses.

(2) Conditions in most sectors of the asbestos industry have greatly improved, and the working conditions 30 or more years ago that caused very high cancer rates among asbestos workers were measured, if at all, with various instruments that counted particles rather than pathogenic fibers. There is no satisfactory uniform conversion factor from particle to fiber counts, and any estimate of dose-specific risk under current working conditions is therefore extremely unreliable.

(3) The observed incidence in lung cancer risk at the same nominal level of exposure varies more than 50-fold between different cohorts, such as chrysotile (white asbestos) miners and U.S. chrysotile textile workers (McDonald et al. 1983); and it is not clear which provides the best estimate for other conditions of industrial or environmental exposure. Dose-specific lung cancer rates are given below to illustrate the qualitative implications of the assumed models; but these figures, although compatible with certain published studies, are not intended as best estimates that can be applied generally.

(4) Crocidolite (blue asbestos) appears to be particularly liable to cause mesothelioma, and it is suspected that at least some mesotheliomas among workers exposed principally to chrysotile, with occasional exposure to crocidolite, are due to the effects of crocidolite. Few formal estimates of the dose-specific mesothelioma risk have been published, however, and the mesothelioma rates assumed below have been chosen to make the predicted mesothelioma risk among men first exposed to asbestos at age 20 approximately half the predicted lung cancer excess, which is similar to the ratio observed among insulation workers exposed to a mixture of fiber types. They may, therefore, be too high for chrysotile but too low for crocidolite.

## Age and Time Dependence

Mesothelioma incidence rises sharply with time since first exposure to asbestos but is unrelated to age at first exposure or smoking, whereas lung cancer incidence is strongly related to both smoking and age, as well as to time since first exposure. The differential effects of these relationships in North American insulation workers are shown in Table 1. The ratio of mesothelioma to excess lung cancer (observed minus expected) was more than 4:1 in nonsmokers, about 1:2 in smokers first exposed to asbestos before age 25, and about 1:4 in smokers first exposed at age 25 or over (Peto et al. 1982). The relative risk for lung cancer (observed/expected) was, however, virtually the same irrespective of age or cigarette smoking, which suggests that asbestos simply multiplies the lung cancer risk caused by natural or other processes. (Note that the expected numbers in Table 1 are smoking-specific; a relative risk of 2 would thus mean that asbestos exposure increases the risk of developing lung cancer from about one in 200 to about one in 100 in nonsmokers, and from about one in ten to about one in five in smokers.)

## Table 1
Observed and Expected Deaths Due to Lung Cancer, and Deaths Due to Mesothelioma, Among North American Insulation Workers

| | Lung cancer | | | | Mesothelioma Obs | Ratio of mesothelioma to excess lung cancer |
| | Obs | Exp[a] | Obs/Exp | Obs-Exp | | |
| --- | --- | --- | --- | --- | --- | --- |
| Smokers aged under 25 at first exposure | 211 | 32.67 | 6.5 | 178.33 | 99 | 0.56 |
| Smokers aged 25 or over at first exposure | 237 | 48.05 | 4.9 | 188.95 | 48 | 0.25 |
| All nonsmokers | 5 | 1.04 | 4.8 | 3.96 | 18 | 4.55 |

Obs = observed; Exp = expected
[a] Expected numbers are smoking-specific
Data from Peto et al. (1982).

## A Model for Lung Cancer

The relative risk for lung cancer increases with both dose and duration of asbestos exposure. A simple model that is now widely accepted, at least as a useful approximation, for the resulting incidence $I_A$ in asbestos workers of a given age, history of smoking, and asbestos exposure is

$$I_A = I_U [k_L(f \cdot d) + 1]$$

where f is the average exposure level in fiber/ml, d is duration of exposure, $k_L$ is a constant that probably depends on fiber dimension and type, and $I_U$ is the normal lung cancer incidence among unexposed individuals of the same age and smoking history (Peto 1978). This model can be modified in various ways to accommodate the delay of about 10 years before the maximum relative risk caused by brief intense exposure is reached (Seidman et al. 1979) and the observation in several cohorts that the relative risk eventually falls (Walker 1984). The effects of such adjustments are, however, likely to be smaller than the uncertainty in the appropriate value of $k_L$.

As the majority of lung cancers in both smokers and nonsmokers occur in old age, this model implies that the lifelong risk caused by asbestos exposure will be virtually independent of age at exposure and will be almost proportional to eventual cumulative dose. It should perhaps be emphasized that the average age at which asbestos-induced lung cancers occur will, under this model, be virtually the same as that of lung cancers in unexposed individuals, even if asbestos exposure occurs only in childhood or throughout life due to ambient exposure.

To illustrate the calculation, suppose that the risk of dying of lung cancer is 0.5% among nonsmokers and 10% among moderate smokers, and that the relative risk for lung cancer is increased by 2.0 (i.e., from 1.0 to about 3.0) by a cumulative

## Table 2
Predicted Excess Numbers of Deaths Before Age 80 per 1000 Men Due to Lung Cancer or Mesothelioma Caused by Asbestos Exposure During Working Hours at 1.0 Fibers/ml[a]

| Age at first exposure (years) | | Duration of exposure (years) | | | |
|---|---|---|---|---|---|
| | | 5 | 10 | 20 | 40 |
| 0 | LC | 3.7 | 7.3 | 14.4 | 28.4 |
| | M | 7.5 | 13.1 | 20.1 | 24.7 |
| 20 | LC | 3.7 | 7.4 | 14.7 | 27.4 |
| | M | 2.1 | 3.5 | 5.0 | 5.6 |
| 40 | LC | 3.7 | 7.3 | 13.2 | 16.8 |
| | M | 0.3 | 0.5 | 0.6 | 0.7 |

LC = lung cancer; M = mesothelioma
[a]Calculated from the models described in the text, using current male death rates (from England and Wales) for lung cancer and all causes.

exposure of 200 fiber/ml years. (This would correspond to 20 years at an average level of 10 fiber/ml, which is typical of the exposure conditions in certain factories 30 or 40 years ago.) Twenty years' exposure to a level of 0.001 fiber/ml (about 10,000 times lower than industrial conditions in the past) throughout the working day would, therefore, produce an increase in relative risk of 2.0/10,000, or 0.0002, and the increase in lifelong lung cancer risk would be about 2 in $10^5$ in smokers and about 1 in $10^6$ in nonsmokers. For ambient exposure at this level 7 days a week throughout the day and night for 20 years, these estimates would be increased by a factor of about 5, and for lifelong ambient exposure by a further factor of about 3 or 4. The lifelong risks for various durations of exposure corresponding to these assumptions are shown in Table 2.

## A Model for Mesothelioma

For both pleural and peritoneal mesothelioma, the incidence appears to be proportional to the third or fourth power of time since first exposure irrespective of duration of exposure, age, or cigarette smoking (Peto et al. 1982), although the magnitude of the risk is, of course, related both to level and to duration of exposure. A simple model that predicts this sort of pattern is that the risk is increased by each day of exposure by an amount proportional to the level of exposure on that day and to the cube of time since that day. For an exposure of duration $T_O$ years at a constant level of f fiber/ml, the incidence T years after first exposure will then be given by the formula

$$I = f \cdot k_M [T^4 - (T - T_O)^4]$$

where $k_M$ is a constant that depends on fiber dimension and type. It is not clear to what extent the incidence of pleural mesothelioma differs between fiber types for a given fiber concentration and size distribution, although peritoneal mesothelioma is almost never caused by exposure to pure chrysotile.

Predicted lifelong risks for different durations of exposure and ages at first exposure are shown in Table 2. These suggest that the mesothelioma risk increases in approximate proportion to duration for exposures of up to about 10 years, but then rises more slowly, and is not greatly increased by continuing exposure beyond about 20 years. The model also implies that the lifelong risk for mesothelioma will be very much greater if exposure occurs early in life. Ambient exposure in childhood may cause similar risks for lung cancer and mesothelioma among smokers; and in nonsmokers, as Table 1 suggests, the mesothelioma risk will probably exceed the lung cancer risk irrespective of age at first exposure.

## NICKEL REFINING

The very high lung and nasal sinus cancer rates suffered in the past by nickel refinery workers provide a further example of site-specific differences in incidence patterns (Table 3) (Peto et al. 1984). Working conditions in this factory had greatly improved by 1930, and high cancer risks occurred only in men first exposed before about 1925. Follow-up began in 1934 and was thus restricted to men whose exposure had virtually ceased. The subsequent absolute excess risk for lung cancer was approximately constant beyond 30 years after first exposure and was unrelated to age at first exposure. In contrast, for nasal sinus cancer the risk was very much higher in those first exposed at older ages and continued to rise sharply for at least 50 years.

## MODELS OF CARCINOGENESIS

The multistage model of carcinogenesis, according to which a normal cell must undergo an ordered sequence of heritable changes to become a cancer cell, predicts

## Table 3
### Estimated Lung and Nasal Sinus Cancer Death Rates in Pre-1925 Welsh Nickel Refinery Workers[a]

| Age at first exposure (years) | | Years since first exposure | | | | |
|---|---|---|---|---|---|---|
| | | Under 20 | 20– | 30– | 40– | 50 or over |
| Under 25 | LC | 1.0 | 2.9 | 5.5 | 6.0 | 4.8 |
| | NS | 1.0 | 4.7 | 6.2 | 12.5 | 16.7 |
| 25–34 | LC | 1.3 | 3.7 | 7.0 | 7.6 | 6.0 |
| | NS | 3.0 | 13.8 | 18.3 | 37.0 | 49.3 |
| 35 or over | LC | 1.3 | 3.7 | 6.9 | 7.5 | 6.0 |
| | NS | 10.0 | 46.8 | 61.9 | 125.4 | 167.2 |

LC = lung cancer; NS = nasal sinus cancer
[a]Relative rates adjusted for period and intensity of exposure (Data from Peto et al. 1984).

that agents acting at the first stage will cause a cancer incidence roughly proportional to a power of time since first exposure, independent of age at exposure, whereas the cancer risk caused by agents acting at a later stage will appear more quickly and will be greater when exposure occurs at older ages (Day and Brown 1980). The pattern of mesothelioma incidence therefore suggests that asbestos acts at the first stage in carcinogenesis, whereas the lung cancer pattern suggests that it acts at a later stage. It is thus impossible to classify carcinogens as early or late acting, except in relation to particular types of tumors. This is a further limitation on any extrapolation from animal data to predict human cancer risks, particularly when the route of administration or tumor type are not the same. Carcinogenicity experiments are rarely conducted on large enough numbers of animals of various ages for such differences to be studied at all, but even if they were, it is not at all certain that the cancer incidence patterns in man would be similar to those observed in the laboratory. Moreover, the striking differences in both age and time dependence between lung cancers and mesotheliomas in asbestos workers and between lung and nasal sinus cancers in nickel refiners, together with laboratory evidence that various carcinogens act at more than one stage in carcinogenesis, suggest that such heterogeneity of effect is probably the rule rather than the exception (Peto 1985).

## Initiation and Promotion

The current fashion for classifying agents as initiators or promoters on the basis of experimental studies and inferring that a certain pattern of dose or time dependence will necessarily be observed in man, and in particular the suggestion that promoters are likely to exhibit a dose threshold, are of dubious relevance to risk assessment. The terms, initiation and promotion, were coined to describe the effect whereby exposure to one agent, followed later by exposure to another, causes a very much greater tumor incidence in experimental animals than the same agents applied in the opposite order. It was, therefore, natural that the same terms should be adopted to describe epidemiological observations suggesting early or late effects in a multistage process, but it cannot be assumed that this speculative analogy implies any particular mode of action.

## Duration of Exposure

The natural incidence of many cancers increases in proportion to the fifth or higher power of age, and the conventional explanation of this phenomenon is that the background rates at which the different cellular accidents postulated by the multistage model occur remain roughly constant throughout life. The implications of this effect in relation to duration of exposure to a carcinogen are, however, uncertain. An agent that acts only at the first stage would be expected to produce a cancer rate similar to that of mesothelioma, rising very sharply with time since first exposure but increasing sublinearly with increasing duration of exposure. For agents that act at several stages, however, the risk will be very much greater when exposure is prolonged, as the lung cancer risk is among continuing smokers. Ionizing radiation provides a nice example of this problem. Conventional calculations of the cancer risk at a given total dose have been based almost entirely on the effects of brief exposure from nuclear weapons or therapeutic irradiation. If the biological effects of radiation were analogous to those of smoking, however, prolonged exposure to the same total dose might cause a very much higher cancer risk than these brief intense exposures. The limited data on humans and animals who have suffered prolonged low-level irradiation do not in fact indicate that the risk at a given total dose is increased enormously; but it is remarkable that this major weakness in the assumptions implicit in the conventional risk calculation should have received so little attention, and further studies of the effects of chronic irradiation would certainly be worthwhile.

## PERCEPTION AND ACCEPTANCE OF RISK

A curious aspect of risk assessment is that the actual value of the calculated risk is almost universally ignored. In view of the dubious nature of such calculations, it could be argued that this is just as well; but until the meaning of a risk of $10^{-1}$, $10^{-3}$, or $10^{-6}$ is better understood, slogans such as "one asbestos fiber can kill" will continue to dominate the public debate. The history of asbestos control provides one example of the irrational way in which risks may be ignored or exaggerated, but there are many others.

### Environmental and Industrial Asbestos Exposure

In the case of asbestos, direct observation showed that about 20 years' exposure at an average level of the order of 10 fibers/ml had caused substantial risks; and the resulting prediction that a working lifetime at 2 fibers/ml (the asbestos standard in force in Britain until 2 years ago) might cause a risk of the order of one in ten therefore seemed unlikely to be wrong in either direction by a large factor (Peto 1978). This dose-specific risk estimate was, however, based on a study in an asbestos textile factory, and subsequent studies in other working environments suggested lower dose-specific risks. Using one of the higher risk estimates and assuming linear dose-response leads to the prediction that the average asbestos levels usually encountered in schools and other buildings containing asbestos will cause a risk of the order of $10^{-5}$ (Ontario Royal Commission 1984). The level in such buildings is usually less than 0.001 fibers/ml, counting fibers longer than 5 $\mu$m and having an aspect ratio exceeding 3:1 with an electron microscope. The same criterion based on optical microscopy is used for industrial measurements; but as very fine fibers cannot be seen with an optical microscope, the "optical equivalent" count in buildings would be even lower. I do not know what proportion of the British or U.S. population live or work in buildings containing substantial amounts of asbestos, but if it is about one in five, a risk of the order of $10^{-5}$ would correspond to about one excess death per year in Britain, and about four in the U.S. The dust levels and extent of exposure assumed in this calculation need to be properly estimated by further surveys;

but unless they can be shown to be much too low, my personal view is that the wholesale removal of asbestos now occurring in Britain and the U.S. is, in most buildings, an unjustified waste of money. I would not object to myself or my own family's being exposed to a risk of this order, nor, I suspect, would most people if they understood what it means. A smoker probably reduces his lifelong risk by about $10^{-5}$ by smoking one less cigarette a year.

This is an interesting example, as the conclusions are of immediate practical importance. It is my personal judgment that the predicted risk is unlikely to be much too low and thus provides a sensible basis for policy decisions. However, I reached this conclusion by offsetting the conservative aspects of the calculation (ignoring the progressive reduction in the relative risk for lung cancer observed after exposure ceases and using one of the highest reasonable dose-specific risk estimates) against its obvious uncertainties (the dubious quality and comparability of the exposure estimates, and linear extrapolation over four orders of magnitude), and such a process cannot be justified formally.

The sequel to the asbestos story is also instructive. The industrial risk, which in my opinion was unacceptably high, was not adequately controlled in Britain until several years after it was recognized, and then only in response to a media scare, whereas the minute environmental risk generated an hysterical overreaction which still continues. Informed public debate would probably have led to the opposite response in both cases, with much quicker industrial action and a more balanced environmental response. Few people have any clear idea of the meaning or magnitude of everyday risks. A substantial proportion of Americans have now rejected smoking; but as saccharin was rejected with almost equal fervor, this can hardly be attributed to a cool appraisal of the evidence, and most smokers are still not aware that about one in four of them will be killed by the habit.

## DISCUSSION

Predicted risks due to agents such as cigarette smoke or asbestos for which there are extensive epidemiological data should certainly be calculated from an appropriate model. For carcinogens for which such data are not available, however, the examples discussed above merely indicate that model-dependent error must be added to the many other uncertainties that such extrapolation entails. It would evidently be prudent to assume a most pessimistic model, and the assumption that the increase in relative risk will remain after exposure ceases may for most carcinogens provide a useful upper limit; but this is of little practical value in relation to agents for which there are no epidemiological data, as relative risks in animals and humans are unlikely to be similar. There are, however, several known carcinogens for which better information on the dependence on age and duration of exposure and the evolution of risk after exposure ceases could be obtained, either by reexamining existing data or by further studies. The collation of such results, together with similar data on the effects of the same agents in animals, would be a useful exercise.

It is very much easier to dismiss risk assessment out of hand than to criticize it constructively, as the mode of carcinogenic action, the measures of dose, and above all the validity of extrapolation from mouse or salmonella to man are for many agents so uncertain that it can be equally plausibly argued either that the risk is unacceptable or that it is negligible. The problem is real, however, and independent scientists can and must be influential in the debate among a conservative industry, erratic regulatory policy, and campaigning zealots, although most of this audience must know from personal experience that it is extremely difficult to be objective when the choice between plausible assumptions is so arbitrary. For the next decade or two, we can only refine the rules of risk assessment, ensure that they are observed and await the day when the molecular basis of carcinogenesis is finally understood. The risk assessment game will then no longer be played, and its passing will be mourned only by those who weren't fit to play it anyway.

## REFERENCES

Day, N.E. and C.C. Brown. 1980. Multistage models and primary prevention of cancer. *J. Natl. Cancer Inst.* 64 **4:** 977.

Doll, R. 1978. An epidemiological perspective of the biology of cancer. *Cancer Res.* **38:** 3573.

Doll, R. and R. Peto. 1978. Cigarette smoking and bronchial carcinoma: Dose and time relationship among regular smokers and lifelong non-smokers. *J. Epidemiol. Community Health* **32:** 303.

McDonald, A.D., J.S. Fry, A.J. Wooley, and J.C. McDonald. 1983. Dust exposure and mortality in an American chrysotile textile plant. *Br. J. Ind. Med.* **40:** 361.

Ontario Royal Commission. 1984. Report of the Royal Commission on matters of health and safety arising from the use of asbestos in Ontario (3 vols.). Ontario Ministry of the Attorney General.

Peto, J. 1978. The hygiene standard for chrysotile asbestos. *Lancet* **i:** 484.

———. 1985. Early and late stage carcinogenesis in mouse skin and in man. In *Models, mechanisms and aetiology of tumour promotion* (ed. M. Borzsonyi, N.E. Day, K. Lapis, and H. Yamasaki), I.A.R.C. Scientific Publications No. 56, p. 359. International Agency for Research on Cancer, Lyon, France.

Peto, J., H. Seidman, and I.J. Selikoff. 1982. Mesothelioma mortality in asbestos workers: Implications for models of carcinogenesis and risk assessment. *Br. J. Cancer* **45:** 124.

Peto, J., H. Cuckle, R. Doll, C. Hermon, and L.G. Morgan. 1984. Respiratory cancer mortality of Welsh nickel refinery workers. In *Nickel in the human environment* (ed. F.W. Sunderman), I.A.R.C. Scientific Publications No. 53, p. 37. International Agency for Research on Cancer, Lyon, France.

Seidman, H., I.J. Selikoff, and E.C. Hammond. 1979. Short-term asbestos work and long-term observation. *Ann. N.Y. Acad. Sci.* **339:** 61.

Walker, A.M. 1984. Declining relative risks for lung cancer after cessation of asbestos exposure. *J. Occup. Med.* **26:** 422.

## COMMENTS

**ALBERT:** Are you suggesting that the asbestos industry ought to be cleaned up, rather than the agent?

**PETO:** When you get risk estimates that differ 100-fold for different sectors of an industry, you can't choose a single exposure standard and apply it across the board because it will be unreasonably stringent in some situations and dangerously lax in others. We obviously aren't measuring the right thing for asbestos, and a more practicable approach is probably to deal with each process separately. The relative risk for lung cancer in asbestos textiles used to be of the order of five in the worst areas, for example, so conditions need to be 20-fold, or 50-fold, or whatever factor you think is appropriate, better than they were 40 years ago. You try to achieve this by reducing particle or fiber counts in textile factories by a factor of 20 or 50, but you can't assume that the risk will be the same at the same nominal level in asbestos mines—in fact, you know that it won't.

**WEINSTEIN:** Did you say that you can't classify asbestos as early or late acting with respect to lung cancer?

**PETO:** No. You can classify asbestos as late acting with some confidence in relation to lung cancer because it increases the lung cancer rate quite quickly. In fact, it behaves almost as if it acts at the last stage, although that seems to me implausible. But it does seem to act late rather than early.

**PURCHASE:** Does the cumulative exposure continue to increase because some of the asbestos fibers stay in the lung after you've stopped inhalation exposure?

**PETO:** The formula predicts that the relative risk is proportional to cumulative dose and the data show whether or not that's approximately true. The mechanisms underlying it are another matter, and they aren't really understood at all. Fibrosis may progress, but the carcinogenic effect may be unrelated to fibrosis.

**ALBERT:** Could that drop-off in the relative risk in lung cancer with the nickel workers be due to change in the process?

**PETO:** They cleaned the place up completely by about 1930. The cohort was followed up until 1981; but in the last 50 years of follow-up there was virtually no exposure, so the cumulative dose was constant.

**PIKE:** If I remember rightly, you said that for lung cancer the cumulative dose is what matters in terms of relative risk, and you also said that age of first exposure didn't matter. You mean age of first exposure given duration?

**PETO:** Yes. Whether you are exposed from age 20–40 or age 40–60, by the time you're 60, which is when lung cancer rates become high, you've got the same cumulative dose. The asbestos insulation workers' data suggest that age at exposure makes almost no difference to the eventual risk, although exposure from age 20–60 must obviously be worse than 40–60.

**WEINSTEIN:** What is the equivalent risk for other industrial hazards?

**PETO:**   It depends on the chemical. You've actually followed up people with high exposure to benzene. Nobody now has such high exposures, so you know that the risk isn't going to be enormous under current conditions, and you can put an upper limit on it with some confidence. For asbestos, it's not so simple because there have been process changes and it's even possible that modern machinery actually produces more very fine, dangerous fibers than the processes that were used 30 years ago. So it's conceivable that we're measuring completely the wrong thing, and the lung cancer risk for some processes will eventually turn out to be as high as it was 20 or 30 years ago. I very much doubt it, but the predictions are certainly less reliable than for a simple chemical.

**WEINSTEIN:**   If you won't define disaster and if you won't use conventional risk extrapolation, is there any point in doing any of this numerically?

**PETO:**   I think that we are developing a better understanding of cancer incidence patterns, a better understanding of carcinogenesis is certainly evolving in the lab, and there's now a good deal of common sense in industry. Some of the older dose-response analyses are quite good, but some of them are terrible, and I think there has been a general raising of standards. The EPA now has a sensible doctrine. It's not that it's scientifically right, but it's scientifically defensible and probably conservative. There's an evolution in the right direction. We still can't guarantee against catastrophe, but we're much less likely to have one now than we were in the days of "safe thresholds."

**PIKE:**   I remember looking at the permissible levels of various compounds in drinking water when TCE was found in some L.A. water supplies. The estimated risks from contamination at these levels varied by several orders of magnitude whichever model you used. I believe that setting permissible levels based on a formal risk estimation procedure will do better than this and will, in general, lead you to prioritize things in roughly the right order. Our risk estimates may be wrong, but I think they are much better than guesswork.

**PETO:**   Some extrapolations based on very dubious models are probably much more robust than they seem at first sight. Take the prediction of mesothelioma rates based on the assumption that the incidence will go on increasing as the cube of time since first exposure to asbestos, for example. The exponent of time may well be five rather than three, and the predicted risk 60 years after first exposure would be proportional to $60^5$, which is orders of magnitude higher than $60^3$. But that isn't the way the calculation works because you've got data on people who have been followed up for about 30 or 40 years, so that point is fixed, and when you compare the third and fifth powers of time passing through that point, there's a difference of less than two in the predicted life-long risk. The model is actually rather robust against errors in the exponent of time. That sort of awareness is important because you want to know which assumptions matter and which ones don't. It should be routine in risk assessment to include a discussion of alternative models of this sort and what their implications are, but it's hardly ever done. You have to have some idea whether errors in the model that you're blithely assuming imply errors of less than two or more than 100 in your risk estimates.

CORN: The question of what constitutes a disaster is very relevant. Everything we're doing is retrospective, and we're detecting the relatively high-risk legacy of the past. But there are some clues as to the risk levels we think we're setting today in areas where there were traditionally high risks. I think the British Coal Standard, which is set on the basis of reasonable dose-response curves at a 1% probability of first-stage detection of pneumoconiosis is representative of what we're trying to say. In the Coke Oven Standard, we also talked about a 1% level of risk for those starting employment today and working a lifetime, as contrasted to higher risks carrying over from the past— 1% is a fairly high risk level.

PETO: I'm not sure that I agree. Risk assessment, particularly in America, has been bedeviled by the assumption that you have to achieve absurdly low risks.

CORN: That's what we're talking about in a nonvoluntary employer-imposed environment. That discussion is current. So, when you compare the power of the methods to what we're setting today or hope we're setting for the future, unless you do much better, you're not going to see anything. With the risk levels we think we're setting today, the disease we'll reap 30 and 40 years from now will require improved epidemiological methods of detecting the excess.

PETO: They'll be completely undetectable. That's the whole point of what John [Kaldor] was saying.

WEINSTEIN: So we'll never know whether the models are correct.

PETO: No. But we'll know they're adequate. If there's a disaster, we'll know. If there isn't a disaster, we'll have no idea whether we're wasting our money.

ALBERT: Could you explain what you meant when you showed those parallel log-log plots of age against incidence for smokers and nonsmokers and asbestos-exposed versus nonasbestos-exposed, one for lung cancer and the other for mesothelioma? Were you saying that both smoking and asbestos exposure were interacting with whatever it is that causes the cancer?

PETO: Yes, and acting at the first stage. The first stage in the lung cancer process is accelerated by smoking, irrespective of the age when you start, so the determinant is duration of smoking; and mesothelioma is initiated by asbestos. For smokers, as Malcolm [Pike] pointed out, the lung cancer risk appears to be proportional to the fourth power of duration of smoking; and for mesothelioma it's the cube of time since first exposure to asbestos. You can't estimate these powers very accurately, but the independence of age indicates that both were initiating the process.

**PURCHASE:** I thought smoking was a late-stage effect because people's incidence falls when they stop.

**PETO:** It's both. John [Kaldor] didn't mention that, but an interesting thing about the dose-response curve that he showed for smoking and lung cancer is that it curves upwards, which is what you'd expect if two stages are affected. There is very good evidence that smoking acts both at the beginning and at a late stage in causing lung cancer. When Richard Doll presented these data in 1971, the dose-response looked linear; and Peter Armitage pointed out that if smoking acts at two stages, the dose-response should be quadratic. When they acquired further data and looked at it more carefully, they found that it was in fact quadratic. It's a rather nice example.

**PIKE:** But Julian [Peto] also knows that it is only quadratic if you ignore the point for very heavy smokers that is way off the curve. There is a reason that those lines appear parallel. It is because smokers have so much more lung cancer than nonsmokers that the background lung cancer rate of smokers can be ignored. If cigarette smoke were not so carcinogenic, you would have to take account of the fact that some lung cancers had already begun before someone had ever smoked, and the lines would not be parallel.

# Session 3:
# Modeling and Extrapolation

# The Impact of Occupational Exposure Patterns on Quantitative Risk Estimation*

DAVID G. HOEL†
Radiation Effects Research Foundation
5-2 Hijiyama Park
Hiroshima 730, Japan

## OVERVIEW

This paper addresses the problem of using short-term epidemiologic exposure and follow-up data in estimating working lifetime cancer risk. Results derived in this study indicate that the true lifetime risk can be significantly under or overestimated, depending on the type of extrapolation model employed; that the situation can be further complicated by consideration of whether the agent of interest acts as an initiator or promoter; and that animal data may provide the best basis for model selection, even when epidemiologic data is also available for risk estimation.

## INTRODUCTION

It is generally held that the most appropriate data for cancer risk estimation is obtained from epidemiological studies. Despite problems of precision, the human study does avoid the very uncertain process of animal-to-man extrapolation. For estimating the quantitative effects of chemical carcinogens, occupational cohort studies are most often used. Two major uncertainties in this particular estimation process are the reconstruction of exposure histories and the use of specific quantitative models. It is this last issue of models which we will briefly explore in this paper.

Possibly the best example of a successful cohort study is the A-bomb follow-up studies of Nagasaki and Hiroshima. The radiation exposures are certainly known with a precision not found with most occupational studies involving chemical carcinogens. Model assumptions, however, are unresolved and contribute significantly to the risk estimates. Specifically, issues of dose-response, dose rate, and interactions with other risk factors are debated. As with radiation, there is a clear need with chemical carcinogens to understand the quantitative implications of model assumptions used in calculating quantitative risk estimates.

The quantitative relationship between cancer rate and dose is often an area of disagreement in risk assessment. Arguments generally revolve around the issue of

---

\* This paper was presented at the Banbury Conference by Dr. Michael Hogan.

† On leave from the National Institute of Environmental Health Sciences, Research Triangle Park, North Carolina

linear versus nonlinear or possible threshold models. Epidemiological data seldom are able to resolve this issue primarily because of exposure uncertainties and limited study size. With radiation, for example, the choice of a linear versus linear-quadratic model continues to be discussed (National Academy of Sciences 1980). Decisions concerning the choice of response curves are thus forced to draw upon quantitative models that speculate about the mechanisms of the cancer process. For most chemical carcinogens neither a large cohort study with good exposure information nor appropriate experimental data is available. What is most often done when quantification is required is to assume linearity and to make other simple assumptions as needed. For example, EPA's analysis of benzene involved estimating the excess relative risk for leukemia and then extrapolating linearly in dose assuming that the relative risk (RR) applied to a lifetime exposure (see Bartman [1982] for discussion).

The quantitative impact of linearity assumptions on a risk estimate is reasonably well understood in most examples. The impact of assumptions concerning the effects of duration of exposure and length of follow-up are not well understood. For example, it was pointed out in the IARC (1982) analysis of benzene that the relative risk for leukemia from the Rinsky et al. (1981) study was 5.6. However, if the cohort is limited to those employees with 5 or more years of presumed exposure, the relative risk increases to 21.1. One is thus faced with the question of which figure, if either, should be used in a risk assessment concerned with a working lifetime exposure of possibly 45 years.

This benzene example illustrates the difficulties in using occupational data that consists of various exposure patterns. Such data makes the task of estimating working lifetime effects of continuous low-level exposures extremely tenuous. The risk estimation process becomes even more complex when this type of occupational data is used to estimate the effects of lifetime environmental exposures.

One solution to this problem is to obtain knowledge of the underlying mechanisms of the disease process itself. For this we need the expertise of the laboratory scientist. Quantitative results will be given to illustrate the utmost importance of the mechanism assumption.

## Epidemiological Models

Both the modeling and statistical analysis of epidemiological data are commonly approached by using regression techniques with regard to the incidence rate or hazard function. Specifically, the incidence rate is written for an individual at time t as $\lambda(t; z)$, where z denotes a vector of the individual's covariates. For the purposes of our discussion, the only covariate of interest will be the exposure function, which is usually expressed as

$$z(t) = \int_0^t x(u)w(t - u)du \tag{1}$$

where $x(t)$ is the dose rate at time t and w is a weighting function. Because of cancer latency, it is often felt that exposure shortly prior to tumor detection does not affect the incidence, hence

$$w(t) = \begin{cases} 0 & t \le C \\ 1 & t > C \end{cases} \tag{2}$$

is a very simple weighting function which takes into account this latency period C. Using this weight function (2), z(t) becomes

$$z(t) = \begin{cases} D(t - C) & t \ge C \\ 0 & t < C \end{cases} \tag{3}$$

for a constant dose rate D. Further discussion of $z(t)$ and other weighting functions can be found in Breslow et al. (1983).

The effect of exposure $z(t)$ on the incidence $\lambda(t; z)$ usually is assumed to follow one of the models:

(i)    $\lambda(t;z) = \lambda_0(t)e^{\beta z}$

(ii)    $\lambda(t;z) = \lambda_0(t)(1 + \beta z)$                   (4)

(iii)   $\lambda(t;z) = \lambda_0(t) + \beta z$

where $\lambda_0(t)$ is the spontaneous or unexposed incidence rate. Models (i) and (ii) are possibly the simplest forms for a multiplicative effect while (iii) represents an additive effect. Several authors (Thomas 1981; Breslow et al. 1983) have considered these models. In particular, Breslow et al. (1983) have argued in favor of (i) partially on the basis of computational ease and partially because the logarithm of the relative risk is linear. They have also analyzed lung cancer data from an occupational cohort exposed to arsenic using models (i) and (iii).

There is a considerable quantitative difference between the additive and multiplicative models using the cumulative dose function $z(t) = Dt$ (for simplicity we ignore the latency period C). Given the typical log-log model $\alpha t^k$ for $\lambda_0(t)$ (Peto 1977) we have from (4)

(i)    $\log \lambda(t;D) = \log \alpha + k \log t + \beta Dt$

(ii)   $\log \lambda(t;D) = \log \alpha + k \log t + \log(1 + \beta Dt)$      (5)

(iii) $\log \lambda(t;D) = \log(\alpha t^k + \beta Dt)$

For the two multiplicative models (i) and (ii) the incidence as a function of time has a greater slope than the background rate on a log scale. This is to be compared with the parallel incidence plots one finds with the multistage model. Also, comparing the additive with the multiplicative models, suppose we set the relative risk at age $t = 40$ to be equal to 4 for each of the three models. Further set $k = 5$, $D = 1$, and $\alpha = 1$. Then we find that the relative risks at $t = 20$ are 2, 2.5, 49, and at age $t = 60$ are 8, 5.5, and 1.6 for the three models, respectively. These values illustrate the considerable difference that can arise with the two types of models in relating effect with time. Functionally, it is clear that on a relative basis the multiplicative models lead to a much greater effect at large values of t.

For an occupational cohort, assume that exposure begins at age $t_0$ and continues at a constant dose rate D until age $t_1$. The simple version (3) of the exposure function $z(t)$ becomes

$$z(t) = \begin{cases} 0 & t \le t_0 + C \\ D(t - t_0 - C) & t_0 + C < t < t_1 + C \\ Dd & t_1 + C \le t \end{cases} \tag{6}$$

where the exposure duration d equals $t_1 - t_0$. Let I denote the cumulative incidence from time $t_0$ until the end of follow-up at time T. In other words

$$I = \int_{t_0}^{T} \lambda(t; z) dt \tag{7}$$

let E denote the corresponding cumulative incidence for background rate $\lambda_0$. Then for the additive model (iii) we find letting C = 0 that

$$I = E + \beta Dd(T - d/2 - t_0). \tag{8}$$

By using the log-log incidence model for $\lambda_0$, it follows that the relative risk is given by

$$RR = 1 + Kd(T - d/2 - t_0)/(T^{k+1} - t_0^{k+1}) \tag{9}$$

Equation (9) shows that this additive model will underestimate the RR for a lifetime exposure based upon limited exposure but complete follow-up. Also, the RR will be overestimated using limited exposure and limited follow-up. The example summarized in Table 1, which assumes that k = 5, illustrates these results.

The displayed values in this table show the possible error in extrapolating relative risk values to lifetime effects if the true underlying model is additive.

For the multiplicative model (ii), the expression for the cumulative incidence is

$$I = E + \frac{\alpha \beta D}{k + 1} [dT^{k+1} - (\frac{1}{k + 2}) (t_1^{k+2} - t_0^{k+2})] \tag{10}$$

and the relative risk becomes

$$RR = 1 + K[dT^{k+1} - \frac{1}{k + 2} (t_1^{k+2} - t_0^{k+2})]/(T^{k+1} - t_0^{k+1}) \tag{11}$$

which is roughly approximated by

$$RR = 1 + Kd[1 - \frac{1}{k + 2} [\frac{t_1}{T}]^{k+1}] \tag{12}$$

Equation (12) indicates that the RR increases somewhat linearly in duration of

## Table 1
## Excess Relative Risk (Additive Model)

| Follow-up | Exposure duration (years) | |
| --- | --- | --- |
| | 20–25 | 20–65 |
| Until age 25 | 5.2 | — |
| Until age 65 | 0.21 | 1 |

**Table 2**
Excess Relative Risk (Multiplicative Model)

| | Exposure duration (years) | |
| --- | --- | --- |
| Follow-up | 20–25 | 20–65 |
| Until age 25 | 0.08 | — |
| Until age 65 | 0.14 | 1 |

exposure d and also increases in length of follow-up time T. Using (11) and the same values used in the previous table, we obtain the results shown in Table 2.

For both examples, long-term follow-up after a short exposure duration results in an underestimate of the appropriate relative risk for a lifetime exposure. For a short-term follow-up, the two models are both in serious error but in opposite directions. These calculations and equations suggest that if there is an appropriate follow-up, it is reasonable to increase the excess relative risk linearly to estimate the risk from exposures longer than those in the study population. This of course assumes that one of these models is, in fact, appropriate.

## Multistage Models

The mathematical models based upon multistage mutation models for cancer have been applied to both toxicological and epidemiological data for purposes of risk estimation and for general quantitative descriptions of time and dose effects. The multistage model is a simple attempt to describe the carcinogenic process as a series of somatic cell mutations leading to a single malignant cell that subsequently develops into a tumor. This model predicts the log-log incidence and age relationship as is observed for many epithelial tumors in man (see Peto [1977] for discussion). The model has, in fact, been used to attempt to decide which stage of the carcinogenic process is affected by a particular carcinogen. Specifically, Brown and Chu (1983) studied the same set of arsenic-exposed workers as did Breslow et al. (1983), but the former used the multistage instead of the multiplicative risk model in order to investigate whether arsenic acted as an initiator or as a promoter. Brown and Hoel (1983) also considered the issue of affected stages and model selection for the very large 2-AAF mouse study involving some 25,000 mice.

For the situation of less than lifetime exposure both Whittemore (1977) and Day and Brown (1980) have derived the mathematical expressions for the incidence rates based upon the multistage model. Mathematically, the expression for the incidence rate is the simplest for the case of either the first stage or the penultimate stage $(k - 1)$ seen as the one affected by the carcinogen. From equation (3) of Day and Brown (1980), we have that the excess incidence over background is proportional to

$$(t - t_0)^{k-1} - (t - t_0 - d)^{k-1} \qquad \text{for } j = 1 \tag{13}$$
$$(t_0 + d)^{k-1} - t_0^{k-1} \qquad \text{for } j = k - 1$$

## EARLY STAGE CARCINOGEN
### Age at first exposure is 0

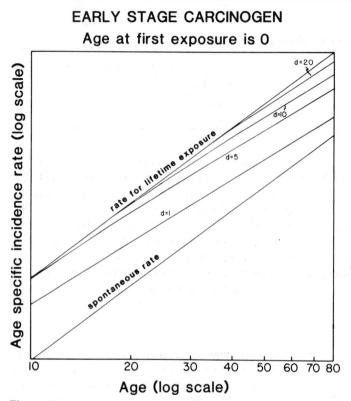

**Age (log scale)**

**Figure 1**

Plot of the age-specific cancer incidence rate versus age on a log-log scale. Age-at-first-exposure equal 0 and the first stage of the multistage model (k = 5 stages) is assumed to be affected. The curves vary depending upon the duration d (years) of exposure.

where $t_0$ is the age at exposure onset, d is the duration of exposure, k is the number of stages in the multistage model, and j is the affected stage. To appreciate the significance of these functions, a number of hypothetical curves which indicate the effects of typical occupational exposures have been plotted.

Figure 1 illustrates the effects of discontinued exposure for several choices of the length or duration of exposure d. What is observed is that a relatively short exposure to an initiator early in life has a lasting effect which is close to the situation of continuous exposure. Figure 2, on the other hand, shows the delayed effect of exposure to an initiator. As is seen, delaying exposure until age 20 clearly reduces the impact on the resultant relative risk. In fact, initial exposure at or beyond age 40 has practically no measurable risk in subsequent years, as is shown in Figure 3. These three figures indicate some of the difficulty in attempting to relate quantitatively a continuous lifetime exposure with a limited occupational exposure.

Dealing with late stage carcinogens or promoters is quite different from the standpoint of risk estimation. The effects are observed soon after exposure is initiated

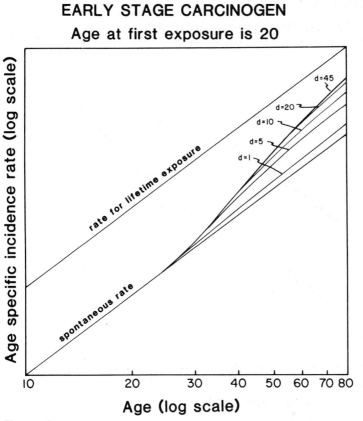

**EARLY STAGE CARCINOGEN**
**Age at first exposure is 20**

**Figure 2**
Same as Figure 1 except age-at-first-exposure is 20 years.

and are rapidly diminished after cessation of exposure. Figure 4 clearly illustrates this point and should be contrasted with the initiator model shown in Figure 2.

In order to consider the impact of the use of occupational exposures to estimate the effects of lifetime environmental exposures, we consider Figures 2 and 4 in somewhat different manners. Let $E_t(t_0,d)$ denote either of the two expressions in equation (13). Then the cumulative risk of background cancers $B_i$ and excess cancers $D_i$ is given by

$$B_i = C_1 \sum_{t=j}^{i} t^{k-1}w_t \tag{14}$$

$$D_i = C_2 \sum_{t=j}^{i} E_t(t_0,d)w_t \tag{15}$$

for age j until age i. Here k is the number of stages in the multistage model and the weighting factor is $w_t = n_t/\Sigma n_j$ where $n_t$ is the population size at age t. Since $E_t(0,t) = t^{k-1}$ it follows that

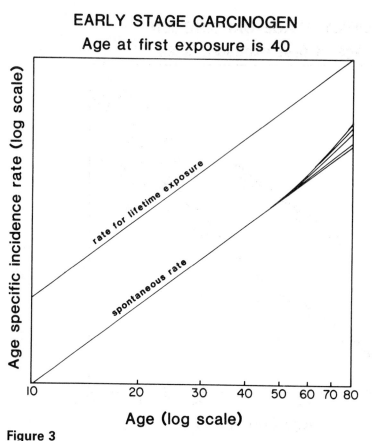

## EARLY STAGE CARCINOGEN
### Age at first exposure is 40

*Age specific incidence rate (log scale)*

rate for lifetime exposure

spontaneous rate

**Age (log scale)**

10   20   30   40   50 60 70 80

**Figure 3**
Same as Figure 1 except age-at-first-exposure is 40 years.

$$\frac{D_i/C_2}{B_i/C_1} \qquad (16)$$

represents the proportion of total excess relative risk one would observe if exposure began at age $t_0$ for a duration d, and follow-up began at age j and continued until age i. The proportion is compared to what one would observe with a lifetime exposure, i.e., $t_0 = 0$, d = t.

In Figures 5 and 6, the cumulative excess risk for less than lifetime exposure is compared with the corresponding excess risk for a lifetime exposure. The curves displayed in these figures, which are plots of equation (16), assume that exposure begins at age 20 and is terminated at the age shown in the figures. To illustrate the use of these curves, suppose that the exposure being studied acts as an early stage carcinogen and that an individual is exposed until age 30 and is followed until age 60. Then the curve labeled 30 in Figure 5 shows that the calculated excess relative risk would be about 10% of the relative risk appropriate for a lifetime exposure at

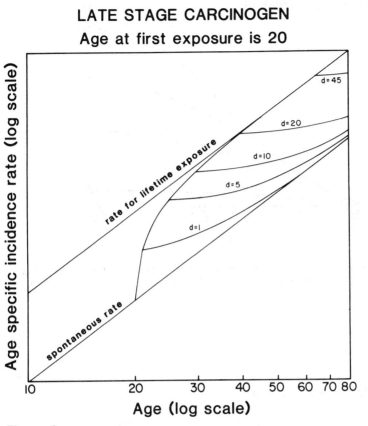

**LATE STAGE CARCINOGEN**
**Age at first exposure is 20**

*Figure labels within chart:* d = 45, d = 20, d = 10, d = 5, d = 1, rate for lifetime exposure, spontaneous rate

*Y-axis:* Age specific incidence rate (log scale)
*X-axis:* Age (log scale) — 10, 20, 30, 40, 50, 60, 70, 80

**Figure 4**
Carcinogen is assumed to affect the penultimate stage (i.e., 4) of the multistage model (k = 5 stages). Age-at-first-exposure is 20 years.

the same exposure rate. The corresponding results for a late stage carcinogen are shown in Figure 6. Figures 5 and 6 indicate quite clearly the degree of error one is likely to encounter in extrapolating from occupational studies to lifetime exposures and vice-versa. Furthermore, it generally will not be known whether one is dealing with an early or late stage carcinogen or even some other unknown model without considerable experimental data to complement the epidemiological study.

## Benzene—An Example

A number of human studies have provided sufficient evidence to establish that benzene is a human leukemogen (IARC 1982). Further, recent experimental studies in rodents have shown benzene to be carcinogenic by both inhalation and gavage (Maltoni et al. 1983; NTP 1984). For quantitative risk estimation, the data that have received the most attention are from the leukemia mortality studies in rubber hydrochloride workers by Rinsky et al. (1981) and Infante et al. (1977). In this

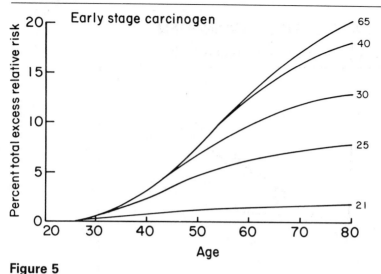

**Figure 5**

Plot of the percentage of excess relative risk versus age for the first stage of a multistage model (k = 5 stages) being affected. Exposure begins at age 20 and the duration of exposure is given on the figure.

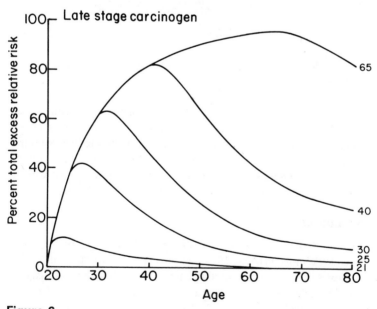

**Figure 6**

Same as Figure 5 except the fourth stage is affected instead of the first stage.

**Table 3**
Observed and Expected Leukemia Deaths from the Benzene Study of Rinsky et al. (1981)

| Length of follow-up beyond exposure period | Duration of exposure (years) | | | | |
| --- | --- | --- | --- | --- | --- |
| | 0–5 | 5–10 | 10 + | Total | RR |
| Current with exposure | 1[a] | 0 | 1 | 2 | 20 |
| | 0.04[b] | 0.02 | 0.04 | 0.10 | |
| 0–5 | 0 | 2 | 0 | 2 | 13 |
| | 0.11 | 0.02 | 0.02 | 0.15 | |
| 5 + | 1 | 1 | 1 | 3 | 3.0 |
| | 0.85 | 0.10 | 0.02 | 0.97 | |
| Total | 2 | 3 | 2 | 7 | 5.6 |
| | 1.0 | 0.14 | 0.09 | 1.25 | |
| RR | 2.0 | 21 | 22 | 5.6 | |

[a] Observed number of cases
[b] Expected number of cases

study, a total of seven cases of leukemia were observed among 748 exposed workers as opposed to 1.25 expected. Workers were exposed in two different plants to various levels of benzene during the 1940s and 1950s and were followed until 1975.

Table 3 summarizes the data from Rinsky et al. (1981). Because only seven cases were observed and are available for the analysis, very little can be concluded about an appropriate statistical model. First, certainly nothing can be concluded about the shape of the dose-response curve. To make inferences about the dose-response curve, one must depend upon assumptions and experimental data. Table 3 does indicate, however, a greatly reduced risk for the group with the smallest duration of exposure. In the IARC (1982) analysis, it was suggested that either the relative risk of 21, which pertained to workers exposed at least 5 years, be used or that the value of 5.6 for the entire cohort be increased linearly. Both methods produced essentially the same working lifetime risk estimate. In a subsequent large-scale industry-wide study of chemical workers by the Environmental Health Associates (1983), a linear relationship was found between cumulative exposure to benzene, e.g., $z(t)$, and relative risk for lymphatic and hematopoietic cancers. Finally, it is worth noting in the data from Risky et al. (1981) (Table 3) that the relative risk decreases from 20 to 13 to 3 as the time interval since the cessation of exposure increases. This would suggest that benzene behaves somewhat like a late stage carcinogen. This conclusion, however, is probably much too strongly stated for the limited data; but the data do indicate that the trend is in this direction. Table 4 compares several risk estimates based upon these data. The major issues that remain today include whether or not the dose-response should be linear and what the appropriate worker exposure histories are.

Some of the experimental animal data is illustrated in Figure 7. For these com-

## Table 4
## Various Lifetime Leukemia Risk Estimates for a 45-year Exposure at 10 ppm Benzene per Working Day[f]

|  | IARC[a] | EPA[b] | OSHA[c] |
|---|---|---|---|
| Upper limit |  |  | 152 |
| Estimate |  | 155[d] |  |
| Lower limit | 14[e] |  |  |

[a] International Agency for Cancer Research (1982)
[b] Environmental Protection Agency Cancer Assessment Group (Bartman 1982)
[c] Occupational Safety and Health Agency (White et al. 1982)
[d] Based upon linear risk with slope B = 0.02407
[e] Obtained by dividing by 10 the risk of 140 at 100 ppm
[f] Leukemia deaths / 1000

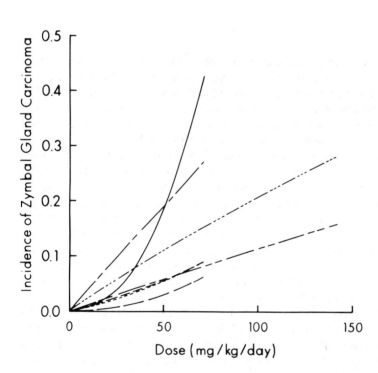

## Figure 7
Fitted linear-quadratic models to the zymbal gland carcinoma incidences due to benzene exposures (mg/kg·day) in the NTP (1984) and Maltoni et al. (1983) studies. It is assumed that 100% absorption takes place with both the gavage and inhalation routes. NTP inhalation: (———) male mice; (——— ———) female mice; (——— – –) male rat; (——— – ) female rat. Maltoni inhalation: (– – – – –) male rat; (— — —) female rat. Maltoni gavage: (——— – – –) female rat.

parisons, gavage and inhalation data have been naively combined assuming 100% absorption and the data has been fitted using a linear quadratic model. Although zymbal gland tumors may not be especially relevant to human leukemia, one does observe that the animal tumor data is reasonably linear. One final observation from the animal tumor data is that a lifetime exposure of 50 mg/kg·day produces a tumor incidence of about 5–10%. From Table 4 we see estimates of about 5–15% for a working lifetime (45 years) exposure of 10 ppm or 1.8 mg/kg·day. Thus the risk estimates based upon the epidemiology suggest that man is more sensitive than the rodent by a factor of at least 25. Therefore, using risk estimates based solely upon the animal data, we would not expect to have seen the excess leukemias that were observed in the study by Rinsky et al. (1981) at the exposure levels used in the analysis of the human data.

## CONCLUSIONS

In the introduction, the statement was made that it is widely held that epidemiological data are to be preferred over toxicological data for risk assessment purposes. This is a valid assumption in an ideal setting with quality exposure and health data, adequate sample sizes, and some knowledge concerning the biology needed for the mathematical models.

What we have attempted to show in this paper is the impact of exposure patterns and mathematical assumptions on risk estimates. We see great differences in estimates generated by early or late stage carcinogens. Further duration of follow-up plays an important part in the estimation process. What all of this suggests is that we need both epidemiological data and laboratory information for risk estimation. This need could include data on the results of various exposure patterns in experimental animals, kinetics and distribution of the compound of interest, and information concerning possible mechanisms of action.

For the benzene example, data concerning the pharmacokinetics, along with exposure fractionation experiments, will go a long way toward settling the questions concerning the risks of benzene. Further occupational studies are not likely to provide more information or insight at this juncture. What is clearly needed is experimental data on underlying mechanisms. In conclusion, I feel that it is of utmost importance to develop methods for combining the epidemiological with the appropriate experimental data so that risk estimation methodology will reflect a more accurate estimate of human risk.

## REFERENCES

Bartman, T.R. 1982. Regulating benzene. In *Quantitative risk assessment in regulation* (ed. L. Lave), p. 99. Brookings Institution Press, Washington, D.C.

Breslow, N.E., J.H. Lubin, P. Marek, and B. Langholz. 1983. Multiplicative models and cohort analysis. *J. Am. Stat. Assoc.* **78:** 1.

Brown, C.C. and K.C. Chu. 1983. Implications of the multistage theory of carcinogenesis applied to occupational arsenic exposure. *J. Natl. Cancer Inst.* **70:** 455.

Brown, K.G. and D.G. Hoel. 1983. Multistage prediction of cancer in serially dosed animals with applications to the $ED_{01}$ study. *Fund. Appl. Toxicol.* **3:** 470.

Day, N.E. and C.C. Brown. 1980. Multistage models and primary prevention of cancer. *J. Natl. Cancer Inst.* **64:** 1977.

Environmental Health Associates. 1983. *An industry-wide mortality study of chemical workers occupationally exposed to benzene.* Report to the Chemical Manufacturer's Association.

Infante, P.F., R.A. Rinsky, J.K. Wagoner, and R.J. Young. 1977. Leukemia in benzene workers. *Lancet* **i:** 76.

International Agency for Research on Cancer (IARC). 1982. Some industrial chemicals and dyestuffs. *IARC monographs on the evaluation of the carcinogenic risk of chemicals to humans,* vol. 27. IARC, Lyon, France.

Maltoni, C., B. Conti, and G. Cotti. 1983. Benzene: A multipotential carcinogen. Results of long-term bioassays performed at the Bologna Institute of Oncology. *Am. J. Indust. Med.* **4:** 589.

National Academy of Sciences. 1980. The effects on populations of exposure to low levels of ionizing radiation. *Report of the Advisory Committee on the Biological Effects of Ionizing Radiations* (BEIR report). National Research Council, Washington, D.C.

National Toxicology Program (NTP). 1984. NTP draft technical report on the toxicology and carcinogenesis studies of benzene (CAS No. 71-43-2) in F344/N rats and B6C3F1 mice (gavage studies). NIH Publication number 84-2545 (NTP TR289). U.S. Department of Health and Human Services, Public Health Service, National Institutes of Health, Bethesda, Maryland.

Peto. R. 1977. Epidemiology, multistage models, and short-term mutagenicity studies. In *Origins of human cancer* (ed. H.H. Hiatt, J.D. Watson, and J.A. Winsten), p. 1403. Cold Spring Harbor Laboratory, Cold Spring Harbor, New York.

Rinsky, R.A., R.J. Young, and A.B. Smith. 1981. Leukemia in benzene workers. *Am. J. Indust. Med.* **2:** 217.

Thomas, D.C. 1981. General relative risk models for survival time and matched case-control analysis. *Biometrics* **37:** 673.

White, M.C., P.F. Infante, and K.C. Chu. 1982. A quantitative estimate of leukemia mortality associated with occupational exposure to benzene. *Risk Analysis* **2:** 195.

Whittemore, A.S. 1977. The age distribution of human cancer for carcinogenic exposures of varying intensity. *Am. J. Epidemiol.* **106:** 418.

# Consequences of Nonlinear Kinetic Dose-response Models on Carcinogenic Risk Assessment

JOHN VAN RYZIN
Division of Biostatistics
Columbia University
New York, New York 10032

## OVERVIEW

This paper discusses the consequences of nonlinear kinetics in risk estimation. It examines this question in the context of a nonlinear kinetic dose-response model based on earlier work by Gehring and Blau (1977), Hoel et al. (1983), and Van Ryzin and Rai (1984). The important consequence for regulatory purposes is that ignoring nonlinear kinetics might lead to either overestimating "safe" doses or underestimating "safe" doses. Furthermore, these may be severe over or under estimates. Finally, linear extrapolation with the one-hit model applied to the inappropriate administered dose may either overestimate or underestimate the virtually safe dose when compared with the one-hit model applied to the appropriate "effective" dose at the target site.

## INTRODUCTION

For regulatory purposes it is often useful to attempt quantification of the risk associated with a low-level exposure to a chemical carcinogen. Usually there is insufficient data in humans to adequately assess the risk. An alternative commonly used method is to estimate the risk at low doses from an animal chronic study. This is then converted to man by means of a conversion factor (OTA 1981). However, even before doing this conversion, one must extrapolate downward from the high-dose levels in the experimental animal to the low-dose levels consistent with the exposure levels in man. This process is known as the low-dose extrapolation problem. The purpose of this paper is to examine the consequences that nonlinear kinetics can have on such low-dose extrapolation.

This issue has already been discussed by Hoel et al. (1983) and by Gehring and Blau (1977). In a recent paper by Van Ryzin and Rai (1984), a dose-response model incorporating nonlinear kinetics was developed based on the model of Gehring and Blau (1977). This model allows for nonlinear kinetics in both the activation and deactivation (repair) phase of the chemical reaction. In this paper we show, by use of the examples of vinyl chloride and saccharin, that the results of such a nonlinear kinetic model could be either to decrease or to increase the risk estimates. To illustrate this, we compare the risk estimates that one obtains with the kinetic model

119

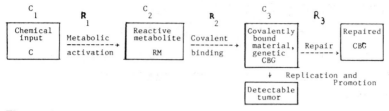

**Figure 1**

A simplified compartment model for a metabolically activated chemical carcinogen. Adapted from Gehring and Blau (1977) and Hoel et al. (1983). ($R_1$) First reaction, nonlinear Michaelis-Menten kinetics; ($R_2$) second reaction, linear kinetics; ($R_3$) third reaction, nonlinear Michaelis-Menten kinetics; ($C_i$) compartment i, i = 1,2,3.

to those obtained from the Weibull and one-hit dose-response models. The Weibull model was taken as typical of a number of dose-response models currently in use which allow for nonlinearity. The one-hit model is linear at low doses.

Finally, based on these examples and other results, we draw some conclusions about what guidelines are prudent in using risk extrapolation estimates for regulatory purposes. In particular, we conclude that nonlinear kinetics suggest that linear extrapolation in the "effective" dose at the target site is a prudent regulatory behavior.

## RESULTS

### Nonlinear Kinetics and Dose-response Modeling

Many chemicals become potential carcinogens only after being metabolized into a reactive metabolite. The reactive metabolite is then capable of covalently binding with DNA. This may then go on to be expressed as genetic damage that is not repaired. Since the metabolic activation process and the repair process may both follow nonlinear kinetic equations, the "effective" dose of the carcinogen is really that amount of covalently bound genetic material which is not repaired. Such a model for the carcinogenic process is illustrated in Figure 1. This figure is a somewhat simplified model adapted from Gehring and Blau (1977) and Hoel et al. (1983). For a further discussion of the biological basis for this model, see these two references and the discussions therein.

In Figure 1, the "effective" dose at the cells of the target organ is the amount of covalently bound genetic material (CBG) in the third compartment ($C_3$) of the figure. The administered dose is proportional to the amount of chemical (C) in the first compartment ($C_1$). However, the amount of "effective" dose in compartment ($C_3$) is dependent on the incoming metabolic activation reaction ($R_1$), the incoming covalent binding reaction ($R_2$) and the outgoing repair reaction ($R_3$). In what follows, we assume that $R_2$, covalent binding, follows first order kinetics. On the other hand $R_1$, metabolic activation and $R_3$, repair, are assumed to follow nonlinear Michaelis-Menten kinetics. For further justification of these assumptions, see Gehring and Blau (1977) and Hoel et al. (1983).

Using this model, if one writes down the differential equations of the transfer of the chemical through compartments and assumes that steady-state conditions have been reached, a simple set of equations relating the substance in each compartment is obtained. This set of equations becomes

$$k_2[RM] = \frac{k_3[CBG]}{b_3 + [CBG]} \quad \text{and} \quad \frac{k_1[C]}{b_1 + [C]} = k_2[RM] \tag{1}$$

Here $k_2$ is a positive constant governing the elimination rate of reaction $R_2$. The constants $k_1$ and $k_3$ are the maximum elimination rates at saturation for the reactions $R_1$ and $R_3$, respectively. Also, $b_1$ and $b_3$ are the respective Michaelis-Menten constants for these reactions. More detailed discussion of the arguments leading to equations (1) can be found in Gehring and Blau (1977), Hoel et al. (1983), and Van Ryzin and Rai (1984).

If the amount of the input chemical [C] as the administered dose is denoted by d and the amount of [CBG] at the target organ as the biologically "effective" is denoted by D, the solution of the steady state equations (1) is

$$D = g(d) = \frac{ad}{1 + bd} \tag{2}$$

where a is a positive constant and b is such that D is positive. For a fuller development of the transformation (2) for any system allowing nonlinear activation and deactivation, see Van Ryzin and Rai (1984).

In the typical chronic laboratory animal experiment, the protocol calls for constant dosing of the animals at $m + 1$ dose levels $d_0 = 0 < d_1 < \ldots < d_m$ ($d_0 = 0$ is control). The resulting biologically "effective" dosing schedule is then $D_0 = 0 < D_1 < \ldots < D_m$, where $D_i = g(d_i)$, $i = 0, 1, \ldots, m$, $g(d)$ given by equation (2). However, in the usual experiment with laboratory animals, the $D_i$ are internal doses at the cellular level at the target site and are unobservable. Thus, the dose-response model one should be using would be a dose-response model given by

$$P(D) = \text{Prob (tumor occurs over a lifetime at dose level D)} \tag{3}$$

that is, P(D) represents the dose-response model yielding the probability that an animal at constant internal D will respond or develop a tumor. Such is typically not available since D is not observable.

Many dose-response models have been suggested in the literature. These include the tolerance distribution models such as the Weibull, logit, and probit models, as well as the biological stochastic models such as the one-hit, multihit, and multistage models. For a fuller discussion of these models, see Rai and Van Ryzin (1979), Krewski and Van Ryzin (1981), or Van Ryzin (1980). Using the Weibull model given by

$$P(d) = 1 - \exp\{-(\alpha + \lambda D^\beta)\} \tag{4}$$

where $\alpha$, $\beta$, and $\lambda$ are all positive constants, Van Ryzin and Rai (1984) combined equation (2) with equation (4) to obtain the model

$$P^*(d) = P(D) = P(g(d)) \tag{5}$$

where $g(d)$ is given by (2). Here, the $P^*(d)$ represents a dose-response model in the administered dose which incorporates the transformation of that dose to the "effective" dose at the target site. The choice of $P(D)$ in equation (4) as the Weibull model is taken because it is a fairly general dose-response model which includes the one-hit model when $\beta = 1$ and approximates the multihit model when $\beta \neq 1$. However, the hits at the target site are now in the transformed or internal dose.

The statistical estimation of the parameters and the corresponding maximum likelihood theory for model (5) can be found in Van Ryzin and Rai (1984). Besides giving the parameter estimation procedures, they also developed statistical tests for the null hypotheses $H_0 : \beta = 1$. This statistical test examines whether or not the one-hit model holds in the transformed data. Van Ryzin and Rai also give the chi-square goodness-of-fit test for the general model of equations (2)-(5). The model with $\beta = 1$ in equation (4) becomes the one-hit model in the transformed dose. The model with $b = 0$ in equation (2) becomes the Weibull model for the administered or untransformed dose. Finally, the model with $b = 0$ in (2) and $\beta = 1$ in equation (4) becomes the one-hit model in the administered dose.

## Application of the Models to Two Sets of Data

All of these models were fit to two sets of data, both of which are quite nonlinear. The first set of data is the vinyl chloride data of Maltoni and Lefemine (1975) on liver angiosarcoma in Sprague-Dawley rats inhaling vinyl chloride for 4 hours/day, 5 days/week for 12 months. The units are in ppm. Table 1 presents these data. Note

**Table 1**
Vinyl Chloride Data and Fitted Models

| Dose (ppm) | Number on test | Number w/tumor | Percent w/tumor | Full model | Effective dose (one-hit model) | Administered dose (Weibull model) | Administered dose (one-hit model) |
|---|---|---|---|---|---|---|---|
| 0 | 58 | 0 | 0.0 | 0.0 | 0.0 | 0.0 | 0.0 |
| 50 | 59 | 1 | 1.7 | 0.9 | 1.3 | 2.8 | 0.1 |
| 250 | 59 | 4 | 6.8 | 4.6 | 4.5 | 4.5 | 0.3 |
| 500 | 59 | 7 | 11.9 | 7.0 | 6.6 | 5.5 | 0.7 |
| 2500 | 59 | 13 | 22.0 | 10.7 | 10.6 | 8.9 | 3.3 |
| 6000 | 60 | 13 | 21.7 | 11.7 | 11.8 | 11.6 | 7.7 |
| 10,000 | 61 | 9 | 14.8 | 12.2 | 12.3 | 13.6 | 12.5 |
| | | | | $p = 0.59$[a] | $p = 0.72$[a] | $p = 0.19$[a] | $p < 0.001$[a] |

[a]$p$ = goodness of fit $p$ value; $p < 0.001$ indicates very poor fit.

**Table 2**
Saccharin Data and Fitted Models

| | | | | Expected number with tumor from model | | | |
| | | | | Full model | Effective dose (one-hit model) | Administered dose (Weibull model) | Administered dose (one-hit model) |
| Dose (% in diet) | Number on test | Number w/tumor | Percent w/tumor | | | | |
|---|---|---|---|---|---|---|---|
| 0.0 | 324 | 0 | 0.0 | 0.0 | 0.0 | 1.3 | 0.0 |
| 1.0 | 658 | 5 | 0.8 | 3.3 | 5.4 | 3.1 | 13.6 |
| 3.0 | 472 | 8 | 1.7 | 14.4 | 15.5 | 11.2 | 28.7 |
| 4.0 | 189 | 12 | 6.3 | 10.3 | 9.9 | 9.9 | 15.2 |
| 5.0 | 120 | 15 | 12.5 | 11.0 | 9.9 | 12.0 | 11.9 |
| 6.25 | 120 | 20 | 16.7 | 20.3 | 17.9 | 22.8 | 14.7 |
| 7.5 | 118 | 37 | 31.4 | 37.6 | 38.4 | 36.7 | 17.2 |
| | | | | $p = 0.13^a$ | $p = 0.12^a$ | $p = 0.28^a$ | $p < 0.001^a$ |

[a] $p$ = goodness-of-fit $p$ value; $p < 0.001$ indicates very poor fit.

that the dose-response curve rises fairly rapidly to a 22% response at 2500 ppm and then levels off. As Gehring et al. (1978) showed, this leveling off is due to saturation of the metabolic activation of vinyl chloride.

The second set of data is the IRDC study of bladder tumors in Sprague-Dawley male rats as reported by Carlborg (1983). The dose units are percent of saccharin in the diet. The data are presented in Table 2. Note that the dose-response curve rises rapidly in a nonlinear manner with the rate of rise increasing as dose increases. This steepness in the dose-response curve has been suggested as possibly being due to saturation of the clearance mechanism of saccharin from the bladder, which would be a nonlinear repair process.

Also given in Tables 1 and 2 are the estimated or expected responses for each of the four models outlined above. As can be seen from the expected numbers columns, all of the models except the one-hit model in the administered dose adequately fit the observed data. In fact, if one examines the goodness-of-fit $p$-values in these tables based on the chi-square theory for these models, we observe that the best fitting model in the vinyl chloride case is the one-hit model with transformed dose ($\beta = 1$ in equation [4]). In the saccharin data, the Weibull model with the administered dose is the best fitting model (b = 0 in equation [2]). However, the one-hit model in the transformed dose ($\beta = 1$ in equation [4]) cannot be ruled out for the saccharin data. In fact, if one does a statistical test of whether or not $\beta = 1$ (one-hit hypothesis for transformed data), this hypothesis is accepted at conventional statistical levels up to a 20% level of significance for both sets of data. This says that either set of data cannot rule out a one-hit phenomenon at the target site in the transformed effective dose. As will be seen below, this will have low-dose extrapolation consequences.

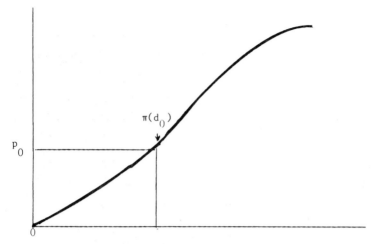

**Figure 2**
Low-dose extrapolation. [$\pi(d)$] Increased risk over background; [$d_o$] virtually safe dose [VSD]; [d] dose.

## Low-dose Extrapolation

The use of a nonlinear kinetic model as given in equations (2)–(5) can have a considerable effect on the low-dose extrapolation. By low-dose extrapolation, we mean the problem of finding a virtually safe dose (VSD) corresponding to some prescribed "acceptable" risk level $P_0$ over background. Specifically, define

$$\pi(d) = P^*(d) - P^*(0) \tag{6}$$
$$= \text{The increased probability (risk) over the background risk of } P^*(0) \text{ due to administered dose d}$$

where $P^*(d)$ is given by equation (5). The virtually safe dose (VSD) at $P_0$ is then defined to be that dose level $d_0$ which satisfies $P_0 = \pi(d_0)$. Specifically, $d_0$ is that dose level leading to a (small) prescribed increased risk $P_0$. To illustrate the method for this low-dose extrapolation, consider Figure 2. If $P_0 = 10^{-6}$, then the dose $d_0$ such that $\pi(d_0) = 10^{-6}$ is that exposure dose leading to an increased probability of one in a million for getting a tumor in the time period of the experiment—a lifetime for chronic studies.

The problem of low-dose extrapolation is then to estimate $\pi(d)$ through the model equations (2)–(6) and obtain the corresponding estimated VSD. The details on how to do this for general dose-response models is discussed in Krewski and Van Ryzin (1981) and, for the model of this paper, in Van Ryzin and Rai (1984).

For the two data sets in Tables 1 and 2, vinyl chloride and saccharin, respectively, we have carried out the low-dose extrapolations at $P_0 = 10^{-4}$ and $P_0 = 10^{-6}$. These are given in Table 3 for vinyl chloride and Table 4 for saccharin for the four models given in Tables 1 and 2. As noted in Table 3, for the case of vinyl chloride the VSD estimates for the one-hit model which allows for nonlinear kinetics (second

## Table 3
### Vinyl Chloride Virtually Safe Dose (VSD) Estimates

| Model | VSD at risk level $P_0$ | |
| --- | --- | --- |
| | $P_0 = 10^{-4}$ | $P_0 = 10^{-6}$ |
| Full model (equation [2]–[5] | 1.6 | $7.6 \times 10^{-2}$ |
| Effective dose one-hit model ($\beta = 1$ in [4]) | $2.1 \times 10^{-1}$ | $2.1 \times 10^{-3}$ |
| Administered dose Weibull model (b = 0 in [2]) | $1.3 \times 10^{-7}$ | $5.3 \times 10^{-14}$ |
| Administered dose one-hit model ($\beta = 1$; b = 0) | 4.3 | $4.3 \times 10^{-2}$ |

row of Table 3) are lower than that of the one-hit model not allowing for kinetics. However, the VSDs are vastly higher than those of the Weibull model (fully 11 orders of magnitude at $10^{-6}$ increased risk). The situation with saccharin is exactly reversed. The models allowing for nonlinear kinetics in Table 4 (first two rows) are now higher than those of the one-hit model for administered dose and lower than those of the Weibull model for administered by as much as three orders of magnitude at increased risk of $10^{-6}$. Since in both data sets the hypothesis of $\beta = 1$ is accepted, we cannot rule out the one-hit model in the transformed dose in either case (row two of Tables 3 and 4). This model gives larger estimates of the VSD than the one-hit model for the untransformed administered dose in the saccharin

## Table 4
### Saccharin Virtually Safe Dose (VSD) Estimates

| Model | VSD at risk level $P_0$ | |
| --- | --- | --- |
| | $P_0 = 10^{-4}$ | $P_0 = 10^{-6}$ |
| Full model (equation [2]–[5]) | $6.4 \times 10^{-2}$ | $2.3 \times 10^{-3}$ |
| Effective dose one-hit model ($\beta = 1$ in [4]) | $1.4 \times 10^{-2}$ | $1.4 \times 10^{-4}$ |
| Administered dose Weibull model (b = 0 in [2]) | $5.7 \times 10^{-1}$ | $1.4 \times 10^{-1}$ |
| Administered dose one-hit model ($\beta = 1$; b = 0) | $4.8 \times 10^{-3}$ | $4.8 \times 10^{-5}$ |

data, but smaller in vinyl chloride. The exact opposite is dramatically true when the one-hit model in the transformed dose is compared with the Weibull model in the administered dose. The consequences of these results for regulatory risk assessment are discussed in the following section.

## DISCUSSION

As evidenced in Tables 3 and 4, the incorporation of nonlinear kinetics into the dose-response model in equation (5) via equation (2) may have a profound effect on the VSD estimates. Since such estimates are often used as a basis for regulatory decisions, it appears that nonlinear kinetics are highly important in regulatory decisons.

Furthermore, it appears that the dose-response model given by equations (2)–(5), although based on a somewhat simplified pharmacokinetic model as outlined above, cannot be dismissed on biological grounds. It is quite consistent with the observed data in these two highly nonlinear data sets. The consequences of this nonlinear kinetic dose-response model for risk assessment include the following:

(1) Dose-response models not incorporating nonlinear repair kinetics may very much underestimate risk and overestimate safe doses. For example, the VSDs at $10^{-6}$ increased risk for saccharin in Table 4 with the model of equation (5) with $\beta = 1$ or arbitrary $\beta$ as compared to the nonlinear, but nonpharmacokinetic Weibull model, is two to three orders of magnitude lower. Therefore, use of the Weibull model, which adequately fits in the observed dose-response range, for extrapolating downward outside this range may in fact allow "safe" doses which are 100–1000-fold too high. Since the goodness-of-fit tests for the two pharmacokinetic models of Table 4 (the full model of equation [5] and the one-hit model in the effective dose with $\beta = 1$ in [4]) are acceptable, we cannot rule out their extrapolated safe dose estimates based on these data alone. Ruling out these estimates would require more understanding of the rat bladder clearance or repair mechanism or possible explanation of the increase at high doses due to increased cell proliferation.

(2) Dose-response models not incorporating nonlinear activation kinetics may very much overestimate risk. This is dramatically clear by comparing the VSD estimates at $10^{-6}$ with the full kinetic model of equation (5) or the restricted one-hit model with $\beta = 1$ in the first two rows of Table 3 with the Weibull-based estimate of the third row. In this case, the work of Gehring et al. (1978), based on a second metabolic experiment, showed that the administered vinyl chloride dose data of the original experiment should be adjusted to the metabolized "effective" dose. When their adjustment is applied to the data of Table 1 and a one-hit model is fitted to the adjusted effective metabolized dose, the fit is quite good. Furthermore, the estimated VSD at increased risk level of $P_0 = 10^{-6}$ if such a procedure is followed is then $1.5 \times 10^{-3}$. For details of these results, see Van Ryzin and Rai (1980). This safe dose estimate compares very closely to our VSD estimate of $2.1 \times 10^{-3}$ given by the one-hit model for the transformed data in Table 3, which suggests very strongly that the estimated VSD of $2.1 \times 10^{-3}$ rather than $5.3 \times$

$10^{-14}$ of the Weibull model is the more correct answer. This is a vast difference in estimates.

(3) Linear extrapolation with the one-hit model ignoring nonlinear kinetics may either overestimate the VSD (underestimate risk), as in vinyl chloride, or underestimate the VSD (overestimate risk), as in saccharin. Compare rows two and four of Tables 3 and 4. In each case the overestimate or underestimate at $P_0 = 10^{-6}$ increased risk was roughly one order of magnitude. Thus, linear extrapolation may not always be protective by overstating risk (understating VSDs).

(4) The use of the dose-response model in equation (5) has the advantage of accounting for nonlinear activation or repair pharmacokinetics using only the administered dose data. The model has the advantage of allowing for estimation of the transformed effective dose at the target site. The model assumes at the target site that the mechanism is approximately multihit including the possibility of one-hit. For more details on this model, see Van Ryzin and Rai (1984). The model is totally consistent with a one-hit mechanism at the target site in the transformed dose in both data sets (vinyl chloride and saccharin) considered here. The model is consistent with nonlinear metabolic activation in the case of vinyl chloride and nonlinear saturable bladder clearance in the case of saccharin.

## ACKNOWLEDGMENT

This work was supported by the National Institute of Environmental Health Sciences on Grant Number ES-02557.

## REFERENCES

Carlborg, F. 1983. Statistical considerations of the design of the IRDC experiment with saccharin. Presentation at *Saccharin: An update,* May 4–6, 1983, Duke University Medical Center.

Gehring, P.J. and G.E. Blau. 1977. Mechanisms of carcinogenesis: Dose response. *Envir. Path. Toxicol.* **1:** 163.

Gehring, P.J., P.G. Watanabe, and C.N. Park. 1978. Resolution of dose-response toxicity data for chemicals requiring metabolic activation: Example—vinyl chloride. *Toxicol. Appl. Pharmacol.* **44:** 581.

Hoel, D.G., N.L. Kaplan, and M.W. Anderson. 1983. Implication of nonlinear kinetics on risk estimation in carcinogenesis. *Science* **219:** 1032.

OTA: Office of Technology Assessment 1981. *Assessment of technologies for determining cancer risks from the environment,* p. 169. U.S. Government Printing Office, Washington, D.C.

Krewski, D. and J. Van Ryzin. 1981. Dose response models for quantal response toxicity data. In *Statistic and related topics* (ed. M. Csorgo et al.), p. 201. North Holland Publishing, Amsterdam, The Netherlands.

Maltoni, C. and G. Lefemine. 1975. Carcinogenicity assays of vinyl chloride: Current results. *Ann. N.Y. Acad. Sci.* **246:** 194.

Rai, K. and J. Van Ryzin. 1979. Risk assessment of toxic environmental substances using a generalized multihit dose response model. In *Energy and health* (ed. N.E. Breslow and A.S. Whittemore), p. 99. Society for Industrial and Applied Mathematics, Philadelphia.

Van Ryzin, J. 1980. Quantitative risk assessment. *J. Occup. Med.* **22:** 322.

Van Ryzin, J. and K. Rai. 1980. The use of quantal response data to make predictions. In *Scientific basis of toxicity assessment* (ed. H.R. Witschi), p. 273. Elsevier/North Holland Biomedical Press, New York.

Van Ryzin, J. and K. Rai. 1984. A dose-response model incorporating Michaelis-Menten kinetics. *American Statistical Association Proceedings of the Biopharmaceutical Section,* p. 59. American Statistical Association, Washington, D.C.

## COMMENTS

**WEINSTEIN:** How did you calculate effective dose?

**VAN RYZIN:** I fit the whole model to the observed data. Remember I said that as a result of the mathematical argument, which I presented, that the internal dose has to be a certain function—namely, this ad/(1 + bd)—and that introduces the parameters a and b. I estimate those parameters from the data. I fit the whole model and that, in a sense gives me estimates of constants a and b.

**WEINSTEIN:** Starting with the assumption of one-hit?

**VAN RYZIN:** No, starting with the full model, which allows for more than one-hit. In Table 3, the second model was forcing it to be a one-hit in the transformed dose or in the internal dose. In the last two models of Table 3, I didn't allow any kinetics to take place at all. I didn't allow any transformed dose. What is administered is what's there at the target site.

**PETO:** Why are the plots of your numbers almost equal? $2.1 \times 10^{-3}$ and $7.6 \times 10^{-2}$ are almost the same for those risks.

**VAN RYZIN:** The full model allows a little bit of nonlinearity in the dose-response curve. Let me point out that if you do a statistical test and ask, "Can you rule out a one-hit model in the transformed dose?", the answer is no. In other words, you cannot rule out the one-hit model in transformed dose over the full model.

**PIKE:** The experiments on metabolism show that the levels didn't flatten at all, that in fact you had resaturation.

**VAN RYZIN:** Yes. That's what Gehring, Watanabe, and Park showed in their 1978 paper.

**WEINSTEIN:** But that doesn't necessarily tell you about metabolic activation at low doses, does it, which is the region of interest?

**VAN RYZIN:** I think it does. They administered radioactive vinyl chloride to the animals at various concentrations and then they collected the excretia from these animals, looked at how much was metabolized, and plotted that. So they could construct that curve, instead of estimating it.

**WEINSTEIN:** But that doesn't tell you how much of the carcinogen is actually bound to critical targets like DNA or removed from the DNA by repair.

**VAN RYZIN:** You can do two different things. You can take their correction factors and apply them to the Maltoni data and you get one answer; you can forget about the correction factor and apply this model. There is only a slight difference; both give basically the same answer.

**PURCHASE:** Do you know whether you get the same answer if you use a slightly different risk: $10^{-4}$ instead of $10^{-6}$?

**VAN RYZIN:** Yes, you do.

**PURCHASE:** So, in other words, it's not that the two endpoints are parallel?

**VAN RYZIN:** No, not at that point. They agree at $10^{-5}$ and $10^{-4}$. It's only a one-hit model; they have to agree. It's one-hit in the transformed dose.

**PIKE:** Then there's no effect of toxicity on the animals; that is, they are not dying at higher rates from other causes?

**VAN RYZIN:** No.

**WEINSTEIN:** Are you assuming that the rate constants of activation of the compound for DNA binding and for DNA excision, and also for conversion to inactive derivatives, are constant across this wide range of dose?

**VAN RYZIN:** No, they could be different at each dose.

**WEINSTEIN:** But DNA repair is an enzymatic reaction and the formation of the active metabolite is an enzymatic reaction; so these reactions are probably a function of substrate and cofactor concentrations. These enzymes may also be species and tissue-specific and inducible at certain levels of substrates or become saturated at other levels. One cannot predict, therefore, a linear response over an arbitrary range without measuring some of these specific parameters.

**J. WILSON:** If you can describe them by the kinetic equation, the coefficients are always the same.

**VAN RYZIN:** I have assumed the same constants at each dose level when in steady state.

**WEINSTEIN:** As a biochemist, I can't assume that.

**GILLETTE:** There are some things about your model that I think should be brought out. Going back to your very simple model, you said you were assuming a steady-state and have assumed no output from the first pool. Is that correct?

**VAN RYZIN:** No.

**GILLETTE:** I'd like to point out that under steady-state conditions, the amount of the compound which is converted to the chemically reactive metabolite that reacts with the DNA is dependent solely on the dose. There's nothing in that model which says that you're changing the fraction of the dose that's converted to the reactive metabolite. As long as you don't have a side pathway, the fraction is independent of whether you approach saturation of the enzyme system. If you had an inactivation reaction going out of the first pool in your model, which was catalyzed by an enzyme system, and if the $k_m$ values for the activation system and the $k_m$ of the inactivation system of the precursor were exactly the same, then, again, the fraction of the dose that ultimately was converted to the chemically reactive metabolite would be independent of whether you approach saturation of the enzymes.

**VAN RYZIN:** The b in my model is the difference between the Michaelis-Menten constant going in and the Michaelis-Menten constant coming out.

**GILLETTE:** I'm not talking about $k_2$ at all. I'm just talking about the side reactions from your first pool. As long as you don't have another way of getting rid of that compound, saturation kinetics are irrelevant. If you have a side pathway, but the $k_m$'s are exactly the same, saturation kinetics again are irrelevant. You have to assume, in order for your model to be correct—and I agree that it is correct —that there is a first order elimination from your central pool which is independent of the dose. Moreover, the side pathway must be the major route of elimination of the parent compound.

**VAN RYZIN:** In the model, there were these two side reactions that were for elimination. I did assume one of those was first order.

**GILLETTE:** Yes, but that has to be a major one. The way Hoel et al. wrote it in their 1983 *Science* paper was very confusing. They don't make these distinctions. I would suggest a much simpler way of looking at it. You should always think of it in terms of the fraction of the dose that ultimately becomes covalently bound to the DNA. Anything that modifies that fraction, or does not modify that fraction, will have an effect or will not have an effect, as the case may be. It's a much simpler way of looking at it, and it takes care of whether approaches to saturation kinetics will affect the amount that ultimately becomes covalently bound to DNA.

**REITZ:** One difference between the way you have presented this material and the way Gehring and Blau presented it is that you have assumed steady-state conditions whereas Gehring and Blau did not.

**GILLETTE:** It really doesn't make too much difference. The calculations come out exactly the same way. What you need to calculate are the areas under the curve of the reactive metabolite. These depend on integrated Michaelis-Menten equations. The equation can be complex when you get two saturable pathways. It is not as simple as the implication here. Indeed, there is no way of predicting a priori whether or not approaches to saturation of enzymes are going to increase or decrease the toxicity because this will depend on which enzyme systems approach saturation first as the dose is increased. If the enzyme that catalyzes the inactivation pathway becomes saturated first, you're going to increase the toxicity.

**REITZ:** I agree with you.

**ALBERT:** Aren't you overlooking an important factor—cell proliferation? What you're assuming is that the target dose is simply the level of DNA adducts. Isn't the effective dose the level of adducts at the time the cells divide? If, in fact, increasing the dose through toxicity increases the rate of cell proliferation, the level of adducts at the time of cell proliferation becomes disproportionately increased.

**VAN RYZIN:** Yes, but if that were first order it would not make any difference.

**WEINSTEIN:** But carcinogen modification of DNA and excision repair are often enzymatic reactions.

**VAN RYZIN:** That could be second order. I do allow for a second order elimination process.

**WEINSTEIN:** But it won't be constant, given all the other variables. Let's assume, as a matter of fact we know, that if you hold cells so they can't divide, then they can repair their DNA and they're in less jeopardy; if you force them to divide, there's big jeopardy. So whether the compound both stimulated proliferation and formed adducts, it's more potent than if the compound formed DNA adducts but was also toxic to cells and they didn't divide for a while. One would compensate for the other. It's hard to believe that all of these things don't change as you go across a wide range of dose.

**SWENBERG:** Yes. But I think in the case of vinyl chloride, at the lower doses, it's not very cytotoxic; so you probably don't have big changes in cell replication.

**WEINSTEIN:** As a matter of fact, in the animal model, vinyl chloride induces proliferation of endothelial cells in the liver.

**SWENBERG:** At low doses?

**WEINSTEIN:** Yes, and also in vinyl chloride exposed workers.

**PIKE:** This argument reminds me of the not very fruitful discussions of the merits of the many explanations that have been put forward over the last 30 years of the straight line relationship you obtain for many epithelial tumors when you plot log incidence against log age. What Dr. Van Ryzin has demonstrated is that saturation-type phenomena can be accommodated in an elegant way into his basic model with the addition of only two parameters. This is really all he has proved, neither more nor less.

**VAN RYZIN:** What I'm trying to point out is that the simpler models, which don't allow for any kinetics at all—Weibull, multistage, one-hit—on which people have been relying quite heavily, give you less believable answers than if you even put in what I call simple possible mechanisms for metabolic activation or nonlinear repair. I think that's why, if one sees these sorts of nonlinearities, that's exactly why one should do side experiments to try to find out the reason. Maybe I should finish the other nonlinearity, which is the saccharin data. The saccharin data goes the opposite way.

**SWENBERG:** I'm intrigued. Your model can predict the biologically effective dose. Is that the bottom line?

**VAN RYZIN:** I wouldn't go that far. I would say it could possibly give an indication of whether it's metabolic activation or not. If you look at the constants, it could give some indication of possible types of mechanisms. It could estimate something, but that something depends on the fact that you've assumed it is one-hit in the biologically effective dose. If indeed it were, it would be estimating the correct constants. If you're assuming that the constants don't change over the dose level and that they describe the mechanism, then it would be predicting that; but I'm not going to be so presumptuous as to say that that is the whole story.

# Uncertainty in Risk Assessment

**RICHARD WILSON, EDMUND CROUCH, and LAUREN ZEISE**
Department of Physics and Energy and Environmental Policy Center
Harvard University
Cambridge, Massachusetts 02138

## OVERVIEW

In this paper we argue that a discussion of uncertainty is central to any risk assessment. If a statement about the uncertainty is not included with the statement of the risk, the decision maker who uses the risk assessment will have inadequate information at best, and misleading information at worst.

## INTRODUCTION

The very word risk implies uncertainty. We think that a proper understanding of uncertainty is central to the use of risk analysis and its subset risk assessment in improving public health and extending life expectancy particularly when the uncertainty in risk is as large as the best estimates of the risk. In many cases such risks are ignored, for example, where something has not been proven a hazard even though it might be a large hazard. If we only attempt to reduce those risks with well-defined magnitude (small uncertainty) we will miss most of the opportunities.

When sanitary engineers insisted on main drainage a century ago, they did so upon general principles, not upon the basis of reliable data showing that failure to remove raw sewage or provide pure water caused bad health; the rule was to provide the best drainage and purest water reasonably possible. There is now no question that this action was correct by almost any standard—even though the benefits at the time must have seemed very uncertain. If today's techniques of risk assessment (e.g., by the Environmental Protection Agency (EPA) for regulation of carcinogens) were used, such improvements might not have happened.

Many of the advances in our civilization have taken place by going ahead in the face of very uncertain risks. Railroad travel and, more recently, road travel have dangers which, although they are now well defined, were initially both uncertain and large (at the opening of the first purely passenger railroad between Liverpool and Manchester, a Member of Parliament was run down and killed). Nevertheless the technologies were allowed to proceed and are now safer (per mile) than those they replaced (horse and canoe).

A decision made without taking uncertainty into account is barely worth calling a decision. The usual way of taking account of uncertainty has been to use "horse sense," but in this paper we want to discuss how decisions can be made more logically. I may say that I have a risk of dying of cancer, meaning that it is uncertain whether or not I will develop cancer and die. If I should develop cancer, the risk

**133**

would at once be changed. It is still not a certainty that I would die of cancer, since (some) cancers can be cured and there is the chance of spontaneous remission. But once all attempts at cure have failed, the risk of death becomes a certainty.

The uncertainties we have just mentioned vary at different points in the tale. Indeed uncertainty has different qualitative meanings at different points. We have discussed various ideas about uncertainty in our book (Crouch and Wilson 1982) on risk-benefit analysis and have found it worthwhile to distinguish several different types of uncertainty. Such ideas arise naturally as soon as you attempt to perform careful calculations of risks or to think about what to do about risks.

Most of the discussion in this paper will concentrate on cancer risks, but we will use other risks in society as well wherever it is appropriate for illustration or illumination of the ideas and distinctions. Most of what is said can be applied to other risks, although it sometimes requires careful thought to realize how general the ideas are.

## DISCUSSION

The first type of uncertainty to consider is the stochastic uncertainty of certain processes—here the cancer process. Some persons exposed to a large dose of carcinogens, for example, lifetime cigarette smoking, will develop lung cancer; others will not. Whether any particular smoker will develop cancer appears to be largely random; there is a stochastic component of uncertainty. Similarly some persons crossing a crowded road blindfolded will be run down and killed, whereas others will not.

It is easy to see that it does not matter in this example whether the onset of cancer is actually a stochastic process or not. (The Oxford English Dictionary traces "stochastic" from the Greek "to aim at a mark, guess"; the decay of a radioactive atom is stochastic.) The details of why a cancer occurs in a particular individual at a particular time is unknown and, with our present and foreseeable knowledge, unknowable in the same sense that in aiming at a mark, we can specify a general distribution of hits but not whether a particular point may be hit. Thus arguments about whether the cancer is "really" started by a hit on an individual molecule are irrelevant at this level.

We can list other examples of stochastic uncertainties. A typical risk assessment may estimate the probability that a person will be killed. For automobile accidents this may be done on the basis of historical experience; of the U.S. population of 225 million persons, approximately 50,000 die in auto accidents each year, giving a (population) average risk of 220 per million per year. This estimate is fairly precise—it varies about 10% from year to year—so the probability of any one individual (randomly chosen from the population) being killed is also precise; but the individual cannot calculate his own time of death or whether he will in fact die from this cause. This uncertainty is inherent in the word "risk," and so we use this word as discussed, for example, in Chapter 3 of Crouch and Wilson (1982). The

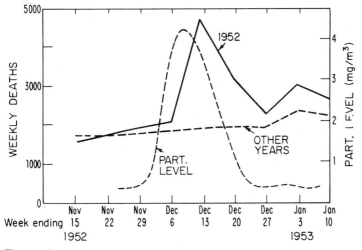

**Figure 1**
Deaths in greater London associated with the air pollution episode of December 5–8, 1952. (Adapted from Goldsmith and Friberg 1977.)

uncertainty here is stochastic— provided the way we have analyzed the historical data is correct.

We will return to this point, but will now take up another thread. For automobile accidents we can count the dead bodies. We are certain that the events described are taking place. But this is not always true for risks we wish to analyze. For example, we know that there was a large risk of premature death or aggravated disease due to air pollution at the high levels of 30 years ago. This can be seen, for example, in Figure 1 (Goldstein and Friberg 1977) where the death rate during the London air pollution of 1952 is compared with that during other years. (See Chapter 5 of Wilson et al. 1980 for greater detail.) At today's levels of air pollution, we do not know that there is any effect. There is no good direct evidence on this problem, and although some of the direct evidence suggests that there is a small risk, this estimate is often based on unreliable data, or on such small populations that no statistically significant effect is seen. In such circumstances, one approach is to see what can be said on the basis of indirect evidence, such as animal data and general biological and chemical principles. The existence of a small effect cannot be disproved. Unfortunately, the largest size of effect that cannot be disproved is large enough that it does have significance for public policies; and the disagreement which exists among scientists over these indirect data implies that there is some chance that disease is caused by, or aggravated by, air pollution at current levels.

Thus we must ask: Does air pollution cause problems at present levels? Similarly we have to ask: Is there a threshold for the effect of this carcinogen? How much radioactive iodine could be released in a serious nuclear accident? Then we should, in principle, incorporate the uncertain answers into any risk estimates.

There are other types of uncertainties which are relevant when using risk assessments (whether for risk management, risk reduction, or other parts of risk analysis). Public perceptions of risk are extremely uncertain as has been extensively explored by Slovic and collaborators (Fischoff et al. 1981) and by Tversky and Hahneman (1981). In addition there are uncertainties of value as discussed by Lowrance (1976), Tversky and Hahneman (1974; 1981), and Chapter 5 of Crouch and Wilson (1982). Most people will accept larger risks voluntarily than they would allow others to impose upon them. Other values are less easy to identify; for instance, it appears that some segments of society place different values on risks of accidents due to natural phenomena compared with accident risks that can be identified with a technological society. A similar dichotomy is often seen betwen values placed on risks from natural chemicals compared with risks from man-made chemicals (sometimes when the two are identical materials!).

With this short and incomplete introduction to some uncertainties, we want to go on and concentrate on how such uncertainties can be calculated, how they might be expressed, and the necessity of their being clearly included in any output from a risk assessment—especially when decisions have to be made on the basis of the assessment.

To illustrate that this is not a trivial exercise, we start at the end and discuss what happens when the uncertainties (particularly the uncertainties of fact) are not all presented to the decisionmaker. Let us ask the question: Is the risk of using a new, untested technology (or chemical) zero (because it has not been shown to be dangerous), or unity (the maximum possible—we only die once—because it has not yet been shown to be safe). This is the dramatic stereotype of the question which has to be answered daily; and we can conjure up stereotypical replies from the industrial manufacturer who says, "Zero," and from the environmental activist who says, "Unity." From previous papers in this volume, we must also include judges of the Fifth Circuit Court of Appeals among those who say zero. The job of the risk analyst is to choose a number somewhere in between, based on all the information available, and to assign an uncertainty to that number. All too often the risk analyst will calculate this number for a case where it turns out to be small, but ignore completely the case where there is great uncertainty but quite possibly greater risk. For example, the Carcinogen Assessment Group (CAG) of the EPA calculates risks only for those chemicals for which a statistically significant effect has been observed in an animal bioassay. This in itself is not bad, provided that limitations are well understood by the users of such risk assessments. But all too often the users neglect all the other chemicals for which bioassays have not been performed or for which the bioassays did not turn up statistically significant effects, even when other information suggests that risks from them may be large enough to be important.

Of course we do not claim that all EPA decisions are wrong. Although no risk analyses are made for chemicals for which there is no bioassay (or for those for which the bioassay produces a statistically insignificant number of tumors), any chemicals which are obviously dangerous are often looked at in other ways.

In our paper on the risks of drinking water (Crouch et al. 1983), we have shown that a more complete procedure may lead one to conclusions different from those of the EPA.

Our procedure is to discuss a risk distribution. The risk (R) at low doses can be written as the product of four factors: the carcinogenic potency ($\beta$) in animals, an interspecies conversion factor $K_{ah}$, the dose or exposure D, and an extrapolation factor E:

$$R = \beta \, KDE$$

The fourth factor is set equal to 1 if proportionality is assumed, and to zero if a threshold is assumed. We assign each of these four a probability distribution derived hopefully from experiments, but if not from theory, and by the usual mathematical folding, get a risk distribution. When we calculate further, we write down more than one risk parameter: the upper 98th percentile of a risk distribution, its mean, and its median. The upper 98th percentile agrees fairly well with the reasonably conservative upper limit that is quoted by the EPA, for those materials which the EPA considers. However, we have added risk calculations for materials such as 1,1,1-trichloroethane, which have been ignored in risk calculations by the EPA (because the bioassays performed on this material have not produced statistically significant results). Including such materials can double the estimated measure of risk—not a big increase.

A more serious difference between us and the EPA comes in the treatment of other halogenated alkanes. In treating all these simultaneously by a regulation specifying the same concentration limit, the EPA implicitly assumes that they are equally carcinogenic. Bromoform, in particular, is assumed to be as carcinogenic as chloroform. In practice, there is reasonably good bioassay data on the latter, but nothing useful on the former.

We examined chemical analogs (Fiering and Wilson 1983), and conclude that bromoform is likely to be considerably more carcinogenic than chloroform. When this larger carcinogenic potency, together with our much larger uncertainty about it, is incorporated into a risk assessment, the estimates of risk (especially the 98th percentiles) are much larger than those of the EPA for those water supplies (chiefly obtained from deep wells) that contain appreciable quantities of bromoform. This procedure, unlike that of the EPA, therefore leads immediately to identification of those water supplies which require further attention and possibly action. The obvious course of action is to immediately start acquiring information about the carcinogenicity of bromoform by performing short-term tests and initiating long-term bioassays, while simultaneously monitoring the water supplies and cleaning up or restricting those supplies which are heavily contaminated. Such a course of action should lead to an orderly reduction of risk, rather than the hiatus that is likely should bromoform turn out to be another case like ethylene dibromide.

A good example of the hiatus that occurred when uncertainty was ignored is the case of saccharin. Establishing that the cancer risk from food additives is low is not easy. The materials must be fed to animals at the highest possible dose—

sometimes as high as 10% of the diet. In the group of dosed animals, an incidence of cancer of 5–10% can just be observed provided the background rate is low. But a food additive may be present in the diet at a level of one in 100,000. So the most sensitive test may just, but only just, be able to detect risks in foodstuffs as low as one in 100,000 per lifetime.

Saccharin has been used for a century without obviously large numbers of cancers occurring. The crudest of all risk analyses therefore tells us at once that the risk cannot be as large as that from cigarettes or alcohol. By 1970 some early bioassays suggested an effect, and prestigious committees of the National Academy of Sciences recommended caution in its general use. But saccharin remained a noncarcinogen until the Federal Register of April 15, 1977, announced the results of more sensitive animal tests. Then a noncarcinogen became a carcinogen overnight, leading to a hiatus in regulation, for carcinogens merit special attention from the law. Yet the name, taste, and use of saccharin remained the same.

A more precise use of words (and a more precise use of risk analysis) would we suggest, have avoided many of the problems. Saccharin should have been called a carcinogen, but one with low potency—less than 0.01 kg·day/mg. But there would have been substantial uncertainty in this statement, uncertainty which should have been incorporated into risk analyses. This uncertainty could have been used in all public policy statements until 1977 when the more precise value for the potency of 0.0003 kg·day/mg (Crouch and Wilson 1979) could be calculated from the more sensitive experiments.

A more serious example of the hiatuses occurring in public policies occurred with formaldehyde. As early as 1975 it was thought by some, on general chemical structural grounds, that formaldehyde must be a carcinogen (S. Lamm, pers. comm.). By 1980, we had noticed that there is a correlation between carcinogenic potency and acute toxicity (Zeise et al. 1984a). The toxicity measurements ($LD_{50}$) available in 1970 were adequate to provide a very rough estimate of carcinogenic potency (0.06 kg·day/mg), which turns out to be within a factor of 2 (0.11 kg·day/mg) of that calculation from the recent experimental results of Albert et al. (1982) (Table 1)—although it is a case of luck to get quite so close.

The risk from exposure to formaldehyde is shown in Table 2. This table also shows how the risk parameters $R_{50}$ and $R_{98}$ change as the new information from

**Table 1**
Carcinogenic Potency of Formaldehyde in the Rat

|  | $\beta(\log_e \beta \pm se)$ in kg-day/mg |
|---|---|
| $LD_{50}$ Extrapolation |  |
|   F344 Rat | 0.054($-2.92 \pm 1.73$) |
|   OM Rat | 0.061($-2.79 \pm 1.29$) |
| NYU Bioassay[a] |  |
|   Sprague Dawley Rat | 0.110($-2.21 \pm 1.84$) |

[a] Albert et al. (1982)

**Table 2**
Yearly Risk of Cancer from Formaldehyde for 24 Hour Exposure

| Average Exposure | Extrapolated from $LD_{50}$-$\beta$ Relation (OM) | | Extrapolated from NYU Bioassay | |
|---|---|---|---|---|
| | $R_{50}$ | $R_{98}$ | $R_{50}$ | $R_{98}$ |
| 1 ppm | $3.7 \times 10^{-4}$ | $1.9 \times 10^{-2}$ | $7 \times 10^{-4}$ | $1.4 \times 10^{-2}$ |
| 1 ppb | $3.7 \times 10^{-7}$ | $1.9 \times 10^{-5}$ | $7 \times 10^{-7}$ | $1.4 \times 10^{-5}$ |

Albert at al. (1982) is added to information from $LD_{50}$. In this case the average value of the risk rises as we go from $LD_{50}$ to the bioassay. But since the risk is determined, the 98th percentile has fallen.

The available prior indicators of possible trouble were ignored when home installation of urea formaldehyde foam was suggested by various state officials as an aid to reducing energy consumption. The release of formaldehyde from this foam, coupled with the reduced air exchange rates now being achieved in well-insulated houses, has resulted in high levels of formaldehyde in some homes—high enough that noncancerous chronic effects are apparent in some cases. The cancer risk in such cases (assuming lifetime occupancy) is quite high. Indeed, this is one case where the choice of low-dose extrapolation of animal results makes scarcely any difference to estimated risks, for in some homes formaldehyde concentrations approach those used in the animal tests. The only people to profit from this experience will be the lawyers as angry homeowners sue the people who encouraged them to save energy.

These examples suggest that there is practical importance (as well as the academic satisfaction of logical completeness) in attempting to include the uncertainties of fact into risk estimates. We have been working on procedures which do this for some time. Our hope is to suggest methods which are simple enough to be used, while accurate enough to be useful. Our procedure for estimating carcinogenic risk when an animal bioassay has been performed has been described in some detail in a series of papers (Crouch and Wilson 1979, 1981; Crouch 1982, 1983; Fiering and Wilson 1983; Crouch et al. 1983; Zeise et al. 1984a). This procedure incorporates the factual uncertainties of animal to human risk extrapolation, but skirts those of low-dose extrapolation. The principal feature of the method is to discuss the probability distribution of a risk coefficient (the ratio of risk to exposure).

At this point we would like to introduce a distinction, which we freely admit is somewhat arbitrary, between objective and subjective risk estimates. The measure of uncertainty in animal to human extrapolations that we derive is based on animal cancer experiments. However, whether such an extrapolation is justified depends on knowledge of biological and chemical mechanisms, and as such is (at present) very subjective. Our risk assessment (as must all risk assessments) leave such subjective questions unanswered as part of their output, for they may sharply influence or be influenced by the uncertainty in values of those using the risk

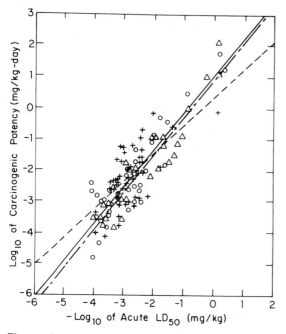

**Figure 2**

Comparison of carcinogenic potency and acute toxicity.

assessments. Alternatively stated, we would like others to consider seriously our procedure for discussing uncertainties, whether or not they agree with the values either for risk or for uncertainty that we select.

A bioassay that produces a result which is not statistically significant, or one in which our best estimate of carcinogenic potency is zero, poses a problem. The EPA addresses this problem by simply ignoring such results, or considering them positive evidence of lack of carcinogenicity. We would argue that one should calculate an upper bound on the risk from such bioassay results, and follow through the risk assessments all the way to the stage where they are to be used in a decision process. If this had been done for saccharin and formaldehyde, their use might have been restricted substantially sooner.

Long-term bioassays have been performed for only a thousand or so of the estimated 60,000 chemicals used in commerce, let alone the 6 million or so recorded by the Chemical Abstracts Service. What is to be done about all the others? We have begun to work on these by discussing the prior estimates based on a number of indicators. We have already mentioned the correlation between carcinogenicity and toxicity displayed in Figure 2. We have been sharply attacked whenever we have pointed out this correlation, but anybody who attempts a little numerical work will find that it obviously has some validity. Aflatoxin $B_1$ is a potent carcinogen and is also fairly toxic. Saccharin is a carcinogen of very low potency and also has very low toxicity. There seem to exist very few or no chemicals (among those tested) which have the toxicity of saccharin but the carcinogenic potency of aflatoxin.

Given such a correlation, it is necessary to ask whether it is useful. Among the chemicals tested in the NCI/NTP program, the correlation can be described by the statement that if an acute $LD_{50}$ is measured, then the probability distribution for carcinogenic potency (should the material be measurably carcinogenic) is roughly log normal with a standard deviation of a factor of 10 about an estimate based on the $LD_{50}$. Such an estimate is fairly uncertain, but since the range of possible potencies is very large (at least a factor of ten million, from saccharin to dioxin) even an estimate with such a large uncertainty can be useful. Many unanswered questions remain concerning this relationship. Is there a biological origin for it? Is it an artifact of the testing process, for example, because some of the observed tumors may be caused by the toxic effects of high doses? Is it a statistical artifact? It has been suggested that this relationship between toxicity and carcinogenicity and the interspecies relationship of potency form a tautology (Bernstein et al. 1984). For a number of reasons too detailed to go into here, we think that neither correlation is tautologous; nor are they statistical artifacts (E.A. Crouch, R. Wilson, and L. Zeise, in prep.). There probably is some biological significance to the correlation although part of the correlation may be an artifact of high-dose testing.

Evidently there are other possible prior indicators that might be used in risk assessments, not least the various short-term tests for mutagenesis (Ames test) and cell transformation assays. Unfortunately, few of these have as yet produced results which quantitatively correlate with the results of animal bioassays, although there is yet hope. Obviously, we should like to continue working on such questions.

We now turn to how "complete" risk assessments can be used to give more useful information to decisionmakers—whether they be ourselves as individuals or those of us entrusted to manage risk in society at large. There are some obvious consequences of the incorporation of different forms of uncertainty into decisions about risks since each decisionmaker might wish to deal with these various types of uncertainty in different ways. An individual must put up with both the stochastic uncertainty and the uncertainties of the type just discussed. Yet to him the distinction may not matter. He clearly does not wish to die and is concerned that the risk of death be kept small, but the particular way of doing this may be of no concern. This is just one example of another type of uncertainty: what measure of risk, or what parameter of a risk distribution, is important in the particular decisionmaking process. In the example given, an individual might be concerned with an average risk. Others may be concerned with the risk to the "most exposed" individual or with some sum of risks to individual members of society (what we have occasionally called the total societal impact). For society as a whole, the stochastic uncertainty may average out (although it is important to note that this is not necessarily true, it depends among other things on the risk measure being used). An individual motorist does not know whether he will get into an accident, but the total number of automobile accidents can be predicted to within about 10%. Similarly, although we do not know well the exposures of individuals to saccharin, we do know the sum of all human exposures since this is relatively easily obtained from the total amount of saccharin produced. Thus, the principal uncertainties for societal decisionmakers may well be factual uncertainties. Risk assessors who fail to provide sufficient information about these various kinds of uncertainties may not be providing enough information for a sensible decision.

It is important to note that any generally useful decision process must be moderately simple and fairly automatic. It is a common misconception that all decisions about chemical risks are made by the EPA, or occasionally by the FDA. In fact, all of us make such decisions about risks every day, whether as individuals or representatives of society. The aim of such decisions is, we hope, generally to reduce risk and improve life expectancy. Such an aim is much more easily improved if there are incentives for doing it built into the decisionmaking processes. For example, some years ago, Schneiderman and Mantel (1977) pointed out that such procedures as the Delaney Clause introduces counterincentives to reducing risk when it is used as a procedure for coping with chemical carcinogens. The counterincentives arose from the requirement for a rigid distinction between carcinogens and noncarcinogens, whereas in practice there is considerable uncertainty about such a distinction. In a similar context, we have taken this into account by suggesting that a particular risk measure be used for policy decisions on carcinogens. This risk measure is chosen so that as uncertainty is reduced, the value of the risk measure is decreased, which gives a strong incentive for obtaining better experimental data. In practice, the value of the measure we suggested (an upper 98th percentile of a risk distribution) is similar to the value that the CAG currently uses, although its interpretation is somewhat different.

Some people have not opposed such an approach because applying it strictly implies that there is some risk from any chemical whatever—a risk which, together with its uncertainty, should be estimated. To some exhausted industry executives (exhausted by what they consider oppressive regulation), this sounds like a plan to extend the EPA's list of regulated chemicals from hundreds to include everything in use. However, this is too pessimistic a view. Any such procedure should be thought of as one for ordering the risks of chemicals. The order cannot be expected to be precise, and indeed we expect the ordering to change as more data on particular chemicals become available. We can expect society to start working on reducing the risks at the top of the list. The procedure may be used to generate different orderings based on different risk measures, for example, using means, medians, and percentiles of the risk distributions, each of which might be more relevant for different decisions.

In practice, of course, some of these ideas are already in use. The Toxic Substances Control Act (TOSCA) mandates that all new chemicals be screened and tested. The present procedures for ordering chemicals for testing and for choosing chemicals for bioassay are similar to what we advocate, although we would replace the dichotomous variables. Our testing list would consist of all of the 60,000 chemicals in commercial use, but we recognize that only the top few hundred would

**Table 3**
Cancers in the U.S. in 1 Year

| | $N_{50}$ | $N_{98}$ | Action |
|---|---|---|---|
| Aflatoxin B1 | 5000 | 50,000 | None |
| Saccharin | 500 | 10,000 | Legislatively accepted |
| 2,4-DAA in | | | Now removed by |
|   hair dyes | | | Clairol |
|   if drunk | 6 | 100 | |
|   if put on hair | $1/100^a$ | $1/5^a$ | |
| Vinyl chloride from | $< 1/10$ | $< 1$ | No decision by FDA |
|   plastic bottles | | | |

[a] More recent absorption estimates would put these a factor of 10 lower.

ever be well tested. The creation of a more complete and better ordered list would effectively serve as a procedure for removing the less important from the list.

An example of such a list could be the chemicals being considered by the FDA in 1977 when saccharin was banned. In Table 3 we show the number of cancers calculated in the U.S. from the use of these chemicals, what we call the societal impact.

Something like this list was available to the Commissioner of FDA in 1977. The Environmental Defense Fund was urging him to ban hair dyes and plastic bottles. But how could he do this without proposing to ban saccharin?

**CONCLUSION**

We conclude this paper by highlighting a recent glaring failure to take account, in the regulatory process, of uncertainties in risk assessments. This is the regulation of ethylene dibromide (EDB) under the Insecticide, Fungicide, and Rodenticide Act (FIFRA). This act differs from TOSCA and other acts in EPA's arsenal in that it demands a risk-benefit analysis. It is therefore one of the acts beloved by the risk analysts.

In this case, one of the most important comparisons of a risk-benefit analysis (i.e., a risk/risk comparison) was omitted. EDB was used to prevent the deterioration of grain and citrus fruits, and part of its action was as a fungicide. Some of the fungi produce mycotoxins; some of which are known to be potent carcinogens (e.g., aflatoxin), while others have not been tested. A relevant question is thus: Is the risk greater from using EDB than it is from not using it? This question has not been discussed in the position document of the EPA. It could turn out that using EDB results in lower risk than not using any fungicide, but it also may be possible to lower the risk further by substituting a "better" fungicide than EDB. It remains a matter of importance to give incentives for finding a better alternative. The position document does not discuss the risks of alternative fungicides, presumably because there are few measurements. According to the current EPA practice, it seems that lack of data leads to an assignment of zero risk.

A brief survey of the literature finds no bioassay data on one alternative—phosphene. Recent measurements (Danse et al. 1984) on another, methyl bromide, suggest that it is at least as carcinogenic as EDB. A mixture of carbon tetrachloride and carbon disulphide has been proposed. Carbon tetrachloride is certainly a carcinogen (albeit a much weaker one than EDB) (Crouch and Wilson 1979), and there is no good data on carbon disulphide.

Since 1977, when it was clear that EDB might have to be regulated, there has been time for detailed animal testing on alternatives. It is disappointing that such tests have not been performed. This testing might have been done had not the regulators preferred a chemical of uncertain, unmeasured risk to one of more certain, measured risk. A proper approach to uncertainty would have given this stimulus.

As we have shown above, we feel that a proper treatment of uncertainty is a logical requirement for any systematic treatment of carcinogenesis.

## REFERENCES

Albert, R., A.R. Sellakumar, S. Laskin, M. Kuschner, N. Nelson, and C.A. Snyder. 1982. Gaseous formaldehyde and hydrogen chloride induction of nasal cancer in the rat. *J. Natl. Cancer Inst.* **68(4):** 597.

Bernstein, L., L.S. Gold, B.N. Ames, M.C. Pike, and D.G. Hoel. 1984. Some tautologous aspects of the comparison of carcinogenic potency in rats and mice. *Fund. Appl. Toxicol.* (in press).

Crouch, E.A.C. 1982. Carcinogenic risk assessment: The consequences of believing models. In *Organ and species specificity in chemical carcinogenesis.* Plenum Press, New York and London.

———. 1983. Uncertainties in interspecies extrapolation of carcinogenic potency. *Environ. Health Perspect.* **50:** 327.

Crouch, E.A.C. and R. Wilson. 1979. Interspecies comparison of carcinogenic potency. *J. Toxicol. Environ. Health* **5:** 1095.

———. 1981. The regulation of carcinogens. *Risk Anal.* **1:** 47.

———. 1982. *Risk/benefit analysis.* Ballinger Publishing, Cambridge, Massachusetts.

Crouch, E., R. Wilson, and L. Zeise. 1983. Risks of drinking water. *Water Resour. Res.* **19:** 1359.

Danse, L.H.J.C., F.L. Van Velsen, and C.A. Vanderheijden. 1984. Methylbromide: Carcinogenic effects in the rat forestomach. *Toxicol. Appl. Pharmacol.* **72:** 262.

Fiering, M. and R. Wilson. 1983. Attempts to establish a risk by analogy. *Risk Anal.* **3:** 207.

Fischoff, B., S. Lichtenstein, P. Slovic, S. Derby, and R. Keeney. 1981. *Acceptable risk.* Cambridge University Press, Cambridge, London, and New York.

Goldstein, J.R. and L.T. Friberg. 1977. Effects on human health. In *Air pollution* (ed. A. Stern). Academic Press, New York.

Lowrance, W. 1976. *Of acceptable risk, science and the determination of safety.* W. Kaufman, Los Altos, California.

Schneiderman, M.A. and N. Mantel. 1973. The Delaney Clause and a scheme for rewarding good experiments. *Prev. Med.* **2:** 165.

Tversky, A. and D. Hahneman. 1974. Judgment under uncertainty: Heuristics and biases. *Science* **185:** 1124.

_____. 1981. The framing of decisions and the psychology of choice. *Science* **211:** 453.

Wilson, R., S.C. Colome, J.G. Spengler, and D.G. Wilson. 1980. *Health effects of fossil fuel burning.* Ballinger Publishing, Cambridge, Massachusetts.

Zeise, L., E.A.C. Crouch, and R. Wilson. 1984a. Use of acute toxicity to estimate carcinogenic risk. *Risk Anal.* **4:** 187.

## COMMENTS

**GILLETTE:** What is the mechanism of toxicity? Are you stating that if you administer catecholamines or something similar, then the $LD_{50}$ is relevant to the carcinogenicity of the compound?

**R. WILSON:** Are you asking how we get the value of $LD_{50}$?

**GILLETTE:** No. I want to know what caused the animals to die. If they died of liver toxicity, what you say may very well be true. Most of the associations of cancer with carbon tetrachloride, for example, appear to be related to the hepatotoxicity of the compound. In other words, the doses that cause cancer are the same doses that cause the liver damage.

**R. WILSON:** In most cases, the $LD_{50}$ was related to the central nervous system; but in many cases, a subsidiary toxicity has been noted in the same organ as that in which the cancer appears. It seems likely to us that the correlation really applies to the subsidiary toxicity. Moreover, the carcinogens found in the NCI series have been accused of being artifactual carcinogens just because the carcinogenicity may be a consequence of the toxic destruction or weakenings of the organ.

**GILLETTE:** I think it really depends on how we define the word promoter. Are all inducers of cytochrome P-450 and all liver toxicants promoters? It's a very simple question.

**R. WILSON:** It is a very simple question, but it's very difficult to get an answer. We are specifically not answering that question, but instead using the following approach: This is a pattern of data. If we look at that data, is it telling something about cancer? We believe it is giving us a red flag to look a little further. That is all we're saying at the moment. In going over this, by the way, we've gone over all the $LD_{50}$ data. We had to go beyond the computations and go back through the literature. It is a long search because part of the $LD_{50}$ data is very badly recorded.

**PURCHASE:** In view of the answer to the previous question, are you implying that all chemicals are carcinogens, but you can't detect carcinogenicity for some of them?

**R. WILSON:** No. I said I will make an assumption that any chemical may be a carcinogen. I always make that assumption. I don't like distinguishing between a noncarcinogen and a carcinogen. I say define a noncarcinogen as a chemical which has a carcinogenic potency less than some defined measured limit. Operationally, that's all one can ever say. I think it is often convenient to be precise about that operational statement because then that avoids the hiatus that we had with saccharin where the chemical suddenly switched from being a noncarcinogen to a carcinogen. If we had asked about the carcinogenic potency in 1970, we would probably have been able to say that it was less than 0.01 kg·day/mg. Now we probably know that the value is 0.0003 kg·day/mg. Those two statements are consistent. The first statement was used to say it's a noncarcinogen; the second statement is used to say it's a carcinogen. I would say it would have been better to be more precise about the first statement to avoid the problem.

**PURCHASE:**   I understand that; but I think you said earlier that the 40% of chemicals not on your graph but which were being tested were so toxic that it would have been impossible to show a carcinogenic effect.

**R. WILSON:**   We said they could be carcinogens of a low potency and the potency could be consistent with this correlation, but on the low side of the correlation. You cannot prove that they're noncarcinogens from that data; but you can prove that they're not very potent carcinogens.

**WEINSTEIN:**   Yet, they were potent toxicants.

**R. WILSON:**   Those that were potent toxicants could have been moderately potent carcinogens; but if they were potent carcinogens, the carcinogenicity would show up.

**WEINSTEIN:**   Certainly there are many things that kill rats that are not carcinogenic.

**R. WILSON:**   Let's go back to that correlation. If the chemicals are potent toxicants, then you cannot measure low carcinogenic potencies. On the other hand, you're not usually very worried about that in any risk analysis because the toxicity discourages you from having a high exposure. So, whether you call this chemical a noncarcinogen, or just a carcinogen of a potency less than a certain defined amount which would be related to its toxicity, is a matter of taste. I am just expressing my taste that from the point of view of avoiding the hiatus in regulation, it is preferable not to use the word, noncarcinogen, because I think we are now capable of more precision in statement than when we made that dichotomous decision between carcinogen or noncarcinogen.

**ALBERT:**   I think a potentially useful application of the relationship of toxicity to carcinogenic potency is in deciding which of the 60,000-odd chemicals that are used—90% of which haven't been tested at all—need to be tested. Usage patterns can be a surrogate for exposure. If the agents with the greatest surrogate exposure are tested for mutagenicity, the most important potential carcinogens will be identified. Their toxicity can be used as a surrogate for carcinogenic potency. Combining the surrogates for exposure and potency, one gets a measure of the relative impact of the agent in terms of cancer induction. That would then provide the means of identifying those agents which might have the greatest likelihood for producing cancer as a basis for doing the very expensive long-term animal bioassays.

**R. WILSON:** Yes. I think that is rather interesting. We've just been going over that a little bit in the following sense: We've gone back over the 200 chemicals tested by the NCI, looking at the uses and the total amount produced; and we made a rough estimate in its use as to how much would actually get into man. Then we would put a cutoff (e.g., "don't worry, if it can't produce more than ten cancers a year in the whole United States' population"), and we would find that it would not have been necessary to test 60% of them. So that is an interesting result already, that under that guideline you test 40% of them, and the other 60% are sort of "luxuries." Maybe we tested the wrong 200, and we should test another set.

**PREUSS:** But that wasn't the purpose of the NCI test, and that's not a fair conclusion.

**R. WILSON:** Of course. I understand.

**SWENBERG:** How did you determine this, from an $LD_{50}$?

**R. WILSON:** Yes, from the $LD_{50}$.

**SWENBERG:** But that doesn't tell you where you are on the potency curve. That just tells you where you are on the X axis.

**R. WILSON:** It tells us the potency curve, provided I assume a correlation.

**WEINSTEIN:** But, the values range over four orders of magnitude of variation. What is "potent"?

**R. WILSON:** This is carcinogenic potency.

**PREUSS:** You don't have that information.

**R. WILSON:** No, in general, I don't have the information on carcinogenic potency. I only have the information on $LD_{50}$. Based on the NCI data, I then assume I have a sort of distribution. It looks like a log-normal distribution: The number of points are clearly equal, on one side or the other of the line. Fitting a log-normal curve seems quite reasonable for that set of data. We fit it, and we have an error ($\sigma$) that is about a factor of ten. I then just ask that question: If I knew in advance of this correlation on the NCI set of chemicals, but did not actually know the particular carcinogenic potencies, how many of the chemicals would I have gone ahead and tested? I would have had priority testing of 40% of them; but there are probably some others not yet tested onto which I would have put a higher priority than the other 60%.

# Session 4:
# Mutagenic Risk in Human Populations

# Attempts to Estimate Genetic Risks Caused by Mutagens to Later Generations

**MARY F. LYON**
MRC Radiobiology Unit
Harwell, Didcot, Oxon OX11 ORD,
United Kingdom

## OVERVIEW

In order to estimate genetic risks to man from exposure to mutagens, it is necessary to extrapolate from animal data. This involves the problems of possible nonlinearity of dose-response, variation among species, and differing sensitivity of various cell types that so commonly occur with this type of extrapolation. Only extrapolation from mammalian germ-cell data is justified for obtaining an estimate of effects on the mutation rate in human germ-cells. It is then necessary to estimate the effect in terms of cases of genetic disease of a given rise in mutation. To do this, one first finds (from animal data) the relative mutagenic effect (RME) of unit dose of the mutagen, then multiplies RME by dose to give the mutation index or percent increase in mutation. This number, in turn, is multiplied by an estimated number of cases of disease resulting from a 1% increase in mutation. Genetic risks due to cytotoxic drugs are estimated as an example. The method is potentially flexible and useful. Its drawback is that it relies heavily on extrapolation.

## INTRODUCTION

As recent advances in medicine have led to a reduction of disease due to such causes as infection or malnutrition, diseases of genetic cause, such as muscular dystrophy or hemophilia, have become of relatively greater importance, particularly during childhood. Some genetic diseases can be prevented by genetic counseling and antenatal diagnosis. However, a substantial proportion of such disease is due to new or recent mutation, the diseases being maintained in the population by a balance between selection tending to eliminate them and new mutation. In addition, mutation can have an adverse effect on the well-being of the population by producing deleterious changes in quantitatively measurable traits such as body size or athletic or intellectual prowess. It is therefore important to guard against increases in the mutation rate. A wide range of environmental agents are mutagenic, there being a strong correlation between mutagenicity and carcinogenicity. Some of these mutagenic agents, such as radiation or cytotoxic drugs, cannot be banned from the environment because of their other beneficial effects or uses; and it is for these that one needs to attempt to estimate the effects in later generations of their mutagenic action.

As is so often the case when one is estimating risks due to hazardous agents, it is not possible to measure the effects of the agents directly in man. It is necessary to extrapolate from data obtained in experimental systems, with all the uncertainties that this entails. In addition, when the extrapolation has been made and an estimate of the possible effect on the human mutation rate has been obtained, it is necessary to predict from this some idea of the risk in terms of additional cases of genetic disease. This again presents formidable problems.

This question has recently been addressed by Committee 4 of the International Commission for Protection against Environmental Mutagens and Carcinogens (Lyon et al. 1983). The committee considered first the various problems associated with extrapolation from experimental data and then suggested a method, termed the mutation index method, for obtaining an estimate of the possible additional number of cases of genetic disease resulting from a given rise in the mutation rate.

## RESULTS

### Extrapolation from Experimental Data

Three main types of extrapolation are involved: (1) from experimental to environmental dose levels, (2) from one cell type to another, (3) from species to species.

As with other types of hazard, the problem of nonlinearity is a major one in dose-to-dose extrapolation. Such nonlinearity may result from metabolism or detoxication of the agent in the body. The dose that reaches the target molecules in the germ cells may be very different from that entering the body, and the relationship may be nonlinear. Further, when the mutagen has reached the target, there is a process of conversion of a DNA lesion to a mutation. This usually involves enzymic steps, possibly using DNA repair enzymes. Here again nonlinearity may occur. In both cases the possibility of a threshold exists. At low doses a zero amount might reach the target area, and even if the agent reaches the target, a cell might have the capacity to repair all DNA lesions up to a certain threshold amount. However, in the absence of experimental proof of the existence of a threshold, it would be imprudent to assume that one exists (Ehling et al. 1983). Ehrenberg et al. (1983) have argued that at low doses the chemical kinetics of the reactions involved approach linearity. Hence, the most appropriate procedure appears to be linear extrapolation from the nearest reliable experimental dose point.

In species-to-species extrapolations there are the usual problems encountered with carcinogens, i.e., that species differ in their metabolism of chemicals. In addition, they may also differ in repair of DNA and in the characteristics of germ-cell populations in terms of sensitivity to mutagens (Lyon et al. 1983).

Extrapolation from one cell type to another is a particularly difficult problem. It is in many cases much easier to obtain data on mutation in somatic cells, such as blood cells or fibroblasts, or in cultured cells, than in the actual germ-cells which will give rise to later generations. However, the evidence is that mutation rates in somatic cells may provide very little guide to those in germ-cells. Furthermore, there may be marked variation among different germ-cell stages and sexes in sensitivity to mutagens (Lyon 1981). The compound ethylnitrosourea (ENU) produces very high mutation rates in spermatogonial stem cells, but only much weaker effects in later stages of spermatogenesis (Russell 1983). Conversely, triethylenemelamine (TEM) is 300–1000 times more effective in spermatids than in spermatogonia (Lyon 1981). At present the basis for such variation in sensitivity with cell stage is not understood. It is therefore very difficult to make any meaningful extrapolations from experimental data, except those obtained in mammalian germ-cells. Mammalian germ-cell tests tend to be laborious and expensive and consequently the relevant data are frequently lacking.

To overcome this problem, various authors have suggested the use of the so-called parallelogram method (Ehrenberg 1979; Bridges 1980; Sobels 1982; Streisinger 1983). The aim is to find a suitable indicator of genetic damage which can be measured in experimental animals and man. In animals one can find the relation between this indicator and the mutation rate in germ-cells, and assuming the same relation in man, one can then predict the effect in human germ-cells. The difficulty lies in finding a suitable indicator. One possibility suggested is the level of alkylation of DNA, but this still requires verification (Lee 1978, 1979; Sobels 1982). For the present, extrapolation from animal germ-cell data is still necessary to obtain an estimate of the likely mutation rate in human germ-cells resulting from exposure to mutagens.

## Extrapolation from Mutation Rate Increase to Disease Incidence

When an estimate of the mutation rate has been obtained, it is then necessary to attempt to translate this estimate into terms of expected effects on incidence of genetic disease. A possible method for doing this is the mutation index method (Lyon et al. 1983). The basis of it is to prepare a table of cases of genetic disease estimated to result from a 1% increase in the mutation rate, and then to multiply this by the actual percent increase expected on the estimates made from the animal data.

In preparing the table of cases of disease, much reliance is placed on work done in estimating the genetic hazards of radiation (BEIR 1980; Oftedal and Searle 1980; UNSCEAR 1977, 1982; Sankaranarayanan 1982). One first needs an estimate of the incidence in the population of genetic diseases maintained by mutation. These include diseases due to autosomal dominant and recessive and X-linked genes, and also those due to chromosome changes, either in structure or number of chromosomes. In addition, there is a large category, including congenital malformations and childhood neoplasms, of diseases which are of complex or uncertain inheritance. Estimates of incidence of genetic disease vary, partly for geographical reasons and partly because of varying criteria for inclusion. One possible estimate derived mainly from UNSCEAR (1977) is shown in Table 1.

In addition to the incidence of genetic diseases, it is necessary to know the

**Table 1**
Incidence of Genetic Disease Expressed as Cases per Million Live Births and Generations of Persistence

|  | Incidence (bpm) | Average persistence (gens) |
|---|---|---|
| Gene mutations |  |  |
| Autosomal |  |  |
| dominant or X-linked | 10,000 | 5 |
| Recessive | 2500[a] | many |
| Complex or uncertain |  |  |
| Congenital malformations | 24,000[b] |  |
| Constitutional and degenerative diseases | 64,600[c] | 10[d] |
| Childhood malignant neoplasms | 1400[b] |  |
| Chromosomal changes |  |  |
| Structural |  |  |
| Balanced | 1900 | 5[e] |
| Unbalanced | 500 | 3[f] |
| Numerical |  |  |
| Sex chromosomes | 2000 |  |
| Autosomes | 1200 | 1 |

bpm = live births per million; gens = generations
[a] Carter (1977)
[b] Leck (1977)
[c] Arrived at by subtraction of Leck's figures from total of 90,000 used by UNSCEAR and others
[d] BEIR (1980)
[e] Evans (1977)
[f] Unbalanced types themselves have a persistence of 1; however ⅔ of unbalanced cases arise not by mutation but by segregation from balanced types (Evans 1977)
Reprinted, with permission, from Lyon et al. (1983).

number of generations these diseases persist in the population after a new mutation. The persistence depends on the harmfulness of the disease. If affected individuals never survive to have children, then a new mutation obviously always dies out in one generation. If, however, some do have children, then the mutation will persist for some generations before dying out. It is estimated (Table 1) that, on the average, dominant genes persist for five generations, but numerical chromosome anomalies, such as Down's syndrome, virtually always cause early death or sterility and have a persistence of only one generation. For conditions with a persistence of $n$ gen-

## Table 2
## Summary of Cases of Genetic Disease per Million Live Births
Resulting from a 1% Increase in Mutation Rate[a]

| | Gen 1 | Gen 2 | Gen 1 + 2 | Sum of all gens (bpm) |
|---|---|---|---|---|
| Range of values | | | | |
| Gene mutation | | | | |
| Autosomal dominant or X-linked | 20 | 16 | 36 | 100 |
| Complex or uncertain | 25–90 | 22–80 | 47–170 | 250–900 |
| Gene mutation total | 45–110 | 38–100 | 80–200 | 350–1000 |
| Chromosome structural changes | 5 | 4 | 10 | 25 |
| Chromosome numerical changes | 33 | — | 33 | 33 |
| All types of change | 80–150 | 40–100 | 120–240 | 400–1100 |
| Mean value | | | | |
| Gene mutation only | 80 | 70 | 150 | 700 |
| Chromosome | | | | |
| Structural | 5 | 4 | 10 | 25 |
| Numerical | 33 | — | 33 | 33 |
| Gene mutation and structural | 85 | 75 | 160 | 700 |
| All types of change | 120 | 75 | 200 | 750 |

bpm = live births per million; gens = generations
[a]Figures have been rounded in some cases to avoid undue impression of precision.
Reprinted, with permission, from Lyon et al. (1983).

erations, the incidence is obviously the product of $n$ previous generations of mutation, and the effect of an increase in mutation rate in one generation will be spread over $n$ generations, with only $1/n$th of the total effect occurring in the first generation.

For the diseases of irregular inheritance, there is the additional problem that it is not clear to what extent these are maintained by mutation. For instance, some congenital malformations have an environmental cause, others may be mainly genetic. At present the uncertainty of the effect of mutation on this class of diseases is unresolved. Table 2 gives an estimated effect of a 1% increase in the mutation rate, in terms of additional cases of genetic disease in the first and later generations of descendants. The uncertainty concerning diseases of irregular inheritance is expressed by giving a range of values.

The actual estimated percent increase in mutation rate resulting from human exposure to a given agent is obtained by first finding the relative mutagenic effect (RME), which is the proportional increase in mutation rate per unit dose, when compared with the spontaneous rate. This value has to be obtained from animal data and can be calculated separately for gene and chromosome changes and for different germ-cell stages. One next finds the exposure dose (D), and this is multiplied by the RME and any relevant factors for sensitivity (S) to give the mutation index (MI). Thus

$$MI = RME \times D \times S \times 100$$

(The factor of 100 is introduced as unit MI corresponds to a 1% mutation rate rise). The MI is then multiplied by the figures in Table 2 to give the estimated additional number of cases of genetic disease resulting from the exposure under consideration (Lyon et al. 1983). The relative risk (RR) can also be estimated.

## Cytotoxic Drugs as Example of Method

As an example of the use of this method, estimates are given below of the possible genetic effects of treatment with some cytotoxic drugs. (A major reason for choosing this example is that animal data are available.) The number of individuals treated with these drugs who subsequently have children is of course small, but it is increasing due to improved survival after treatment of types of cancer that occur in children or young adults. Thus the question of the genetic effects of these drugs does have a medical relevance.

In Table 3 the RME has been calculated separately for gene and chromosome changes and for treatment of spermatogonia and postmeiotic germ-cells. The latter would contribute to conceptions occurring in the first 3 months after treatment, and the former to all later conceptions. There is great variation among the drugs and in their relative effects in the different germ-cell stages. The mutation indices (Table 4), calculated on the basis of some possible doses received, again show great variation. When the MIs are used to calculate the estimated resulting increased cases of genetic disease (Table 5), it is noticeable how low the relative risks (RR) are in the first generation, particularly for spermatogonial exposure. Even though the total number of cases occurring over all future generations may be around three times the normal incidence per generation, the relative risk in the first generation may be only 1.2–1.3 and therefore difficult to pick up in surveys of offspring of treated patients. For postmeiotic cells, and thus for conceptions occurring within 3 months of treatment, however, the risk is, in some cases, sufficiently high as to justify advising patients against conception.

## DISCUSSION

The method described here provides a possible means of estimating the likely effects of mutagens in later generations and could potentially be used with a variety of environmental agents. The method is sufficiently flexible to deal with problems in complex situations. If the dose-response is nonlinear, and widely different doses are being received in different instances, separate RMEs can be calculated for different dose ranges. The RMEs for different types of genetic change can be

## Table 3
## Relative Mutagenic Effect (RME) of Some Cytotoxic Drugs for Spermatagonia and Postmeiotic Stage of Male Mice

| Drug | Spermatogonia | | | Postmeiotic | | References |
|---|---|---|---|---|---|---|
| | Specific locus | Sperm abs | Trans | Specific locus | Trans | |
| Adriamycin | — | — | 4.11[b] | — | 1.07 | 1 |
| Cyclophosphamide | 0.002 | 0.008 | 0.0 | 0.039 | 0.557 | 2,3,4,5 |
| Mitomycin C | 0.81 | 0.77 | 0.0 | 0.0 | 2.32 | 2,4,6 |
| Myleran | 0.284[a] | 0.069 | — | — | — | 2,3 |
| Natulan | 0.009 | 0.008 | — | 0.0075 | 0.1275 | 2,3,7,8 |
| TEM | 3.09 | — | 0.0 | 51.5 | 1200 | 3,4 |
| Thio TEPA | — | 0.5 | 12.3 | — | 42.2 | 2,9 |

Unit dose = 1 mg/kg
Trans = Translocations; Sperm abs = sperm abnormalities
[a] Upper fiducial limit
[b] Based on aberrations in spermatocytes
Reprinted, with permission, from Lyon et al. (1983).
1. Au and Hsu (1980)
2. Wyrobek and Bruce (1978)
3. Ehling (1978)
4. Ehling (1982)
5. Generoso et al. (1980)
6. Ehling (1980)
7. Ehling and Neuhauser (1979)
8. Sharma et al. (1979)
9. Malashenko and Surkova (1974)

calculated separately, and in cases of mixed exposure, RMEs from the various agents can be totaled.

It is to be noted that the method can be used to calculate either the risk to the individual's descendants or the population risk. In considering protective measures, the aim should be to keep both individual and population risk to a minimum. Which of the two becomes overriding obviously depends on the situation. For the case of cytotoxic drugs, where relatively few individuals receive high doses, the individual risk will be more important. In occupational exposure, either individual or population risk may be overriding, depending on the number of workers exposed.

A major drawback to the method is the need to extrapolate from animal germ-cell data. On the one hand, these data are extremely sparse, and on the other, there are all the uncertainties inherent in such extrapolation. It would be very valuable if the method could be tested by comparison with the results of known human exposure, such as that to cytotoxic drugs. Various surveys have been made of the offspring of patients treated with such drugs, but there are numerous difficulties (Blatt et al. 1980; Mulvihill 1982; Rustin et al. 1984). In most cases the treated patients were females, whereas the animal data were derived from treated males, giving an obvious extrapolation problem. The human doses were received in multiple

## Table 4
## Mutation Index of Some Cytotoxic Drugs at Doses Equal to About
## 3 Months Human Treatment

| | | Gonia | | Postmeiotic | |
|---|---|---|---|---|---|
| Drug | Dose assumed (mg/kg) | Gene mutation | Trans | Gene mutation | Trans |
| Adriamycin | 9.6 | 200[a] | 3950 | 50[a] | 1030 |
| Cyclophosphamide | 300 | 60 | 0.0 | 1170 | 16,700 |
| Mitomycin C | 1.0 | 80 | 0.0 | 12[a] | 230 |
| Myleran | 4.55 | 31 | — | — | — |
| Natulan | 250 | 225 | — | 187 | 3190 |
| TEM | 1.0 | 309 | 0.0 | 5150 | 120,000 |
| Thio TEPA | 2.0 | 100[a] | 2450 | 422[a] | 8440 |

Figures have been rounded to avoid undue impression of precision.
[a] Assumed values on the basis that MI of gene mutation is $\frac{1}{20}$ of translocation
Reprinted, with permission, from Lyon et al. (1983).

small fractions, as opposed to the large single doses to the animals, and fractionation may reduce the mutagenic effect (Russell 1983). Another problem is that the numbers of offspring in each survey were very low in relation to the numbers needed to demonstrate any effect. They were commonly below 100 and in a recent large survey were only 281 (Rustin et al. 1984). This is too low to show a relative risk of only 1.2–1.3. Furthermore, the endpoint commonly measured is congenital malformations. As previously mentioned, there is doubt concerning the extent to which these are mutationally dependent. In addition, the persistence of the genes concerned is thought to be fairly high, and hence the relative risk in the first generation would be correspondingly lower.

Thus, to conclude, the method suggested here provides an attempt to estimate mutagenic risks to later generations. However, it relies heavily on extrapolation from animal data and far better methods of extrapolation are urgently needed.

## REFERENCES

Au, W.W. and T.C. Hsu. 1980. The genotoxic effects of adriamycin in somatic and germinal cells of the mouse. *Mutat. Res.* **72:** 351.

BEIR. 1980. *The effects on populations of exposures to low levels of ionizing radiation.* National Academy of Sciences, Washington, D.C.

Blatt, J., J.J. Mulvihill, J.L. Ziegler, R.C. Young, and D.G. Poplack. 1980. Pregnancy outcome following cancer chemotherapy. *Am. J. Med.* **69:** 828.

Bridges, B.A. 1980. An approach to the assessment of the risk to man from DNA damaging agents. *Arch. Toxicol. Suppl.* **3:** 271.

Carter, C.O. 1977. Monogenic disorders. *J. Med. Genet.* **14:** 316.

Ehling, U.H. 1978. Specific locus mutations in mice. In *Chemical mutagens* (ed. A. Hollaender and F.J. de Serres), vol. 5, p.233. Plenum Press, New York.

## Table 5
## Cases of Genetic Disease Expected to be Induced per $10^6$ Births by About 3 Months Treatment with Some Cytotoxic Drugs and Relative Risk

| Drug | First 3 months (postmeiotic stages) | | | | Total all gens | |
|---|---|---|---|---|---|---|
| | Generation 1 | | Generation 2 | | | |
| | Cases | RR | Cases | RR | Cases | RR |
| Adriamycin | 9,000 | 1.09 | 7,600 | 1.07 | 60,000 | 1.6 |
| CP | 180,000 | 2.7 | 150,000 | 2.4 | 1,200,000 | 12 |
| MMC | 2,100 | 1.02 | 1,800 | 1.02 | 14,000 | 1.1 |
| Myleran | — | — | — | — | — | — |
| Natulan | 31,000 | 1.3 | 26,000 | 1.25 | 210,000 | 3.0 |
| TEM | 1,000,000 | 10 | 840,000 | 9.0 | 6,600,000 | 64 |
| Thio TEPA | 76,000 | 1.7 | 63,000 | 1.6 | 510,000 | 5.9 |
| After 3 months interval (spermatogonial stages) | | | | | | |
| Adriamycin | 36,000 | 1.3 | 30,000 | 1.3 | 240,000 | 3.3 |
| CP | 4,800 | 1.05 | 4,200 | 1.04 | 42,000 | 1.4 |
| MMC | 6,400 | 1.06 | 5,600 | 1.05 | 56,000 | 1.5 |
| Myleran | 2,500 | 1.02 | 2,200 | 1.02 | 22,000 | 1.2 |
| Natulan | 18,000 | 1.2 | 16,000 | 1.2 | 160,000 | 2.5 |
| TEM | 25,000 | 1.2 | 22,000 | 1.2 | 220,000 | 3.1 |
| Thio TEPA | 20,000 | 1.2 | 17,000 | 1.2 | 130,000 | 2.2 |

RR = relative risk, assuming normal incidence of 105,000 cases of genetic disease per $10^6$ live births
Results have been rounded to two significant figures
CP = cyclophosphamide; MMC = mitomycin C
Reprinted, with permission, from Lyon et al. (1983)

_____. 1980. Induction of gene mutations in germ cells of the mouse. *Arch. Toxicol.* **46:** 123.

_____. 1982. Risk estimation based on germ cell mutations in mice. In *Environmental mutagens and carcinogens* (ed. T. Sugimura et al.), p.709. University of Tokyo Press, Tokyo and Alan R. Liss, New York.

Ehling, U.H. and A. Neuhauser. 1979. Procarbazine-induced specific locus mutations in male mice. *Mutat. Res.* **59:** 245.

Ehling, U.H., D. Averbeck, P. Cerutti, J. Friedman, H. Greim, A.C. Kolbye, and M.L. Mendelsohn. 1983. ICPEMC Publication No. 10. Review of the evidence for the presence or absence of thresholds in the induction of genetic effects by genotoxic chemicals. *Mutat. Res.* **123:** 281.

Ehrenberg, L. 1979. Risk assessment of ethylene oxide and other compounds. In *Banbury Report 1: Assessing chemical mutagens: The risk to humans* (ed. V.K. McElheny and S. Abrahamson), p.157. Cold Spring Harbor Laboratory, Cold Spring Harbor, New York.

Ehrenberg, L., E. Moustacchi, and S. Osterman-Golkar. 1983. Dosimetry of genotoxic agents and dose response relationships of their effects. *Mutat. Res.* **123:** 121.

Evans, H.J. 1977. Chromosome anomalies among livebirths. *J. Med. Genet.* **14:** 309.

Generoso, W.M., J.B. Bishop, D.G. Gosslee, G.W. Newell, C.J. Sheu, and E. von Halle. 1980. Heritable translocation test in mice. *Mutat. Res.* **76:** 191.

Leck, I. 1977. Congenital malformations and childhood neoplasms. *J. Med. Genet.* **14:** 321.

Lee, W.R. 1978. Dosimetry of chemical mutagens in eukaryotic germ cells. In *Chemical mutagens* (ed. A. Hollaender and F. de Serres), vol. 5, chap. 8, p.177. Plenum Press, New York.

_____. 1979. Dosimetry of alkylating agents. In *Banbury Report 1: Assesssing chemical mutagens: The risk to humans* (ed. V.K. McElheny and S. Abrahamson), p.191. Cold Spring Harbor Laboratory, Cold Spring Harbor, New York.

Lyon, M.F. 1981. Sensitivity of various germ cell stages to environmental mutagens. *Mutat. Res.* **87:** 323.

Lyon, M.F., I.D. Adler, B.A. Bridges, L. Ehrenberg, L. Golberg, D.J. Kilian, S. Kondo, E. Moustacchi, A. Putrament, K. Sankaranarayanan, F.H. Sobels, R.J. Sram, G. Streisinger, and K. Sundaram. 1983. Committee 4 Final Report. Estimation of genetic risks and increased incidence of genetic disease due to environmental mutagens. *Mutat. Res.* **115:** 255.

Malashenko, A.M. and N.I. Surkova. 1974. The mutagenic effect of thio-TEPA in laboratory mice I. Chromosome aberrations in somatic and germ cells of male mice. *Sov. Genet.* **10:** 51.

Mulvihill, J.J., E.A. McKeen, F. Rosner, and M.H. Zarrabi. 1982. Pregnancy outcomes in women with cancer. *Amer. J. Hum. Genet.* **34:** 75A.

Oftedal, P. and A.G. Searle. 1980. An overall genetic risk assessment for radiological protection purposes. *J. Med. Genet.* **17:** 15.

Russell, W.L. 1983. Relation of mouse specific-locus tests to other mutagenicity tests and to risk estimation. In *Symposium on utilization of mammalian specific locus studies in hazard evaluation and estimation of genetic risks* (ed. F.J. de Serres and W. Sheridan), p.109. Plenum Press, New York.

Rustin, G.J.S., M. Booth, J. Dent, S. Salt, F. Rustin, and K.D. Bagshawe. 1984. Pregnancy after cytotoxic chemotherapy for gestational trophoblastic tumours. *Brit. Med. J.* **288:** 103.

Sankaranarayanan, K. 1982. *Genetic effects of ionizing radiation in multicellular eukaryotes and the assessment of genetic radiation hazards in man.* Elsevier, Amsterdam, The Netherlands.

Sharma, R.K., G.T. Roberts, F.M. Johnson, and H.V. Malling. 1979. Translocation and sperm abnormality assays in mouse spermatogonia treated with procarbazine. *Mutat. Res.* **67:** 385.

Sobels, F.H. 1982. The parallelogram: An indirect approach for the assessment of genetic risks from chemical mutagens. In *Progress in mutation research* (ed. K.C. Bora et al.), vol. 3, p. 323. Elsevier-North Holland, Amsterdam, The Netherlands.

Streisinger, G. 1983. Extrapolation from species to species and from various cell types in assessing risks from chemical mutagens. *Mutat. Res.* **114:** 93.

UNSCEAR. 1977. *Sources and effects of ionizing radiation.* United Nations, New York.

UNSCEAR. 1982. *Ionizing radiation: Sources and biological effects.* United Nations, New York.

Wyrobek, A.J. and W.R. Bruce. 1978. The induction of sperm-shape abnormalities in mice and humans. In *Chemical mutagens* (ed. A. Hollaender and F.J. de Serres), vol. 5, p. 257. Plenum Press, New York.

## COMMENTS

**CORN:**  The tables were all point estimates. Is it possible to include uncertainties, that is, to bracket your numbers? If so, what would that look like?

**LYON:**  It is possible, yes. You can get wide variation. I'm not sure what it means because the main problem, of course, is the extrapolation, the fact that you're going from one species to another. I don't see how, at the moment, you can estimate what the error is in going from mouse to man.

**ALBERT:**  How about mouse to rat, can you do that?

**LYON:**  In radiation, various species have been compared, and you certainly do get variation. It's not orders of magnitude; it's factors of two and four. With chemicals, it has largely not been done.

**PERERA:**  In the beginning, you presented a parallelogram approach with animal and human data. Could you compare parallel animal testing and human monitoring data on somatic cell mutation (for example, mutant lymphocytes or chromosomal aberrations) with markers of germ-cell damage, such as alterations in sperm?

**LYON:**  The chromosome aberration approach has been tried and it doesn't work. Van Buul has looked at chromosome aberrations in lymphocytes of mice and monkeys and compared them with aberrations in the germ-cells of mice and monkeys, and it didn't work out at all. Whether things like DNA alkylations would work out still remains to be tested.

**ALBERT:**  You mentioned that a direct-acting alkylating agent, such as ethylmethanesulfonate, produces markedly different mutagenic effects on different types of cells. Is there any speculation as to the basis for that, because the DNA adducts should be comparable?

**LYON:**  It's very strange. In EMS, it is suggested that it is producing its effects not by acting on the DNA, but that it's acting on the sperm proteins, which in turn is affecting the DNA.

**ALBERT:**  Is there any evidence for that?

**LYON:**  Yes. Sega at Oak Ridge has evidence for that. But that doesn't explain the phenomena in general. Sega also raised the question: "Does the agent actually get to the cells of the testes?" That's a possible explanation for something like ENU, which has a stronger effect on the spermatogonia than it does on the later stages; it could be it reaches the spermatogonia but not the later stages. However, it doesn't explain the ones that act the other way around, where you get the stronger effect in the later stages. If it reaches the later stages, it must be able to reach the spermatogonia. As I said, there is no rational basis for it.

# Some Aspects of Quantifying and Acting upon the Risks of Radiation Exposures

JAMES V. NEEL
Department of Human Genetics
University of Michigan Medical School
Ann Arbor, Michigan 48109

## INTRODUCTION

This paper will be limited to the questions of how we can better define the genetic risks to humans of a wide variety of environmental contaminants, especially radiation, and of how we then use the data. I will use the term, genetic risk, in the strict sense, as applying to changes in the hereditary material which are transmitted to the next generation, not in the all too prevalent looser sense, of changes in the genetic material of the somatic cells of the exposed individual, such as an increase in chromosome breaks, sister chromatid exchanges, or directly measured DNA damage. Although the latter types of findings create the presumption that transmissible genetic damage has been induced in germ-cells, there are simply no data permitting quantification of this presumption in humans at present.

At the outset let me suggest that the issue is as complicated as any with which the mind of man has grappled thus far in human history. The evaluation of genetic risk, it is now clear, demands not only some rather difficult measurements in human populations and the preferred human surrogate, laboratory mice, but, in the ultimate, an understanding of the very complicated nature of our genetic material and how it maintains its integrity. The use of this knowledge, in turn, requires a wisdom which our species is still struggling to acquire.

As a historical aside, I should mention that I had the privilege of serving, from 1955 to 1956, on the first of the several Committees of the National Academy of Sciences which attempted to evaluate the somatic and genetic effects of radiation and to suggest reasonable limits on human exposures. That group recommended, on the basis of the then current genetic information, that members of the general population should not receive up to age 30 an accumulated dose beyond background of more than 10 rem of ionizing radiation. Subsequently it was suggested that half of this potential exposure be allocated to those medical diagnostic procedures that result in a radiation exposure, with the other half to be accounted for by all the remaining man-made sources of radiation. The Committee was very explicit in the view that this amount of radiation was not harmless and was the maximum they could justify on any reasonable risk-benefit analyses. The hope was expressed that exposures could be held substantially lower than this permissible maximum. These recommendations have been only slightly altered over the years by various official

**163**

bodies. Our Committee, however, was untroubled by the responsibility of implementing that decision. What has become clear in the past three decades is how difficult that implementation will be.

## RISK-BENEFIT ANALYSIS AS VIEWED BY THE GENETICIST

Since I am a geneticist, I would like to present a brief introduction to the data base that is available to the geneticist when he or she approaches the evaluation of genetic risks from radiation or chemicals. As most people are aware, this matter has been the subject of many reports by a number of national and international committees or commissions (in addition to that mentioned above) and it is a bit presumptuous to attempt to condense these reports into a few brief pages. From the outset, the cornerstone of genetic thinking (as reported in the 1956 report of the Committee of the U.S. National Academy of Sciences mentioned above) has been that there is no threshold in the genetic effects of radiation. Thus, any exposure to radiation carries some risk. These risks must be justified by the benefits stemming from the exposures. However, too often these days, considerations of risk and benefits are divorced; and this provides tempting targets for the fearful or uninformed who wish to obtain all of the benefits associated with technical advances but incur none of the risks. When these matters come to litigation, the adversarial atmosphere of the judiciary system requires both the plaintiff and defendant to assume exaggerated positions. Realizing full well how naive I may sound, I wonder if we couldn't identify, some place in our complex society, a respected focus which could issue objective risk-benefit analyses in language that a motivated individual of average education would be able to understand.

## RELATIVE GENETIC RISKS VERSUS ABSOLUTE GENETIC RISKS

Genetic (and somatic) risks can be stated either in absolute or in relative terms. In my opinion, the absolute approach lends itself to abuse and misinterpretation much more easily than the relative approach. The former results in a free-floating figure with no familiar landmarks to assist in placing it in perspective. An extreme example is provided by EPA's statement (40 CFR Part 191 [Proposed]) that the radiation exposures permitted by the plan recommended for the disposal of high-level radioactive waste will result in 1000 adverse health effects over the next 10,000 years. Given their treatment of the issue, "health effects" was essentially a euphemism for fatal cancer, although genetic effects were included in their appraisal. Elsewhere in this document, we learn that the escape of radionuclides from the planned geological repositories should be less than if the corresponding amount of radioactive material had remained in place, unmined. These adverse health effects are thus not an additional health burden that the disposal system places on the population, but the substitution of one source of morbidity/mortality for another. Is this "risk" as the term is usually defined? These comments are not meant to be critical of EPA; as it interpreted its mission, EPA had no really viable alternative approach.

The relativistic approach to radiation risk usually draws upon the concept of a doubling dose, i.e., the amount of radiation required to produce the same frequency of mutations or cancer as the spontaneous frequency, a frequency and an impact with which both the scientist and the public have some familiarity. The doubling dose can vary according to the endpoint; the tendency is to work with the average of a variety of pertinent endpoints, an average whose derivation involves judgments as to how the data should be weighted. This is a more demanding approach than the absolute since it requires not only the derivation of an absolute effect, but also an estimate of the normal background level with which this induced effect may be compared. For example, if it is stated that a given genetic effect will be 1/1000 of that occurring spontaneously, i.e., 1/1000 of that resulting from a doubling dose, a frame of reference is provided, which can be converted to an absolute effect if deemed necessary. The example quoted in the previous paragraph assumes a somewhat different perspective when it is considered that these 1000 "health effects" are 0.0003% of those of this type, which, by the same approach, can be calculated to occur in the U.S. population over that same 10,000-year period from the omnipresent background radiation.

## THE PRESENT STATE OF THE DATA BASE ON HUMAN GENETIC RISKS FROM ENVIRONMENTAL AGENTS

The major current difficulties in genetic risk quantification and the regulatory policy appropriate to these risks can be very simply stated. First, with respect to radiation, there are major uncertainties in the existing experimental and human data. Second, most of the risk estimates demanded of regulatory agencies require extrapolations to exposures some three orders of magnitude below the exposure levels at which the existing data were collected, such extrapolations, of course, substantially expanding the uncertainties. With respect to chemical agents, not only is the data base much inferior to that for radiation, but the evaluation of gonadal doses is infinitely more difficult.

Experiments on mice have provided the primary data base from which estimates of the genetic risks of radiation in humans are derived. The reasons are obvious: A mouse is an easily manipulated animal with a relatively short life cycle, concerning whose genetic characterization a great deal is known. On the basis of an enormous amount of careful work, extensively reviewed in the various reports of the United Nations Scientific Committee on the Effects of Atomic Radiation (1977), it has been estimated that for the mouse the average doubling dose for genetic phenomena resulting from acute gamma radiation is about 40 r. One of the early, unexpected findings in this field was that when a given (high) dose was fractionated or delivered as a chronic dose, the genetic yield was reduced by a factor of about 3 (Russell et al. 1958). Most of the radiation humans will experience in their lifetimes, barring a nuclear catastrophe, will come in the form of small pulses or more or less continuously at very low levels. Because of this fact, as well as the many possible sources of error in the experiments, it has been suggested, on the basis of these murine experiments, that the doubling dose of intermittently received radiation for humans was between 50 and 250 rem (BEIR III). A good deal of the uncertainty reflected in that range arises from a growing awareness that the genetic loci and strains employed in the experiments may not be adequately representative.

The chief source of data on humans derives from the atomic bombings of Hiroshima and Nagasaki. I would like to present an approximate picture of the present status of the ongoing studies of the most reliable indicators of a genetic radiation effect. I say approximate for two reasons: (1) The estimated exposures to radiation are under revision; and (2) there is a large amount of data just becoming available. Expressed as a regression, two of the studies indicate an effect and two do not, but none of the regressions depart significantly from zero. If we make the assumption that there was indeed a genetic effect, and pool the regression estimates into one average, we arrive at a preliminary estimate of 156 rem to the gonad for the doubling dose of acute radiation (Schull et al. 1981), an estimate that will have to be scaled down by some presently unknown factor because of a reevaluation now in progress of the amount of radiation received by the survivors. My current guess is that the new dose will, on average, be about 75% of the old. Precise upper and lower bounds could not be set on this estimate of 156 rem. If the abovementioned factor of 3, derived at higher gonadal doses than those on average sustained by the survivors of the atomic bombings, can be applied to this situation, we may suggest that the doubling dose for chronic radiation would be about 350 rem, with a lower bound which could overlap with the upper portion of the range given for the mouse, and an upper bound of at least 700 rem.

If I seem to be projecting considerable uncertainty in our doubling dose estimates for both mouse and man (and the absolute estimates no less), this is not by accident. How much worse the situation with regard to chemical agents! The relatively few experiments with mammals have been conducted with massive doses of the chemical agent under study, and there is not a single study on the offspring of humans exposed to a chemical mutagen that meets contemporary epidemiological standards.

## IMMEDIATE PROSPECTS FOR IMPROVING THAT DATA BASE

The prospects are excellent in the next decade for substantial amelioration of some of these uncertainties regarding the genetic effects of radiation, if society is willing to make the necessary investment. Further experiments with mice, and continuing observations in Hiroshima and Nagasaki, should substantially lessen some of the present ambiguities. Even more important is the fact that the study of mutation is about to participate fully in the technical advances characteristic of modern molecular biology. Specifically, there are two upcoming technologies which appear particularly promising. One is known as two-dimensional polyacrylamide gel electrophoresis, which, coupled with sensitive protein stains, permits visualizing and inspecting for certain types of abnormality a substantial fraction of the many proteins of a cell type, tissue, or body fluid, in a detail previously unthinkable (Neel et al. 1984). Computer algorithms are under development which have the potential for substantially relieving the tedium of the visual scoring of these gels (Skolnick 1982; Skolnick et al. 1982). In a genetic monitoring setting, the objective is to identify protein variants present in a child but not in the parents; a successful algorithm must be able to recognize any unique aspect of a child's protein pattern in relation to the patterns of the parents. The second new technology would draw upon all of the recent developments in our ability to characterize lesions in DNA. The development of computer algorithms for analyzing the preparations should substantially alleviate the tedium inherent in scoring the required large number of DNA preparations. However, this approach is not quite as close to hand as the former method mentioned.

## THE USES OF BETTER DATA: REGULATION OF PERMISSIBLE EXPOSURES TO THE GENERAL POPULATION

As mentioned above, the "permissible" exposure of 170 mrem/year (the annual equivalent of 5 rem accumulated to age 30) has never been considered harmless; it has been regarded as an absolute upper limit to a necessary trade-off in view of the benefits accruing from the human activities that result in these exposures. In response to the conviction of all the responsible bodies considering the matter of exposures, that the less exposure the better, the related ALARA concept has been widely adopted. This requires that exposures be held As Low As Reasonably Achievable. It is becoming clear that the term, reasonable, is subject to many interpretations.

I regard the permissible exposure, however defined, as a resource, to be used in a wise and coordinated manner. It would be imprudent to delay regulatory action as commitments against this resource pile up; but, in the complex technological world in which we function, extremism in efforts to reduce presumed radiation risks may carry an unreasonable humanistic and financial price tag, especially when the price is viewed in relation to the total problem of risk regulation in our complex society. Unfortunately, no one seems to be in charge of relating commitments against this resource to the totality of the risk commitments characteristic of an industrialized society. Let us put aside the matter of occupational exposures to radiation, which involve relatively few persons, and consider only the population exposures. I am aware of only four official commitments against that resource, namely, the proposed regulations of the Environmental Protection Agency regarding exposures (1) from the disposal of high-level radioactive waste (40 CFR Part 191), (2) from the disposal of low-level waste (40 CFR Part 193), (3) from uranium and thorium mill tailings (40 CFR Part 192), and (4) from ambient radionuclides (40 CFR Part 61 [AH-FR1 2324-3]). All are quite stringent and are to be met (if not modified) at considerable financial cost. Some of these sets of regulations were promulgated in response to very specific situations, the waste disposal standards following passage of the Nuclear Waste Policy Act (PL 97-425) by Congress, and the radionuclide standard after the Sierra Club in 1981 filed a brief with the U.S. District Court for the Northern District of California that such regulation was mandatory under the provisions of Section 112 of the Clean Air Act. As I study the documents, I am impressed that they reflect the ALARA approach much more than a reasoned risk-benefit analysis. I sugggest the time has come to proceed, not on an ad hoc, case-by-case basis, but as a result of surveying all the man-made exposures to which general populations are subjected, somewhat as was done in the 1977 report of the United Nations Scientific Committee on the Effects of Atomic Radiation (UNSCEAR) or by the Nuclear Regulatory Commission (1980), to visualize the total setting in the U.S. within which the regulatory agencies should function. This should be followed by an appraisal of where exposures can be lowered at a reasonable cost as well as where the cost would be excessive. A significant step in this direction was taken by a subcommittee of EPA's Science Advisory Board (1984), which found the exposure limits placed upon the depositories for high-level waste so much more stringent than the general approach to radiation exposures that they recommended a tenfold relaxation in these standards.

## THE USES OF BETTER DATA: THE EXPOSED INDIVIDUAL

Let us now consider some aspects of genetic risk quantification for the individual. There will from time to time be individuals whose accidental exposures apparently substantially exceed the permissible, as allegedly illustrated by some members of the general population living downwind from the Nevada Test Site (Johnson 1984). Given the frequency with which abortion, miscarriage, stillbirth, congenital defect, and genetic defect occur in the general poulation, such unfortunate outcomes of pregnancy will occasionally occur, and even seem to cluster, in the offspring of persons with no mutagenic exposures; presumably they will cluster at some increased rate following an exposure to a mutagen. How most equitably to meet the actions seeking indemnification for genetic injury which are certain to arise? In this regard, I find myself following with great interest the principle of "proportionate risk" being developed with respect to malignancy (Bond 1959, 1981, 1982), whereby, given an estimate of the doubling dose of radiation for carcinogenesis, indemnification occurs on a sliding scale related to exposure, according to tables still being drawn up under the provisions of proposed legislation (S 921, 98th Congress, Radiogenic Cancer Compensation Act of 1983). However, although this is an attractive concept, and as equitable as any I can envision, once one departs from genetic outcomes clearly to be attributed to chromosomal or point mutation in the preceding generation, the manifestations of induced genetic damage can be so various that implementation of the concept presents extreme difficulties.

## THE CARCINOGEN-MUTAGEN AXIS

Almost all agents that are mutagenic are carcinogenic and vice-versa. Although there is still debate over some of the details of this correlation, its general truth is widely accepted. The implication is that a mutation-like event plays a primary role in initiating a malignancy. I mentioned above that a cornerstone of genetic thought was the belief that there was no threshold to the genetic effects of radiation; for the chemical mutagens, the question is more open. There is, however, even for radiation and certainly for chemicals, room for debate as to the nature of the dose-effect curve at very low doses. These same considerations carry over to carcinogenesis, where there is even more lively debate as to the question of threshold and curve shape at very low doses. The conservative course of action in setting limits on exposure to carcinogens has been to assume linearity and no threshold in the dose-effect relationship, and this is what has usually been done.

The organ dose of acute radiation which will double the likelihood of developing cancer in the average organ can, from the Japanese experience to date (Kato and Schull 1982; Kato et al. 1982; Wakabayashi et al. 1983), be placed, very approximately, at 170 rad (TR65 dose schedule). (I am indebted to Dr. E.P. Radford for this calculation.) The cancer doubling dose thus appears to be very similar to the genetic doubling dose, as discussed above. It must be emphasized that both these doubling doses are the average of a multiplicity of endpoints; this is a crude comparison but probably sufficiently robust for the generalization we wish to draw. In many respects, difficult though it has been to estimate cancer doubling doses, it is somewhat less difficult than to measure genetic doubling doses. The cancer doubling dose for man is thus on a more secure footing than the genetic doubling dose. On a pragmatic level, one can argue that regulations which adequately protect the public from the standpoint of malignancy should also provide adequate genetic protection, although because of the 20-year lag between radiation and the development of malignancy for most cancers (except leukemia), genetic damage may have occurred before the cancer warning system is effective.

Although this is a reasonable rule-of-thumb, there are at least three aspects of the genetic problem which require that the quest for better data continue. First, genetic risks should be set on the basis of genetic data. There is a very real possibility that evolutionary pressures have resulted in superior genetic repair systems in the germ line, in consequence of which the genetic doubling dose is substantially higher than the doubling dose for the event in somatic cells which initiates carcinogenesis. Second, in the case of the individual who somehow receives an excessive dose of radiation and, on the basis of subsequent reproductive outcomes, claims genetic damage, an equitable settlement is best based on genetic data. The third reason is somewhat more subtle. Radiation-induced damage to somatic cells that results in malignancy does not carry over to the next generation, but an induced mutation with deleterious effects may persist for many generations. In the event of a long-term increase in radiation exposure, extending over many generations, the frequency in the population of disease-producing genes maintained by mutation pressure f will rise to a new equilibrium value in accordance with the following expression:

$$f = m/s$$

where m = mutation rate, and s = average selection against the conditions produced by these genes.

If s is high, the cumulation will be low; but if s is low—and continuing improvements in medical care should lower s—then the cumulation could be considerable. The better the knowledge of m and s, the better the ability to predict the long-range consequences of an altered mutation rate.

## CONCLUSION

It is apparent from the foregoing that the data base for quantifying the genetic risks of radiation and a variety of chemical agents recently introduced into the environment is still inadequate for more than rough guidelines, despite a rather extensive research program over the past 40 years. Interest is repeatedly expressed by the scientific community concerning the regulation of genetic exposures on the basis of the much more easily obtained data on such effects on the genetic material of somatic cells as chromosome breaks or measurable alterations in DNA. Although this procedure has an appealing simplicity, it would be wholly unscientific, since we do not know the appropriate conversion factor between somatic cell and germ-cell damage for any potential mutagen—even radiation.

The only viable course of action, once superior approaches to evaluating genetic damage has been developed, is for nations to sponsor the appropriate studies on those populations (worldwide), which have sustained a particularly impressive, presumptively mutagenic exposure. If properly designed studies fail to reveal evidences of genetic damage, a source of deep public concern will have been alleviated. If, on the other hand, genetic effects are found, extrapolation can proceed from a much more secure base than now exists. The alternative is a continuation of the present attitude of fear which sometimes approaches hysteria. Once again, the genie is out of its bottle.

## REFERENCES

Bond, V.P. 1959. The medical effects of radiation. In *Proceedings Thirteenth Annual Convention, National Association Claimant's Counsel of America*, p. 117. W.H. Anderson, Cincinnati, Ohio.

———. 1981. The cancer risk attributable to radiation exposure: Some practical problems. *Health Phys.* **40:** 108.

———. 1982. Statement. *Hearings on radiation exposure compensation act of 1981* (S. 1483), p. 242. Government Printing Office, Washington, D.C.

Committee on the Biological Effects of Ionizing Radiation. 1980. *The effects on populations of exposures to low levels of ionizing radiation: 1980* (BEIR III), pp. xv and 524. National Academy Press, Washington, D.C.

High-level Radioactive Waste Disposal Subcommittee Advisory Board, U.S. Environmental Protection Agency. 1984. *Report on the review of proposed environmental standards for the management and disposal of spent nuclear fuel, high-level, and transuranic radioactive waste* (40 CFR 191), p. 26 and appendices.

Johnson, C.J. 1984. Cancer incidence in an area of radioactive fallout downwind from the Nevada Test Site. *J. Am. Med. Assoc.* **251:** 230.

Kato, H. and W.J. Schull. 1982. *Life span study report. Study report 9, part 1*, p. 39. *Cancer mortality among atomic bomb survivors, 1950–1978*. Radiation Effects Research Foundation Tech. Report 12–80.

Kato, H., C.C. Brown, D.G. Hoel, and W.J. Schull. 1982. *Life span study report 9, part 2*, p. 27. *Mortality from causes other than cancer among atomic bomb survivors, 1950–1978*. Radiation Effects Research Foundation Tech. Report 5–81, Hiroshima.

Neel, J.V., B.B. Rosenblum, C.F. Sing, M.M. Skolnick, S.M. Hanash, and S. Sternberg. 1984. Adapting two-dimensional gel electrophoresis to the study of human germline mutation rates. In *Methods and applications of two-dimensional gel electrophoresis of proteins* (ed. J.E. Celis), chap. 9, p. 259. Academic Press, New York.

Russell, W.L., L.B. Russell, and E.M. Kelly. 1958. Radiation dose rate and mutation frequency. *Science* **128:** 1546.

Schull, W.J., M. Otake, and J.V. Neel. 1981. A reappraisal of the genetic effects of the atomic bombs: Summary of a thirty-four year study. *Science* **213:** 1220.

Skolnick, M.M. 1982. An approach to completely automatic comparison of two-dimensional electrophoresis gels. *Clin. Chem.* **28:** 979.

Skolnick, M.M., S.R. Sternberg, and J.V. Neel. 1982. Computer programs for adopting two-dimensional gels to the study of mutation. *Clin. Chem.* **28:** 969.

United Nations Scientific Committee on the Effects of Atomic Radiation (UNSCEAR). 1977. *Sources and effects of ionizing radiation.* p. 725. United Nations, New York.

U.S. Nuclear Regulatory Commission 1980. *The feasibility of epidemiologic investigations of the health effects of low-level ionizing radiation* (NUREG/CR-1728), pp. xxiii & 421. U.S. Nuclear Regulatory Commission, Washington, D.C.

Wakabayashi, T., H. Kato, T. Ikeda, and W.J. Schull. 1983. *Life span study report 9, part 3*, p. 31. *Tumor registry data, Nagasaki 1959–1978*. Radiation Effects Research Foundation Tech. Report 6–81.

# Session 5:
# Toxicology and Biological Mechanisms

# Carcinogenic Risk Assessment: A Toxicologist's View

IAIN F. H. PURCHASE
Imperial Chemical Industries PLC
Alderley Park, Macclesfield
Cheshire, United Kingdom

## OVERVIEW

The drive for better quantitative methods of assessing carcinogenic risk has led to the development of a number of mathematical models for extrapolating data derived from animal experiments, usually conducted at high doses, to the risk that is likely to occur with substantially lower exposure levels. From a toxicologist's point of view, these methods are inadequate. Two examples are used to illustrate the way in which simple mathematical extrapolation provides estimates of risk at low dose which are clearly incompatible with the existing knowledge of mechanisms of action or from epidemiology. In the case of vinyl chloride, which has been studied in numerous animal studies, mathematical models are used to extrapolate from each of the animal studies a dose likely to produce a risk of one in $10^{-6}$. The range of doses produced was so wide that the utility of the procedure is called into question. A second example, that of trichlorethylene carcinogenesis, is used to illustrate that information on the mechanism of carcinogenic action can provide evidence that mathematical extrapolation methods are unsuitable. The evidence of lack of susceptibility of human tissues—in vitro—together with knowledge of the nongenetic mechanisms of carcinogenesis for this compound, indicate that the mouse data is unsuitable for risk assessment in man. Current use of mathematical models aims to be conservative by selecting data and the means of calculating risk which provides an upper limited (overestimate) of risk. However, the early stages of risk assessment are scientific processes and, therefore, should not lead to either over or under estimation of risk as either could act against the best interests of society.

## INTRODUCTION

Risk quantitation is but one step in the overall process of risk management aimed at protecting the health of those exposed to chemicals. Discussions of this topic are beset by problems of terminology, particularly the distinction between hazard and risk.

Risk assessment and management is a complex process which for ease of discussion may be set out as a series of sequential steps. Table 1 is a modification of a scheme by Sors (1982), which originally provided an overall framework of decisionmaking for environmental risk management. For the purposes of this paper, it has been modified to a scheme of risk management for a single chemical. Different

**175**

## Table 1
## Scheme for Risk Management

| | Components of risk management |
|---|---|
| 1. Identify broad nature of the hazard. | Hazard identification |
| 2. Establish dose-effect relationship in animal studies. | |
| 3. Assess potential dose-effect relationship for the chemical in man by extrapolation from (2) using all available data and taking into account likely exposure, (4), and/or by direct observation in man. | Hazard assessment |
| 4. Define conditions of exposure (level, route, target groups, time). | |
| 5. Relate likelihood, nature, and extent of effect (3) to exposure (4). | Risk assessment |
| 6. Evaluate costs, risks, and benefits of chemical. | Risk evaluation |
| 7. Evaluate the acceptable level of risk to the various targets. | |
| 8. Specify the type and level of control required to achieve acceptable risk. | |
| 9. Implement and enforce controls. | Control measures |
| 10. Review actual risk levels and effectiveness of controls. | |

ie - Science first

disciplines contribute to each of the stages. Hazard identification and assessment and risk assessment are primarily scientific; risk evaluation, particularly the evaluation of the acceptability of risk (Table 1, step 7), involves nonscientists and may be a political rather than a scientific stage; and control measures involve governmental and industrial components.

The first (scientific) stages of risk management are the subject of this volume, and hence the distinction between hazard and risk is pertinent. Hazard is an event or act which holds adverse consequences; for chemicals it is the likelihood that the substance will cause adverse effects (at various expected exposure levels). Risk is a statistical concept defined as the expected frequency of undesirable effects arising from a particular exposure to a chemical. Carcinogenic risk assessment begins with an assessment of the hazard and relates it to the actual circumstances of exposure. In most cases, this requires estimation of the hazard at doses well below those which are of practical use in laboratory experiments and then, as a separate process, the judgment of the relevance of the hazard to man and a projection of its magnitude.

The majority of data produced for regulatory purposes (and, for example, by the National Toxicology Program) is adequate to fulfill step 1 (hazard identification) in Table 1. There is frequently insufficient data to fully define the dose-response relationship in animals (Table 1, step 2) nor to understand the mechanisms of action and comparative toxicity necessary to assess the potential dose-response in man (Table 1, step 3). Mathematical models have been used widely in the low-dose estimation and are frequently incorrectly assumed to provide accurate numerical point estimates of risk. The low-dose extrapolation using these models is confined, at best, to estimation of hazard and, as currently applied, takes insufficient account of the complexities of the biological processes in carcinogenesis and frequently uses inadequate experimental data. A rational basis for risk assessment is a necessary component of regulatory processes and the following two examples are selected to illustrate the pitfalls of using these models.

## VINYL CHLORIDE: RISK ASSESSMENT BASED ON EXTENSIVE HUMAN AND ANIMAL DATA

Since the discovery of the carcinogenicity of vinyl chloride in the early 1970s, its carcinogenic effects (inducing angiosarcoma of the liver and other cancers) in man and animals have been the subject of extensive studies. Vinyl chloride is carcinogenic to all species tested adequately, and epidemiological studies on over 50,000 exposed workers provide one of the most extensive sets of data available. The experimental studies in rodents which are of most use for quantitative assessment are several inhalation and gavage studies carried out by Maltoni (Maltoni et al. 1981), an ingestion study by Feron (Feron et al. 1981), and an inhalation study in mice by Lee (Lee et al. 1978). Previous calculations of risk using a variety of mathematical models provided estimates between $3.9 \times 10^{-7}$ ppb (Food Safety Council 1980) and 1000 ppb (Anderson 1980) as the exposure for a lifetime risk of $10^{-6}$ (Table 2). The higher values were derived from models which included consideration of the saturable nature of vinyl chloride metabolism to its reactive proximate carcinogen (chloroethylene oxide) while the lower values used conservative models without incorporating adjustment for metabolism. In all cases, however, there is difficulty in checking the accuracy of the models because of the low frequency phenomenon being studied. What can be done, however, is to compare the results of extrapolation using various mathematical models or from various experimental data on a single compound. The results of hazard and risk estimations carried out with this purpose in mind (Purchase et al. 1985) are given in Table 3. The results of this comparison, giving an extremely wide range of estimations, calls into question the reliability of these methods for estimating risks and leads directly to the need to test the methods in other ways.

One obvious test is to compare the results from low-dose extrapolation with epidemiological studies in man. There have been 21 epidemiological studies carried out on about 50,000 exposed people (Purchase et al. 1985). These studies confirm that vinyl chloride produces angiosarcoma of the liver (and brain tumors) but do not provide adequate information on dose-response due to the paucity of accurate exposure data. However, studies of the distribution of angiosarcoma in the general population in relation to the location of vinyl chloride manufacture (Barr 1982) and the absence of cases in the PVC fabrication industry with measurable exposure to

**Table 2**
**Summary of Quantitative Risk Assessments for VCM (by Inhalation)**

| Author | Species | Exposure for $10^{-6}$ lifetime risk (ppb) | Comments |
|---|---|---|---|
| Schneiderman et al. | Rat | 73 | Probit (slope = 1, Mantel) |
| (1975) | | 119 | Logit (slope = 3.45) |
| | | 2 | Logit (slope = 2.3, 1 hit) |
| Kuzmack and | Rat | 14 | Linear through zero |
| McGaughy (1975) | Man | 140–1400 | Log-probit |
| Gehring et al. (1979) | Rat | > 1000 | Biotransformation data included |
| | Man | | Linear or log-probit |
| Food Safety Council | Rat | 20 | One-hit |
| (1978; 1980) | | 20 | Armitage Doll |
| | | $2.1 \times 10^{-6}$ | Weibull |
| | | $3.9 \times 10^{-7}$ | Multihit |
| Anderson (1980) | Rat | > 1000 | DNA binding used for dosimetry |
| | Man | | |
| Gaylor and Kodell | Rat | 0.7 | Upper 97.5% confidence limit of |
| (1980) | | | linear model |
| | | 0.5 | Armitage Doll |
| Carlborg (1981) | Rat | $2.5 \times 10^{-5}$ | Weibull |
| Barr (1982) | Man | > 100 | Derived from Barr's negative epidemiology. |
| Purchase et al. (1984) | Rat | 0.025–9.16 | Log-probit including |
| | Mouse | $2 \times 10^{-15}$ | biotransformation data |
| | Man | 0.63–90 | Log-probit including biotransformation data for man. |
| | Rat | $2 \times 10^{-3} - 2 \times 10^{-8}$ | Weibull including |
| | Mouse | $6 \times 10^{-43}$ | biotransformation |
| | Man | 0.067–8.14 | Weibull including biotransformation for man |

Data from Barr (1982).

much larger population groups provides satisfactory evidence that the dose in man likely to produce a risk of $10^{-6}$ is likely to be in excess of 100 ppb. This estimate is not unrealistic in the light of the knowledge of the metabolism of vinyl chloride and provides a direct challenge to the much higher estimates of risk derived from mathematical models, particularly those not using corrections for nonlinear kinetics of metabolism (Table 2).

## Table 3
Quantitative Hazard and Risk Estimations Derived from Animal Experiments and Expressed as the Dose of Vinyl Chloride Calculated to Give a Life-time Incidence of $10^{-6a}$

| Experimental data[b] | Exposure for rodents | | Exposure for man | |
|---|---|---|---|---|
| | (a) | (b) | (a) | (b) |
| Sprague-Dawley Rats Inhalation | $2.5 \times 10^{-2}$ ppb | $2 \times 10^{-8}$ ppb | 0.63 ppb | $6.7 \times 10^{-2}$ ppb |
| Male Wistar Rats Inhalation | t9.16 ppb | $2 \times 10^{-3}$ ppb | 90 ppb | 8.14 ppb |
| Sprague-Dawley Rats Ingestion | $9 \times 10^{-4}$ mg/kg | $4 \times 10^{-6}$ mg/kg | — | — |
| Wistar Rats Ingestion | $3 \times 10^{-5}$ mg/kg | $9 \times 10^{-14}$ mg/kg | — | — |
| Mice Inhalation | $2 \times 10^{-15}$ ppb | $6 \times 10^{-43}$ ppb | $3 \times 10^{-2}$ | $9 \times 10^{-3}$ ppb |

[a] Data from Purchase et al. 1985.
[b] From Maltoni et al. 1981; Feron et al. 1981 and Lee et al. 1978.
(a) Based on log-probit analysis, estimated using maximum likelihood.
(b) Based on generalized linear model, estimated using maximum likelihood.

## TRICHLOROETHYLENE: INTERSPECIES COMPARISONS OF MECHANISMS OF ACTION PROVIDE ALTERNATIVE ESTIMATES OF RISK

Trichloroethylene (TRI) administered by gavage to mice at doses of 1000 mg/kg·day or greater produced hepatocellular carcinomas, but similar doses in rats (Osborn-Mendel, and Fischer 344) produced no hepatocarcinogenic effects (NCI 1976; NTP 1983). The Carcinogen Assessment Group of the EPA calculated an upper bound of 26.9μg/L drinking water corresponding to a lifetime risk level of $10^{-5}$ (Anderson 1982). These calculations assumed a daily intake of 2 L of drinking water and 6.5 ozs edible fish for a 70 kg man. This figure provided guidance for water quality criteria and, although it is stated that "the weight of biomedical evidence varies enormously for the chemicals . . . and this information should not be ignored in applying these target concentrations . . .", no modification of the target concentration is offered.

We became interested in TRI carcinogenicity because of the substantial difference in response in rats and mice and because pure trichloroethylene is only marginally mutagenic or nonmutagenic and binding of metabolites to DNA occurs only at insignificant levels. A better understanding of these differences would allow a more accurate assessment of the mechanisms of action and ultimately the potential carcinogenicity to man.

The key observations made on these studies (Elcombe 1985; Green and Prout 1985; Prout et al. 1985) can be summarized as follows:

(1) The primary active metabolite of TRI in rats and mice is trichloroacetic acid (TCA).

(2) In rats, the metabolism to TCA is saturable and reaches a maximum at TRI doses of about 500 mg/kg and above. In mice, formation of TCA follows linear kinetics with increasing levels of TCA as the dose of TRI is increased up to 2000 mg/kg. Consequently at 1000 mg/kg, the TCA blood levels are seven times those found in the rat.

(3) TCA induces peroxisomal proliferation in the liver of both rats and mice at doses of 50 mg/kg and above; but because of the differences in metabolic kinetics, peroxisomal proliferation after TRI administration occurs only in the mouse.

(4) Isolated mouse hepatocytes produce 30-fold greater amounts of TCA from TRI than rat hepatocytes which, in turn, are threefold more active than human liver cells.

(5) TCA induces a roughly equivalent level of peroxisomal proliferation in rats and mouse hepatocytes (i.e., results similar to those obtained in vivo), whereas no stimulation of peroxisomes was observed in human hepatocytes.

(6) The peroxisomal proliferation in mice resulted in dose-dependent stimulation of oxidation (up to 700% of control values) but no effect on peroxisomal catalase.

On the basis of these observations, it is proposed that TCI is carcinogenic by a nongenetic mechanism (epigenetic or nongenotoxic carcinogenesis) that involves the stimulation of hepatic peroxisomes. The precise steps involved in neoplastic transformation after peroxisomal proliferation are unclear, but it has been suggested that it is by reactive oxygen species (Reddy and Lalwai 1983). It can be concluded that the lack of responsiveness of the rat is due to the much lower capacity of the rat to metabolize TRI to TCA than the mouse, although the rat is capable of responding to TCA by peroxisomal proliferation. In man, the hepatocyte is less able to metabolize TRI to TCA (90 times less than the mouse), nor does it respond to TCA by peroxisomal proliferation; it is therefore reasonable to deduce that man is not susceptible to the hepatocarcinogenicity of TRI. In addition, as peroxisome proliferation has a threshold dose below which no effect is seen even in susceptible species, a threshold in the carcinogenic dose-response can be anticipated.

There remains doubt as to the exact mechanisms of action of TRI as a carcinogen as there is doubt about the mechanisms of all carcinogens. The hypothesis that TRI is a nongenotoxic carcinogen is as well developed as any current mechanistic hypothesis. The arbitrary application of a mathematical model to TRI carcinogenesis gives an upper bound for a $10^{-5}$ risk of 26.9 μg/L or about 0.77 μg/kg daily dose. Doses of 1000 mg/kg (about $3 \times 10^5$ higher) produce no effect in rats, a species susceptible to effects of the major metabolite. In man, with no discernible susceptibility to the effects of TCA and a lower capacity to metabolize TRI to TCA, this means of calculating risk has no justifiable basis.

# A DESCRIPTION OF RISK ASSESSMENT PROCEDURES

## Hazard Identification

A variety of experimental data can lead to a presumption of potential carcinogenicity. This is most frequently from considerations of chemical structure, results of short-term tests for carcinogens or results of life-time animal experiments; greater confidence is placed on data from experimental systems and particularly from animal studies. Risk assessment based on this evidence of carcinogenicity and human exposure is often inaccurate and should be considered preliminary.

## Hazard Assessment

Careful conduct and evaluation of life-time animal carcinogenicity may provide adequate dose-effect data. Too often the results are equivocal and judgment of the presence or absence of carcinogenic effects is required. Supporting evidence from mutagenicity and other short-term tests may be useful.

The next step, namely to assess the potential dose-effect relationship in man using all available data, is the most difficult. The assessment of potency (a function of dose and intensity of effect) for carcinogens has been oversimplified to the calculation of an $ED_{50}$. This is inadequate because it fails to take account of frequency, magnitude, duration and route of exposure, and the many parameters needed to express cancer incidence adequately (including proportion of tumor-bearing animals, the multiplicity of tumors in one organ or animal, time to development of tumors, cell type affected, and the growth rate and behavior of the cells). Simple $ED_{50}$ type expressions of potency are likely to be misleading even when used for comparative purposes.

In assessing carcinogenic potency, the following have been proposed as the important characteristics of experimental data (ECETOC 1982):

"Key information to be derived from such a study includes:
a) The proportion of animals bearing neoplasms at each exposure level.
   The number of neoplasms per animal.
   The number of different types of neoplasms.
   The number of species affected.
b) The magnitude of the dose at which the carcinogenic response occurs.
c) The organ or target tissue in which the carcinogenic response occurs. It should be recognised that an increase in the number of tumours of a type which occurs spontaneously in a high proportion of the strain of animal being used (e.g., liver tumours or pulmonary adenomas in certain strains of mice) carries less weight in the estimation of potency than does the appearance of tumours in other organs.
d) The latency period before tumour development. The shorter the latency period the more potent is the chemical.
e) The sensitivity of the experimental model.
f) Further information obtained from other toxicological studies such as kinetic and metabolic data. The significance of these in the estimation of potency to

man is not clear in every case. Fundamental differences in genetic make-up between animals and man, which can lead to wide variations in response to the action of chemicals, include differences in immune and hormonal status, among others. Only in those situations where it can be demonstrated that the active metabolite (or ultimate carcinogen) and the mechanism of action are the same in an animal and man, and where similarities in exposure conditions, kinetic, metabolic pathways and defence mechanisms have been established, would a quantitative extrapolation of potency have more meaning."

Knowledge of metabolism and mode of action, as has been demonstrated above, can be of particular importance in this context. Recent evidence of carcinogens acting without evidence of genetic effects leads to the view that clear thresholds may be present for genotoxic carcinogens, and for nongenotoxic carcinogens, the threshold may be determined economically by establishing the threshold for the primary toxic event.

The use of mathematical models to extrapolate the incidence at high-dose levels to the practical lower dose levels encountered by man is no more accurate than other estimates. There is a danger that the outcome from such calculations, often a number expressing risk at a given dose (or vice versa), provides a point estimate which is viewed as reliable. However, the selection of which model to use has as large an influence on the estimate as the experimental data; there is no guidance for selecting the "best" model on the basis of a knowledge of mechanism of action of carcinogens (because this is imperfectly understood) or on goodness-of-fit (because all models can be made to fit by suitable selection of variables).

Differences in the fate and rate of metabolism between high and low doses may also distort the estimates of most of the available models. Finally, such calculations can at best only provide a first estimate of incidence at low-dose levels in the strain and species under investigation.

Extrapolation from experimental data to the human situation is frequently assumed to be quantitatively and qualitatively identical (apart from some adjustment for differences in body size). In cases where a potent effect is observed in several species, it may be reasonable to assume that man behaves as do other species; in many cases this is not so. The evidence, although limited, is that substantial interspecies differences in response occur, and careful and painstaking scientific investigation is necessary to provide data for extrapolation.

## Risk Assessment

Ultimately, data derived from human observation provides the most relevant risk estimation, but unfortunately epidemiological studies suffer from two drawbacks: small size, which limits statistical power, and inadequate quantitative estimates of exposure. Where the human data can be combined with extrapolation from animal experiments and compatible risk estimates result, there is much greater confidence in the estimates.

The important stage in risk assessment is the definition of the conditions of exposure (Table 1, stage 4). The intrinsic properties of the substance (volatility, dustiness) have an important bearing on the route and likely level of exposure. The extent of exposure is also influenced by the use of the substance and the precautions taken to control exposure in that use. Detailed studies are needed to determine the level of exposure and even then we have no validated method of integrating intermittent or variable exposures or exposures by more than one route.

Finally, the integration of information derived from experimental work, epidemiology, and extent of exposure (Table 1, step 5) provides an overall risk assessment. This task relies on scientific data and judgment from a variety of experts, and there is no substitute for expert opinion and judgment at our present state of development.

## DESIRABLE CHARACTERISTICS OF RISK ASSESSMENT FOR REGULATORY PURPOSES

The single most important attribute of the risk assessment process is that it should provide an accurate assessment of risk. "Uncertainties in the risk estimation process should not lead to either over- or under-estimation of risk, as either could act against the best interests of society" (ECETOC 1980).

Risk assessment should share the other characteristics of scientific activities including reproducibility and compatibility with other knowledge (e.g., with known mechanisms of action). The ability to test the assumptions on which the assessment process is based is also an important attribute.

Currently available methods of risk assessment do not have all these attributes. In particular, the use of mathematical models is misleading because these models use a number of conservative assumptions (e.g., low-dose linearity, no threshold, and upper 95% confidence limits), which are untestable but designed not to provide an accurate estimate. They are frequently used in a way that disregards other biological and chemical knowledge and gives a spurious impression of precision as has been illustrated with vinyl chloride and trichloroethylene.

Regulatory policymakers do not yet have available to them a method that meets the criteria of accuracy, reproducibility, and compatibility outlined above. The step-by-step analysis using a consensus of scientific opinion is the best available method; indeed the similarity in national standards in Organization for Economic Cooperation and Development (OECD) countries provides encouragement for this pragmatic approach.

## REFERENCES

Anderson, N.L. 1982. Quantitative methods in use in the United States to assess cancer risk. Workshop on Quantitative Estimation of Risk to Human Health from Chemicals. Rome, Italy.

Anderson, M.W., D.G. Hoel, and N.L. Kaplan. 1980. A general scheme for the incorporation of pharmacokinetics in low-dose risk estimation for chemical carcinogens: Example —Vinyl chloride. *Toxicol. Appl. Pharmacol.* **55**: 154.

Barr, J.T. 1982. Risk assessment for vinyl chloride in perspective. Presented at the 75th Annual Meeting of the Air Pollution Control Association, New Orleans, U.S.A.

Carlborg, F.W. 1981. Dose-response functions in carcinogenesis and the Weibull model. *Food Cosmet. Toxicol.* **19**: 255.

ECETOC (European Chemical Industry Ecology and Toxicology Centre). 1980. *A contribution to the strategy for the identification and control of occupational carcinogens,* p. 1. European Chemical Industry Ecology and Toxicology Centre, Brussels, Belgium.

_____. 1982. *Risk assessment of occupational chemical carcinogens,* p. 1. European Chemical Industry. Ecology and Toxicology Centre, Brussels, Belgium.

Elcombe, C.R. 1985. Species differences in carcinogenicity and peroxisome proliferation due to trichloroethylene; a biochemical human hazard assesssment. *Arch. Toxicol.* (in press).

Feron, V.J., C.F.M. Hendrikson, A.J. Speek, H.P. Til, and B.J. Spit. 1981. Lifespan oral toxicity of vinyl chloride in rats. *Food Cosmet. Toxicol.* **19**: 317.

Food Safety Council Final Report. 1978. Proposed system for food safety assessment. *Food Cosmet. Toxicol.* **16(2)**: 1.

Food Safety Council Scientific Committee. 1980. Proposed system for food safety assessment. Food Safety Council, Washington, D.C.

Gaylor, D.W. and R.L. Kodell. 1980. Linear interpolation algorithm for low-dose risk assessment of toxic substances. *J. Environ. Pathol. Toxicol.* **4**: 305.

Gehring, P.J., P.G. Watanabe, and C.N. Park. 1979. Risk of angiosarcoma in workers exposed to vinyl chloride as predicted from studies in rats. *Toxicol. Appl. Pharmacol.* **49**: 15.

Green, T., and M.S. Prout. 1985. Species differences in response to trichloroethylene II. Biotransformation in rats and mice. *Toxicol. Appl. Pharmacol.* (in press).

Kuzmack, A.M. and R. E. McGoughy. 1975. Quantitative risk assessment for community exposure to vinyl chloride. Dec. 5, 1975. U.S. EPA, Washington, D.C.

Lee, C.C., J.C. Bhandari, J.M. Winston, W.B. House, and J.S. Woods. 1978. Carcinogenicity of vinyl chloride and vinylidine chloride. *J. Toxicol. Environ. Health* **4**: 15.

Maltoni, C., G. Lefimine, A. Ciliberti, G. Cotti, and D. Caretti. 1981. Carcinogenicity bioassays of vinyl chloride monomer: A model of risk assessment on an experimental basis. *Eviron. Health Perspect.* **41**: 3.

National Cancer Institute (N.C.I.). 1976. Carcinogenesis of bioassay of trichloroethylene. DHEW Publ. No. (NH) 76-802.

National Toxicology Program (N.T.P.). 1983. NTP draft report abstracts on nine chemical carcinogenesis bioassays. *Chem. Reg. Reporter* **6**: 767.

Prout, M.S., W.M. Provan, and T. Green. 1985. Species differences in response to trichloroethylene I. Pharmacokinetics in rats and mice. *Toxicol. Appl. Pharmacol.* (in press).

Purchase, I.F.H., J. Stafford, and G.M. Paddle. 1985. Vinyl chloride: A cancer case study. In *Toxicological risk assessment* (ed. D.B. Clayson). CRC Press, Boca Raton, Florida.

Reddy, J.K. and N.D. Lalwai. 1983. 1. Carcinogenesis by hepatic peroxisome proliferators: Evaluation of the risk of hypolipidemic drugs and industrial plasticizers to humans. *Crit. Rev. Toxicol.* **12(1)**: 1.

Schneiderman, M.A., N. Mantel, and C.C. Brown. 1975. From mouse to man—or how to get from the laboratory to Park Avenue and 59th Street. *Ann. N.Y. Acad. Sci.* **246**: 237.

Sors, A.I. 1982. Risk assessment and its use in management—A state-of-art review. In

*Evaluation and risk assessment of chemicals* (ed. A. Gilad et al.). Interim document No. 6, World Health Organization, Copenhagen.

## COMMENTS

**ALBERT:** You're assuming that trichloroacetic acid is the ultimate carcinogen for trichloroethylene. I understand you have a bioassay going on that.

**PURCHASE:** I wouldn't call it a bioassay. We don't have the resources available to the NTP, but we have a small long-term experiment, yes. It's only been running for about 25 or 30 weeks.

**ALBERT:** Is that showing any increase in peroxisomes?

**PURCHASE:** It shows an increase in the level of peroxisomes, but I don't know how much.

**PREUSS:** On the subject of peroxisome proliferation by trichloroethylene, if you had to do an assessment now for the compound, how would you take those data into account?

**PURCHASE:** The simple answer to that is that I would handle it as a toxic chemical and not as a carcinogen; and I would use the procedures which are used for liver toxicity or any other type of toxicity which don't involve mathematical models, but simpler methods such as safety factors.

**WEINSTEIN:** Why isn't it a carcinogen?

**PURCHASE:** Dr. Preuss asked me how we would take this information into account. I'm saying that, on the basis of the evidence we have so far, and if it is confirmed, one can conclude that humans are not going to be a responsive species to tricholoroethylene carcinogenesis.

**ALBERT:** But the idea of peroxisomes is Reddy's. He, himself, considers this a speculative mode of action.

**PURCHASE:** Absolutely, just the same sort of speculation as the DNA damage theory for genotoxic carcinogens being applied to nongenotoxic carcinogens.

**REITZ:** I'd like to comment that experience with hypolipidemic drugs in the pharmaceutical industry has suggested that, at least in animals, there is a correlation between peroxisome proliferation and increased incidence of hepatic cancer. That's another reason for suggesting that that mechanism may be involved.

**PREUSS:** Yes, there clearly is a correlation with the hypolipidemic drugs, but there's no demonstration that it's mechanistically involved, and there's no demonstration of anything beyond the simple correlation. In addition to which, you come to the question of whether the markers that you're using for peroxisome proliferation are sensitive enough. With some of the markers which initially led us to believe that there was no proliferation of peroxisomes, I have the feeling that the recent literature is showing some peroxisome proliferation at low dose.

**PERERA:** Regarding a point mentioned earlier, since TCE does induce protein, DNA, and RNA binding, I just don't know whether you can say, "That information isn't relevant; we'll put it aside and look only at this other mechanism."

**PURCHASE:** The degree and level of binding are so low that it is unlikely that it can explain the effect in mouse liver. Furthermore, DNA binding in vivo has been shown to be at or below the levels of detection.

**WEINSTEIN:** I wonder if it isn't a tumor promoter. Has it been tested in the Peraino liver tumor induction model?

**ALBERT:** No, it hasn't.

**SWENBERG:** Other agents that cause peroxisomal proliferation have, and they fail to induce increased numbers of altered ($GGt^+$) foci.

# Application of Model Systems in Pharmacokinetics*

**ROBERT L. DEDRICK**
Biomedical Engineering and Instrumentation Branch
Division of Research Services
National Institutes of Health
Bethesda, Maryland 20205

## OVERVIEW

Physiological pharmacokinetics provides a natural and clearly articulated basis for the integration of data from various sources. These may include pharmacokinetic studies in experimental animals, observations on man during the development of drugs or following accidental or occupational exposure to environmental contaminants, and a variety of thermodynamic and kinetic studies performed with tissues, cells, extracts, and other systems in vitro. The concepts are illustrated by a discussion of a pharmacokinetic model of cytosine arabinoside (Ara-C) in several species, one of several published examples of the use of in vitro data in pharmacokinetic models. Appropriate models can provide considerable insight into the definition of pharmacokinetic time scales. They can assist in the extrapolation from one biological system to another; and, in conjunction with pharmacodynamic ideas, they can strengthen the plausibility of risk estimation.

## INTRODUCTION

Allometry, the study of the relative growth of parts of organisms, has been one of the major unifying concepts in biology. Extension of the essentially morphometric ideas to the comparison of homologous physiological processes occurred relatively recently in an historic time scale, but the literature is now extensive and strongly interrelated (Adolph 1949; Stahl 1963; Schmidt-Nielsen 1970; Lindstedt and Calder 1981). Discussion continues with recognition of the theoretical problems of applying dimensional analysis to complex biological systems (Rosen 1983) and the empirical fact that a remarkably simple power function of body weight correlates much physiological data over a wide range of body sizes. This was illustrated in careful detail recently for the components of kidney structure and function (Calder and Braun 1983).

Application of allometric concepts to pharmacokinetics has been explored to a much more limited extent (Kleiber 1965; Dedrick et al. 1970; Bischoff et al. 1971;

---

* Condensed from paper presented at Workshop on Toxicokinetics in the Safety Evaluation of Chemicals, Electric Power Research Institute, San Diego, California. November 30–December 2, 1983 (Dedrick 1985).

Dedrick 1973). Such concepts appear to be useful for many purposes, but the range of applicability has not been validated in any general terms, and limitations on application of body-weight correlations to xenobiotic metabolism are well recognized.

Despite the strong influence of allometry in the development of biology and an underlying belief that experimental systems provide useful information about humans, disproportionate emphasis has been placed on species differences. This appears to derive from the culture of biology because differences among species have often been more interesting than similarities and because these differences can provide important information on the development of species. The differences have led to the recognition that no animal is the same as man in any general biological sense and that insistence on "sameness" in a model system is illusory.

I propose that we adopt more of an engineering-design view when we develop experimental systems in pharmacokinetics and attempt to use data from these systems for predictive purposes. If we do this, we are comforted by the fact that, in engineering systems as in biology, the model is never the same as the prototype. Interpretation is always required. In some simple engineering systems, concepts of similitude and dimensional analysis place design on a sound theoretical basis. But in more complex situations, rigorous similitude may not be attainable. In these cases, it is often possible to model parts of a complex system and use the model-dependent information in a design process which incorporates sound theoretical principles but often contains judgment and experience as well.

In this paper some of the interrelationships among model systems are illustrated by a specific pharmacokinetic example, and a few ideas are elaborated on the application of pharmacokinetics to toxicology. We hypothesize that it should be possible to use what is known or what is measurable in model systems in connection with physiological models to predict many pharmacokinetic events in other experimental systems and in man.

## RESULTS

Classical pharmacokinetics has been developed to describe the time course of drug and metabolite concentrations or amounts in accessible fluids and tissues, usually blood and urine. Statistical concepts are used to obtain parameters such as compartment sizes, intercompartment transport parameters, reaction rates, and clearances. In general, the parameters are mathematical ideas which are not easily related to the underlying anatomy and physiology. Classical pharmacokinetic models have been the mainstay of clinical pharmacology and have clearly shown their usefulness in adjustment of dose and schedule and in answering questions concerning bioavailability of particular dose forms. Linear one- and two-compartment open models have been used almost exclusively.

### Physiological Pharmacokinetics

Physiological pharmacokinetics derives from the assumption that the distribution and disposition of a foreign chemical in the body result from a complex set of

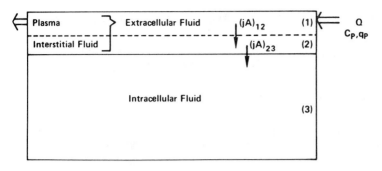

**Figure 1**
Diagram of compartment for pharmacokinetic analysis. Reprinted from Dedrick et al. (1973a).

physiological processes and biochemical interactions. It is generally assumed that the model parameters are measurable and have explicit meaning that may be independent of the particular drug or other chemical such as blood flow rates or organ sizes. Extensive didactic presentations are available (Lutz et al. 1980; Collins and Dedrick 1982; Gibaldi and Perrier 1982); so, only the basic principles are listed here.

A physiological pharmacokinetic model is based on anatomic compartments such as shown in Figure 1 (Dedrick et al. 1973a). The chemical enters the compartment with the blood flowing at a rate, $Q$. The state of the chemical may be characterized by the free concentration, $C$, or the total concentration, $q$. After it is inside the tissue, it may cross capillary membranes at a rate $(jA)_{12}$ and cell membranes at a rate $(jA)_{23}$. The chemical may bind to tissue components or may undergo a variety of chemical reactions or physiological processes such as excretion. In principle, each of the thermodynamic and rate processes can be described mathematically. Then, if a group of compartments is correctly organized anatomically, the set of implied mass-balance equations constitutes the pharmacokinetic model, and its solution provides the concentration of the chemical and its metabolites as a function of time in each compartment.

The structure of physiological models may be similar to that of classical pharmacokinetic models, but physiological models are generally more complex and require a significantly greater number of parameters. The complexity is the price for generalizability. Complexity is not as great as implied by the full model structure. Often one or a very small number of the rate processes are substantially slower than the others so that valid limiting model behavior is probable. Also, many of the parameters are independent of the particular chemical that is being studied or can be obtained from independent experiments designed for that purpose.

## Pharmacokinetic Example—Cytosine Arabinoside

There are now a substantial number of examples of the application of physiological pharmacokinetic principles to elucidate mechanism, account for species differences, and assist in the design of clinical trials. Many of these have been reviewed (Chen and Gross 1979; Himmelstein and Lutz 1979; Gerlowski and Jain 1983). The pharmacokinetics of cytosine arabinoside (Ara-C) illustrate the principles of physiological modeling and the operational basis for incorporating data from model systems.

Ara-C is a widely used anticancer drug that also appeared to be a good model compound with which to attempt in vitro–in vivo prediction (Dedrick et al. 1972; Dedrick et al. 1973b). The deaminase that catalyzes its inactivation to uracil arabinoside (Ara-U) varies considerably in its location and kinetic characteristics among mammalian species. Human liver deaminase has been studied thoroughly. It is specific in its substrate requirements, and no cofactor requirements or direct regulatory mechanisms have been demonstrated. Furthermore, plasma and tissue binding appears not to be significant so that thermodynamic difficulties are obviated. The resulting flow diagram is shown in Figure 2 in which the compartments have been chosen based on their size, physiological function, biochemical activity, or site of toxicity. Figure 3 presents the predicted concentrations of Ara-C and of total radioactivity (Ara-C plus Ara-U) in the plasma of a patient given Ara-C by intravenous injection and compares these predictions with experimental data. The only parameter used from this patient was the dose per unit body weight. All enzyme levels were based on in vitro studies of tissue homogenates.

Examination of the deaminase activities listed in Table 1 shows the futility of attempting a traditional allometric correlation of metabolism. However, if the kidney clearances, based on a physiological process, are plotted versus body weight on log-log paper, as shown in Figure 4, a good linear correlation with a slope of 0.80 is obtained. This slope may be compared with the value for inulin of 0.77 obtained by Adolph (1949) or 0.72 cited by Calder and Braun (1983).

## DISCUSSION

Pharmacokinetics has recently attracted considerable attention in risk assessment. This attention results from the supposition that toxicity produced by foreign chemicals in the body is generally mediated by essentially chemical processes. Usually chemical concentrations in animals can be measured with much greater sensitivity than bioassays involving whole organisms.

### Extrapolation from One Biological System to Another

Physiological pharmacokinetics provides a natural framework for use of information determined in various model systems, and there is a growing literature on in vitro–in vivo correlations. Although the subject has not been explored in great detail, there is considerable evidence that many thermodynamic and kinetic data from in vitro systems can be used successfully for quantitative prediction in intact animals if properly constructed mathematical models are employed. Predictions may be tested explicitly for drugs, such as Ara-C discussed above, because therapeutic

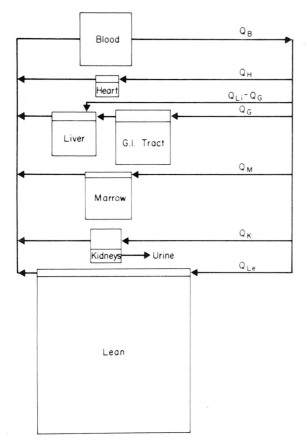

**Figure 2**
Compartmental model for Ara-C pharmacokinetics. The compartment volumes are approximately proportional to areas in the figure. Reprinted from Dedrick et al. (1973b).

intent allows ethical pharmacokinetic studies in humans. Toxic chemicals with no known therapeutic applications pose a different problem. Our working hypothesis is that thermodynamic factors such as tissue-to-blood distribution ratios are more likely to be similar among mammalian species than intrinsic rates of metabolism. The suppositions concerning both thermodynamics and metabolism would be very greatly strengthened if supported by comparative studies on human and animal tissues. The in vitro studies would provide a way to adjust parameter estimates and revise pharmacokinetic predictions.

## Assessing Time Scales of Interest

For many purposes, detailed pharmacokinetic calculations are not required. Questions arise concerning the appropriate schedule for sampling during a pharmacokinetic study, the accumulation of a chemical during extended feeding studies, the

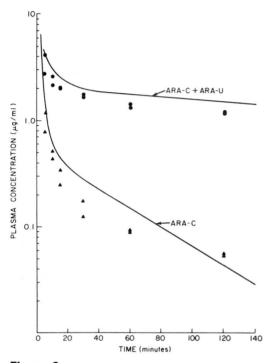

**Figure 3**

Predicted concentrations of Ara-C and total radioactivity in the plasma after a pulse dose of 1.2 mg/kg, i.v. Data points represent two different injections of Ara-C in a 70 kg woman. Reprinted from Dedrick et. al. (1972).

time required for distribution into a compartment or redistribution among compartments, and the likelihood of a chemical's persistence for long periods of time. Even in the absence of a detailed pharmacokinetic model, some rather powerful statements can be made about pharmacokinetic time scales, and these show an extraordinary range. At one end of the scale, certain activated chemical intermediates are so short lived that their probability of even leaving the cell where they are produced is small, and adequate methodology to observe the kinetics needs to be developed. At the other end of the time scale, some very persistent materials would not be significantly eliminated from the body of the host during a lifetime.

The structure of a pharmacokinetic model suggests a natural time scale (T) which has the form of a volume (V) divided by a flow (Q) or a volume divided by a clearance (k)

$$T = RV/Q \text{ or } RV/k$$

where R is the tissue-to-blood or tissue-to-plasma distribution coefficient. The product RV represents the physiological volume of distribution. In a one-compartment approximation, the volume of distribution of the whole animal can be obtained by summing the RV terms for all tissues.

## Table 1
Model Parameter for Cytosine Arabinoside in Several Species

| Parameter | Mouse | Monkey | Dog | Man |
|---|---|---|---|---|
| Body wt (g) | 22 | 5000 | 10,000 | 70,000 |
| Michaelis constant ($\mu$g/ml $H_2O$) | 283 | 39 | 115 | 39 |
| Deaminase activity ($\mu$g/g-min) | | | | |
| Blood | | 1.6 | | |
| Liver | 4.6 | 80.2 | 7 | 119 |
| Gut | 8.3 | | | |
| Heart | | 57.0 | | 6 |
| Kidney | 91.5 | 71.8 | | 20 |
| Lean | | 34.3 | | |
| Marrow | | | | |
| Kidney clearance (ml/min) | 0.18 | 14 | 32 | 90 |

Reprinted from Dedrick et al. (1973b).

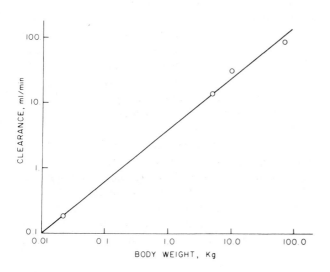

## Figure 4
Kidney clearance of Ara-C and Ara-U vs. body weight for mice, monkeys, dogs, and humans. Reprinted from Dedrick et al. (1973b).

## Pharmacodynamic Models

Pharmacodynamic models describe drug effects. There is a limited but significant literature on the pharmacodynamics of drugs which could be adapted to other agents; however, relatively little has been done for environmental contaminants. At the biochemical level, interactions may be expected to be some function of concentration of an active species and time (pharmacokinetics), but the function may not be simple. A reversible inhibitor may need to be present above an inhibitory level for a period of time before any biological effect can be demonstrated. This can lead to extreme schedule dependence so that the concept of dose-response is not generally valid. Schedule dependence has been well documented in the literature on anticancer drugs. For example, an infusion of 3 mg/kg of the folic acid antagonist methotrexate during 96 hours is more toxic to mice than a single dose of 350 mg/kg (Zaharko 1974). The biochemical effect of an irreversible reaction, such as alkylation, may be correlated better with the area under the concentration-time curve. Again, there may not be a close temporal relationship between the biochemical interaction and observed biological effect.

## Risk Estimation

If the parent chemical is the toxic species, then pharmacokinetic models for the parent can be used in conjunction with pharmacodynamic models to estimate biological effect. If a metabolite is the toxic species, then the details of the chemistry can, in principle, be incorporated into the pharmacokinetic model. For example, Morrison et al. (1975), realizing that the triphosphate of Ara-C (Ara-CTP) is the active species, modified the Ara-C model described to include the appropriate metabolic steps. Their model showed that Ara-CTP concentrations follow a very different time course than the parent drug.

The metabolic activation of many environmental contaminants to more toxic forms is well established. The kinetic implications have been discussed (Gillette 1976, 1977), and numerical simulations including nonlinear reactions have been described by Gehring and Blau (1977). It has been suggested that risk estimation could incorporate the amount of chemical metabolized (Gehring et al. 1978), covalent binding to macromolecules (McKenna et al. 1977; Dedrick 1979), or specific levels of DNA adduct formation (Hoel et al. 1983).

Xenobiotic metabolism may involve a rather complex set of chemical steps. Rates of individual reactions within the set and even qualitative features may vary considerably among species. Because of this, we will not be able to explore the metabolism of very many chemicals in the detail required to describe all of the intermediate reactions and their kinetic characteristics. However, we may be able to uncover some general behaviors of biochemical networks by means of mathematical analyses that would not require complete elucidation of every individual step.

# REFERENCES

Adolph, E.F. 1949. Quantitative relations in the physiological constitutions of mammals. *Science* **109:** 579.

Bischoff, K.B., R.L. Dedrick, D.S. Zaharko, and J.A. Longstreth. 1971. Methotrexate pharmacokinetics. *J. Pharm. Sci.* **60:** 1128.

Calder, W.A. and E.J. Braun. 1983. Scaling of osmotic regulation in mammals and birds. *Am. J. Physiol.* **244** (*Regulatory Integrative Comp. Physiol.*) **13:** R601.

Chen, H.-S.G. and J.F. Gross. 1979. Physiologically based pharmacokinetic models for anticancer drugs. *Cancer Chemother. Pharmacol.* **2:** 85.

Collins, J.M. and R.L. Dedrick. 1982. Pharmacokinetics of anticancer drugs. In *Pharmacologic principles of cancer treatment* (ed. B.A. Chabner), p. 77. W.B. Saunders, Philadelphia.

Dedrick, R.L. 1973. Animal scale-up. *J. Pharmacokinet. Biopharm.* **1:** 435.

_____. 1979. *Environ. Health Perspect.* **28:** 311.

_____. 1985. Application of model systems in pharmacokinetics. In *New directions in the extrapolation of animal data to man,* vol. 2. *Toxicokinetics* (ed. A. Silvers and G.W. Newell). Electric Power Research Institute, Palo Alto, California. (In press).

Dedrick, R.L., K.B. Bischoff, and D.S. Zaharko. 1970. Interspecies correlation of plasma concentration history of methotrexate (NSC-740). *Cancer Chemother. Rep.* **54:** 95.

Dedrick, R.L., D.D. Forrester, and D.H.W. Ho. 1972. In vitro-in vivo correlation of drug metabolism—Deamination of 1-β-D-arabinofuranosylcytosine. *Biochem. Pharmacol.* **21:** 1.

Dedrick, R.L., D.S. Zaharko, and R.J. Lutz. 1973a. Transport and binding of methotrexate in vivo. *J. Pharm. Sci.* **62:** 882.

Dedrick, R.L., D.D. Forrester, J.N. Cannon, S.M. El Dareer, and L.B. Mellett. 1973b. Pharmacokinetics of 1-β-D-arabinofuranosylcytosine (Ara-C) deamination in several species. *Biochem. Pharmacol.* **22:** 2405.

Gehring, P.J. and G.E. Blau. 1977. Mechanisms of carcinogenesis: Dose response. *J. Environ. Pathol. Toxicol.* **1:** 163.

Gehring, P.J., P.G. Watanabe, and C.N. Park. 1978. Resolution of dose-response toxicity data for chemicals requiring metabolic activation: Example—Vinyl chloride. *Toxicol. Appl. Pharmacol.* **44:** 581.

Gerlowski, L.E. and R.K. Jain. 1983. Physiologically based pharmacokinetic modeling: Principles and applications. *J. Pharm. Sci.* **72:** 1103.

Gibaldi, M. and D. Perrier. 1982. *Pharmacokinetics,* 2nd ed., p. 355. Marcel Dekker, New York.

Gillette, J.R. 1976. Application of pharmacokinetic principles in the extrapolation of animal data to humans. *Clin. Toxicol.* **9:** 709.

_____. 1977. Kinetics of reactive metabolites and covalent binding in vivo and in vitro. In *Biologically reactive intermediates* (ed. D.J. Jallow et al.), p. 25. Plenum Publishing, New York.

Himmelstein, K.J. and R.J. Lutz. 1979. A review of the applications of physiologically based pharmacokinetic modeling. *J. Pharmacokinet. Biopharm.* **7:** 127.

Hoel, D.G., N.L. Kaplan, and M.W. Anderson. 1983. Implications of nonlinear kinetics on risk estimation in carcinogenesis. *Science* **219:** 1032.

Kleiber, M. 1965. In *Handbook of physiology—Respiration II,* p. 927. American Physiological Society, Washington, D.C.

Lindstedt, S.L. and W.A. Calder. 1981. Body size, physiological time, and longevity of homeothermic animals. *Q. Rev. Biol.* **56:** 1.

Lutz, R.J., R.L. Dedrick, and D.S. Zaharko. 1980. Physiological pharmacokinetics: An in vivo approach to membrane transport. *Pharmacol. Ther.* **11:** 559.

McKenna, M.J., P.G. Watanabe, and P.J. Gehring. 1977. Pharmacokinetics of vinylidine chloride in the rat. *Environ. Health Perspect.* **21:** 99.

Morrison, P.F., T.L. Lincoln, and J. Aroesty. 1975. Disposition of cytosine arabinoside (NSC-63878) and its metabolites: A pharmacokinetic simulation. *Cancer Chemother. Rep.* **59:** 861.

Rosen, R. 1983. Role of similarity principles in data extrapolation. *Am. J. Physiol.* **244** (*Regulatory Integrative Comp. Physiol.*) **13:** R591.

Schmidt-Nielsen, K. 1970. Energy metabolism, body size, physiological time, and longevity of homeothermic animals. *Fed. Proc.* **29:** 1524.

Stahl, W.R. 1963. The analysis of biological similarity. In *Advances in biological and medical physics* (ed. J.H. Lawrence and J.W. Gofman), vol. 9, p. 335. Academic Press, New York.

Zaharko, D.S. 1974. Pharmacokinetics and drug effect. *Biochem. Pharmacol.* (Suppl.) **2:** 1.

## COMMENTS

**WEINSTEIN:** One of the most difficult things to assess is the role of specific metabolites. Dr. Purchase described species differences in the conversion of TCE to TCA. Unless you know that this occurs, that part of your model contains a major unknown. In the case of Ara-C, you'd have to know that the active metabolite is ara-C-triphosphate. Thus, in assessing these chemicals, and there are so many to assess, to do the mathematical modeling correctly, you would have to make each assessment a biochemical project.

**DEDRICK:** Perhaps for a complete model—but not necessarily for a "correct" model. I think that there probably are some simplified, perhaps even simplistic, ways of thinking through the model structure without knowing all the details. Certainly that's going to be necessary, because there's no way that a full Ara-C type workup is going to be done on each of the thousands of chemicals of potential concern.

**WEINSTEIN:** Although if it is an important chemical of major economic value, then maybe it's best to stop and do a complete assessment of metabolism.

**PIKE:** For human risk assessment from animal work, it has never been assumed that the affected organ had to be the same. Iain's [Purchase] discussion of metabolic pathway differences in the liver of man and various animal species may only be very important if we have to assume that liver cancer is what we have to be concerned with for that chemical in man as well as in the experimental animals. However, apparently in contrast to the situation in many animals, liver is a very resistant organ in man, and risk assessment procedures have instead considered cancer in the whole animal. It has, of course, been recognized that this attitude is rather unbiological. Iain [Purchase] is recommending that we do risk assessment organ by organ. This would be a profound change in attitude. It does, however, have a great deal of merit.

**WEINSTEIN:**   That could be good or bad. It might be that certain species have a specific type of liver metabolism which makes a compound a liver carcinogen in that species, whereas in other species another tissue is the target for carcinogenic action.

**PIKE:**   But you wouldn't know that.

**CORN:**   Isn't that what we've been saying for years—that the target organ is what we're really interested in, but we don't know how to get to it, so we'll talk about the whole animal? Thus, it's just a natural evolution with some promise of getting to the target organ. This modeling is a first step. You indicate that once you're at the target organ you have to go further.

**R. WILSON:**   Dr. Purchase might find a difference in metabolic processes between rat and mouse or some other animal. Then, by looking at a particular indicator, he might say, "Humans are not as sensitive to trichloroethylene as rats." This might be used to modify the usual animal-to-man extrapolation. But then I worry about the following: The standard statement one makes in using animal tests to estimate the risk to man is that an animal in its life of 2 years will get about as much cancer as a man in his 70-year life, within a factor of ten or so, if fed the same amount relative to its weight (or surface area). Now, if I note that cancer varies with the fourth power of age, and I make a much simpler assumption that a piece of flesh is the same whether it's in a mouse or in a man, that should be a factor of $(70/2)^4 \times (70\ kg/400\ g)\ 35^4$ or about a factor of 100 million difference in carcinogenic sensitivity. So somehow the differences in metabolism in some way or another make up for this factor of 100 million. Are these differences that Dr. Purchase found in trichloroethylene just part of that expression of the metabolism, or are they something additional? Because, if it is something additional, it should be included in the risk assessment; if it is part of the overall difference in metabolism, we have already included it somehow. I'm worried about the double counting effect.

**PURCHASE:**   All I can say is for other toxic phenomena it is possible on occasions to mimic the situation in animals and humans quite precisely. Take for example the accumulation of paraquat into the lung after a single dose; what happens in the human happens in the human tissue in vitro, and you can measure kinetics comparable to those in the rat. The whole thing fits together very well indeed.

**R. WILSON:**   So this would be additional to the metabolic factor of 100 million that is somehow needed in going from an animal to a human for an average chemical?

**PURCHASE:**  I don't know about that.

**DEDRICK:**  We have extrapolated the metabolic clearance of 2,3,7,8-TCDF to man from studies in mice, rats, and monkeys. Based on very limited published data for man, I don't think that our prediction was greatly in error, but I'd feel much more comfortable if we had comparative studies done on human liver and liver from any one of those other species. Relevant to the point on lifespan made by Dr. Wilson, a fairly good correlation is found between lifespan and body size of mammals. If you plot the lifespan versus the body weight on a log-log scale, you obtain a reasonable correlation from mice to elephants. But the human is an outlier. We live longer than a 70-kg mammal should. This observation may have some implications for human risk estimation.

**NEEL:**  I think the point that Dr. Wilson has just made is going to come up consistently at this meeting. The cancer incidence curves of humans and mice have the same shape, but there is an enormous difference in lifespan. Therefore, if I believe a mutagenic type of event touches off cancer, the human must have evolved pretty good repair mechanisms to live as long as he does and to get by with as few offspring as he has. There is one piece of evidence that tends to back that up. Now that we can use the same sorts of indicators—namely proteins—for mutation rates, the rates in *Drosophila,* mouse and man per generation are emerging within a factor of two or three of each other, despite the enormous differences in lifespan and body temperature.

# Biological Variation: The Unsolvable Problem in Quantitative Extrapolations from Laboratory Animals and Other Surrogate Systems to Human Populations

JAMES R. GILLETTE
Laboratory of Chemical Pharmacology
National Heart, Lung, and Blood Institute
National Institutes of Health
Bethesda, Maryland 20205

## OVERVIEW

One of the difficulties in making quantitative estimates of the rate of occurrence of toxicities in the human population solely from data obtained with laboratory animals is the heterogeneity that exists in the human population. Since for good reasons toxicity studies are almost invariably performed with homogeneous strains of animals kept under carefully controlled environmental conditions, there is no way that any given strain of animals can adequately mimic the entire human population. Nevertheless, there is no reasonable alternative to the use of data obtained with homogeneous animal strains together with arbitrary safety factors in making first approximations of acceptable risks.

## INTRODUCTION

The obvious objective of risk assessment is to estimate the rate of occurrence of a given biological response at any given dose of a given substance in the human population or in the populations of other organisms in the environment. For many theoretical as well as practical reasons, however, this objective is virtually unattainable, even for compounds that are already present in the environment.

## SOURCES OF VARIANCE

Whether a given individual within the human population manifests a disease caused by an environmental substance present in air, water, soil, food or drugs, and cosmetics depends on the answers to four fundamental questions: (1) How much of the substance is present in the environment of the individual human? (2) How much of the substance in the environment reaches action sites within the individual? (3) Is the amount or concentration of the substance at action sites sufficient to evoke a significant response of the substance at its action sites? (4) In the individual, does

**199**

the transduction system that relates the action of the substance on action sites to the manifestation of the toxicity make the individual unusually sensitive or resistant to the substance?

Many of the difficulties in answering the first question are obvious. The distribution of any substance on earth can differ markedly from one location to another and usually changes with time. Moreover, any given individual is exposed to several different environments not only from year to year, but even within the same day. Indeed, even with drugs prescribed by physicians, the dose is uncertain because the patient may not have taken the drug exactly as prescribed.

For any given individual at any given time, the concentration of the parent substance at putative action sites may be assessed by standard pharmacokinetic techniques (Gibaldi and Perrier 1975; Rowland and Tozer 1980). Many of the pharmacokinetic parameters, however, can be highly variable, even in the same individual. For example, the rate and even the extent of absorption of a substance from the gastrointestinal tract may depend not only on the physical state of the ingested substance and the emptying time of the stomach but also on the physicochemical properties of the substance, the volume of the intestinal contents, the motility of the intestinal tract, and the presence or absence of transport systems. After the substance enters the blood, the rate and extent of distribution of the substance to various cells within organs in turn depends on the diffusivity of the substance through various membranes, the extent to which the substance is reversibly bound to various extracellular and intracellular components, and sometimes the blood flow rate through the various organs. The rate at which the compound is eliminated from the body depends on the principal mechanisms of elimination. For substances that are eliminated predominantly by renal excretion, rate and the total body clearance of the substance will obviously depend predominantly on renal function. For such substances, the rate of elimination of the substance by an individual may change with age and with the presence of acute and chronic renal disease. For substances that are eliminated by the bile, the rate of elimination and the total body clearance of the substance will depend on the rate and extent of enterohepatic circulation of the substance (Smith 1973; Gillette and Pang 1977). For substances that are eliminated predominantly by conversion to metabolic products, the rate of elimination and the total body clearance of the substance will depend predominantly on the activities of the enzymes that catalyze the metabolism of the substance in various organs and, to a certain extent, on the blood flow rates through the organs (Gillette and Pang 1977). The blood flow rates through organs, however, may be changed by cardiovascular diseases and the administration of cardiovascular drugs. Moreover, the activity of the enzymes may be altered by various inducers and inhibitors (Conney 1967), but owing to the plethora and diversity of substrate specificity of these enzymes in the body (Jakoby 1980; Sato and Kato 1982), induction or inhibition of given isozymes of these enzymes usually will alter the metabolism of different substances to different extents.

Although the pharmacokinetic factors that govern the concentration of the parent substance at putative action sites will also affect the pharmacokinetic factors that govern the maximum, minimum, and average concentrations of any of the metabolites of the substance, they are not the only factors (Gillette 1980; 1982). Thus, pharmacokinetic studies of the parent compound rarely provide sufficient information to describe the pharmacokinetics of metabolites. Since many toxicities are mediated to various extents by metabolites of environmental substances, more extensive pharmacokinetic studies may be needed to describe this part of the mechanism of toxicity.

A substance may exert a biological effect in many different ways. Some exert their action by promoting the release of endogenous substances from storage sites. Some combine reversibly with receptor sites and thereby either mimic or block the actions of endogenous substances. Some act by inhibiting either reversibly or irreversibly enzymes that synthesize vital endogenous substances, thereby altering the concentrations of these endogenous substances. Some react irreversibly with various intracellular components, including DNA, and thereby alter cellular biochemistry and replication. Whether the magnitude of the response is more closely related to the maximum, minimum, or average concentration of the environmental substance depends on the mechanism of response at putative action sites (Gillette 1984). To relate the pharmacokinetics of substances at putative action sites to a magnitude of response of the altered action sites thus requires at least some knowledge of the mechanism by which the active form of the substance alters the sites. Whatever the mechanism, however, there is little doubt that there can be marked individual differences in the action sites and the kinetics by which the substance alters the sites.

After the active form reacts with the action sites, a series of biochemical, physiological, and morphological changes usually occur, which result in the manifestation of the response. These transduction mechanisms obviously depend on the response. Frequently, however, the magnitude of the response may be either increased or decreased by altering one or more of the intermediate changes. For example, the manifestation of a carcinogen depends not only on the amount of substance that becomes covalently bound to DNA, but also on the effectiveness of DNA repair mechanisms and the presence and effectiveness of various promotors of carcinogenesis. Again there can be marked individual differences in these transduction mechanisms, but the magnitude of the variances may differ with the kind of response.

## VARIANCES IN HUMANS

Variations in the factors represented by each of the parts of a toxic mechanism contribute to the total variance of the human population. The relative contributions of each of the parts, however, may vary with the subpopulation and the toxicant.

It is now known that there are marked differences in the activities of the enzymes that catalyze the metabolism of environmental chemicals among individuals in the human populations. Indeed, it is not uncommon to find 20-fold or even 50-fold differences in the total body clearances of a substance even in small groups of test subjects (Rowland and Tozer 1980). With other substances, the variances appear to be relatively small. Since the variances can differ markedly with the substance, studies demonstrating the variance with one substance are not particularly useful in predicting the variances of other substances. Some variations in pharmacokinetic factors are due to genetic differences which result in different relative and total amounts of isozymes of the enzymes whereas other variances are due to genetic differences which govern the way an individual responds to various environmental factors including inducers and inhibitors. Moreover, individuals possessing these heritable differences are heterogenously distributed on earth. Thus it seems unlikely that the variance in the metabolism and elimination of any environmental substance will ever be exactly known. Since there are now about 4 billion of us on earth, however, it seems likely that the range of values for the total body metabolic clearances could be quite large.

## ANALYSIS OF VARIANCES

In many instances, the variances in the kinetics of the reaction of substances with action sites and the subsequent events that lead to the manifestation of the toxicity may be as large as or even larger than the variances in the pharmacokinetic factors. The relative contributions of the variance in the pharmacokinetic factors and the variance in these pharmacodynamic factors, however, will undoubtedly vary with the kind of response, with the toxicant, and with the population. In some instances, the variance in the factors that govern the pharmacokinetic relationship (pharmacokinetic factors) and the variance in the factors that govern the responsiveness of the human population to the substance (pharmacodynamic factors) may be about the same (Fig. 1). Thus at any given dose of a toxicant, an individual in group A would manifest the toxicity, whereas individuals in groups B, C, and D would not manifest the toxicity, but for different reasons. With some toxicants, however, the variance in the pharmacokinetic factors may be considerably less than the variance of the pharmacodynamic factors or vice versa. In addition, however, the total human population may comprise two (or more) markedly different subpopulations which may result in bimodal or multimodal dose-response curves. Thus at a given dose, a substance may evoke the toxicity in subpopulation A in Figure 2, but not in other subpopulations B, C, and D in Figure 2.

It should be kept in mind that a substance may cause several different responses by different mechanisms. Thus several different diagrams representing each of the responses may be drawn to show the relative contributions of the variances of the pharmacokinetic and pharmacodynamic factors. A given individual, however, may be located in different parts of each of the diagrams, especially when the responses are caused by different metabolites of the substance and by different mechanisms. Thus, there is no assurance that the order of appearance of the various responses with increasing doses will be the same for all individuals in the human population.

Because various human subpopulations are heterogenously distributed on earth, there is no assurance that all of the subpopulations would be represented in a small group of human subjects selected for clinical investigation. Thus, a failure to observe

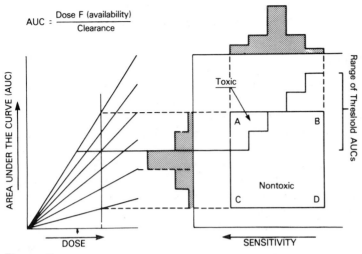

**Figure 1**

An analysis of variance of the effects of a dose of a hypothetical toxicant in the human population. A, B, C, and D represent either individuals in the human populations or surrogate strains of animals that represent different subpopulations.

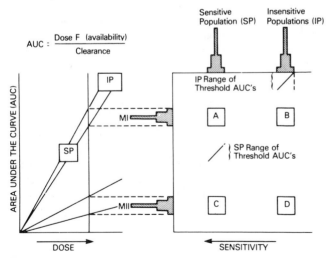

**Figure 2**

An analysis of variance of the effects of a dose of a hypothetical toxicant in either different human subpopulations or in different strains of different species of animals.

a toxicity in such studies does not always mean that a given substance would fail to cause toxicities in subpopulations not represented in the study. As Carl Sagan (1977) has written, ". . . absence of evidence is not evidence of absence."

## ANIMAL STUDIES

Because of the difficulty in evaluating the variance in the human population for substances already in the environment and the impossibility of predicting it for substances not in the environment, toxicologists have turned their attention to toxicity studies in animals and other surrogate systems. Unfortunately, the purposes and limitations of such studies have not always been clear to many investigators. Obviously, the initial and sometimes the sole purpose of such studies is to determine whether a substance can cause, either directly or indirectly, biochemical, physiological, or morphological changes in the test system under the conditions of the experiment. Because large variations in the normal values of biological systems would decrease the sensitivity of the experiment, the animals or surrogate systems are specifically selected to be as homogenous as possible. Moreover, because the number of animals is limited in such studies, usually no more than 100 to 1000, the lowest detectable incidence rate would be within this range, and thus doses of the substance used in the experiment are likely to be large.

## EXTRAPOLATION MODELS

Of course, one would like to be able to extrapolate the information obtained with a single experiment with one strain of an organism to populations of other organisms including the human population, but the validity of such extrapolations depends on the question asked. It is one kind of extrapolation to suggest that a substance that causes a biological response in a homogenous strain of test animals might cause a similar response in at least some individuals of a heterogeneous population of another animal species including the human population. But it is quite another kind to attempt to predict accurately ($\pm$ 50%) from test animal data alone the incidence rate of the response at any given dose of the substance in the heterogeneous population in various heterogenous environments.

Various investigators have suggested different mathematical models as aids in making extrapolations from high doses to low doses and from small experimental animals to the human population. Most of these models, however, have been based on the assumptions that there is no variance within the populations of experimental animals and humans and no differences in the $ED_{50}$ values between populations. Other models estimate the variances of the population of the test animals but, of course, cannot predict the variance in the human population.

The size of the variances for both the pharmacokinetic factors and the pharmacodynamic factors are undoubtedly smaller for the homogeneous test animals than for the total human population in uncontrolled and widely diverse environments. Toxicity studies with different groups of test animals of different species or even of different strains may provide markedly different dose-response curves, but each group may represent some human subpopulation. This might be represented by overlaying Figure 2, which may represent the results of the four test groups, on Figure 1, which may represent the human population. The problem is that there would be no way of knowing a priori which, if any, of the groups represented the major portion of the human population. Since clinical trials of drugs are also performed with small groups, it should be no surprise that some investigators have concluded that "animal studies, no matter how exhaustive, do not predict the outcome of administering a new drug to humans" (Goldstein et al. 1968).

In any effort to improve the predictability, some investigators have sought "animal species that metabolize drugs similar to man," but I wonder what they mean. The metabolism of a substance in any homogeneous strain of an animal species could represent only a portion of the human population and not the entire human population. Moreover, different strains or species may metabolize the substance quite differently and still represent different human subpopulations.

## SAFETY FACTORS

It is prudent to accept the view that a substance which causes a toxicity in any animal species might cause the toxicity in a human subpopulation. But attempts to predict accurately the rate of occurrence of the toxicity caused by any given dose of the substance are doomed to failure. Most investigators have suggested the use of safety factors (usually $10^{-2}$–$10^{-3}$) to predict the rate of occurrence of toxicities in humans. To the extent that such safety factors follow the maxim that "The smaller the dose of a substance, the lower the incidence of response," they are valid. Although some investigators have inferred that given safety factors have a universally valid rational basis, such arguments, like a matador's cape, attract much attention but in reality have little substance. At best, safety factors provide only first guesses of the doses that we hope will result in acceptable risks. Nevertheless, it is essential that a consensus for an arbitrary safety factor be obtained. Since they will inevitably fail with some substances, however, they will never replace the need for epidemiological studies and toxicity reporting programs.

## REFERENCES

Conney, A.H. 1967. Pharmacological implications of microsomal enzyme inducton. *Pharmacol. Rev.* **19**: 317.

Gibaldi, M. and D. Perrier. 1975. *Pharmacokinetics*. Marcel Dekker, New York.

Gillette, J.R. 1980. Kinetic aspects of metabolism and elimination of foreign compounds in animals. In *Enzymatic basis of detoxication* (ed. W.B. Jakoby), vol. 1, p. 9. Academic Press, New York.

———. 1982. The problem of chemically reactive metabolites. *Drug Metab. Rev.* **13**: 941.

———. 1984. Solvable and unsolvable problems in extrapolating toxicological data between animal species and strains. In *Drug metabolism and drug toxicity* (ed. J.R. Mitchell and M.G. Horning), p. 237. Raven Press, New York.

Gillette, J.R. and K.S. Pang. 1977. Theoretical aspects of pharmacokinetic drug interactions. *Clin. Pharmacol.* **22:** 623.

Goldstein, A., L. Aronow, and S.M. Kalman. 1968. *Principles of drug action: The basis of pharmacology,* p. 793. Harper and Row, New York.

Jakoby, W.B. 1980. *Enzymatic basis of detoxication.* Academic Press, New York.

Rowland, M. and T.N. Tozer. 1980. *Clinical pharmacokinetics: Concepts and applications.* Lea and Febiger, Philadelphia.

Sagan, C. 1977. *The dragons of Eden. Speculations on the evolution of human intelligence.* Ballantine Books, New York.

Sato, R. and R. Kato. 1982. *Microsomes, drug oxidations and drug toxicity.* Wiley-Interscience, New York.

Smith, R.L. 1973. *The excretory function of bile: The elimination of drugs and toxic substances in bile.* Chapman and Hall, London, England.

## COMMENTS

**NEEL:**   As somebody who has made a living dealing with human variations for the past 30 or so years, I can fully applaud what you just said. But, as you've already heard me be critical of the generality of the results based on any one inbred strain, with respect to genetic endpoints, I would also be critical on the toxicological front. In the next several decades, what are the chances of the people who are doing lab work shifting over to using non-inbred strains? It would, of course, increase the numbers of animals in experiments. Would the use of outbred strains be a step in the right direction?

**GILLETTE:**   No, I don't think so, because it is going to be impossible to predict the variance in the human population from animal experiments, whether outbred or inbred strains are used. You also sacrifice the power of the test when the variance within the strains of animals used in toxicity studies is increased.

**NEEL:**   But you lose the power to get a false answer.

**GILLETTE:**   No. It depends on the objective of the experiment. As far as I'm concerned, an animal test has only one major initial objective and that is to determine whether a given chemical can cause a toxic response under the defined conditions of the experiment. To achieve this objective, the population of the animals used in the study should be as homogeneous as possible.

**NEEL:**   But the more homogeneous your population, the greater the likelihood that you'll get an atypical answer.

**GILLETTE:**   Atypical with whom? With 4 billion of us in the world, we would have 4 billion different answers. Everybody's going to respond to a compound a little bit differently. The point I wish to make here is that the objectives of animal studies should be very limited. The first objective of a toxicology test, in fact the sole objective in some cases, is to determine whether a compound can cause a toxicity. The second objective is to determine how the compound causes the toxicity. Such studies raise the possibility that they might have relevance in another population, but the relevance would have to be confirmed by studies in the other population.

**PURCHASE:** In a sense, the discussion you've just been having is a bit illusory because the difference between inbred and outbred strains of the commonly available laboratory animals is not that great for most of these phenomena. Most outbred strains have an inbreeding of 20% by the time you've had them in the lab for 30 or 40 years, and there's not that much evidence to suggest that they are so much better in the terms that Dr. Neel is talking about than the inbred strains.

**WEINSTEIN:** There are certainly examples of major differences in drug metabolism between inbred strains, such as in aryl hydrocarbon hydroxylase.

**GILLETTE:** But there would be no way of predicting a priori which strain is going to predict the effects in the majority of the human population.

**WEINSTEIN:** Are you completely pessimistic about establishing some general patterns of species differences in certain drug-metabolizing enzymes? Aren't there such patterns in the literature?

**GILLETTE:** The variations between two strains of animals of the same species can be as great as the variations between species. Thus, it is not entirely accurate to say that one species does this and the other species does that. Moreover, the range of differences in the human population in the metabolism of drugs is unknown, but it could be very large.

**ALBERT:** How do you explain that people are still using animals?

**GILLETTE:** The principal reasons are to establish general principles and to demonstrate the plausibility of different mechanisms. As one of my friends, Dr. Gerhard Levy, once said, "We extrapolate knowledge, we don't extrapolate numbers." If a compound is capable of causing a toxicity, then it must cause it by a certain mechanism. If you understand that mechanism, then you may be able to suggest that the general mechanism might occur in other mammalian systems. Elucidation of the key elements of the mechanism presumably should alert investigators to search for those elements in other mammalian species.

**PETO:** The trouble with all these adjustments, such as metabolism, is that you can alter the extrapolation from animal experiments to human risk prediction in any direction you choose. You need an agreed list of ways in which the risk assessment procedure should be formally modified because otherwise anybody can come along and pick the ones that give the answer he or she wants.

**GILLETTE:**   At the time you wish to make those adjustments, however, it is probable that knowledge of the relative contributions of metabolism and pharmacodynamic factors to the variability within the human population is going to be too poor with most compounds. Therefore, it is difficult to determine whether metabolism is going to be an important factor.

**PETO:**   Well, take trichloroethylene, there's an example where there seem to be large differences.

**GILLETTE:**   But most compounds are not as well studied as is trichloroethylene. Assessments of most compounds are based on minimal studies.

**J. WILSON:**   There are many important cases where much more than the minimum is done.

**GILLETTE:**   I would agree. But we also must have pragmatic approaches for economic reasons. As I said, two fundamentally different approaches for studying toxicology have been developed over the years. I think it important to understand the differences between the objectives of the two approaches. As we get more and more information about the mechanisms of toxicity, then we can use the information to predict the toxicities of other substances that act through that mechanism. Thus, if the variance in the pharmacodynamic factors within the human population are known for one toxicant, then variance in these factors would also be known for all toxicants that act through exactly the same mechanism. To elucidate the mechanism for any toxicant, however, can be slow, expensive, and frequently inconclusive. At the present time, the mechanistic approach is not suitable for screening vast numbers of substances for all the possible toxicities that they may evoke. For that purpose, we must retain the safety factor approach for the foreseeable future.

**WEINSTEIN:**   Would you agree that until we have more mechanistic information, the use of a few divergent species is the best way to encompass these variations, and that prudence would dictate that the most sensitive species be used to assess potential human risks?

**GILLETTE:**   Let's say you've got a prediction that's based on the guinea pig, for example, and you've got another prediction based on a particular strain of pigs. What do you do with the two numbers?

**WEINSTEIN:**   You're saying that there is not a body of data in the literature which says "the human will resemble the pig with respect to the metabolism of certain compounds."

**GILLETTE:**   What I am driving at is that there's no way of predicting what strain or what species is going to predict the toxicity of a substance in a human subpopulation when nothing is known about the toxicity of the substance in the subpopulation or about the mechanism of toxicity.

**ALBERT:** Are you saying that the human population is homogeneous with respect to mechanisms of response?

**GILLETTE:** No, I'm not saying that at all. Let us assume that we have established that a substance causes a toxicity through the combination of a chemically reactive metabolite with DNA. The mechanism would be general for all individuals manifesting the toxicity and, presumably, the kinds of factors that govern the manifestation of the toxicity would be qualitatively the same. Quantitatively though, all of the factors that govern the amount of DNA that is going to be altered by the chemically reactive metabolite may vary markedly from one individual to another. Knowing the mechanism, however, helps us to identify the relevant pharmacokinetic parameters that should be studied in individuals.

# Potential Methods to Monitor Human Populations Exposed to Carcinogens: Carcinogen-DNA Binding as an Example

FREDERICA P. PERERA,* REGINA M. SANTELLA,† AND
MIRIAM C. POIRIER†
*Division of Environmental Sciences
School of Public Health
Columbia University
New York, New York 10032
†Laboratory of Cellular Carcinogenesis and Tumor Promotion
National Cancer Institute, NIH
Bethesda, Maryland 20205

## OVERVIEW

Molecular epidemiology holds promise as a new approach to detecting and quantifying carcinogenic risks to humans. By directly measuring the biologically effective dose of carcinogen instead of relying exclusively on ambient or workplace monitoring data, such studies could identify groups or individuals potentially at risk of cancer, thereby generating dosimetry data useful to policymakers. Another advantage is that many of the same markers of biologically effective dose can be applied to cell culture systems, laboratory animals, and human subjects in order to improve risk extrapolation between systems and species.

This paper reviews progress in the field and focuses specifically upon methods to detect carcinogen-DNA adducts. Data are presented on results in animal and human studies using immunoassays with antibodies to benzo[a]pyrene-DNA adducts.

## INTRODUCTION

A new area of joint interest to epidemiologists, laboratory researchers, and regulators concerned with carcinogens is molecular epidemiology or, more particularly, human monitoring to detect and quantify dose and preclinical response to carcinogens (Perera and Weinstein 1982). Why? Because more precise and sensitive methods are clearly needed for early detection and assessment of human risk. We won't go into the limitations of animal bioassays, in vitro tests, and epidemiological methods or their justification as the best currently available methods for purposes of risk assessment. Instead, we will discuss in a general way the potential usefulness of biomonitoring in the context of its present state of development, limitations, application in human studies to date, and research needs. Then we will present some data on carcinogen-DNA binding as an illustration of these points.

Before continuing, let us define some terms. Exposure refers to the estimated concentration of a substance or agent in the individual's immediate environment (e.g., air, water, food) in contrast to internal dose, which is the amount of a parent compound or activated metabolite in body fluids. Indicators of biologically effective dose reflect the amount of substance or agent that has reacted with critical cellular targets such as DNA, RNA, and protein as distinct from indicators of risk or preclinical response, which measure biological or biochemical changes in target cells correlated with occurrence of cancer. Other important terms are (1) susceptibility: predisposition to cancer because of inherited host factors (e.g., XP, Bloom's syndrome), acquired factors (Hepatitis B), or a combination of inherited and acquired factors (AAH); (2) risk: increased odds of developing cancer as a result of elevated exposure and/or susceptibility; (3) biomonitoring: measurement of internal or biologically effective dose or preclinical response in a human population; and (4) screening: preexposure testing of an individual for traits that predispose to cancer.

Our emphasis will be on the monitoring of biologically effective dose (or carcinogen dosimetry) rather than risk or susceptibility since at the present time we lack prospective data from human and animal studies definitively linking any individual biomonitoring measurements to occurrence of cancer. Therefore, biomonitoring methods are currently restricted to providing information on the average effective dose in a group of exposed individuals.

An immediate goal is the identification of groups or individuals at potentially higher risk of cancer in time to prevent the disease. This information would shape more effective health protective policies and regulations. We stress the value of early detection in preventing risks such as those demonstrated in asbestos, vinyl chloride, and benzene workers 10–30 years after first exposure. Specifically, knowledge of the relationship between exposure and biologically effective dose in a population can flag the need for protective measures, and/or increased surveillance. For example, in the same way that patients on chemotherapy have been experimentally monitored for cis-platinum-DNA adducts as a guide in dose setting (M.C. Poirier et al., pers. comm.), one might test workers or community populations exposed to specific substances or complex mixtures for evidence of a carcinogenic hazard. (Hazard identification refers to the qualitative determination of an actual or potential toxic effect.) This type of dosimetry information is more precise than workplace or ambient monitoring data since it is capable of relecting cumulative exposure interacting both with background and with factors influencing susceptibility.

A second major goal is to use biomonitoring methods in conjunction with data from cell culture systems, laboratory animals, and epidemiology to provide a more rational basis for risk extrapolation between different systems. For example, comparable biologically effective dose/preclinical response data in a human population and in experimental animals for whom tumor incidence is known can assist in extrapolation of risk from animal to human. One can also envision relating biomonitoring data from a population with historical data on increased relative risk of

**Table 1**
Examples of Markers of Internal and Biologically Effective Dose

| Internal dose | Biologically effective dose |
|---|---|
| Mutagenicity of urine | DNA, RNA, protein adducts |
| | Sister chromatid exchange |
| | Chromosomal aberrations |
| | Somatic cell mutation |
| | Sperm abnormalities |
| | (May reflect a genetic or phenotypic change) |

cancer (e.g., coke oven workers) and one with similar exposure whose relative risks were unknown as a guide in risk estimation.

We are still a long way from achieving these goals. Most methods are experimental. Furthermore, most methods now under development pertain to interaction with the genetic material; hence they measure relatively early or initiating events in the carcinogenic process and omit promotion, progression, or what the epidemiologists call late-stage events. For this reason, they may at best turn out to be partial predictors of risk since variation in later stages of the carcinogenic process will influence the individual's or group's risk and hence the predictive value of the test. Other problems are the lack of information on the persistence of the effects measured, the large number of confounding variables that must be accounted for in study design and analysis, and the difficulty in selecting an appropriate control group. Moreover, the cells and body fluids available for human monitoring—although they comprise a long list—are usually remote from the target tissue and therefore give an indirect measure of the biologically relevant dose.

## METHODS/OVERVIEW

Moving from the abstract to the specific, Table 1 shows some methods now considered to be among those most promising for biomonitoring (Bloom 1981; Legator 1981; Bridges et al. 1982; Perera and Weinstein 1982; N.T.P. 1984) including indicators of internal dose or biologically effective dose as defined earlier.

We recognize that classification of these markers is somewhat arbitrary and subject to revision as further information becomes available. Without going into detail, these methods have yielded positive results in a number of human studies (Table 2).

Table 3 shows a reasonable correlation between data from in vitro genetic toxicity tests, animal bioassays, human biomonitoring, and epidemiological studies for five substances or classes of chemicals.

## Table 2
## Some Positive Results in Human Populations

| Population | MU | CA | SCE | Covalent Adducts | MUT L | SM |
|---|---|---|---|---|---|---|
| Chemotherapy patients | + | | + | + | + | |
| Cigarette smokers | + | + | + | + | | + |
| Oncology nurses | + | + | + | | | |
| Cancer patients | | | + | + | | + |
| Workers: | | | | | | |
|   Epichlorohydrin | + | + | | | | |
|   Vinyl chloride | | + | + | | | |
|   Organic solvents | + | | + | | | |
|   Pesticides/herbicides | | + | + | | | |
|   Ethylene oxide | | + | + | +(P) | | |

MU, mutagenicity of wire; CA, chromosomal aberrations; MUT L, mutant lymphocytes; SM, sperm morphology; P, protein

## IMMUNOASSAY FOR BENZO[A]PYRENE-DNA (B[a]P-DNA) ADDUCTS AS A PROTOTYPE

### Background and Rationale

DNA binding is considered a highly relevant dosimeter because an extensive data base indicates that most carcinogens are metabolically activated to electrophilic species capable of covalently binding to cellular macromolecules (DNA, RNA, protein) and that such binding is a critical early event in chemical carcinogenesis (Miller 1978). Furthermore, in laboratory animals, the carcinogenic potency of a series of polycyclic aromatic hydrocarbons (PAHs) and direct-acting alkylating

## Table 3
## Correlation Between Experimental and Epidemiological Findings

| Method/endpoint | Agents | | | | |
|---|---|---|---|---|---|
| | Cigarette smoke | Hair dyes | Anesthetic agents | Cytostatic drugs | Ethylene oxide |
| In vitro genotoxicity | + | + | + | + | + |
| Bioassay/carcinogenicity | + | + | •• | + | + |
| Human studies | | | | | |
|   Agent in body fluids | + | + | + | + | + |
|   Mutagenicity of urine | + | + | ± | + | •• |
|   Covalent adducts | + | •• | •• | + | + |
|   Chromosomal changes | + | + | •• | + | + |
| Epidemiology/cancer | + | ± | ± | + | (+) |

+ Positive data; (+) suggestive; ± contradictory; •• no data
Modified from Vainio 1983.

agents correlates with their ability to form covalent adducts with DNA (Brookes and Lawley 1964; Lutz 1979; Pelkonen et al. 1980; Bartsch et al. 1983). Moreover, a correlation has been observed between DNA adduct formation and mutagenicity for B[a]P (Theall et al. 1982).

B[a]P is a potent animal carcinogen and a pervasive environmental contaminant (in cigarette smoke, workplace and ambient air, food and water) (N.A.S. 1972; I.A.R.C. 1973; Gelboin and Ts'o 1978). As a constituent of cigarette smoke and effluent from gas work, coke ovens, and tar roofing operations, B[a]P is associated with increased risk of lung cancer in humans (Bridbord and French 1978; Redmond et al. 1981).

B[a]P is activated to an electrophilic intermediate which has been shown to form covalent adducts with DNA. The major carcinogenic/mutagenic metabolite of benzo[a]pyrene—the dihydrodiolepoxide, BPDE I, (specifically, 7β,8α-dihydroxy-9α,10α-epoxy-7,8,9,10-tetrahydrobenzo[a]pyrene), binds to deoxyguanosine in DNA both in vitro and in vivo (Harris et al. 1978; Cohen et al. 1979; Jeffrey et al. 1979; Hsu et al. 1981; Perera et al. 1982; Shamsuddin et al. 1985).

Immunoassays are generally rapid, reproducible, highly sensitive, and—unlike methods which use radiolabeled carcinogens—can be used in human studies. Further advantages of B[a]P-DNA immunoassays are their biological relevance, their sensitivity (they can detect one carcinogen residue per $10^7$ nucleotides), their ability to provide chemical-specific data allowing comparisons with ambient monitoring data for B[a]P, and their applicability to many different populations. Among the disadvantages are that B[a]P-DNA adducts relate only to the initiating or early stage of carcinogenesis. As with all assays in Table 1, there appears to be significant individual variation. (Studies of human cells or tissues exposed to B[a]P in vitro have shown 12–100-fold variation between individuals with respect to B[a]P-DNA binding levels (Harris et al. 1978; Cohen et al. 1979). Moreover, the persistence of lesions in various human tissues (dependent on DNA repair and cell turnover) is not known. (Information on rates of repair is limited largely to in vitro and other experimental studies which suggest that the BPDE-DNA adduct can be fairly persistent (Cerrutti et al. 1978; Feldman et al. 1980). In addition, there is a long list of potential confounding variables in a human study.

Dr. I.B. Weinstein's group at Columbia, collaborating with Dr. M.C. Poirier et al. at N.C.I., have developed a rabbit antibody to BPDE I-modified DNA (Poirier et al. 1980). This antibody has been used in a highly sensitive, enzyme-linked immunosorbent assay (ELISA) to detect as little as 3 fmole of BPDE I-dG adduct in 50 μg of DNA (Hsu et al. 1981). This is equivalent to approximately one carcinogen residue per $10^7$ nucleotides. The human cell has about $2 \times 10^9$ nucleotides so that, with this level of sensitivity, it is feasible to monitor human populations having exposure to B[a]P.

## Methods

Figure 1 gives the schematic of the competitive enzyme-linked immunosorbent assay (ELISA). In vitro modified BPDE I-DNA (5 ng) is coated on 96 well mi-

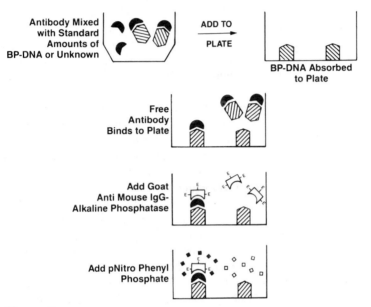

**Figure 1**

Competitive ELISA (color development inversely proportional to amount of B[a]P-DNA in test sample).

croplates. In separate tubes the antibody is mixed with either known amounts of in vitro modified B[a]P-DNA or unknown DNA. All samples contain 50 µg of DNA. The combined antibody and competitor are then transferred to the 96 well plate. With increasing amount of competitor antigen in the tube, decreasing amounts of antibody are free to react with the antigen on the plate. The amount of antibody attached to the plate is then quantitated using a second antibody coupled to alkaline phosphatase. Goat antirabbit IgG-alkaline phosphatase is used with polyclonal antibody and goat antimouse IgG-alkaline phosphate is used with the monoclonals. The substrate for the enzyme, p-nitrophenylphosphate, is then added and the color development at 405 nm determined. Standard curves of percent inhibition of antibody binding to the plate versus fmole B[a]P-dG can be constructed. This allows the determination of the fmole of B[a]P-DNA in an unknown sample from its percent inhibition.

The standard curve using the competitive ELISA with the B[a]P-DNA polyclonal antibody is shown in Figure 2.

## Animal Studies

Using the ELISA with the polyclonal antibody described earlier, a dose-response was seen in lung DNA of mice injected i.p. with 0.1–1 mg of [³H]-B[a]P where

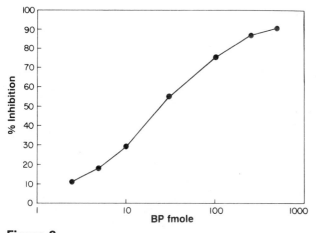

**Figure 2**
Standard curve using polyclonal competitive ELISA.

dose was the amount of B[a]P administered and response was the concentration of adducts in lung. A plateau was observed at doses from 1–3 mg B[a]P-mouse (Figure 3). No adducts were seen in DNA of control mice. There was a correspondence between adduct levels in the mouse measured by ELISA and by radioactive methods

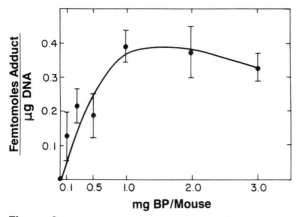

**Figure 3**
B[a]P-DNA adduct formation in lung DNA of mice injected i.p. with benzo[a]pyrene.

**Table 4**
**Examples of Substances or Agents Which May Affect B[a]P**
**Metabolism in Humans**

| |
|---|
| Inducers |
|   Foods (charbroiled meat, ethanol) |
|   Drugs (sedatives) |
|   Other environmental chemicals/mixtures (cigarette smoke, PCBS) |
| Inhibitors |
|   Foods (methylxanthines) |
|   Drugs (steroids) |
|   Other environmental chemicals/mixtures (solvents, spray paints) |

Data from Conney (1982) and Dossing (1982)

respectively, as well as with those seen in rabbit lung at an equivalent dose (Perera et al. 1982). the lower limit of detectability was established at 0.08–0.10 fmole/$\mu$g DNA. This is equivalent to about one BPDE adduct per $10^7$–$10^8$ bases in DNA. By contrast, no significant differences were seen in blood cell DNA from dogs exposed to less than 0.3 $\mu$g daily of B[a]P on smoke inhalation machines as compared to controls.

## Human Studies

The same ELISA with polyclonal antibody was used to assay lung tumor and/or normal lung DNA from 14 lung cancer patients and 13 patients without lung primaries. Exposure histories taken by questionnaire provided information on sources and duration of exposure to B[a]P (smoking, occupation, diet, ambient air) and to agents believed to modify B[a]P-DNA binding (Table 4).

Four of the lung cancer patients (and none of the controls) had significant levels of adducts defined as greater than 30% inhibition. In this small sample, there was no clear relationship between either cigarette smoking or other B[a]P exposures and results in the assay (Table 5).

Table 6 combines these results with those obtained by Shamsuddin et al. (1985) using the same polyclonal antibody specific for the BPDE I-DNA adduct.

More recently, we have developed monoclonal antibodies to BPDE I-DNA to be used in monitoring experimental animals and humans for exposure to B[a]P (Santella et al. 1984). Figure 4 shows a standard curve for the competitive ELISA with the monoclonal antibody 5D11. In collaboration with Dr. R. Everson at NIEHS, this assay was applied to placental samples of 14 women for whom smoking data were available. By a one-sided Mann-Whitney Rank Test, the increase in binding in the smokers compared with that in nonsmokers is significant at the 0.025 level (Figure 5). However, this relationship did not hold when these data were later pooled with the results from 47 additional placental samples.

Since the pilot study in lung cancer patients, we have undertaken larger scale parallel studies in laboratory animals, in cigarette smokers and nonsmokers, lung

**Table 5**
Positive Results of Assay of Lung DNA from Lung Cancer Patients

| Patient | Sample | DX | ELISA % inhibition | Fmol adduct/ μg DNA | Exposure to cigarette smoke* |
|---------|--------|-----|---------|---------|---------------|
| 1 | NT | AC | NS | NS | − A, − P(FS) |
|   | T |   | 36 | 0.17 |  |
| 2** | NT | AC | 38 | 0.18 | − A, − P(FS) |
|   | T |   | 38 | 0.18 |  |
| 3** | NT | AC | 36 | 0.17 | − A, + P |
|   | T |   | 32 | 0.14 |  |
| 4 | NT | AC | NS | NS | − A, − P(FS) |
|   | T |   | 35 | 0.17 |  |

AC, adenocarcinoma; NS, nonsignificant; NT, non-tumor lung tissue; T, tumor tissue; A, active; P, passive; FS, former cigarette smoker
*Exposure during 2 years prior to study
**Positive results in peripheral blood DNA

cancer patients and controls, and coke oven workers with controls. In these ongoing studies, we are investigating short-term persistence of adducts in smokers.

Finally, an interesting question prompted by recent studies of human tumors (Pulciani et al. 1982; Santos et al. 1984) is whether there is a relationship between carcinogenic DNA-interaction as evidenced by adducts, SCEs, and oncogene activation in the same tissue. We are now pursuing this question in pilot studies.

## FUTURE DIRECTIONS

One of the most challenging problems is the validation of such methods as indicators of biologically effective dose and indicators of risk. Validation of markers of biologically effective dose might be accomplished by animal studies which assess the relationship between the administered dose and the effective dose of carcinogen

**Table 6**
B[a]P-DNA Adducts in Humans by Immunoassay (Polyclonal)

| Populations studied | Tissue | Number positive |
|---------------------|--------|-----------------|
| Roofers | Lymphocytes | 7/28 |
| Foundry workers | Lymphocytes | 7/20 |
| Smokers/nonsmokers | Lung tissue | 7[a]/23 |
| Volunteers | PAMS | 3[a]/5 |
| Lung cancer patients | Lung tissue | 4/14 |
| Lung cancer controls | Lung tissue | 0/13 |

[a] All smokers
Data from A.M. Shamsuddin et al. (1985) and Perera et al. (1982)
PAMS, peripheral alveolar macrophages

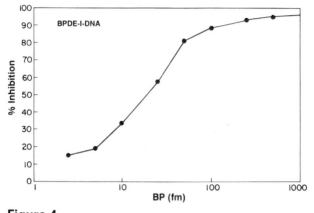

**Figure 4**
Standard curve using monoclonal competitive ELISA.

to target cells and by studies relating workplace monitoring data to measurements of biologically effective dose in workers pre- and postexposure.

In order to validate indicators of risk, one might conduct prospective studies in laboratory animals to determine the relationship between carcinogen dosimetry data and tumor incidence and to relate this information to parallel data from human

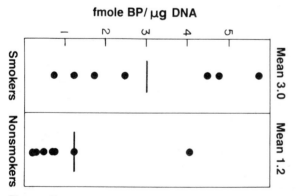

**Figure 5**
Binding in human placental tissue: Smokers and nonsmokers (in collaboration with Dr. R. Everson, NIEHS).

populations with exposure to the same substance. Ideal human populations for study would be chemotherapy patients (who have a 5–10% chance of secondary cancers) and high-risk industrial groups. A further possibility is to conduct a nested case control or retrospective case control study in which one would assay biological samples that had been taken at the start of a large scale prospective study in order to compare cancer cases with controls with respect to potential indicators of risk. This highly cost-effective method was recently used with stored blood samples from participants in the Hypertension Detection and Follow-Up Program (Kolata 1984).

A creative approach suggested by Albertini (1984) to establish the credibility of a positive result is to test an ideal population with a series of assays, each time retesting only those samples which were positive in the previous test. The problem is that a carcinogen may exert its effect through a specific mechanism detected only by one of the tests used; however such an agent and test would be discounted under this system.

In conclusion, early results using this and other methods are promising. They should encourage the necessary validation studies.

## REFERENCES

Albertini, R. 1984. Presentation at the Annual Meeting of the Environmental Mutagen Society. Montreal, Canada.

Bartsch, H., B. Terracini, C. MaLaveille, L. Tomatis, J. Wahrendorf, G. Brun, and B. Dodet. 1983. Quantitative comparison of carcinogenicity, mutagenicity, and electrophilicity of 10 direct-acting alkylating agents and of the initial 0:7-alkylguanine ratio in DNA with carcinogenic potency in rodents. *Mutat. Res.* **110:** 181.

Bloom, A.D. (ed.). 1981. Guidelines for studies of human populations exposed to mutagenic and reproductive hazards. March of Dimes Birth Defects Foundation, White Plains, New York.

Bridbord, K. and J.G. French. 1978. Carcinogenic and mutagenic risks associated with fossil fuels. In *Carcinogenesis: Polynuclear aromatic hydrocarbons* (ed. P.W. Jones and R.I. Fruendenthal), vol. 3, p. 451. Raven Press, New York.

Bridges, B.A., B.E. Butterworth, I.B. Weinstein (eds.). 1982. *Banbury report 13: Indicators of genotoxic exposure*. Cold Spring Harbor Laboratory, Cold Spring Harbor, New York.

Brookes, P. and P.D. Lawley. 1964. Evidence for the binding of polynuclear aromatic hydrocarbons to the nucleic acids of mouse skin: Relation between carcinogenic power of hydrocarbons and their binding to DNA. *Nature* **202:** 781.

Cerutti, P.A., F. Sessions, P.V. Hariharan, and A. Lusby. 1978. Repair of DNA damage induced by benzo(a)pyrene diol-epoxides I and II in human alveolar tumor cells. *Cancer Res.* **38:** 2118.

Cohen, G.M., R. Mehta, and M. Meredith-Brown. 1979. Large interindividual variations . in metabolism of benzo(a)pyrene by peripheral lung tissue from lung cancer patients. *Int. J. Cancer* **24:** 129.

Conney, A.H. 1982. Induction of microsomal enzymes by foreign chemicals and carcinogens by polycyclic aromatic hydrocarbons. *Cancer Res.* **42:** 4875.

Dossing, M. 1982. Changes in hepatic microsomal enzyme function in workers exposed to mixtures of chemicals. *Clin. Pharmacol. Ther.* **32:** 340.

Feldman, G., J. Remsen, T.V. Wang, and P. Cerutti. 1980. Formation and excision of covalent deoxyribonucleic acid adducts of benzo(a)pyrene diol-epoxide I in human lung cells A549. *Biochemistry* **19**: 1095.

Gelboin, H.V. and P.O.P. Ts'o (ed.). 1978. *Polycyclic hydrocarbons and cancer*, vols. 1 and 2. Academic Press, New York.

Harris, C.C., H. Altrup, and G. Stoner. 1978. Metabolism of benzo(a)pyrene in cultured human tissues and cells. In *Polycyclic hydrocarbons and cancer* (ed. G. Stoner, H.V. Gelboin, and P.O.P. Ts'o), vol. 2, p. 331. Academic Press, New York.

Hsu, I.C., M.C. Poirier, S.H. Yuspa, D. Grunberger, I.B. Weinstein, R.H. Yolken, and C.C. Harris. 1981. Measurement of benzo(a)pyrene-DNA adducts by enzyme bioassays and radioimmunoassay. *Cancer Res.* **41**: 1090.

I.A.R.C. 1973. *Certain polycyclic aromatic hydrocarbons and heterocyclic compounds*, vol. 3. IARC Monograph on the evaluation of carcinogenic risk of chemicals to man. International Agency for Research on Cancer, Lyon, France.

Jeffrey, A.M., K. Grzeskowiak, I.B. Weinstein, K. Nakanishi, P. Roller, and R.G. Harvey. 1979. Benzo(a)pyrene, 7,8-dihydrodiol 9,10-oxide adenosine and deoxyadenosine adducts: Structure and stereochemistry. *Science* **206**: 1309.

Kolata, G. 1984. A new kind of epidemiology. *Science* **224**: 481.

Legator, M.S. 1981. A holistic approach to monitoring high-risk populations by short-term procedures. In *Banbury report 9: Quantification of occupational cancer* (ed. R. Peto and M. Schneiderman), p. 335. Cold Spring Harbor Laboratory, Cold Spring Harbor, New York.

Lutz, W.K. 1979. In vivo covalent binding of organic chemicals to DNA as a quantitative indicator in the process of chemical carcinogenesis. *Mutat. Res.* **65**: 289.

Miller, E.C. 1978. Some current perspectives on chemical carcinogens in humans and experimental animals: Presidential address. *Cancer Res.* **38**: 1479.

N.A.S. 1972. *Biological effects of atmospheric pollutants: Particulate polycyclic organic matter*. National Academy of Science, Washington, D.C.

N.T.P. 1983. *Report of the ad hoc panel on the National Toxicology Program (N.T.P.) carcinogenicity testing program*. August 17, 1984. NIEHS, Research Triangle Park, North Carolina.

Pelkonen, O., K. Vahakangas, and D.W. Nebert. 1980. Binding of polycyclic aromatic hydrocarbons to DNA: Comparison with mutagenesis and tumorigenesis. *J. Toxicol. Environ. Health* **6**: 1009.

Perera, F. and I.B. Weinstein. 1982. Molecular epidemiology and carcinogen-DNA adduct detection: New approaches to studies of human cancer causation. *J. Chronic Dis.* **35**: 581.

Perera, F.P., M.C. Poirier, S.H. Yuspa, J. Nakayama, A. Jaretzki, M.M. Curnen, D.M. Knowles, and I.B. Weinstein. 1982. A pilot project in molecular cancer epidemiology: Determination of benzo(a)pyrene-DNA adducts in animal and human tissues by immunoassay. *Carcinogenesis* **3**: 1405.

Poirier, M.C., R. Santella, I.B. Weinstein, D. Grunberger, and S.H. Yuspa. 1980. Quantitation of benzo(a)pyrene-deoxyguanosine adducts by radioimmunoassay. *Cancer Res.* **40**: 412.

Pulciani, S., E. Santos, A.V. Lauver, L.K. Long, S.A. Aaronson, and M. Barbacid. 1982. Oncogenes in solid human tumors. *Nature* **300**: 539.

Redmond, C.K. 1981. Cancer mortality among coke oven workers. Presented at the Second Annual Symposium on Environmental Epidemiology, April 27–29, 1981.

Santella, R.M., C.D. Lin, W.L. Cleveland, and I.B. Weinstein. 1984. Monoclonal antibodies to DNA modified by a benzo(a)pyrene diol epoxide. *Carcinogenesis* **5:** 373.

Santos, E., D. Martin-Zanca, E. Premkumar Reddy, M.A. Pierotti, G. Della Porta, and M. Barbacid. 1984. A mutational event responsible for the malignant activation of a k-ras oncogene occurs in tumor but not in normal tissue of a patient with a squamous cell lung carcinoma. *Science* **223:** 661.

Shamsuddin, A.K.M., N.T. Sinoploi, K. Hemminki, R.R. Boesch, and C.C. Harris. 1985. Detection of benzo[*a*]pyrene: DNA adducts in human white blood cells. *Cancer Res.* **45:** 66.

Theall, G., I.B. Weinstein, D. Grunberger, S. Nessnow, and G. Hatch. 1982. Quantitative relationships between DNA adduct formation and biological effects. In *Banbury report 13: Indicators of genotoxic exposure* (ed. B.A. Bridges et al.), p. 231. Cold Spring Harbor Laboratory, Cold Spring Harbor, New York.

Vainio, H., M. Sorsa, and K. Hemminki. 1983. Biological monitoring in surveillance of exposure to genotoxicants. *Am. J. Ind. Med.* **4:** 87.

## COMMENTS

**GOLDSTEIN:** Are you looking at any of your studies in relationship to dose? In your coke oven workers, do you know what they're being exposed to? Can you link the adducts back to the exposure?

**PERERA:** This is a part of a collaborative study involving the University of Pittsburgh and Brookhaven National Laboratory. We understand that some exposure data is available through researchers at the University of Pittsburgh who are working with the unions and have monitoring data from the plants. I should also mention that these same samples are being tested for sister chromatid exchange (SCEs) at Brookhaven, so we'll have two measures of carcinogen-DNA interaction in the same subject and can relate both of those to exposure.

**GOLDSTEIN:** Unless you can relate these measurements to exposure, it's really not of much value to risk assessment.

**PERERA:** I agree. This group is a good one for study because we will have some monitoring data. Cigarette smokers, of course, are ideal, or as ideal as we can get, because we can quantify reasonably well their exposure to benzo[*a*]pyrene, taking into account details such as butt length and brand.

**PURCHASE:** Did you do that in the study in which the placental DNA was measured?

**PERERA:** Smoking histories were obtained by researchers at NIEHS. These were not detailed, however.

**PURCHASE:** You had data from lung cancer patients and lung cancer controls and it was obtained from lung tissue. How did you get the lung tissue from the controls?

**PERERA:** We took a number of surgical cases without cancer. But, as you know, with the present diagnostic methods, there are few lung surgery cases without cancer. We therefore included several autopsy patients.

**NEEL:** I'd like to make one addition to your future agenda. We have absolutely no way to translate these somatic cell indicators of genetic damage into estimates of transmitted genetic damage at the present time. I would hope that within the next decade studies are initiated that begin to look at the offspring of the persons who show the highest degrees of somatic damage that you can identify. This is what I've been calling at various meetings the "worst cases approach," where we try to identify by your technique those groups with the most genetic damage to somatic cells and then initiate follow-up studies on the children. The numbers of children are not going to be large, which is why we need the kind of methodological improvements that I discussed previously.

**PERERA:** That's a very good point. I think the answer is to conduct prospective studies, not just to follow the individual, but to follow the offspring as well.

**WEINSTEIN:** I think this approach is analogous to the parallelogram approach of others; but this one provides another parameter. We would like to know what dose of benzo[a]pyrene produces how many adducts and obtain this information in two or three species, at least in humans and a rodent species. We would also like to have information on the levels of carcinogen-DNA adducts that cause cancer. We already know that a carcinogenic dose of benzo[a]pyrene in rodents produces about one adduct per $10^5$ nucleotides; this is a useful "ballpark" figure. In the past, this type of data was was obtained mainly by radioactive assays. In the human, you can't administer the radioactive material; but where there has been human exposure to the compound in question, immunoassays can be used to detect and quantitate DNA adducts.

**PURCHASE:** Is that in the target organ?

**WEINSTEIN:** It is not exclusively in the target organ, since the DNA in tissues that don't develop cancer can still contain carcinogen-DNA adducts, presumably because other steps in the carcinogenic process are limiting.

**SWENBERG:** If you use alkylating agents, there's a pretty good correlation between the amount of a promutagenic adduct, such as $O^6$-ethylguanine or $O^4$-ethylthymidine, the amount of cell replication, and initiation of carcinogenesis. There are cell-specific differences, and the target cells for cancer have shown a greater effect. In fact, I think the only troubling example that really comes to mind is the gerbil brain, which has similar amounts of DNA adducts as the rat brain, and yet it doesn't get any brain tumors.

**WEINSTEIN:** However, with other compounds there isn't always a simple relationship between the number of adducts formed in the tissue and the susceptibility of that tissue to cancer. This approach does begin to assess at least an initial and presumably critical event, and then other events—promotion, late stage events—may be additional determinants. In this sort of parallelogram approach, one would also like to obtain the equivalence between DNA adducts and yield of mutants. These numbers are becoming available in tissue culture and in bacteria and could probably be obtained in intact rodents, although that becomes more complicated. One would also like to know the equivalence between adducts and chromosomal aberrations, or any other genotoxic marker that one thinks is relevant, and the equivalence of adducts to oncogene mutations. It will still be necessary to assess factors related to tumor promotion and progression, but at least this approach provides a beginning.

**ALBERT:** It's not going to be so easy, because with the mouse skin, there is a linear dose-response between B[*a*]P adducts in the epidermis and applied dose, over four orders of magnitude. It goes along with a linear dose-response for initiation, but not with carcinogenesis, which has a power of dose of somewhere between two and three. You still have to know the shape of the dose-response in order to translate adducts into effect.

**WEINSTEIN:** Yes. DNA adduct dosimetry is admittedly complex, but it will be, I think, a major advance beyond just feeding the carcinogen to animals and seeing how many tumors you get. It also opens the door to new methods of risk extrapolation. The extrapolation is not done on the basis just of cancer incidence, but one measures in the human markers which can be put into the risk extrapolation. Maybe one will also have to take into account species differences with respect to extent and effect of DNA adduct formation.

**KALDOR:** Are there noncarcinogens which form adducts?

**WEINSTEIN:** I don't know of any.

**KALDOR:** Then it's accepted that if an agent forms adducts it's likely to be a carcinogen?

**WEINSTEIN:** That's a good assumption, but the reverse is not true. There are carcinogens which do not form detectable DNA adducts. Thus, as Dr. Perera emphasized, this will be an assay for only one category of factors that influence cancer risk; but it is a major category. Ionizing radiation produces DNA strand breaks, rather than DNA adducts, but there is renewed interest in the fact that it can also result in modified bases (thymine glycol, 5-hydroxymethyl cytidine). Immunoassays for these modified bases might be developed and also used for dosimetry, thus extending the concept of using cellular DNA as a dosimeter.

**PURCHASE:** In partial answer to Dr. Kaldor's question, one of the complications is the fact that you do get adducts in organs which don't get cancer. That could be just a difference in potency.

**WEINSTEIN:** Perhaps persistence of adducts is an important factor in determining organ susceptibility. Dr. Swenberg, why don't you describe the phenomenon of persistence?

**SWENBERG:** It is well known that different tissues have different levels of repair, and even different amounts of repair for different adducts within the same cell type. For instance, the rodent liver is very good at removing $O^6$-alkylguanine, but it's not very good at removing $O^4$-alkylthymine. So, you have differential repair of different adducts in different tissues. The rodent brain, on the other hand, is very poor at repairing $O^6$-alkylguanine. Furthermore, if you measure DNA adducts following chronic administration, you find that adducts reach a steady state. If you stop exposure to the carcinogen, DNA adducts come down to about one-half of that level after which repair becomes much slower. This suggests that some portion of the adducts persists, either in sensitive cells, or in core versus linker DNA.

**WEINSTEIN:** It's a very curious phenomenon. If you administer certain labeled carcinogens, measure the initial number of DNA adducts, and express it as 100%, within the first 24–48 hours perhaps 50% are removed, but the remainder can persist for a long time. And yet, the cells divide happily. This is seen both in bacteria and mammalian cells. The level of persistence can vary between experimental systems. The extent to which this occurs in humans is not known, but immunoassays will make it possible to assess this. Dr. Perera is measuring persistence in lymphocytes obtained from cigarette smokers after they stop smoking.

**PETO:** Do you mean that cells divide and the adducts remain?

**WEINSTEIN:** Apparently. Thus, there is an opportunity for the DNA-bound material to continue to function for several cell cycles.

**NEEL:** But, to follow up on that, has anybody looked at persons receiving therapeutic doses of radiation 30 years ago for the frequency of persistent adducts?

**WEINSTEIN:** The tools aren't available yet. You need antibody to thymine glycol, and the levels of modified bases are probably very low. On the other hand, as you know, lymphocytes can retain evidence of radiation-induced chromosomal abnormalities for many years after the exposure.

**NEEL:** That's precisely what I was thinking of. It seems to me that would be a high priority for study.

**WEINSTEIN:** Perhaps in dormant lymphocytes DNA repair enzymes are at a very low level, so there may be subpopulations in the body which would store these DNA adducts for a very long time.

**PETO:** What proportion of the adducts are likely to be formed by the sorts of things that people are going to be exposed to in the development of the chemical industry over the next 50 years?

**WEINSTEIN:** Anything that's Ames assay positive is likely to form an adduct.

**J. WILSON:** But what if there has been no human exposure to the compound in question?

**WEINSTEIN:** Then the method can't be applied except in human tissue culture systems; but there are many examples of human exposure where further assessment of risk is required.

**PETO:** What proportion of the adducts that are likely to be formed in the general industrial environment are going to be caused by agents whose carcinogenic effects are known at all? Presumably it's a very small proportion.

**PERERA:** Very few.

**KALDOR:** The question is whether adduct measurements can be extrapolated to estimate cancer risk.

**PERERA:** We don't know at the moment. I have discussed adducts primarily as indicators of biologically effective dose in humans. We do not yet know what they're telling us about risk. Since risk is a combination of exposure and susceptibility, you can say, "Well, if you're getting hit with a large amount of this material and it's interacting with your DNA, presumably you are at some higher risk than you were before exposure"—but that's as far as you can go without further prospective animal and human studies linking adducts to health outcome.

**KALDOR:** It's no use to risk assessment if a quantitative relationship cannot be established.

**WEINSTEIN:** As a minimum, it's no worse than the Ames assay. The endpoint in an Ames assay is also based on DNA damage. But, the advantage of the DNA adduct method is that you can do it in humans, under ambient conditions of human exposure, so you don't have to extrapolate from a bacterial system. Experimental data indicate that it's not healthy to have one adduct per $10^5$ nucleotides on your DNA; that's often associated with a carcinogenic event. Noncarcinogens show less than one adduct per $10^{10}$ nucleotides. Further dosimetry of this type could be useful in quantitative risk extrapolation.

**PIKE:** But you're suggesting then that it doesn't matter what the adduct is; that a B[a]P adduct is the same as any other adduct?

**WEINSTEIN:** The type of adduct may determine potency, organ specificity, and so forth. But a methyl group on DNA is a carcinogen, and so is aflatoxin. That's a dilemma in the field—why such diverse adducts can be carcinogenic.

**J. WILSON:** This is very interesting and exciting work, and I think it's going to be very useful in trying to explain some of the mechanisms of cancer, but you have much further to go before using these methods as predictive tools in any kind of prospective risk assessment. There are many simpler ways to get these data.

**WEINSTEIN:** Wouldn't it already be useful, for example, in the case of vinyl chloride?

**J. WILSON:** But with vinyl chloride we know the answer.

**WEINSTEIN:** However, one could use this approach to assess risk more precisely. For example, one might use this approach to determine whether a reduction in exposure to vinyl chloride in the workplace has led to a reduction to a negligible level of DNA adducts in the exposed workers. Thus, it might serve as an on-line monitor.

**R. WILSON:** We heard a statement earlier that, for vinyl chloride, there was a big difference between the Wistar rats and the Sprague-Dawley rats. Have people looked to see if they could find interstrain differences in adducts? That would be a very simple and useful thing to do.

**WEINSTEIN:** It hasn't been done, to my knowledge, with vinyl chloride.

**SWENBERG:** It has been done with other agents. Strain and species differences have been shown for liver cancer with nitrosamines. A single dose will cause hepatocellular carcinomas in hamsters but not in rats. In hamsters, the $O^6$-alkylguanine persists for much longer than in the rat. This is a very productive field for future research. Some of the questions you're asking are very good. There are some techniques that are emerging, such as the postlabeling technique, where you can demonstrate adducts, even though you have not identified them. With a radioimmunoassay, you have to start with purified adduct.

**ALBERT:** This adds the dimension of metabolism onto exposure assessment. It's going to raise some curious situations because if you go into a population exposed to a given level of a carcinogen and you find some individuals with a markedly higher effective dose, you're going to be identifying individuals who have a hyperactive metabolism. In a sense, it's going back to the screening approach.

**WEINSTEIN:** But I think the more information you have, the better your judgment will be. You must realize that this is no different than any other short-term test. I'm convinced that we cannot continue to use cancer as the experimental endpoint for predicting cancer risks because (1) you want to be predictive; (2) the methods for detecting cancer are too insensitive in the human population; and (3) the latent period is too long. So, the only way to advance the field—and one must make some commitments—is to use markers (biochemical, molecular), which are predictive of cancer risk, and use these for risk extrapolation. This is analogous to approaches in the field of infectious diseases, where you don't necessarily wait for the person to get the full-blown disease, but you rely on serum titers and culture techniques.

**ALBERT:** Years ago, Lederberg suggested that the level of control ought to be at the level of the DNA, and maybe standards ought to be set on the basis of the number of adducts, regardless of the endpoint.

**WEINSTEIN:** I think so. There may be surprises. Perhaps all of us have our DNA mixed up with a certain level of chemical adducts, without any obvious health effects. Maybe that's the background level. But we should assess this and then try to go further.

**GOLDSTEIN:** You're focusing on the hazard side again. When you get out of the workplace and you do risk assessment on the general environmental type of problems, the great uncertainty is exposure, not hazard. Although hazard assessment is fine and we can talk about all the interesting mechanistic things that this provides us, your approach also, in a sense, gives you a biological monitor or dosimeter. It really doesn't matter what the adduct is—that adduct could be hemoglobin. To find out whether people living around a hazardous waste dump are in fact exposed or not exposed, forgetting about the implication of risk, this could still be a very powerful tool. I think you have to look at it from that point of view as well.

**WEINSTEIN:** Absolutely. DNA is a wonderful internal chemical "trap" to ask how many substances or agents are around that can cause genetic damage. Fortunately, it has a relatively simple structure and anything present other than the four major bases is suspect.

# The Relevance of Tumor Promotion and Multistage Carcinogenesis to Risk Assessment

**I. BERNARD WEINSTEIN**
Division of Environmental Sciences
School of Public Health and the Cancer Center
Columbia University
New York, New York 10032

## OVERVIEW

Carcinogenesis is a multistage process involving at least three distinct phases: initiation, promotion, and progression. These stages are enhanced by different types of agents and involve qualitatively different cellular and molecular mechanisms. They also display different dose-response relationships. Furthermore, certain human tumors may be due to synergistic interactions between environmental chemicals and viruses. These aspects considerably complicate attempts to do quantitative risk assessment based on simple mathematical models. Current studies on the mechanism of action of tumor initiators and promoters may, however, provide new approaches to risk extrapolation. Evidence is reviewed indicating that the primary target for initiating agents is cellular DNA, whereas the target for the phorbol ester tumor promoters, and related compounds, is the phospholipid-dependent enzyme protein kinase C. Recent findings on the mechanism of action of tumor promoters suggest new types of short-term assays for these compounds. Hopefully, the development of such assays will provide some of the additional tools that are needed for more accurately assessing the potential risks of various types of environmental agents.

## INTRODUCTION

Carcinogenesis is a multistep process that displays at least three distinct steps: initiation, promotion, and progression. The individual steps can be influenced by different factors, both environmental (e.g., exogenous) and endogenous (genetic, hormonal), and these steps may involve different cellular and biochemical mechanisms (Weinstein et al. 1984a). It is probable that the individual steps also differ in their dose-response relationships, as well as in their intertissue and interspecies variations. The likelihood that cancer will result following exposure to a single agent or a group of agents is, therefore, dependent upon a summation of these events. These aspects considerably complicate any quantitative attempts at risk assessment. Indeed, in view of this complexity, one wonders whether it will ever be possible to do quantitative risk assessment with any precision, particularly across a wide range of diverse compounds, species, and tissues. Furthermore, such risk

**231**

assessments are often done in the absence of detailed dose-response data on the particular compound in question, when tested alone and in combination with possible cofactors.

## INITIATING CARCINOGENS AND COMPLETE CARCINOGENS

It is known that a number of chemicals that act as initiators of the carcinogenic process yield highly reactive metabolites that bind covalently to cellular DNA (Weinstein et al. 1984a). It is often assumed, therefore, that they obey one-hit kinetics and that this simplifies the process of quantitative risk assessment for these agents. However, a number of variables could influence the efficacy of a given dose of such chemicals. These variables include: (1) uptake, tissue distribution, and excretion of the parent compound; (2) the extent of metabolism of the compound, in terms of either the formation of metabolites that bind to DNA or of detoxification products; (3) the efficiency and fidelity of DNA repair; (4) the efficiency of conversion of the promutagenic damage to DNA to stable heritable alterations in the cellular genome; and (5) the likelihood that subsequent stages (promotion and progression) in the multistage carcinogenic process will occur. We should also emphasize that simple one-hit kinetics might not apply to initiating carcinogens if they act via inducible cellular, or "SOS"-like, cellular responses (Ivanovic and Weinstein 1980; Lambert et al. 1983; Weinstein et al. 1984a). Recent studies of activated oncogenes in tumor cells (Bishop 1983) indicate not only simple point mutations, but also gene amplifications, gene transpositions, and chromosome translocations. Little is known about the molecular mechanisms underlying the latter changes. Thus it is difficult to predict the kinetics of such activation. Extensive studies with in vitro assays for potential carcinogens have also made it apparent that there is no simple quantitative correlation between the potency of a chemical as a mutagen and its potency as a carcinogen (National Academy of Sciences 1984).

Most of the known carcinogens produce multiple effects. In fact, when given at sufficient dosage, the genotoxic chemicals (or initiators) are usually complete carcinogens and, therefore, probably produce both tumor-initiating and tumor-promoting effects (Ivanovic and Weinstein 1982). Simple tests for genotoxicity may fail to assess the promoting capacity of these compounds. This and other factors severely limit attempts to predict the mechanisms of action and relative potencies of carcinogens when findings based simply on genotoxic activity are used. The paradigm of random point mutation as a basis for understanding the carcinogenic action of agents that display genotoxic effects may itself be antiquated, in view of the multistage aspects of the carcinogenic process, probable synergistic (and sometimes inhibitory) multifactor interactions, and the possibility that carcinogenesis involves more complex genomic changes (i.e., gene rearrangements, chromosomal translocation, oncogene activation, and altered DNA methylation) (Weinstein et al. 1984a).

## TUMOR PROMOTION

Let us now specifically consider the process of tumor promotion and its implications with respect to quantitative risk assessment. Tumor promoters can be defined as

## Table 1
Examples of Two-stage Carcinogenesis in Experimental Animals[a]

| Tissue | Species | Initiator | Promoter |
|--------|---------|-----------|----------|
| Phorbol related examples | | | |
| Skin | Mouse | Polycyclic hydrocarbons, MNNG, β-propiolactone, urethane | Croton oil, phorbol esters, teleocidin |
| Ovary | Mouse | DMBA | TPA |
| Forestomach | Mouse | DMBA | TPA |
| Stomach | Rat | MNNG | Croton oil |
| Liver | Mouse | DMN | Phorbol |
| Lung | Mouse | DMN | Phorbol |
| Non-phorbol examples | | | |
| Skin | Mouse | Polycyclic hydrocarbons | Anthralin, iodoacetate, tweens, citrus oil, surface-active agents |
| Liver | Rat | AAF, DEN, 3'-methyl-N,N-dimethyl-4-aminoazo-benzene | Phenobarbital, DDT, BHT, TCDD |
| | Mouse | DEN | PCB |
| Lung | Mouse | Urethane | BHT |
| Colon | Rat | MNNG | Bile acids |
| Bladder | Rat | MNU | Cyclamate, saccharin, normal urine |
| Mammary gland | Rat | Neutron, γ-radiation | Prolactin |
| Thyroid | Rat | N-bis(2-hydroxypropyl)-nitrosamine | 3-amino-1,2,4-triazole |
| Intestine | Rat | 1,2-Dimethylhydrazine | Sodium barbiturate |

See Hecker et al. (1982) and Greenebaum and Weinstein (1981) for individual references
Modified from Yamasaki and Weinstein (1985).
MNNG = N-methyl-N'-nitro-N-nitrosoguanidine; DMBA = dimethylbenz($a$)anthracene; DMN = dimethylnitrosamine; AAF = N-acetylaminofluorene; DEN = diethylnitrosamine; MNU = methyl-nitrosourea; TPA = 12-0-tetradecanoyl phorbol-13 acetate; DDT = α,α-bis(p-chlorophenyl)-β,β,β-trichlorethane; BHT = butylated hydroxytoluene; TCDD = 2,3,7,8-tetrachlorodibenzo-p-dioxin

compounds that have very weak or no carcinogenic activity when tested alone, but markedly enhance tumor yield when applied repeatedly following a low or subop-timal dose of a carcinogen (initiator) (Berenblum 1982). Although the phenomenon has been studied most extensively on mouse skin, there is considerable evidence that it applies to various tissues (including liver, bladder, and breast) and to a variety of species (Table 1). Table 2 contrasts the properties of tumor initiators and pro-moters, based on studies on mouse skin. Two points bear emphasis. The first has to do with the differences in dose-schedule effects between initiators and promoters.

## Table 2
Biologic Properties of Initiating and Promoting Agents

| Initiating agents | Promoting agents |
|---|---|
| 1. Carcinogenic by themselves—"solitary carcinogens" | 1. Not carcinogenic alone |
| | 2. Must be given after the initiating agent |
| 2. Must be given before promoting agent | 3. Require repeated exposure |
| 3. Single exposure is sufficient | 4. Action reversible (at early stage) |
| 4. Action "irreversible" | 5. Possible threshold |
| 5. No apparent threshold | 6. No evidence of covalent binding |
| 6. Yield electrophiles—bind covalently to cell macromolecules | 7. Not mutagenic |
| 7. Mutagenic | |

For additional details, see Berenblum (1982), Hecker et al. (1982), Weinstein et al. (1984a)

The second is that, in contrast to initiators, tumor promoters do not appear to act by producing direct damage to cellular DNA. Detailed studies with the phorbol ester tumor promoters, and with two other types of promoters (teleocidin and aplysiatoxin), indicate that their primary sites of action are cell membranes (Weinstein et al. 1984a, b). These promoters induce several changes in membrane function, including altered ion flux, nutrient uptake, phospholipid metabolism, and the function of receptors for certain growth factors. At the cellular level, they can produce three types of effects: (1) modulation of differentiation, (2) mimicry of transformation, and (3) enhancement of cell transformation initiated by chemical carcinogens or certain viral agents. An exciting, recent finding is that for at least three classes of tumor promoters (the phorbol esters, teleocidin, and aplysiatoxin) the cellular receptor is the membrane-associated enzyme protein kinase C (PKC). These compounds also markedly enhance the activity of this enzyme. Thus, PKC may be the initial effector for the action of these compounds on target cells (Castagna et al. 1982; Nishizuka 1984; Weinstein et al. 1984b). It remains to be determined to what extent other types of tumor promoters also exert their effects, either directly or indirectly, on PKC or other cellular protein kinases. If studies on protein kinases indicate a unitary mechanism for tumor promotion, this would suggest simple assays for their detection and for risk extrapolation studies.

Certain tumor promoters, such as the phorbol esters (Hecker et al. 1982) and 2,3,7,8-tetrachlorodibenzo-$p$-dioxin (TCDD) (Kociba et al. 1978), can induce a significant number of tumors in animals, even without prior application of an initiating carcinogen. In addition, there are a few studies suggesting that, although the primary target of the phorbol ester tumor promoters is cellular membranes and PKC, rather than DNA, these compounds may indirectly inflict chromosomal damage, perhaps via the generation of activated forms of oxygen, and that this damage might contribute to the process of tumor promotion (Kennedy et al. 1984). If this is the case, then tumor promoters would also have genotoxic activity, albeit through an indirect effect. This would further complicate the process of risk extrapolation.

It is often assumed that tumor promoters and other agents that might act through epigenetic mechanisms will, in contrast to initiating and genotoxic carcinogens, display a threshold in their dose-response. The experimental data on dose-response relationships with tumor promoters like 12-O-tetradecanoyl phorbol-13 acetate (TPA), TCDD, and phenobarbital (PB) are limited and do not establish a threshold. Nor is there evidence for a threshold or nonlinear dose-response for tumor promoters in humans. Even if this were the case, how would we know how to extrapolate, from a specific set of data, the threshold level in a heterogeneous human population?

It is true that the known tumor promoters require repeated application to exert their tumor-promoting effects, whereas the single application of certain initiating carcinogens is sufficient. This may reflect a dose-schedule effect rather than a true threshold (Yamasaki and Weinstein 1982). Nor does it necessarily imply a comfortable margin of safety for tumor promoters, because for many substances that are of concern (such as water pollutants, industrial chemicals, and food additives), there is likely to be repeated and prolonged human exposure. Moreover, some of these substances are very lipophilic or are only slowly degraded. They can, therefore, persist or even accumulate in body tissues or the general environment.

There is the impression that tumor promoters are much less potent than initiating carcinogens and, therefore, are less hazardous. This is not necessarily the case. On a molar basis, TPA is about two orders of magnitude more potent in exerting biologic effects than benzo[a]pyrene (B[a]P), and TCDD is even more potent than TPA (Hecker et al. 1982; Poland et al. 1982; Knutson and Poland 1984). We know that nature has evolved specific defense mechanisms against some of the genotoxic agents, including conjugation and detoxifying mechanisms and DNA excision repair. We do not know to what extent humans have evolved protective mechanisms against tumor promoters. I do not doubt that such mechanisms exist, but at the present time we do not know their properties or relative efficiencies.

A final reason for being concerned about the potential health hazards of tumor promoters and other carcinogenic cofactors that do not appear to act by directly damaging cellular DNA is the evidence that a major fraction of human cancer is due to lifestyle factors and dietary factors and that many of these may not act as simple genotoxic agents (Doll and Peto 1981). It is essential, therefore, that we not overemphasize our concerns with genotoxic agents, downplay the potential health hazards of other types of agents, and thus distort priorities in our efforts at primary cancer prevention.

Unfortunately, at the present time there do not exist well-validated, short-term, or in vitro assays for tumor promoters. This is a serious limitation in the area of environmental monitoring and risk assessment. As discussed above, there are, however, promising leads on the cellular and molecular mechanisms of action of tumor promoters. These leads might be used to develop such assays. A tentative list of such assays is given in Table 3. I should emphasize that all of these assays require further development and validation.

## MULTISTAGE AND MULTIFACTOR CARCINOGENESIS IN HUMANS

There is considerable evidence for multistage carcinogenesis in humans and for synergistic interactions between various types of agents in the causation of human

## Table 3
## Possible Rapid Assays For Tumor Promoters[a]

1. Enhancement of in vitro cell transformation—initiated by carcinogens, radiation, viruses, or oncogene transfection
2. Inhibition or enhancement of cellular differentiation
3. Membrane changes
   a. Altered adhesion
   b. Inhibition of cell-cell metabolic cooperation or electric coupling
   c. Increased phospholipid turnover
   d. Altered activity of membrane-associated receptors
4. Induction of ornithine decarboxylase or plasminogen activator
5. Altered activity or cellular distribution of protein kinase C; altered profile of cellular phosphoproteins

[a]It should be stressed that all of these assays require more extensive study and validation and that they may not be specific for tumor promoters. For further details see text, Hecker et al. (1982), Weinstein et al. (1984b), Hsiao et al. (1984).

cancer (Greenebaum and Weinstein 1981; Yamasaki and Weinstein 1985). Examples of the latter include: (1) synergy between asbestos and cigarette smoking in the causation of lung cancer (Selikoff and Hammond 1979); (2) synergy between hepatitis B virus infection and aflatoxin in the causation of liver cancer (Linsell and Peers 1977; Sherman and Shafritz 1984); (3) a possible synergy between an environmental tumor promoter and EBV virus in the causation of nasopharyngeal cancer in South China (Ito and Hirayama 1981); and (4) synergy between cigarette smoking and alcohol consumption in the causation of esophageal, larynx, and oral cavity cancers (Tuyns 1979). These types of synergistic interactions also call into question the usual mathematical models used for quantitative risk extrapolation. Obviously, it would be extremely difficult to make such extrapolations in those cases where synergistic interactions exist, particularly if one of the agents is a replicating virus (Fisher and Weinstein 1980; Greenbaum and Weinstein 1981). We must recognize, therefore, that the current mathematical models used for quantitative risk extrapolations make a number of biologic assumptions that are either untested or not warranted, particularly in view of the complexities of multistage and multifactor carcinogenesis.

## REFERENCES

Berenblum, I. 1982. Sequential aspects of chemical carcinogenesis: Skin. In *Cancer: A comprehensive treatise* (ed. F.F. Becker), vol. 1 (2nd ed.). Plenum Publishing, New York.

Bishop, J.M. 1983. Cancer genes come of age. *Cell* **32:** 1018.

Castagna, M., U. Takai, K. Kaibuchi, K. Sano, U. Kikkawa, and Y. Nishizuka. 1982. Direct activation of calcium-activated, phospholipid-dependent protein kinase by tumor promoting phorbol esters. *J. Biol. Chem.* **257:** 7847.

Doll, R. and R. Peto. 1981. *The causes of cancer.* Oxford University Press, Oxford.

Fisher, P.B. and I.B. Weinstein. 1980. Chemical-viral interactions and multistep aspects of cell transformation. In *Molecular and cellular aspects of carcinogen screening tests* (ed. R. Montesano, L. Bartsch, and L. Tomatis), p. 113. IARC Scientific Pub., No. 27. IARC, Lyon, France.

Greenebaum, E. and I.B. Weinstein. 1981. Relevance of the concept of tumor promotion to the causation of human cancer. In *Progress in surgical pathology* (ed. C.M. Fenoglio and M. Wolf), p. 27. Masson Publishing USA, New York.

Hecker, E., N.E. Fusenig, W. Kunz, F. Marks, and H.W. Thielmann. 1982. *Carcinogenesis: A comprehensive survey*, vol. 7. Raven Press, New York.

Hsiao, W-L.W., S. Gattoni-Celli, and I.B. Weinstein. 1984. A tumor promoter enhances oncogene-induced transformation of C3H 10T½ cells. *Science* **226:** 552.

Ito, Y. and T. Hirayama. 1981. A new view of the etiology of nasopharyngeal carcinoma. *Prev. Med.* **10:** 614.

Ivanovic, V. and I.B. Weinstein. 1980. Genetic factors in *Escherichia coli* that affect cell killing and mutagenesis induced by benzo(a)pyrene-7,8-dihydrodiol 9,10-oxide. *Cancer Res.* **40:** 3508.

Ivanovic, V. and I.B. Weinstein. 1982. Benzo[*a*]pyrene and other inducers of cytochrome $P_1$-450 inhibit binding of epidermal growth factor to cell surface receptors. *Carcinogenesis* **3:** 505.

Kennedy, A.R., W. Troll, and J.B. Little. 1984. Role of free radicals in the initiation and promotion of radiation transformation in vitro. *Carcinogenesis* **5:** 1213.

Knutson, J.C. and Poland, A. 1984. 2,3,7,8-Tetrachlorodibenzo-p-dioxin: Examination of biochemical effects involved in the proliferation and differentiation of XB cells. *J. Cell. Physiol.* **121:** 143.

Kociba, R., D. Keyes, J. Beyer, R. Carreon, E. Wade, D. Dittenber, R. Kalnins, L. Grauson, D. Park, S. Barnard, R. Hummel, and C. Humiston. 1978. Results of a two-year chronic toxicity and oncogenicity study of 2,3,7,8-tetrachlorodibenzo-p-dioxin (TCDD) in rats. *Toxicol. Appl. Pharmacol.* **46:** 279.

Lambert, M.E., S. Gattoni-Celli, P. Kirschmeier, and I.B. Weinstein. 1983. Benzo[*a*]pyrene induction of extrachromosomal viral DNA synthesis in rat cells transformed by polyoma virus. *Carcinogenesis* **4:** 587.

Linsell, C.A. and F.G. Peers. 1977. Field studies on liver cell cancer. In *The origins of human cancer* (ed. H.H. Hiatt, J.D. Watson, and J.A. Winsten), vol. 4, p. 549. Cold Spring Harbor Laboratory, Cold Spring Harbor, New York.

National Academy of Sciences, Committee on Chemical Environmental Mutagens. 1984. The correlation between mutagenic and carcinogenic potencies: A feasibility study.

Nishizuka, Y. 1984. The role of protein kinase C in cell surface signal transduction and tumor promotion. *Nature* **308:** 693.

Poland, A., D. Palen, and E. Glover. 1982. Tumor promotion of TCDD in skin of HRS/J hairless mice. *Nature* **300:** 271.

Selikoff, I.J. and E.C. Hammond. 1979. Asbestos and smoking (Editorial). *J. Am. Med. Assoc.* **242:** 458.

Sherman, M. and D.A. Shafritz. 1984. Hepatitis B virus and hepatocellular carcinoma: Molecular biology and mechanistic considerations. *Sem. Liv. Dis.* **4:** 98.

Tuyns, A.J. 1979. Epidemiology of alcohol and cancer. *Cancer Res.* **39:** 2840.

Weinstein, I.B., S. Gattoni-Celli, P. Kirschmeier, M. Lambert, W. Hsiao, J. Backer, and A. Jeffrey. 1984a. Multistage carcinogenesis involves multiple genes and multiple mechanisms. In *Cancer cells 1. The transformed phenotype* (ed. A. Levine, G. Vande

Woude, J.D Watson, and W.C. Topp), p. 229. Cold Spring Harbor Laboratory, Cold Spring Harbor, New York.

Weinstein, I.B., J. Arcoleo, J. Backer, A.M. Jeffrey, W. Hsiao, S. Gattoni-Celli, P. Kirschmeier, and E. Okin. 1984b. Molecular mechanisms of tumor promotion and multistage carcinogenesis. In *Cellular interactions by environmental tumor promoters* (ed. H. Fujiki et al.), p. 59. Japan Science Society Press, Tokyo, Japan.

Yamasaki, H. and I.B. Weinstein. 1985. Cellular and molecular mechanisms of tumor promotion and their implications with respect to risk assessment. In *Methods for estimating risks of chemical injury: Human and non-human, biota and ecosystems* (ed. V.B. Vouk, G.C. Batler, O.G. Hall, and D.B. Peakall). John Wiley, New York. (In press).

## COMMENTS

**J. WILSON:** A couple of thoughts occurred to me about promoters. First, obviously the theory is very attractive. It explains a large variety of observations in a satisfactory way. Second, it seems entirely possible that a number of the compounds that are shown to be carcinogenic at high levels of feeding in some of these NTP-type studies are acting by a promotion mechanism.

**WEINSTEIN:** Yes. I think that halogenated organics and the pesticides that score positive in the mouse liver and do not have clear genotoxic activity are probably going to turn out to be promoters. Some of the halogenated organics which are positive in the mouse for liver carcinogenesis and negative in the rat are positive in the rat if you first treat the rat with diethylnitrosamine.

**ALBERT:** But one of the hallmarks of promoter action is the production of benign tumors. You see this in the skin. Henry Pitot tells me that you see this in the liver too; the tumors that are brought out by phenobarbitol or other promoters are benign.

**WEINSTEIN:** It depends on how long you feed the compound.

**ALBERT:** They take 6–9 months to become cancer. If you look at an agent like trichloroethylene, you see that there's a very high proportion of cancers. On the face of it, it doesn't look like a promoter action.

**WEINSTEIN:** You would know that if you continued to expose the animal to the promoter. The promoter enhances their appearance. If you give diethylnitrosamine and keep feeding the phenobarbitol, you can get liver carcinomas, likewise with TCDD.

**ALBERT:** It takes a long time.

**WEINSTEIN:** It takes longer, right. Maybe we're stopping the assays too soon.

**PETO:** What about the division of promotion into two stages? There are two sorts of papilloma, the reversible ones which appear very quickly, and the irreversible ones which are more likely to convert to carcinoma and appear later.

**WEINSTEIN:** Yes, I've oversimplified. Mouse skin promotion itself has a minimum of two phases. There are certain agents which will act in the first phase of promotion and others in the second stage. There are also two types of papillomas, some of which will regress when you stop the promoter and some which won't. The other aspect about promotion is that the early stages, both in liver and in mouse skin, are often reversible.

**PETO:** I think it's worth mentioning that epidemiologists don't mean the same thing as animal experimenters when they talk about promotion. Promotion in the laboratory usually means enhancing papilloma production. When epidemiologists talk about promotion, they mean that a late stage in carcinogenesis is affected, which is inferred because the cancer risk increases with age at exposure to the carcinogen. We shan't know the relationship between these phenomena until analogous experiments are done with animals.

**WEINSTEIN:** That's because you have stolen a term and are using it the wrong way. We claim priority. The term "promotion" was invented by Peyton Rous in 1939, and subsequently used by Berenblum, and there's a long literature that defines it. I think, as a matter of fact, when you say "promotion" you probably mean progression. I think what the epidemiologists mean is a late-stage process. But I don't know that there's any evidence that what the epidemiologist refers to is the same as promotion in the experimental model.

**PURCHASE:** I have a question about the threshold dose in regard to promoters. A single dose of TPA on mouse skin does not promote, does it?

**WEINSTEIN:** No. The dose on mouse skin is extremely low.

**PURCHASE:** So that, in effect then, is a threshold of a type.

**WEINSTEIN:** Well, a single low dose of benzo[a]pyrene doesn't either. You don't get tumors with a low dose of benzo[a]pyrene, at a detectable level, within the lifespan and with a limited number of animals, unless you subsequently apply a promoter.

**SWENBERG:** We now have models for promotion in quite a number of tissues besides skin, such as liver, kidney, thyroid, colon, and lung. It's a field that is really just starting to emerge. The other thing that we have to keep in mind when we talk about the bioassays is that we have many spontaneous tumors in the control animals, and these chemicals could be acting as promoters of spontaneous tumors. We don't have to think of it any differently than had they been initiated by DEN or any other compound.

**R. WILSON:** DDT is probably a promoter. The animal data look very much that way.

**PIKE:** How do hormones fit into this? Events like age of menarche affect breast cancer risk for the rest of a woman's life.

**WEINSTEIN:** I've always thought of promotion as a subclass of hormonal carcinogenesis. It looks as if TPA is really a hormone-like substance. TPA affects differentiation and proliferation and so do hormones. Hormones are not genotoxic.

**PIKE:** But why would you expect events at age 30 or 40 to affect cancer incidence at age 65?

**WEINSTEIN:** In breast cancer, within the paradigm of initiation-promotion, I would assume that there is an initiator yet to be discovered for breast cancer—in Hiroshima it was radiation—and that this is followed by promotion, which is probably due to endogenous estrogens and prolactin, i.e., hormones.

**PIKE:** I agree about the hormones probably involved, but I find it hard to accept that events like menarche are acting solely as promoters in the conventional sense for tumors that occur 50 years later.

**WEINSTEIN:** In Hiroshima it looks as though the optimum time for initiation is at a very early age. It might be that in the breast you have to get the initiator in there before the duct epithelium of the breast has reached a certain stage of maturity. So, the mammary tissue in a very young child might be most susceptible to initiation, and after that a prolonged period of repeated promotion, including estrogen activity (early menarche/late menopause provides a long period of estrogen stimulation) and perhaps prolactin activity and dietary lipid as well, might be necessary.

**PERERA:** Which of those five possible assays for promoters that you mentioned earlier is potentially applicable to human studies?

**WEINSTEIN:** I think ornithine decarboxylase is. People are beginning to look at biopsy tissue from colon and so forth. Bob Bruce has evidence that the colonic epithelium of individuals on a high-fat diet is, in a sense, hyperproliferative.

# Mechanistic Considerations in the Formulation of Carcinogenic Risk Estimations

**RICHARD H. REITZ and PHILIP G. WATANABE**
Toxicology Research Laboratory
Dow Chemical Company
Midland, Michigan 48640

## INTRODUCTION

A cancer cell may be defined as a living cell which responds abnormally to bio-chemical signals controlling cellular growth and division. Since this altered response is passed on from generation to generation, it is tempting to speculate that a cancer cell has undergone one or more permanent changes in its genetic make-up (i.e., experienced a mutation). In fact, many potent mutagens are also carcinogens, and it is common practice to use various in vitro mutagenicity tests to identify agents with high carcinogenic potential.

The somatic mutation theory of carcinogenesis is often cited as a theoretical basis for adopting a particular type of extrapolation procedure during the formulation of carcinogenic risk estimations. It has been suggested that if one or more hits on the genetic material are sufficient to initiate carcinogenesis, then the induction of cancer can be modeled as a simple statistical process subject to the laws of mathematics. However, any model of carcinogenesis that fails to consider the effects of DNA repair mechanisms is unlikely to be very accurate, since these systems play a crucial role in determining whether potential genetic damage is, in fact, expressed.

Maher et al. (1979) have shown that fibroblasts from normal individuals are capable of soaking up a finite amount of ultraviolet light before lethality, mutations, or transformations are observed. This hockey stick type of dose-response curve is observed in DNA repair competent cells, but cells from individuals deficient in DNA repair mechanisms (*Xeroderma pigmentosum*) do not exhibit this behavior.

Russel et al. (1979; 1982a,b) studied the effect of ethylnitrosourea (ENU) on transmitted gene mutations in the mouse. They found that the dose-response curve for this agent showed significant deviations from linearity at low doses, in spite of the fact that the production of DNA adducts was demonstrated to be a linear function of dose. They concluded that saturation of DNA repair mechanisms was responsible for this nonlinearity. Thus the expression of any potentially mutagenic (or carcin-ogenic) lesion is dependent upon the relative rates of DNA repair and DNA rep-lication in the affected organ, and these factors should be included in any mechanistically based extrapolation model.

Gehring and Blau (1977) described a procedure for visualizing the effects of saturable DNA repair systems upon the production of genetic damage. The details of this model are summarized in Figure 1.

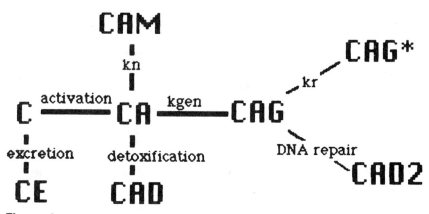

**Figure 1**
Hypothetical model of the fate of a chemical carcinogen in the body. This model requires bioactivation, covalent binding to genetic material, and subsequent replication of damaged DNA for initiation of carcinogenesis. (C) Chemical; (CE) chemical excreted; (CA) chemical bioactivated; (CAD) bioactivated chemical after detoxification; (CAG) bioactivated chemical bound to DNA; (CAD2) CAG after DNA repair; (CAG*) CAG after cell replication.

Chemical is deposited into the model without consideration of the input functions, and a series of differential equations are formulated to describe the disposition of the chemical. Chemical (C) is either excreted (CE) or activated to a reactive species (CA). CA, in turn, may be detoxified (CAD), react with noncritical macromolecules (CAM), or react with genetic material (CAG). The genetic adducts may be repaired (CAD2) or undergo consolidation during replication of damaged DNA (CAG*). Some of these reactions (excretion, activation, detoxification, and DNA repair) are assumed to be enzymatic in nature, and the rates of these reactions are described by the Michaelis-Menten equation. The reaction of CA with noncritical macromolecules or genetic materials is assumed to be diffusion limited with rate constants of kn and kgen respectively. The replication of cells is naively assumed to occur at a constant rate throughout, so that the formation of CAG* is also a first order process with a rate constant of kr. The formation of CAG* is assumed to be a crucial event in the initiation of carcinogenesis in this model since replication of the damaged DNA may lead to an alteration of nucleotide sequence which is no longer recognized as damage by DNA repair systems. Realistic values of the various rate constants were chosen for the simulation. The reader is referred to Gehring and Blau (1977) for further details of this model.

The series of differential equations describing these processes may be numerically integrated on a digital computer. Unlike the frail animal, the maximum tolerated dose for a computer is infinity, so a wide variety of doses may be evaluated. Normalized binding of chemical to noncritical macromolecules (CAM/C0), genetic material with subsequent replication (CAG*/C0), and genetic material with sub-

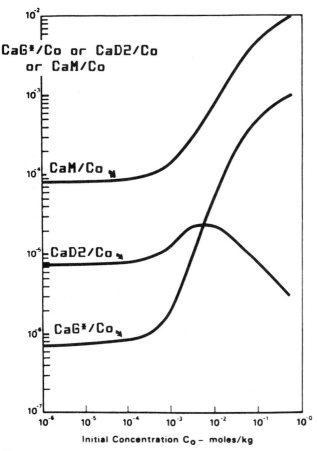

**Figure 2**

Calculated amounts (normalized for dose, CO) of chemical bound to nongenetic macromolecules (CAM/CO), and chemical bound to genetic material and subsequently replicated (CAG*/CO). Values are those calculated by the computer at very long time periods (i.e., after establishment of steady state).

sequent repair (CAD2/C0) at various doses are depicted in Figure 2. Several important concepts can be derived from this hypothetical model:

1. When the dose exceeds $10^{-4}$ moles/kg, a disproportionate amount of the chemical is bound to critical receptors.
2. Measurement of alkylated molecules (CAM and/or CAG) will give a more realistic dose-response relationship than administered dose.
3. In this model, DNA damage consolidated by repair (CAG*) increases more rapidly than noncritical alkylated macromolecules, due to the saturation of DNA repair systems.

It is also important to realize that events other than direct alteration of DNA may also affect the tumorigenic process. For example, the rate of cellular replication in animals exposed to chemicals is frequently altered by the administered chemical. Reitz et al. (1982) administered chloroform to B6C3F1 mice and found that the rates of cellular division in liver and kidneys were increased by 1400% and 2480%, respectively. Observations such as these may explain how agents which lack direct genotoxicity can increase the tumor yield in animal bioassays.

This may also be visualized in the model of Gehring and Blau with a few relatively minor changes. First, we assume that the rate of replication is not fixed, but may vary as a function of chemical treatment, which is often the case when the rate of destruction of nongenetic targets (macromolecules) exceeds their rate of resynthesis. This results in death of a portion of the cells with subsequent replacement by cellular regeneration. Second, we assume that agents other than the administered chemical may produce low levels of genetic damage in both the control and treated animals (i.e., there is a background rate of genetic damage). Third, we set the rate constant for CA binding to genetic material (kgen) to zero to simulate a material with no direct genotoxicity.

Under these circumstances it can be shown that CAG* will increase slowly throughout the lifetime of control animals, even without any exposure to chemical (Fig. 3, line A). Episodic exposures to genotoxic chemicals throughout the lifetime of an animal will lead to a more rapid accumulation of CAG* in a stairstep fashion (Fig. 3, line B). Similarly, more rapid accumulation of CAG* is seen when a cytotoxic chemical stimulates cellular regeneration (Fig. 3, line C), even when this chemical has no direct effect upon DNA.

There appear to be agents that increase the incidence of tumors in animal bioassays through indirect mechanisms such as recurrent cytotoxicity. Sodium orthophenyl phenate (SOPP) is an example of such an agent.

Hiraga and Fujii (1981) reported that F344 rats consuming diets with high levels of SOPP developed tumors of the urinary tract, especially bladder tumors. Reitz et al. (1983) studied the metabolism of SOPP in F344 rats and found a pronounced dose-dependency in the metabolic pathways. At low doses (0.017 mM/kg–0.17 mM/kg) most of the SOPP given by gavage was eliminated as glucuronide or sulfate conjugates of SOPP. However, when higher doses of SOPP (1.7 mM/kg) were administered, 25–30% of the urinary radioactivity was recovered in the form of more highly oxidized species. The more oxidized species are similar to the metabolites identified as metabolites of benzene and hypothesized to be responsible for benzene toxicity (Tunek et al. 1978).

Reitz et al. (1984) subsequently found that in vivo macromolecular binding of 14C-SOPP rose disproportionately as the primary metabolic pathways were saturated (Table 1) and suggested that the toxicity of SOPP was related to production of the more highly oxidized metabolite of SOPP. Rates of cellular division in bladder epithelial cells (visualized by microautoradiography) increased 5000–7000% after administration of 1.7 mM/kg SOPP (Reitz and Watanabe 1983).

However, the reactive intermediate formed from SOPP is apparently not genotoxic because SOPP was not mutagenic in the Ames test and did not induce unscheduled

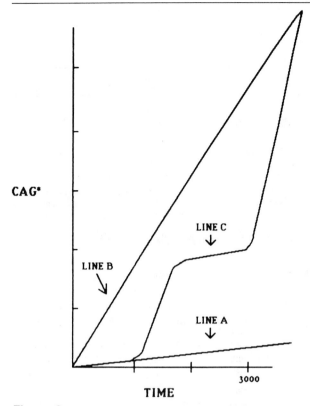

**CAG***

TIME

**Figure 3**
Calculated amounts of replicated genetic damage (CAG*) as a function of time in a modified Gehring/
Blau model with a nonzero background of genetic damage and a variable rate of cellular replication.
(*Line A*) CAG* buildup in control animals; (*Line B*) CAG* buildup during the same time period with
two exposures to a genotoxic chemical; (*Line C*) CAG* buildup with an altered rate of cellular replication,
but no input of CAG other than background genetic damage.

DNA synthesis in primary rat hepatocytes. Furthermore, no covalent binding of
14C-SOPP to DNA of bladder was detected after administration of 1.7 mM/kg SOPP
(detection limit one alkylation per million nucleotides) (Reitz et al. 1983).

Consequently, the increased incidence of bladder lesions observed by Hiraga
and Fujii (1981) after administration of SOPP is likely related to the induction of
recurrent cytotoxicity rather than to any direct effect upon the genome. Since
cytotoxicity would not be expected at low levels where the rate of replacement of
cytoplasmic components would greatly exceed their rate of destruction, it does not
seem logical to perform a linear extrapolation of data from high doses over several
orders of magnitude for human risk estimations. How then are we to proceed in
such cases?

The processes of carcinogenesis appear to be complex enough so that they will
probably never be totally amenable to rigorous mathematical analysis. Nevertheless,
the individual components of the process can often be modeled in a meaningful

## Table 1
In Vivo Macromolecular Binding in Tissues of Male F344 Rats Dosed with 14C-SOPP

|  | Liver | Kidney | Bladder |
|---|---|---|---|
| SOPP (mM/kg) |  |  |  |
| 0.19 | 3.7 ± 0.6 | 4.9 ± 0.5 | 1.9 |
| 0.38 | 9.0 ± 0.6 | 8.8 ± 2.4 | 2.4 |
| 0.75 | 28.0 ± 11[a] | 37.0 ± 5.5 | 24.0 |
| 1.90 | 485.0 ± 210[a] | 200.0 ± 22.0 | 400.0[a] |

Values reported are n moles/mg of protein ± standard deviation for radioactivity remaining in tissues after extensive extraction with 5% TCA and 80% methanol. N = 4 for liver and kidney data unless otherwise noted. Bladders from three to four animals were pooled for a single determination in bladder tissue.
[a]Indicates significant deviation from linearity by regression analysis ($p < 0.05$)

way (e.g., the use of pharmacokinetics to predict internal dose). Park and Snee (1983) have recently suggested an approach that offers sufficient flexibility to incorporate a variety of pertinent information into risk extrapolations without becoming unreasonably complex. The conceptual basis of their procedure is outlined below:

1. First the positive data from one or more bioassays are extrapolated over a limited range to estimate a 1% incidence level (ED01). In general, any of the commonly used models will give reasonable fit to experimental data over a narrow extrapolation range.
2. Then an initial estimate of the safe dose is calculated as:

Initial Estimate = ED01 × 1/F

where F is a safety factor whose size depends upon the nature of the risk being estimated. Historically F has varied from 10 to 1000 in most cases.
3. Finally the initial estimate of the safe dose is adjusted by a series of additional multiplicative factors based on our additional knowledge of the compound:

Safe Dose = Initial Estimate × (A1 × A2 × . . . Ai)

4. Park and Snee (1983) have commented that "The evaluation of Ai will be subjective and will require an agreement of expert opinion to arrive at quantification. Scientific judgment and the use of extrapolation factors are a better approach, however, than burying biological issues in mathematical sophistication."

In the case of SOPP it is clear that several of the factors would suggest that the safe dose should be considerably higher than the initial estimate. These include the dose-dependency of the metabolic pathways, the lack of genotoxicity, and the species specificity. Hagiwara et al. (1984) failed to observe bladder tumors in B6C3F1 mice consuming diets supplemented with high levels of SOPP.

This composite approach, although lacking the mathematical elegance of a single unified model, allows the input of data from a variety of sources into the risk assessment process. It should provide a motivation for conducting the supplemental studies that are vital to increasing the accuracy of quantitative risk assessments.

## REFERENCES

Gehring, P.J. and G.E. Blau. 1977. Mechanisms of carcinogenesis: Dose response. *J. Environ. Pathol. Toxicol.* **1:** 163.

Hagiwara, A., M. Shibata, M. Hirose, S. Fukushima, and N. Ito. 1984. Long-term toxicity and carcinogenicity study of sodium O-phenylphenate in B6C3F1 mice. *Food Chem. Toxicol.* **22:** 809.

Hiraga, K. and T. Fujii. 1981. Induction of tumours of the urinary system in F344 rats by dietary administration of sodium O-phenylphenate. *Food Cosmet. Toxicol.* **19:** 303.

Maher, V.M., D.J. Dorney, A.L. Mendrala, B. Konze-Thomas, and J.J. McCormick. 1979. DNA excision-repair processes in human cells can eliminate the cytotoxic and mutagenic consequences of ultraviolet radiation. *Mutat. Res.* **62:** 311.

Park, C.N. and R.D. Snee. 1983. Quantitative risk assessment: State-of-the-art for carcinogenesis. *Amer. Statis.* **37:** 427.

Reitz, R.H. and P.G. Watanabe. 1983. Importance of nongenetic mechanisms in carcinogencity. In *Developments in the science and practice of toxicology* (ed. A.W. Hayes et al.), vol. 11, p. 163. Elsevier Science Publishers, Amsterdam, The Netherlands.

Reitz, R.H., T.R. Fox, and J.F. Quast. 1982. Mechanistic considerations for carcinogenic risk estimation: Chloroform. *Environ. Health Perspect.* **46:** 163.

Reitz, R.H., T.R. Fox, J.F. Quast, E.A. Hermann, and P.G. Watanabe. 1983. Molecular mechanisms involved in the toxicity of orthophenylphenol and its sodium salt. *Chem. Biol. Interact.* **43:** 99.

――――. 1984. Biochemical factors involved in the effects of orthophenylphenol (OPP) and sodium orthophenylphenate (SOPP) on the urinary tract of male F344 rats. *Toxicol. Appl. Pharmacol.* **73:** 745.

Russel, W.L., E.M. Kelley, P.R. Hunsicker, J.W. Bangham, S.C. Maddux, and E.L. Phipps. 1979. Specific-locus test shows ethylnitrosourea to be the most potent mutagen in the mouse. *Proc. Natl. Acad. Sci. U.S.A.* **76:** 5818.

Russel, W.L., P.R. Hunsicker, G.D. Raymer, M.H. Steele, K.F. Stelzner, and H.M. Thompson. 1982a. Dose-response curve for ethylnitrosourea induced specific locus mutations in mouse spermatogonia. *Proc. Natl. Acad. Sci. U.S.A.* **79:** 3589.

Russel, W.L., P.R. Hunsicker, D.A. Carpenter, C.V. Cornett, and G.M. Guinn. 1982b. Effect of dose fractionation on the ethylnitrosourea induction of specific locus mutations in mouse spermatogonia. *Proc. Natl. Acad. Sci. U.S.A.* **79:** 3592.

Tunek, A., K.L. Platt, M. Przybylski, and F. Oesch. 1978. Microsomal metabolism of benzene to species irreversibly binding to microsomal protein and effects of modifications of this metabolism. *Mol. Pharmacol.* **14:** 920.

## COMMENTS

**ALBERT:**   Are those curves based on exponential removal of adducts?

**REITZ:**   Yes. We picked a set of constants that seemed biochemically reasonable for use in the model. We also assumed that the processes which have names in Figure 1 are likely to be governed by Michaelis-Menten kinetics (i.e., saturable). These processes are activation, excretion, detoxification, and DNA repair. We further assumed that the activated intermediate, CA, would react nonenzymatically (i.e., nonsaturably) with noncritical and critical targets in the cell. Since we did not know anything about the processes of cellular replication, we assumed that this would proceed at a constant rate throughout. Now the model predicts for us what the behavior of the various species shown will be under those particular conditions. I've simply chosen a couple of concentrations of administered dose to show what those predictions are.

**WEINSTEIN:** How do you choose the parameters?

**REITZ:** We looked at several sets of possible parameters and chose some which would demonstrate the possibilities for nonlinear responses.

**WEINSTEIN:** That was arbitrary, right?

**REITZ:** It was absolutely arbitrary. It was not real data but was just done for demonstration purposes.

**WEINSTEIN:** Did you attempt to obtain parameters from the studies of Veronica Maher and Justin McCormack?

**REITZ:** No, we haven't done that yet. That would be a very interesting thing to do. That data ought to be accessible, since they have measured concentrations of DNA adducts.

**ALBERT:** What about the point that cell proliferation stops when you get to high doses? Your endpoint there is that CAG*, which is essentially DNA damage following proliferation. Don't you have to consider the fact that the agent itself is slowing down proliferation?

**REITZ:** Actually, many of the complete carcinogens speed up cell proliferation at higher doses. For example, if you give 10 mg/kg of dimethylnitrosamine (DMN) to a mouse, you can see hyperplasia in the liver within 48 hours. A dose of 1 mg/kg DMN generally has no effect upon the rate of cellular replication, but probably does produce genetic lesions. So the dose of 10 mg/kg may be producing genetic lesions and "promoting" them by increasing cell proliferation as well: a synergistic effect from the two different processes.

**ALBERT:** It seems to me this approach is fine for laying out the general possibilities, but the actual results depend on the realities of the circumstances.

**REITZ:** Precisely. I'm not suggesting that we do a risk extrapolation using this model. I'm just saying that I think this model graphically illustrates the kind of information we need to obtain. That's the point I'm making.

**ALBERT:** Did you demonstrate macromolecular binding with the C14 label?

**REITZ:** Yes, we did.

**ALBERT:** In the bladder?

**REITZ:** Yes, in vivo. In that experiment, we gave the animals the radioactive form of the chemical, took the bladders out, and extracted them repeatedly with trichloroacetic acid and methanol to remove all noncovalently-bound radioactivity. Then we solubilized that material and counted the macromolecular binding to everything—protein, RNA, glycogen, whatever. In contrast, in the DNA studies, we used the Marmur procedure to isolate the DNA and purify it from all RNA and protein contaminants. When we did that, we purified away all the radioactivity. So the SOPP metabolite binds, but it doesn't bind to DNA.

**ALBERT:** Is it only at the high doses that you obtained a metabolic pathway which is electrophilic?

**REITZ:** I guess we wouldn't say "only." I think we'd have to say we get a disproportionate amount of it. We couldn't detect it in the experiments we did with lower doses.

**ALBERT:** When you gave a radioactive material, were you giving it at a high dose?

**REITZ:** Absolutely. We gave it at 500 mg/kg down to 50 mg/kg. We saw a big change in the amount that bound to the tissues between those two doses.

**ALBERT:** Were you were making the point that you were getting electrophiles at high doses, but they were too reactive to get to the DNA?

**REITZ:** Exactly. We think these metabolites influence the carcinogenic process by destroying the cells in the bladder. One other experiment is pertinent here. We actually measured the rate of cellular regeneration in animals after administration of 500 mg/kg of SOPP and found that the epithelial cells were dividing from 40 to 60 times as fast as in control animals.

**J. WILSON:** You think that's an effect on proliferation?

**REITZ:** Yes, it's an effect on proliferation and not an effect on the genetic material.

**WEINSTEIN:** It sounds like a promoter.

**PERERA:** Your safety factor approach up to now has been used for reversible toxicity, so what you're proposing is something quite new and different for carcinogenicity, which involves a self-replicating lesion. This approach includes the concept of threshold or "safe" level of exposure to carcinogens. Am I correct?

**REITZ:** Let me point out that if you do a linear extrapolation down to the $10^{-5}$

level, or if you extrapolate down to the 1% level and then apply a 1000-fold safety factor, you get the same answer. You come up with virtually the same safe dose, or allowable dose, or whatever.

**PERERA:** Then what is the benefit of using this method?

**REITZ:** The benefit is that you can modify that safety factor to take advantage of the other information. For example, we had another species that was bioassayed and it was negative. How could you put that into a mathematical model if you're performing linear extrapolation? You don't use that information at all in that case.

**PERERA:** That's an important point. What is the value or weight one gives to a negative study? We just heard about the different responses between species and strains and that the prudent policy is to take the response in the most sensitive species.

**REITZ:** I guess that I disagree with you. I think if you have a material that has five bioassays that are all clearly positive, then you have to be more concerned about that material than one for which some bioassays are positive and others are negative. You have to give some sort of weight to that when you are rank-ordering the risk potential. That's not to say that you ignore positive bioassays when there's a negative bioassay either.

**GOLDSTEIN:** As you pointed out, this would be a less formal approach than the approach usually used. How are you going to prevent someone from deciding what number is wanted in advance, and then using specific safety factors to get that number?

**REITZ:** I think that it should be relatively clear how to use pharmacokinetic data. In other cases, such as weighting negative bioassays, scientific judgment would have to be used. In a practical sense, I think that's what really goes on when you do a risk assessment anyway. When IARC sits as a body and decides if there's sufficient evidence for carcinogenicity or limited evidence for carcinogenicity or whatever, they're weighing all these factors in their minds. This approach simply says, "Here are all the factors we are weighing and here's how important we think they are to the overall risk assessment." Let's put this out in the open where everybody can see what we're doing.

**PREUSS:** But the big policy question is whether you go up or down from $10^{-5}$. In other words, you mentioned that if you have a couple of negative bioassays versus a chemical that had five positive bioassays, you might weight them differently. Of course, at that point I don't think it's a scientific question; I think it's a policy question in terms of public health protection—whether or not you want to add an additional safety factor for each positive one, so that for the one that had five positive bioassays you'd go down to $10^{-6}$ or $10^{-7}$, or whether you'd be going up from $10^{-5}$ to some higher level. I don't think there's any science that would guide you in that discussion or in those decisions. We are back to exactly the same point that Bernie [Goldstein] made, which is, "(a) how would you prevent manipulation of the system; and (b) how would you get the two of us to agree on what those factors are?"

**REITZ:** One of the things that I like about this approach is that it eliminates all the controversy about which model is right and which model is wrong. Almost all of the models will fit the data reasonably well when you're just extrapolating to the 1% effect level, and outside that range, we're just guessing anyway. This approach says, "Here's as far as we can reasonably go with the data we have, and now here's our best guess as to what the real risk is, with some indication of why we think that." That's the best we can do—let's be honest about it.

**ALBERT:** The formation of electrophiles that are so reactive that they don't get to the DNA is not unique to this material. Dioxin is a good example of that. But they do react with macromolecules. Now, we heard earlier from Dr. Lyon that Sega at Oak Ridge seems to have evidence that interaction with proteins can cause mutations. How does that come about—because it's relevant to this apparently nongenotoxic agent.

**LYON:** He says that the interaction of the EMS with the proteins distorts the DNA and causes the damage.

**WEINSTEIN:** It seems to me that you should go one step further in your analysis in the direction taken by Iain Purchase. How does human liver handle this compound? Perhaps you will find that it forms this quinone at very low doses or maybe only at very high doses. The critical question is, how do humans respond to this material?

**REITZ:** I think that's a very important point.

**WEINSTEIN:** Unless you go further, I don't think you have provided us with any reassurance as to what the safe dose is.

# Session 6:
# Specific Case Histories

# A Scientific Approach to Formaldehyde Risk Assessment

JAMES A. SWENBERG, HENRY d'A. HECK, KEVIN T. MORGAN,
AND THOMAS B. STARR
Chemical Industry Institute of Toxicology
Research Triangle Park, North Carolina 27709

## OVERVIEW

Mathematical models for quantitative risk assessment are being used increasingly by regulatory agencies. These models, estimated primarily with tumor incidence data gathered at high-administered exposure levels, are extrapolated downward to predict potential results at low exposures. No appropriate data bases exist that would allow a true validation of the models. Furthermore, these models give no explicit consideration to factors such as saturable homeostatic mechanisms including deposition, absorption, detoxification, and DNA repair. It is proposed that quantitative risk assesment models should incorporate as much mechanistic data as possible to increase their accuracy. In the case of formaldehyde, relevant data include the dose-response relationships for cell proliferation and covalent binding to DNA, and the fact that airborne concentration rather than cumulative exposure exerts the greatest influence on toxicity. By itself, incorporation of data on DNA covalent binding as the measure of internal exposure reduces the multistage model's maximum likelihood estimate of nasal cancer risk by a factor of 53 at concentrations of 1 ppm or less. Since accurate quantitative risk assessments can be of great value in the regulatory decisionmaking process, it is urged that new models which incorporate such data be developed and utilized.

## INTRODUCTION

As is apparent from the subject of this volume, regulatory policy regarding toxic substances is making greater and greater use of quantitative risk assessment in the decisionmaking process. Data from animal bioassays are often employed in a number of mathematical models to extrapolate to low-dose risk estimates. Since high-dose animal data can be incorporated into several different models, such risk estimates can and frequently do vary by several orders of magnitude. The real dilemma is that such models are highly theoretical, with no real data base by which to critically evaluate them. At the present time, the $ED_{01}$ study of 2-acetylaminofluorene-exposed mice provides the largest data set (Staffa and Mehlman 1979); yet even this study covered a dose range of less than one order of magnitude. Thus, drawing conclusions on the presence or absence of "no effect or threshold levels" using animal bioassay data is meaningless when stated in the context of risk extrapolations covering

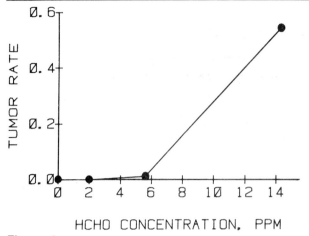

HCHO CONCENTRATION, PPM

**Figure 1**
Formaldehyde concentration response for the induction of squamous cell carcinoma of the Fischer 344 rat nasal passages. Adapted from Starr et al. (1985).

exposures several orders of magnitude lower. The paucity of available quantitative data on which to judge models for quantitative risk assessment or the presence or absence of thresholds represents a serious gap in our scientific data base.

This poses a real dilemma for the regulatory agencies since they are mandated the task of protecting human health from unreasonable risks. How does one prioritize risks from competing factors so that those posing the greatest hazard are dealt with first? This is a place where quantitative risk assessment could be of great value, but accurate estimates must be utilized if the process is to be effective. Unfortunately, the present mathematical models used in quantitative risk assessment cannot be evaluated for their accuracy due to the lack of an appropriate data base. One can use human epidemiology data to put upper and lower bounds on risk estimates when human data are available. In most cases, however, the epidemiologic data are inadequate for this task. A second alternative is to relate the bioassay tumor response to an internal dosimeter, such as DNA adducts, so that factors such as absorption, distribution, metabolic activation, detoxification, and DNA repair can be incorporated (Hoel et al. 1983). Since many of these factors represent saturable processes, their influence probably differs greatly between high- versus low-dose exposures. Consideration of such effects is particularly important when observed tumor data from animal bioassays are nonlinear (Hoel et al. 1983). This is the case for formaldehyde, where less than a threefold increase in ambient air concentration (5.6 ppm versus 14.3 ppm) resulted in a 50-fold increase in the incidence of squamous cell carcinoma in rats (Fig. 1). Since the completion of this bioassay, a great deal of research has been conducted on the mechanisms involved in the toxicity and carcinogenicity of formaldehyde. These data have been reviewed recently (Swenberg et al. 1983a; Starr et al. 1984), therefore, only the highlights will be described below. While much future research is necessary to fully understand the exact mechanisms involved, it is presently clear that many of the factors that control internal dosimetry are affected greatly by the ambient air concentration of formaldehyde. Thus, to avoid bias, low-dose risk estimates should incorporate comparisons of squamous cell carcinoma incidence with the dose of formaldehyde that reaches critical target macromolecules. As discussed in the paragraphs below, the best measure of this target site dosimetry at the present time is the amount of DNA cross-linking that occurs in the respiratory epithelium of the rat nasal passages.

## RESULTS

Much of the initial research on mechanisms involved in formaldehyde's toxicity and carcinogenicity focused on the marked species difference in squamous cell carcinoma incidence (Table 1) (Kerns et al. 1983; Swenberg et al. 1983a; Starr et al. 1984). Whereas 103/232 rats exposed to 14.3 ppm formaldehyde developed squamous cell carcinomas, there were only two such neoplasms in 215 mice. The incidence of nasal cancer in mice exposed to 14.3 ppm formaldehyde was remarkably similar to the 2/235 squamous cell carcinomas diagnosed in rats exposed to 5.6 ppm formaldehyde. When respiratory depression due to sensory irritation was examined in rats and mice, an important mechanism which could account for the marked species difference became clear. After normalizing by the two species' nasal passage surface area, the amount of formaldehyde inhaled per unit time by rats was nearly twice that inhaled by mice when animals were exposed to 15 ppm formaldehyde (Chang et al. 1983). Furthermore, the amount of formaldehyde inhaled per unit time by mice exposed to 15 ppm formaldehyde was similar to that inhaled by rats exposed to 6 ppm. Parallel dose/species response relationships were demonstrated for cytoxicity and cell proliferation. Thus, the correlation between ambient air concentration and both acute and chronic toxic response is poor even for two closely related species.

The relationship between ambient air concentration and toxic response is also critical within a species. One of the factors that may be responsible for this relationship is the interaction of formaldehyde with the nasal mucociliary apparatus. The mucociliary apparatus is a complex and dynamic system that warms, humidifies, and cleanses incoming air. That portion of the rat nose that developed squamous cell carcinomas is normally covered by a continuous blanket of mucus that flows over the respiratory epithelium and is swallowed (Fig. 2) (Morgan et al. 1984). Since formaldehyde is a highly reactive compound, it should readily bind to mucus components such as glycoproteins and other proteins and in part be carried away from the nose and swallowed in a bound form. Experiments by Morgan and coworkers (1983a,b) have shown that exposure of rats to high concentrations of formaldehyde (15 ppm) causes physical changes in mucus, mucostasis, and ciliastasis in those locations where cytotoxicity and squamous cell carcinomas are produced following chronic exposures to similar airborne concentrations. The extent of these changes is time and concentration dependent as shown in Figure 3. It should be noted that no inhibition of mucociliary function was detected at 0.5 ppm formaldehyde. Thus, at this and lower concentrations, the ability of the nasal

**Table 1**
Summary of Neoplastic Lesions in the Nasal Cavity of Fischer 344 Rats and B6C3F1 Mice Exposed to Formaldehyde Gas

| Exposure group | 0 ppm | | | | 2.0 ppm | | | | 5.6 ppm | | | | 14.3 ppm | | | |
|---|---|---|---|---|---|---|---|---|---|---|---|---|---|---|---|---|
| Species | Mouse | | Rat | | Mouse | | Rat | | Mouse | | Rat | | Mouse | | Rat | |
| Sex | M | F | M | F | M | F | M | F | M | F | M | F | M | F | M | F |
| Number of nasal cavities evaluated | 109 | 114 | 118 | 114 | 100 | 114 | 118 | 118 | 106 | 112 | 119 | 116 | 106 | 109 | 117 | 115 |
| Squamous cell carcinoma | 0 | 0 | 0 | 0 | 0 | 0 | 0 | 0 | 0 | 0 | 1 | 1 | 2 | 0 | 51 | 52 |
| Nasal carcinoma | 0 | 0 | 0 | 0 | 0 | 0 | 0 | 0 | 0 | 0 | 0 | 0 | 0 | 0 | 1[a] | 1 |
| Undifferentiated carcinoma or sarcoma | 0 | 0 | 0 | 0 | 0 | 0 | 0 | 0 | 0 | 0 | 0 | 0 | 0 | 0 | 2[a] | 0 |
| Carcinosarcoma | 0 | 0 | 0 | 0 | 0 | 0 | 0 | 0 | 0 | 0 | 0 | 0 | 0 | 0 | 1 | 0 |
| Polypoid adenoma | 0 | 0 | 1 | 0 | 0 | 0 | 4 | 0 | 0 | 0 | 6 | 0 | 0 | 0 | 4 | 1 |
| Osteochondroma | 0 | 0 | 1 | 0 | 0 | 0 | 0 | 0 | 0 | 0 | 0 | 0 | 0 | 0 | 0 | 0 |

[a] A rat in this group also has a squamous cell carcinoma.

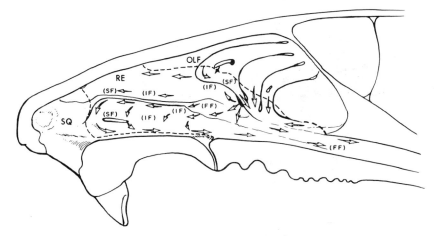

## Figure 2

Diagrammatic sketch of a rat nose opened adjacent to the midline, with the septum removed to expose the turbinates. Arrows indicate the direction of mucus flow. Flow rate is indicated by letters in parentheses: (FF) fast flow (> 6 mm/min); (IF) intermediate flow (2–6 mm/min); (SF) slow flow (< 2 mm/min). Adapted from Morgan et al. (1984).

mucociliary apparatus to remove formaldehyde prior to its contact with the nasal respiratory epithelium is unaffected by formaldehyde exposure. It therefore follows that ambient air concentration is nonlinearly related to target site exposure.

That portion of inhaled formaldehyde that penetrates into nasal tissues must escape local detoxification via intracellular metabolism if it is to interact biochemically with cellular macromolecules. Formaldehyde is a normal metabolic intermediate that is present in all biological tissues (Heck and Casanova-Schmitz 1984). In its active form ($N^5,N^{10}$-methylene-tetrahydrofolate), it is used by mammalian cells in the biosynthesis of purines, thymine, methionine, and serine. It is produced from serine, glycine, and other compounds containing $N$-, $O$-, and $S$-methyl groups, and specific enzymatic pathways exist for its detoxification. Formaldehyde dehydrogenase catalyzes the nicotinamide adenine dinucleotide ($NAD^+$)-dependent oxidation of the reversible formaldehyde adduct, $S$-hydroxymethylglutathione, to $S$-formyl glutathione. Some isozymes of aldehyde dehydrogenase also catalyze the $NAD^+$-dependent oxidation of formaldehyde to formate. Enzymes catalyzing the production and detoxification of formaldehyde are widely distributed in tissues including rat nasal mucosa (Dahl and Hadley 1983; Heck and Casanova-Schmitz 1984), so that rapid metabolism of inhaled formaldehyde is expected.

Only that portion of the formaldehyde in ambient air that does not get bound to mucus or detoxified should be available for cytotoxic and carcinogenic effects. Thus a measure of the amount of formaldehyde that actually binds to critical cellular macromolecules would be of great value in more accurately extrapolating risk across species and concentrations. In mammalian cells, formaldehyde has been shown to cause DNA-protein cross-links which are rapidly repaired (Ross and Shipley 1980;

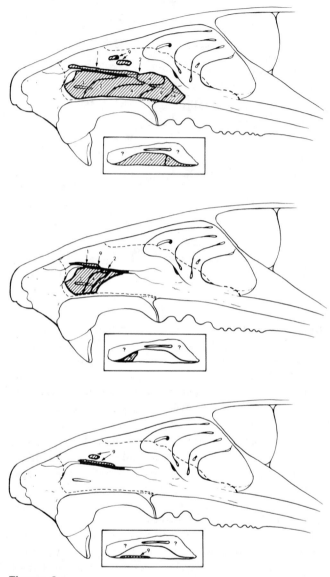

## Figure 3

Diagrams which summarize the results of experiments reported previously (Morgan et al. 1983a). Cross hatching indicates areas of ciliastasis in rats (F-344). The numbers indicate days of exposure (6 hr/day, 5 days/wk) for each exposure group (6 rats/group). The inset shows the lateral aspect of the nasoturbinate. Mucociliary function was assessed at the end of the last exposure using a previously described procedure (Morgan et al. 1983b). Note extensive ciliastasis at 15 ppm, which progresses posteriorly with increasing days exposure. These effects are also present at 6 ppm, but there is much less progression, while at 2 ppm ciliastasis was confined to small areas in animals exposed for 9 days. At 0.5 ppm, ciliastasis was not observed in rats exposed for up to 9 days, indicating a no-effect level. (*Top panel*) 15 ppm formaldehyde; (*middle panel*) 6 ppm formaldehyde; (*bottom panel*) 2 ppm formaldehyde.

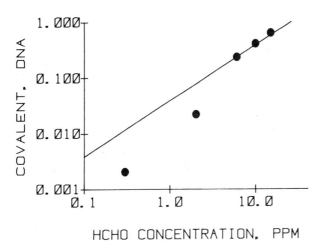

HCHO CONCENTRATION. PPM

### Figure 4

Plot of the concentration of formaldehyde covalently bound to Fischer 344 rat respiratory mucosal DNA (ng/mg DNA) versus airborne formaldehyde concentration following two daily 6-hour exposures. Observed values are denoted by dark circles. The straight line passes from the origin through the level of binding observed at 6 ppm and represents predicted binding levels based on the assumption of linear proportionality between administered and delivered doses. Adapted from Starr et al. (1985).

Grafstrom et al. 1983). Exposure of rats to formaldehyde vapor caused concentration-dependent increases in DNA-protein complexes in the respiratory mucosa of the nasal passages (Casanova-Schmitz and Heck 1983). More recently, similar experiments utilizing [$^{14}$C]- and [$^3$H]-formaldehyde have provided a mechanism to differentiate between covalent binding and metabolic incorporation in the labeling of DNA (Casanova-Schmitz et al. 1984).

These studies involved rats that had been pre-exposed for 1 day to a selected concentration of unlabeled formaldehyde (0.3, 2, 6, 10, or 15 ppm), followed by a single exposure (6 hours) to the same concentration of labeled formaldehyde. It was observed that, although most of the labeling of DNA in the respiratory mucosa was due to normal metabolic incorporation, a small percentage was caused by covalent binding. The latter was identifiable with DNA-protein cross-links.

Of considerable interest was the observation that the concentration of covalently bound formaldehyde in respiratory mucosal DNA depended nonlinearly on the airborne formaldehyde concentration (Fig. 4). These concentrations are shown in Table 2, the last column of which presents normalized concentrations, i.e., amounts of formaldehyde bound to DNA per ppm of airborne formaldehyde. Analysis of these data using Newman-Keuls' multiple range test shows that the normalized concentrations at 0.3 ppm and 2 ppm are not significantly different from each other, nor are those at 6 ppm, 10 ppm, and 15 ppm. Inasmuch as the linear hypothesis would require that all such normalized concentrations have the same value, these data provide strong evidence that covalent binding of formaldehyde to DNA is nonlinearly dependent upon the airborne formaldehyde concentration.

## Table 2

Absolute Concentrations of Covalently Bound [$^{14}$C]-Formaldehyde in Respiratory Mucosal DNA and Concentrations of Covalently Bound Formaldehyde Relative to the Inhaled Formaldehyde Concentration

| Airborne formaldehyde concentration (ppm) | Absolute concentration of covalently bound [$^{14}$C]-formaldehyde[a] (nmole/ mg of DNA) | Concentration of covalently bound [$^{14}$C]-formaldehyde per ppm inhaled formaldehyde[a] |
|---|---|---|
| 0.3 | 0.002 ± 0.003 | 0.007 ± 0.009 |
| 2 | 0.022 ± 0.006 | 0.011 ± 0.003 |
| 6 | 0.233 ± 0.023 | 0.039 ± 0.004 |
| 10 | 0.406 ± 0.099 | 0.041 ± 0.010 |
| 15 | 0.631 ± 0.064 | 0.042 ± 0.004 |

[a]Covalently bound formaldehyde was calculated using the equations given in Appendix 2 of Casanova-Schmitz et al. (1984). Values shown are mean ± s.e. $n = 3$ groups of rates at each concentration, four animals per group.

The nonlinear relationship between administered and delivered formaldehyde doses can have a substantial impact on quantitative estimates of risk associated with low-level exposures. This is readily illustrated by comparing estimates of risk obtained with administered dose (airborne formaldehyde concentration) as the measure of exposure to corresponding estimates obtained with delivered dose (the concentration of covalently bound formaldehyde in target tissue DNA).

In order to convert the delivered dose results to equivalent airborne formaldehyde exposure levels below 2 ppm, the concentration of covalently bound formaldehyde in respiratory mucosal DNA was assumed to be linearly dependent on airborne concentration in this range, with the slope of the relationship given by the normalized value of binding observed at 2 ppm, namely 0.011 nmole/mg DNA/ppm (Table 2). Note that this assumption is likely to overestimate the amount of covalent binding that occurs below 2 ppm, since the observation at 0.3 ppm is about 36% lower than is predicted by this linear relationship.

Results from multistage model analyses of the CIIT bioassay data for Fischer 344 rats as reported by Starr and Gibson (1984) are summarized in Table 3. It is readily apparent that the risk estimates based on delivered dose are smaller than the corresponding estimates based on administered dose. The maximum likelihood estimates are reduced by a factor of approximately 53, whereas the upper 95% confidence bounds are reduced by a factor of about 2.5. Similar but generally larger reductions in both the maximum likelihood risk estimates and their upper 95% confidence bounds (not shown) were obtained from analyses employing the probit, logit, and Weibull quantal response models (Starr and Buck 1984). These results indicate that risk estimates derived with the administered dose as the measure of exposure are conservatively biased, irrespective of the dose-response model employed.

**Table 3**
Multistage Model Estimates of Risk of Squamous Cell Carcinoma in Rats Based on Administered Dose and Delivered Dose at Selected Airborne Formaldehyde Concentrations.

| Airborne concentration (ppm) | Dose measure | Maximum likelihood risk estimate | Upper 95% confidence bound |
|---|---|---|---|
| 1.0 | Administered | $251 \times 10^{-6}$ | $16.0 \times 10^{-4}$ |
| | Delivered | $4.7 \times 10^{-6}$ | $6.2 \times 10^{-4}$ |
| 0.5 | Administered | $314 \times 10^{-7}$ | $8.1 \times 10^{-4}$ |
| | Delivered | $5.9 \times 10^{-7}$ | $3.1 \times 10^{-4}$ |
| 0.1 | Administered | $251 \times 10^{-9}$ | $15.6 \times 10^{-5}$ |
| | Delivered | $4.7 \times 10^{-9}$ | $6.2 \times 10^{-5}$ |

It is, however, important to recognize that use of the covalent binding data as a measure of exposure rests on two critical assumptions that need to be validated with laboratory experiments. First, as was noted earlier, covalent binding was measured following just two 6-hour exposures to airborne formaldehyde. It must therefore be assumed that these observations are representative of the steady-state distribution and pharmacokinetics that prevail throughout the course of a long-term bioassay. Since formaldehyde is a very highly reactive chemical, there is no obvious reason to suppose that this is not the case, but on the other hand, there is at present no direct evidence that the steady-state is achieved after just 2 days of exposure.

Second, it must also be assumed that the covalent binding of formaldehyde to target tissue DNA is an important factor in nasal tumor induction. This is not implausible, since formaldehyde has been shown to have genotoxic activity in a variety of test systems. Furthermore, Hoel et al. (1983) have argued convincingly that it is likely to be "biologically more meaningful to relate tumor response to concentrations of specific DNA adducts in the target tissue than it is to relate tumor response to the administered dose of a chemical." Again, however, the assumption that covalent binding is directly relevant to nasal tumor induction remains to be validated in the laboratory.

## DISCUSSION

While the incorporation of target site dosimetry data would appear to improve the accuracy of low-dose extrapolation, the estimates reported herein probably remain overly conservative for several reasons. First, these estimates assume that the amount of formaldehyde that is covalently bound to DNA at low concentrations remains proportional to that bound at 2 ppm. If the proportion of formaldehyde that penetrates the mucus blanket decreases further with decreasing concentration, or if a greater proportion of that reaching the respiratory epithelium is detoxified, the amount available for covalent binding will be reduced to an even greater extent. Present methods do not permit accurate measurements of formaldehyde covalent binding to DNA at concentrations of 0.1 ppm or less. Thus, an important area for future research will be the development of ultrasensitive techniques for quantitating formaldehyde-DNA adducts.

A second factor that has not been incorporated into the low-dose risk estimates is cell replication. Cell replication should play a direct role in "fixing" mutations due to formaldehyde-DNA adducts, as well as in expanding initiated cell populations. Current theories on multistage carcinogenesis invoke the requirement for sequential mutational events in such expanded cell populations (Hennings et al. 1983; Potter 1980, 1981, 1984; Moolgavkar and Knudson 1981). Cell replication was probably a major factor in the nonlinear concentration response for squamous cell carcinoma induction between 5.6 ppm and 14.3 ppm formaldehyde (Swenberg et al. 1983b; Starr et al. 1984). However, it is not likely to be a major factor in exposures to concentrations less than 2 ppm. The only aspect of the increase in cell replication that is incorporated into the molecular dosimetry approach to risk assessment is the possible effect of increased amounts of single-stranded DNA and subsequent increases in formaldehyde-DNA binding.

Recent risk assessments on formaldehyde have assumed that different exposure regimens with the same product of airborne concentration and duration of daily exposure will produce identical responses (Cohn 1981; EPA 1984). We have shown with both acute and chronic exposure of rats that this is not true (Kerns et al. 1983; Swenberg et al. 1983a,b; Starr et al. 1984). Instead, airborne concentration is the dominant factor in the induction of cytotoxic, proliferative, and hyperplastic cellular alterations in the respiratory epithelium of the nasal passages. Therefore, in a quantitative risk assessment, airborne concentration should be given greater weight than the concentration-duration product would indicate.

It is clear that one could always use more information to improve the accuracy of risk assessments. However, one cannot continually postpone regulation. The scientific and regulatory communities need to develop methods that utilize bases broader than the number of tumor bearing animals per exposure group. In the case of formaldehyde, considerable information is available including cell replication and molecular dosimetry over a limited exposure range. These observations should be employed in risk assessments and utilized in the regulatory process to set interim exposure limits. Periodic review of new findings can then be used to fine tune regulatory decisions. Such an approach has several advantages including (1) more accurate and defensible risk assessment; (2) more rapid regulation of perceived hazards; (3) the fostering of basic and applied research; and (4) greater flexibility in the regulatory process.

## REFERENCES

Casanova-Schmitz, M. and H. d'A. Heck. 1983. Effects of formaldehyde exposure on the extractibility of DNA from proteins in the rat nasal mucosa. *Toxicol. Appl. Pharmacol.* **70:** 121.

Casanova-Schmitz, M., T.B. Starr, and H. d'A. Heck. 1984. Differentiation between metabolic incorporation and covalent binding in the labeling of macromolecules in the rat nasal mucosa and bone marrow by inhaled [$^{14}$C]- and [$^{3}$H]-formaldehyde. *Toxicol. Appl. Pharmacol.* **76:** 26..

Chang, J.C.F., E.A. Gross, J.A. Swenberg, and C.S. Barrow. 1983. Nasal cavity deposition, histopathology, and cell proliferation after single or repeated formaldehyde exposures in B6C3F1 mice and F-344 rats. *Toxicol. Appl. Pharmacol.* **68:** 161.

Cohn, M.S. 1981. Revised carcinogenic risk assessment of urea-formaldehyde foam insulation: Estimates of cancer risk due to inhalation of formaldehyde released by UFFI. U.S. Consumer Product Safety Commission, Washington, D.C., October 26, 1981.

Dahl, A.R. and W.M. Hadley. 1983. Formaldehyde production promoted by rat nasal cytochrome P-450 dependent monooxygenases with nasal decongestants, essences, solvents, air pollutants, nicotine and cocaine as substrates. *Toxicol. Appl. Pharmacol.* **67:** 200.

Grafstrom, R.C., A.J. Fornace, Jr., H. Autrup, J.F. Lechner, and C.C. Harris. 1983. Formaldehyde damage to DNA and inhibition of DNA repair in human bronchial cells. *Science* **220:** 216.

Heck, H. d'A. and M. Casanova-Schmitz. 1984. Biochemical toxicology of formaldehyde. *Rev. Biochem. Toxicol.* **6:** 155.

Hennings, H., R. Shores, M.L. Wenk, E.F. Spangler, R. Tarone, and S.H. Yuspa. 1983. Malignant conversion of mouse skin tumors is increased by tumor initiators and unaffected by tumor promoters. *Nature (Lond.)* **304:** 67.

Hoel, D.G., N.L. Kaplan, and M.W. Anderson. 1983. Implication of nonlinear kinetics on risk estimation in carcinogenesis. *Science* **219:** 1032.

Kerns, W.D., K.L. Pavkov, D.J. Donofrio, E.J. Gralla, and J.A. Swenberg. 1983. Carcinogenicity of formaldehyde in rats and mice after long-term inhalation exposure. *Cancer Res.* **43:** 4382.

Moolgavkar, S.H. and A.G. Knudson, Jr. 1981. Mutation and cancer: A model for human carcinogenesis. *J. Natl. Cancer Inst.* **66:** 1037.

Morgan, K.T. 1983a. Localization of areas of inhibition of nasal mucociliary function in rats following in vivo exposure to formaldehyde. *Am. Rev. Respir. Dis.* **127:** 166.

Morgan, K.T., D.L. Patterson, and E.A. Gross. 1983b. Formaldehyde and the nasal mucociliary apparatus. In *Formaldehyde: Toxicology, epidemiology and mechanisms* (ed. J.J. Clary et al.), p. 193. Marcel Dekker, New York.

Morgan, K.T., X.Z. Jiang, D.L. Patterson, and E.A. Gross. 1984. The nasal mucociliary apparatus: Correlation of structure and function in the rat. *Am. Rev. Respir. Dis.* **130:** 275.

Potter, V.R. 1980. Initiation and promotion in cancer formation: The importance of studies on intercellular communication. *Yale J. Biol. Med.* **53:** 367.

_____. 1981. Commentary: A new protocol and its rationale for the study of initiation and promotion of carcinogenesis in rat liver. *Carcinogenesis* **2:** 1375.

_____. 1984. Use of two sequential applications of initiators in the production of hepatomas in the rat: An examination of the Solt-Farber protocol. *Cancer Res.* **44:** 2733.

Ross, W.E. and N. Shipley. 1980. Relationship between DNA damage and survival in formaldehyde-treated mouse cells. *Mutat. Res.* **79:** 277.

Staffa, J.A. and M.A. Mehlman. 1979. *Innovations in cancer risk assessments* (ED$_{01}$ study). Pathotox Publishers, Park Forest South, Illinois.

Starr, T.B. 1985. The role of mechanistic data in dose-response modeling. In *Assessment of risk from low level exposure to radiation and chemicals: A critical overview* (ed. A.D. Woodhead). Plenum Publishing, New York.

Starr, T.B. and R.D. Buck. 1984. The importance of delivered dose in estimating low-dose cancer risk from inhalation exposure to formaldehyde. *Fundam. Appl. Toxicol.* **4:** 740.

Starr, T.B. and J.E. Gibson. 1984. The importance of delivered dose in quantitative risk estimation: Formaldehyde. *Toxicologist* **4:** 30.

Starr, T.B., J.E. Gibson, C.S. Barrow, C.J. Boreiko, H. d'A. Heck, R.J. Levine, K.T. Morgan, and J.A. Swenberg. 1984. Estimating human cancer risk from formaldehyde: Critical issues. Am. Chem. Soc. (Environmental Chemistry Section). In *Formaldehyde toxicology and analytical chemistry* (ed. V. Turoski). Advances in Chemistry Series. American Chemical Society, Washington. (In press)

Swenberg, J.A., C.S. Barrow, C.J. Boreiko, H. d'A. Heck, R.J. Levine, K.T. Morgan, and T.B. Starr. 1983a. Nonlinear biological responses to formaldehyde and their implications for carcinogenic risk assessment. *Carcinogenesis* **4:** 945.

Swenberg, J.A., E.A. Gross, H.W. Randall, and C.S. Barrow. 1983b. The effect of formaldehyde exposure on cytotoxicity and cell proliferation. In *Formaldehyde: Toxicology, epidemiology, and mechanisms* (ed. J.J. Clary et al.), p. 225. Marcel Dekker, New York.

U.S. Environmental Protection Agency. 1984. Formaldehyde: Determination of significant risk. *Red. Reg.* **49(101):** 21870.

## COMMENTS

**GILLETTE:** Do you have enough radioactivity to permit an amino acid analysis to determine whether or not formaldehyde is incorporated in the carbon pool?

**SWENBERG:** There would be plenty to do that.

**GILLETTE:** Was radioactivity associated with serine and methionine?

**SWENBERG:** We haven't done amino acid analyses. We have actually taken the DNA and digested it to nucleosides.

**GILLETTE:** But were the ring carbons labeled or were the bases really methylated?

**SWENBERG:** Recent HPLC studies have shown that the radioactivity in aqueous DNA is predominantly incorporated into normal deoxynucleosides.

**ALBERT:** How much of the DNA activity is from the metabolic pool?

**SWENBERG:** The radioactivity in the aqueous DNA is all considered metabolic pool. Radioactivity in the interfacial DNA is due to metabolic incorporation and covalent binding. As a result, the interfacial DNA has a higher $^3H/^{14}C$ ratio than the aqueous DNA. If you give glutathione inhibitors to these animals, the $^3H/^{14}C$ ratio in the interfacial DNA will go up to 0.99, indicating that it is all due to covalent binding. Thus, if you wipe out the detoxification mechanisms in the cell, the amount of formaldehyde that is covalently bound increases.

**ALBERT:** Are you saying there's no metabolic incorporation of the formaldehyde into the DNA?

**SWENBERG:** No. You had a ratio in the aqueous DNA of about 0.5.

**WEINSTEIN:** Into the normal purines? And the other half is adducts?

**SWENBERG:** No. The ratio of 0.5 is not a direct measure of adducts. I would refer you to Casanova-Schmitz et al. for details.

**WEINSTEIN:** What do you think the level of adduct formation is?

**SWENBERG:** Dr. Heck did some rough calculations. At 2 ppm, it approaches one per $10^5$.

# Description of a Carcinogenic Risk Assessment Used in a Regulatory Proceeding: Formaldehyde*

MURRAY STEVEN COHN
Directorate for Health Sciences
U.S. Consumer Product Safety Commission
Washington, D.C. 20207

## OVERVIEW

Carcinogenic risk assessment is an uncertain, controversial process largely due to the nature of the toxicological data available. In the case of formaldehyde, data from animals exposed at high concentrations are used as a basis for estimates of human risk at much lower concentrations. Depending upon the assumptions made regarding such extrapolations, ultimate estimates of risk may vary by orders of magnitude. Assumptions are usually made with consideration of what little data are available and attempt to take into account the prevailing theories on carcinogenic mechanism of actions. Much needs to be accomplished in terms of research and discussion before confidence in the procedures for risk estimation is achieved.

## INTRODUCTION

The United States Consumer Product Safety Commission (CPSC) promulgated the ban of a formaldehyde-emitting product, urea-formaldehyde foam insulation in 1982 (CPSC 1982a). One of the technical pieces prepared by the CPSC staff that was important to this regulatory proceeding was a carcinogenic risk assessment which contained an analysis of the risk of cancer due to human exposure to formaldehyde, exposure information regarding the estimated levels of formaldehyde experienced by residents of homes containing the foam insulation, and the resulting estimated carcinogenic risk projected to residents of such homes (CPSC 1982b). The upper bound on carcinogenic risk, in the case of residents of homes with such foam insulation, was about one in 20,000.

Though various industry trade associations, such as the Formaldehyde Institute and the Chemical Industry Institute of Toxicology (CIIT), found fault with many aspects of the CPSC risk assessment, none of the comments led to a substantial alteration of the CPSC staff's position (CPSC 1982b). After the ban of urea-formaldehyde foam insulation was issued, the action was challenged by the industry

---

* The author is employed by the Consumer Product Safety Commission. Since this paper was written in his official capacity, it is in the public domain and may be freely copied or reprinted. The opinions expressed by the author do not necessarily represent the views of the Commission.

in the Fifth Circuit Court of Appeals. Briefs filed by counsel for the Formaldehyde Institute and other parties to the suit noted these same and other criticisms of the CPSC carcinogenic risk assessment as well as other Commission documents. After reviewing oral and written arguments from both sides, the Court vacated the ban in April 1983 (Fifth Circuit 1983). The Commission filed a petition for rehearing with the same court, noting a number of errors in the science dealing with the risk assessment included in the decision, but the petition was largely rejected. When the Solicitor General, after a request by the Commission to appeal the Fifth Circuit Court decision to the Supreme Court, decided against this action in August 1983, the ban was officially vacated.

A detailed discussion of the Fifth Circuit Court's decision with respect to the carcinogenic risk assessment is presented elsewhere (Ashford et al. 1983). A noteworthy concept introduced by the Court, however, was that imprecise data, such as that in CPSC's exposure database, or in the CIIT formaldehyde cancer bioassay, was not compatible with a mathematical risk assessment model, which demands precision. "To make precise estimates," observed the Court, "precise data are required." For example, the Court stated that the error in using a response of 103 rats with nasal cancer out of 240 at risk is inherently large. It indicated that had 20 fewer, or 20 more, rats developed this lesion, the risk predicted by the risk assessment model would be altered drastically (Fifth Circuit 1983). The Court, however, failed to explain why risk estimates must be precise and did not provide acceptable limits on precision. Without guidance as to the amount of variation that is allowed in the databases used for subsequent regulatory purposes, it cannot be known until after judicial challenge whether or not "proper" rulemaking procedures have been adhered to.

Because of the controversy surrounding the adverse health effects of formaldehyde in general, a forum to discuss, and hopefully reach, a scientific consensus on the issues involved was set up under the auspices of the National Center for Toxicological Research. Known as the Consensus Workshop on Formaldehyde, the conference met in October 1983. This paper presents the Commission's current approach to carcinogenic risk assessment in the case of formaldehyde, which is similar to that prepared for the foam insulation ban, and explains how the positions preliminarily reached by the Risk Estimation Panel of the Consensus Conference on Formaldehyde relate to this approach.

## RESULTS

### Use of the CIIT Bioassay on Formaldehyde for Risk Estimation

Although several bioassays have been performed on formaldehyde (Federal Panel on Formaldehyde 1980), the only study containing adequate information for risk estimation is that performed under contract to CIIT on rats (CIIT 1981). The recently completed New York University bioassay (Albert et al. 1982; Sellakumar et al. 1983) was also of the quality needed for risk estimation purposes, but only one dose level (15 ppm) was utilized. Since the CIIT study demonstrated, through the use of multiple exposure levels, that the dose-response curve is nonlinear below 15 ppm, simple linear extrapolation from the single 15 ppm point is inappropriate. The Consensus Conference similarly concluded that the CIIT study contained adequate information for risk estimation purposes and that no other study is, at the present time, quantitatively usable.

The CIIT long-term formaldehyde bioassay is, however, complicated by a series of scheduled sacrifices (at 6, 12, 18, 24, 27, and 30 months) and the cessation of exposure at 24 months, leading to animals being at risk for different periods of time, and none of the animals (except for early deaths) being exposed for lifetime. To account for these factors, all rats sacrificed on schedule are eliminated from this analysis except for those sacrificed at 24, 27, or 30 months (i.e., animals which were sacrificed on schedule before the end of the 2-year exposure period and thus had a shortened observation period compared to the bulk of the animals under study were excluded).

Since exposure ceased at 24 months, all animals are assumed to have been exposed for this period of time. Animals exposed to a given concentration in the CIIT study (i.e., 24 months of exposure, 5 days per week, 6 hours per day is about 0.13 of lifetime) (CPSC 1982b) are assumed to be at 0.13 of the risk that they would be at had they been exposed to that level over lifetime. The only response considered in this risk assessment is squamous cell carcinoma of the nasal cavity. Benign tumors of the nasal cavity (polypoid adenomas) are not combined with nasal squamous cell carcinomas, the major reason being that at the Consensus Conference the opinion was expressed that polypoid adenomas would be precursors to adenocarcinomas, not to squamous cell carcinomas. Conventionally, tumor types are not combined unless they are related. However, there were eight polypoid adenomas (as presently diagnosed) observed at 2.0 ppm in the 159 animals examined histopathologically versus one observed in 157 controls. This difference is statistically significant ($p = 0.019$, one-tailed Fisher Exact Test). The authors of the CIIT study have stated that these tumors are likely related to formaldehyde exposure (CIIT 1981). Though the polypoid adenomas are not used in this risk assessment, an additional cancer risk, stemming from the presence of these benign tumors, may occur as a result of exposure to formaldehyde.

Elimination of animals sacrificed on schedule before 24 months and animals not histopathologically examined in the nasal cavity leads to the data given in Table 1.

## Methodology for Risk Estimation

This risk assessment makes use of the multistage model and linearity at low-dose at the upper 95% confidence limit (UCL) generated by the computer program Global83 (Howe and Crump 1983) to produce the upper estimate of risk, and makes use of the maximum likelihood estimate (MLE) from the same or other models to produce the lower estimate of risk. Global83 is flexible in fitting the CIIT study data, i.e., it does not restrict the power to which dose is raised when determining the MLE.

## Table 1
CIIT Study Data Used for Risk Modeling

| Exposure level | Rats at risk | Number of rats developing squamous cell carcinoma of the nasal cavity |
|---|---|---|
| 0 ppm | 157 | 0 |
| 2.0 ppm | 159 | 0 |
| 5.6 ppm | 155 | 2 |
| 14.3 ppm | 145 | 95 |

The UCL generated by Global is linear at low-dose, whereas the MLE from any independent background model which adequately fits the formaldehyde data is nonlinear throughout the entire dose-response range. The MLE is most likely in a mathematical sense only and would only be most likely in a risk estimation sense if every event caused by formaldehyde at high exposure levels in the CIIT study was also caused entirely by formaldehyde at low exposure levels, i.e., the effects caused by formaldehyde are completely background independent. Even a small amount of interaction with background would be expected to lead to low-dose linearity (Hoel 1980). Since a number of studies show that formaldehyde is genotoxic (Federal Panel on Formaldehyde 1980; Swenberg et al. 1983a) and can interact with agents which affect carcinogenesis in processes such as initiation, promotion, and viral transformation (Boreiko and Ragan 1983; Frazelle et al. 1983; Hatch et al. 1983), it can be concluded that formaldehyde is extremely likely to interact with background carcinogenic processes; linearity at low-dose follows as a consequence.

Linearity at low-dose would likely be more applicable to the human situation as compared to rats, since the population, which is genetically heterogeneous (as opposed to inbred rats), exhibits a background cancer rate at many sites, including the lung, upper respiratory tract, the oral cavity, and nasal cavities (the 1973–1977 U.S. incidence rate for the latter is 0.8/100,000/year [National Cancer Institute 1981]). Thus, it is likely that a risk estimate based upon the UCL is closer to the true risk than that based upon an MLE in the case of formaldehyde. The Risk Estimation Panel of the Formaldehyde Consensus Conference decided that in order to estimate the carcinogenic risk of exposure to formaldehyde, two mathematical modeling procedures can be used to produce the range of the potential risk. One incorporates linearity at low-dose and is consistent with that used to produce the upper estimate of risk used here. The other, which involves a choice of nonlinear-at-low-dose models, includes the model used to produce the lower estimate of risk used here.

With respect to carcinogenesis, humans and rats are assumed to respond similarly to a given lifetime formaldehyde exposure level, all other influences being equal. This assumption is also reflective of the Consensus Conference, which noted that although there are differences in formaldehyde carcinogenicity among different species, at present there is no reason to assume that humans would be more or less susceptible than the rat. Another assumption, which was not discussed at the Consensus Conference, is that risk is related to proportion of lifetime exposed. These assumptions are made since they are reasonable and plausible in the absence of information to the contrary.

In any dose-response analysis to be used in risk assessment, it is important to know the relationship between effective dose, or that dose which is present at a target site, and the dose administered to the animal or human. The use of the administered dose in a risk analysis is precluded only if it has been demonstrated that the ratio of "administered" to "effective" dose is not constant as the exposure level changes in the range of exposures considered.

Some have suggested that the ratio is not constant for the case of the nasal cavity because, at low levels of formaldehyde, the mucous layer would absorb the formaldehyde and transport it away from the nasal mucosa. At high levels, the formaldehyde would "break through" the mucous layer and reach the nasal mucosal target (Frazelle et al. 1983; Gibson 1983). This argument, however, is not supported by the present evidence. Existing data, indeed, support an alternative viewpoint, that the ratio is relatively constant regardless of exposure level. The Consensus Conference noted that the nonlinear response to dosage seen in the CIIT study is in contrast with the linear response of DNA-protein cross-links at 6 ppm and above. The actual data are discussed in detail elsewhere (CPSC 1984).

Another hypothesis that has been advanced is that when rats are exposed to high levels of formaldehyde, ulceration and heightened cellular turnover/proliferation are observed (Swenberg et al. 1983a; Frazelle et al. 1983); any tumors seen subsequently are dependent upon this early cytotoxicity. As a result, since the ulceration is not seen at lower exposure levels, no carcinogenic response would occur (i.e., a threshold for the carcinogenic effects of formaldehyde).

However, ulceration was only observed in a short-term (less than 2 weeks) study (Swenberg et al. 1983b) which showed that initial destruction of the respiratory epithelium at 15 ppm was followed by replacement of these cells with squamous cells (thus increased cellular proliferation is observed). Once this more resistant layer is formed, further ulceration and resulting heightened cellular turnover would be unlikely (no ulceration was observed at 6, 12, 18, or 24 months at 14.3 ppm formaldehyde in the CIIT bioassay). This squamous cell layer is the target tissue; and it is from this layer, not the original respiratory epithelium, that the large number of observed carcinomas arise. None of the experiments performed at CIIT address cellular turnover after the nasal mucosa reaches equilibrium for a given exposure regimen with respect to cell type. Thus, the original cytotoxicity may well simply change the target layer as opposed to being a prerequisite for carcinogenic development. No tumors were found in the CIIT study at 6 months; it was under the conditions of the continuing exposure to formaldehyde over 1–2 years that the tumors observed were produced (indeed, when exposure ceased, the promoting process also ceased as indicated by a reversal of the squamous metaplasia) (CIIT 1981).

The original target layer is also susceptible to the carcinogenic effects of formaldehyde at lower concentrations, since a significant benign tumor response, as well as squamous metaplasia, was observed at 2.0 ppm where ulceration would not be expected to occur (Swenberg et al. 1983b). All observations are consistent with the dose-response curve being upwardly curved at high exposure due to the combined initiation and promotion (possibly including the initial cytotoxicity) effects of formaldehyde. It is therefore unlikely that the initial cytotoxicity/ulceration is a prerequisite for carcinogenesis.

One must keep in mind the uncertainty attendant to the process of risk estimation. Each assumption referred to in this section is made in the absence of data sufficient to warrant the assumption unnecessary. Obviously, the estimates of risk will vary as do these assumptions. The two assumptions most likely to affect estimates of risk are those used in extrapolating between species, and those used in extrapolating risks at high to low formaldehyde concentrations.

## Calculation of Unit Estimates of Risk

Two estimates of risk using the multistage model are calculated for a given exposure. These two estimates can be placed into perspective by comparing them with the results of using various other models in additive background (using UCLs of those models) and independent background (using MLEs of those models) modes. Values (except for the multistage) were obtained from the computer program RISK81 (Kovar and Krewski 1981). Table 2 displays the exposure levels which, under the conditions of the CIIT bioassay, give a predicted excess cancer risk of $1.0 \times 10^{-5}$. The table illustrates that the major factor affecting final estimates of risk is not the choice of a mathematical extrapolation model, but rather whether or not background (as included in a UCL) is taken to be additive or independent. The table also illustrates that use of the multistage UCL is not the most conservative of the estimates from

## Table 2
Comparison of Various Mathematical Risk Estimation Models

| | Formaldehyde level (ppm)[a] for an estimated risk of $1 \times 10^{-5}$ | |
| Model[b] | MLE (independent background)[c] | UCL (additive background)[d] |
|---|---|---|
| Logit | 1.5 | 0.000012 |
| gamma-Multihit | 2.1 | 0.0071 |
| Multistage | 1.1 | 0.0028 |
| Probit | 2.7 | 0.0018 |
| Weibull extreme value | 1.2 | 0.000033 |

[a] Under conditions of the CIIT bioassay (formaldehyde exposure 6 hours/day, 5 days/week for 2 years)

[b] The linear and one-hit models are not included as they do not provide an adequate fit to the CIIT formaldehyde bioassay data. All models were fitted using RISK81 except the multistage, which was fitted using Global83. Input data are shown in Table 1.

[c] Maximum likelihood estimate

[d] 95% upper confidence limit based on variance of log dose

the various other model additive background UCLs (it should be noted that the additive background UCL for the logit and Weibull models may be overestimated by one to two orders of magnitude, due to the way RISK81 handles data if there is no experimental background).

The first of the two estimates for this assessment is derived from the maximum likelihood estimate output by Global83 based on the input data given in Table 1. This estimate, which is simply a "best fit to the data" estimate, is expected to apply in the case that formaldehyde cannot interact with background carcinogenic processes and other environmental carcinogens. The equation for the MLE (at nonsaturating risks) is

Lifetime Estimated Excess Risk (MLE) $= 0.00000481E^4 + 0.00000144E^5$

where E is the level of exposure administered 6 hours per day, 5 days per week over a 2-year period. Values of the calculated maximum likelihood estimates are displayed in Table 3. Dividing by the proportion of lifetime (0.13) that the rats were exposed (CPSC 1982b), the MLE (at nonsaturating risks) is

Lifetime Estimated Excess Risk (MLE) $= 0.000037L^4 + 0.0000011L^5$

where L is the level of exposure administered for lifetime.

The second estimate of risk uses the upper 95% confidence limit output by Global83 based on the input given in Table 1. This estimate, which incorporates linearity at low-dose, is expected to apply in the case that formaldehyde can interact with background processes or with exposures to other chemicals. The equation for this estimate, in the linear portion of the curve (which applies below 1 ppm) is

Lifetime Estimated Excess Risk (UCL) $= 0.0036E$

where E is the level of exposure administered 6 hours per day, 5 days per week over a 2-year period. Values of the calculated upper (95% upper confidence limit from Global83) estimates are displayed in Table 3. Dividing by the proportion of lifetime exposed (0.13), the upper estimate (applying below 1 ppm) is

Lifetime Estimated Excess Risk (UCL) $= 0.028L$

**Table 3**
Estimated Human Carcinogenic Risks (Lifetime Exposure)

| Exposure level | Upper estimate of risk | Lower estimate of risk |
| --- | --- | --- |
| 5.0  ppm | $1.7 \times 10^{-1}$ | $5.8 \times 10^{-2}$ |
| 2.0  ppm | $5.5 \times 10^{-2}$ | $9.5 \times 10^{-4}$ |
| 1.0  ppm | $2.8 \times 10^{-2}$ | $4.8 \times 10^{-5}$ |
| 0.10 ppm | $2.8 \times 10^{-3}$ | $3.8 \times 10^{-9}$ |
| 0.05 ppm | $1.4 \times 10^{-3}$ | $2.4 \times 10^{-10}$ |
| 0.01 ppm | $2.8 \times 10^{-4}$ | $3.7 \times 10^{-13}$ |

where L is the level of exposure administered for a lifetime.

Differences in assumptions can lead to orders of magnitude differences in risk estimates, as demonstrated by the upper and lower formaldehyde risk estimates calculated here.

## DISCUSSION

The procedure for estimating human carcinogenic risks based on animal data is complex and difficult, encompassing many disciplines, and is subject to a large uncertainty due to assumptions based on data and scientific hypotheses. One of the most controversial issues is the modeling of the dose-response curve, which is fit to the data from a long-term animal bioassay. Since these data are usually obtained at doses higher than those experienced by the population at risk, mathematical extrapolation models are employed to project the risk at lower levels of exposure. If, such as in the case of formaldehyde, the dose-response curve is nonlinear at the higher exposure levels, a much lower risk is estimated for humans if such nonlinearity is continued throughout the entire dose-response curve, as compared to a risk based on the dose-response curve becoming linear at low-dose.

The experience that the CPSC has had with formaldehyde has demonstrated how little has been accomplished in resolving the difficulties, such as that posed by the example above, inherent in the process of risk estimation. In spite of the relatively large amount of information gathered on formaldehyde in terms of its genotoxicity, pharmacokinetics, metabolism, interaction with other carcinogens and mutagens, and carcinogenicity (the latter including one of the largest multidose bioassays ever conducted), markedly different risk estimation methodologies and corresponding interpretations of the underlying data and theory have been proposed. The conclusions of the Consensus Conference on Formaldehyde are illustrative of the uncertainty regarding risk estimation. In some cases, alternatives (and accompanying reasons supportive of their consideration) are delineated for an issue (e.g., linear or nonlinear modeling at low formaldehyde exposure levels). For others, an assumption is recommended as tenable as a consequence of the paucity of data available. Clearly, much needs to be accomplished in terms of research and discussion before the mechanisms of carcinogenesis, and other areas germane to risk estimation, are understood.

## REFERENCES

Albert, R., A.R. Sellakumar, S. Laskin, M. Kuschner, N. Nelson, and C.A. Snyder. 1982. Gaseous formaldehyde and hydrogen chloride induction of nasal cancer in the rat. *J. Natl. Cancer Inst.* **68:** 597.

Ashford, N.A., C.W. Ryan, and C.C. Caldart. 1983. A hard look at federal regulation of formaldehyde: A departure from reasoned decisionmaking. *Harvard Environ. Law Review* **7:** 297.

Boreiko, C.J. and D.L. Ragan. 1983. Formaldehyde effects in the C3H10T½ cell transformation assay. *In Formaldehyde toxicity* (ed. J.E. Gibson), p. 63. Hemisphere Publishing, Washington, D.C.

Chemical Industry Institute of Toxicology (CIIT). 1981. Final report on a chronic inhalation toxicology study in rats and mice exposed to formaldehyde. Chemical Industry Institute of Toxicology, December 31, 1981.

Consumer Product Safety Commission (CPSC). 1982a. Ban of urea-formaldehyde foam insulation, withdraw of proposed information labeling rule, and denial of petition to issue a standard. *Federal Register* **47**: 14366.

_____. 1982b. Briefing package prepared for the Commissioners of the U.S. Consumer Product Safety Commission regarding the proposed ban of urea-formaldehyde foam insulation. January 29, 1982.

_____. 1984. Comments of the U.S. Consumer Product Safety Commission Staff to the Department of Housing and Urban Development's proposed revisions of the Manufactured Home Construction and Safety Standards (24 CFR Part 3280).

Federal Panel on Formaldehyde. 1980. *Report to the Consumer Product Safety Commission.* November 21, 1980.

Fifth Circuit Court of Appeals. 1983. *Gulf South Insulation v. CPSC.* 701 F.2d 1137. 1143.

Frazelle, J.H., D.J. Abernethy, and C.J. Boreiko. 1983. Weak promotion of C3H/10T½ cell transformation by repeated treatments with formaldehyde. *Cancer Res.* **43**: 3236.

Gibson, J.E. 1983. Risk assessment using a combination of testing and research results. In *Formaldehyde toxicity* (ed. J.E. Gibson), p. 295. Hemisphere Publishing, Washington, D.C.

Hatch, G.G., P.M. Conklin, C.C. Christensen, B.C. Casto, and S. Nesnow. 1983. Synergism in the transformation of hamster embryo cells treated with formaldehyde and adenovirus. *Environ. Mutagen.* **5**: 49.

Hoel, D. 1980. Incorporation of background in dose-response models. *Fed. Proc.* **39**: 73.

Howe, R.B. and K.S. Crump. 1983. Global83 (Sept. 1983). Science Research Systems, Inc., 1201 Gaines Street, Ruston, LA 71270.

Kovar, J. and D. Krewski. 1981. RISK81: A computer program for low dose extrapolation of quantal response toxicity data. Health and Welfare Canada. April, 1981.

National Cancer Institute. 1981. Surveillance Epidemiology End Results (SEER). Incidence and mortality data: 1973–77. U.S. Department of Health and Human Resources, Public Health Service, National Institutes of Health, *Natl. Cancer Inst. Monogr.* 57, June, 1981.

Sellakumar, A., R. Albert, and C. Snyder. 1983. Inhalation carcinogenicity of formaldehyde in Sprague-Dawley rats. AACR Abstracts, 1983.

Swenberg, J.A., C.S. Barrow, C.J. Boreiko, H. d'A. Heck, R.J. Levine, K.T. Morgan, and T.B. Starr. 1983a. Non-linear biological responses to formaldehyde and their implications for carcinogenic risk assessment. *Carcinogenesis* **4**: 945.

Swenberg, J.A., E.A. Gross, J. Martin, and J.A. Popp. 1983b. Mechanisms of formaldehyde toxicity. In *Formaldehyde toxicity* (ed. J.E. Gibson), p. 132. Hemisphere Publishing, Washington, D.C.

## COMMENTS

**REITZ:** I have a comment on the use of upper confidence limits in risk extrapolation. When you use the upper confidence limits, you will predict a finite risk even when there is absolutely no difference in tumor incidence in treated and control animals, and I don't feel this is a valid thing to do.

**COHN:** Remember, these numbers are by no means exact. The finite number reflects the uncertainty in the number zero. We fully realize that the risk, by this model, can be as high as the finite number, and it could be lower. What would you say should be the alternative?

**ALBERT:** Use the benign tumors, which increases your risk by a factor of nine.

**COHN:** Yes, it does increase the risk, if one were to consider the response at the lowest dose: eight tumors at 2.0 ppm versus the one in the control.

**SWENBERG:** What does that do to the maximum likelihood estimate?

**COHN:** It increases the upper confidence limit by a factor of about seven, and the maximum likelihood estimate by a similarly large factor, that is, it brings the maximum likelihood estimate to a factor of two to threefold from that of the upper confidence limit.

**R. WILSON:** That number is for the average exposure in these 1000 homes, right?

**COHN:** Right.

**R. WILSON:** The FDA has a rule that they have to take account of the gluttonous individual or some similar phrase. Why don't you take account of the most exposed individual who might be exposed in one of these places? Why do you take the average individual?

**COHN:** We were trying to determine the average risk to the population. You're right; some individuals will be at much higher risk, and some will be at much lower risk.

**SWENBERG:** Isn't that already taken care of in using the 95% upper confidence limit?

**COHN:** You are essentially correct. An important consideration is that the calculations are not in the nonlinear portion of the curve for any urea-formaldehyde foam insulation exposure situation using the upper confidence limit.

**CORN:** Why not take the 95% and the 5% exposure confidence level to put confidence limits on exposure?

**COHN:** We considered this, but we realized that the error in exposure would be trivial compared to the errors in estimating human risk at these exposure levels.

**PURCHASE:** You were referring to a point that the court made about the "robustness" of the data, how reliable it was. I would have thought that a lay person, looking at all these numbers and seeing the endpoint of rats dying of cancer, would want to know just how reliable and robust those figures are. Thus, asking you to do calculations with slightly different numbers of animals or proportions of tumors sounds to me quite a sensible way of approaching the problem.

**PIKE:** But they didn't ask before they made their decision. They should have asked as part of the case.

**COHN:** I agree, it might have been a good idea to perform such a sensitivity analysis initially; but, in fact, after we obtained the Fifth Circuit Court opinion, we responded with these calculations in a petition for rehearing, and that didn't seem to make a difference.

**SWENBERG:** The important question is, as Murray [Cohn] said, where do we go from here. I think maybe that is a more productive way of spending our time. If we look at UFFI, it's no longer a viable product. We still have homes that have UFFI, but the amount of formaldehyde is continually decreasing. What's of more concern to me is why there hasn't been something done with the OSHA levels. My research has shown that concentration is extremely important. Yet, we can still have exposure of five parts per million for 30 minutes every day.

**COHN:** It's three parts per million time-weighted average.

**SWENBERG:** I find it very hard to understand this aspect of it because that's in the observable range for our animal data.

**PREUSS:** A panel set up by Irving Selikoff at Mt. Sinai for the American Cancer Society said their concern was that the animal exposures were so close to the levels at which people were exposed. This wasn't the usual bioassay where there were three or four orders of magnitude difference between the animal exposures and what people were exposed to, but only an order of magnitude in some cases. As Jim [Swenberg] says, in the occupational setting, perhaps they are only a factor of five higher.

**J. WILSON:** But if occupational exposures have been as high as that for such a long time, and yet the epidemiology is inconclusive, what does it mean?

**SWENBERG:** The best study is the Acheson study. It is a pretty good study, published in *Lancet,* and it doesn't show any effect.

**COHN:** That the Acheson study shows no effect is debatable.

**J. WILSON:** If this is as potent a carcinogen as is now suggested it is, at the kinds of concentrations which you say are present or have been present for as long as they have been, why aren't we seeing an effect?

**COHN:** You're using the word "potent." Do you think $50 \times 10^{-6}$ is potent? By assuming representative exposure levels and applying the upper confidence limit of the multistage model to the number of people exposed in all of the available epidemiological studies, I have found that no excess cancers would be predicted.

**PREUSS:** I would suggest that those of you who are interested in this epidemiological question wait for another week or so to see the report of the Consensus Conference on Formaldehyde. There was a panel on epidemiology, which Acheson, the author of this paper that Jim [Swenberg] just mentioned, chaired. As I understand it, there was significant disagreement between him and other members of his panel concerning what his study showed because, in fact, in the one largest factory that he looked at, with 7000 workers, there was an apparent dose-response relationship for lung cancer related to levels of exposure and duration of exposure to formaldehyde. When he combined it with the other plants in his study, that excess of lung cancer disappeared. So, there was a fair amount of disagreement as to whether or not that study showed or did not show effect. I frankly don't think it will be cleared up until we get the results of the NCI study now underway, it is looking at approximately 25,000 workers.

**PERERA:** I have a comment on the epidemiology that was considered by the NTP and the IARC panels. IARC noted that the power of three PMR studies to detect a threefold excess of mortality from nasal cancer was on the order of 7–12%, so that they told very little about human risk.

**COHN:** I think you had to have a relative risk somewhere over 30 for nasal cancer before an effect could be observed.

**PERERA:** Because of the very small numbers of subjects studied and the problem of not really knowing what the exposures had been, epidemiological studies of formaldehyde to date have been inadequate as a basis for assessing human risk. I think that is really the answer to the question, "Well, if it's so bad why haven't we seen some cases?"

**J. WILSON:** It's a powerless negative of epidemiology. It says that if the exposures are high enough to worry somebody that either it is not as active as everybody is concerned or something else is going on.

**PREUSS:** I think you're misinterpreting. If it is as active as we say it is in our risk assessment, all of those epidemiological studies that have been done so far essentially have no power of discrimination and have been completely inadequate in terms of the number of people that they've examined.

**COHN:** In other words, if you were to have five excess cases of lung cancer, you'd miss them.

**SWENBERG:** I would just add that I think formaldehyde is an extremely interesting compound for us to consider. We're going to learn a great deal in the future that will allow us to understand this compound and to understand both the epidemiology and the animal data that's coming out. The epidemiology and the animal data are not necessarily in conflict. We have a biological mechanism in the case of the mucociliary clearance mechanism that may account for a lower risk of cancer than for chemicals that are absorbed and metabolized. However, the data are yet to come in.

# Human Exposure Estimates for Hazardous Waste Site Risk Assessment

**MORTON CORN AND PATRICK N. BREYSSE**
Department of Environmental Health Sciences
School of Hygiene and Public Health
The Johns Hopkins University
Baltimore, Maryland 21205

## OVERVIEW

A model is presented for exposure of populations at risk to waste site chemicals. Chemicals migrate from the site primarily via air, water, and/or soil. Internal exposure results when there is absorption of a chemical into the body following external exposure; acute or chronic health effects are manifested after chemical interaction with tissue. Because of the large number of chemicals migrating from many sites, surrogate chemicals may be used to represent mixtures of chemicals that can potentially affect health. Dose to those individuals potentially exposed can be estimated from knowledge of exposure concentration and intakes of air or water per day. In the absence of accurate exposure data, maximum measured or estimated exposure concentration can be used to obtain a "worst case" risk estimate. In the absence of any exposure data, biological indices of exposure may reveal if exposure has occurred. The formidable difficulties associated with reliable retrospective exposure estimates suggest that great emphasis be immediately placed on surveillance or prospective monitoring of exposure for those potentially exposed to waste site chemicals.

## INTRODUCTION

The purpose of this paper is to discuss issues associated with past and present exposures of the population to uncontrolled waste disposal sites and potential future exposures to new sites regulated under the Resource Conservation and Recovery Act (RCRA) of 1976. Old sites and their remediation are addressed by the Comprehensive Environmental Response, Compensation and Liability Act (CERCLA), also known as Superfund. Although public concern for hazardous wastes is great, there has not been a single defensible epidemiological investigation of the effects on health, if any, of residents in proximity to hazardous waste disposal sites.

Methodological difficulties with such a study are formidable (Heath 1983). Mitre (1983) recently analyzed the data available for substances released from and observed in the vicinity of the 546 National Priority List (NPL) sites identified as mandated under CERCLA (Superfund). Concentrations of the substances were not reported, but there are listings of the total number of sites at which individual chemicals have been observed. Of the chemicals or chemical mixtures tabulated by reported observation at the NFL sites, 173 were reported in groundwater, 162 in surface water, and 65 in air. The chemicals observed in the environment at the greatest number of sites were reported to be trichloroethylene, released to groundwater at 110 NPL sites; lead, released to surface water at 64 NPL sites; and benzene, released to air at 17 NPL sites.

The numbers of people affected by NPL facilities exhibiting releases of hazardous substances to the environment were estimated to be about 5,103,000 people at sites with groundwater releases, about 4,033,000 people at sites with surface water releases, and 803,000 people within a 4-mile radius of sites with air releases (Mitre 1983).

Quantitative risk assessment requires measures of exposure in order to estimate dosages received by those exposed. Knowledge of dosage permits one to refer to a dose-response curve, if it exists, in order to anticipate the expected detrimental effects on health, if any, or to correlate exposure with observed effects on health stemming from an epidemiological investigation.

Population exposure to chemicals from hazardous waste sites is yet one more manifestation of potential chronic effects on health caused by the ubiquitous presence of chemicals in the environments of a modern society. The population is exposed to community air and water pollution, products of tobacco combustion (personal pollution), possible workplace exposures and personal usage of chemicals. Sorting out the effects of each requires a model or schema to differentiate exposures in each setting. Manifestations of ill health which are of primary concern are usually nonspecific in nature, that is, multiple causes can result in the same disease state.

A model of hazardous waste site exposure will be initially presented. Its translation to exposure estimates for old sites and its utilization in investigations of the health status of residents will then be discussed.

## Exposure Model and Results

The sequence of events associated with the development of early indicators of ill health or frank symptoms of disease from exposure to a hazardous waste facility must occur as depicted in Figure 1. The first step in the sequence involves migration of chemicals from the site, causing an external exposure to individuals living in proximity to the facility. If the movement of chemicals from the site brings them in proximity to or in contact with individuals, then this results in an external exposure. Absorption of these chemicals into the body creates an internal exposure; absorption can occur following inhalation, ingestion, or passage through the skin  The final

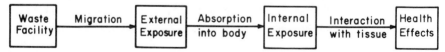

**Figure 1**

Sequence of events leading to health effects due to migration of chemicals from a hazardous waste facility

step in the sequence is the interaction of an absorbed chemical with body tissues, resulting in a toxic response or symptoms of ill health, i.e., a health effect. Health effects can be either acute or chronic. In some cases the sequence depicted in Figure 1 is not followed and a health effect can be caused by a chemical without absorption into the body. An example of this is a dermatitic reaction.

In order to prevent detrimental effects on health, one must intervene in the sequence depicted in Figure 1; the external exposure must be prevented or maintained at an acceptable, i.e., safe level. Therefore, the emphasis must be on preventing or controlling the migration of chemicals from the facility.

Figure 2 is a diagrammatic representation of the media or pathways by which chemicals can migrate from a waste facility and affect people and the environment. The migration of chemicals from a waste site facility is a complex process involving movement of chemicals in the atmosphere, lithosphere, hydrosphere, and biosphere. Superimposed on this movement of chemicals between environmental compartments are other concerns that need to be addressed with respect to public health. These are transportation of wastes, critical events, such as explosions, fires, spills, and other factors such as odor and noise. Each of the pathways between these environmental compartments and concerns is numbered and identified in Table 1.

The potential health effects from existing uncontrolled or abandoned hazardous waste sites have been addressed, but a generalized approach to either exposure or effects assessment has not emerged (JRB Associates 1980; Lowrance 1981; Janerich

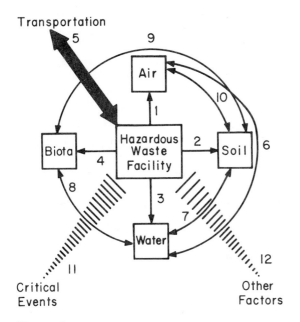

**Figure 2**
Model illustrating media or pathways for a hazardous waste facility to affect people and the environment

## Table 1
Identification of Pathways and Other Areas of Concern Associated with Hazardous Waste Facilities

1. Movement of chemicals from the facility directly to the air via gaseous and particulate emissions
2. Movement of chemicals from the facility directly to the soil through spills
3. Movement of chemicals from the facility to water leaching, runoff, or direct spills
4. Biological accumulation of chemicals from the facility due to spills, pests, direct contact
5. Contamination of community and environment through bulk transport of wastes to and from the site
6. Contamination of water due to washout and fallout of gaseous and particulate air pollutants and contamination of air due to evaporation from polluted water
7. Contamination of soil from contact with contaminated water and contamination of water from contact with contaminated soil
8. Contamination of biota due to contact and ingestion of contaminated water and contamination of water due to contaminated biota
9. Contamination of biota due to contact with contaminated soil and contamination of soil due to contaminated biota
10. Contamination of soil due to fallout from air pollution and contamination of air due to suspension of contaminated soil
11. Release of chemicals from the site or during transportation resulting from a critical event such as fire, explosion, or spill
12. Other factors which may affect public health such as noise or odor

et al. 1981). Hazardous waste sites frequently contain hundreds of toxic chemicals, as judged by the composition of leacheate, stormwater runoff, or drill cores. Furthermore, chemical transformation of dumped chemicals can occur during their storage or transport from the site to the receptors, yielding products of either greater or lesser potential to affect health.

The estimation of risk to residents of communities adjacent to waste sites necessitates estimation of exposure and dosage. Each route of entry to the body (e.g., inhalation, gastrointestinal, skin) must be considered to obtain the total dose to those exposed. For example, if the inhalation route is considered, the dosage per day (mg) to the respiratory tract from inhalation of an airborne agent is

$$D = \int_{0}^{t} \int_{C_1}^{C_2} \int_{I_1}^{I_2} dICdt \qquad (1)$$

where $I$ = inhalation rate in $m^3$/unit of time; $C$ = agent average concentration in air, $mg/m^3$; $f$ = fraction absorbed in the respiratory tract (assume constant).

Equation (1) can be simplified by assuming average values for $I$ and $C$ (Equation 2):

$$D = fICt \qquad (2)$$

Here $I$ is expressed as $m^3$/day.

The major difficulty is with the estimation of $C$, the agent concentration. Complex mathematical models have been developed to estimate $C$ in the media of air, water, and soil at given distances from the emission source (Bonazountas and Fiksel 1982). These models are subject to large errors and should probably be considered order of magnitude estimators. The techniques for dosage estimation from inhalation are well developed for aerosols, where C is known.

The dose from water can be estimated from agent concentration in water and the amount of water consumed by an individual per day. Once again, the retrospective knowledge of agent concentrations is not known in virtually all cases.

Agents also enter the G.I. tract in food contaminated with site chemicals. Contaminated fish have been a frequent result of waste site contamination.

## Quantitative Risk Assessment: "Worst Case" Approach

One approach to deriving a quantitative risk assessment for a hazardous waste site is to assume that the highest concentrations known for a given media are applicable to the case in hand, yielding a "worst case" estimator.

Fred C. Hart Associates (1982) evaluated data available for 929 sites that had been selected based on the following criteria: The sites were either active or inactive disposal sites for which laboratory sampling data were available; the sites were operated as storage facilities; the sites had been scored by Mitre; and there was a likelihood of environmental releases of the stored chemicals. Concentration data were available for many of the chemicals released to the environment at some of the sites. These data are summarized in Table 2 (note that values are variously reported in units of mg/L, µg/L, or ng/L). Concentrations of certain chemicals were very high at certain sites (for example, the maximum concentration observed at any site for trichloroethylene in groundwater was 315 mg/L; for dichloromethane in surface water was 250 mg/L; and for benzene in groundwater and surface water was 80 mg/L and 22 mg/L, respectively). The wide ranges for these values suggest that different volumes of chemicals have been disposed at each site and that conditions resulting in chemical release and environmental transport are different for each waste disposal site; these site-specific factors make it impossible to estimate "average exposure concentrations" for the population of the United States. Use of the highest concentrations listed for a quantitative risk assessment is obviously an incorrect, but probably defensible, procedure in the light of current knowledge to very liberally estimate the risk. It is a prudent public health procedure.

## Biological Indices of Exposure

If exposure has occurred, many chemicals can potentially be detected in the body. Thus, lead in blood, cadmium in urine, PCBs in sera are examples of well-accepted indices of exposure to these materials. In this way, confirmation of exposure and a rough estimate of body burden can be made, although the time sequence for exposure cannot be reconstructed. A difficulty with this approach is that there are far fewer biological indices for specific chemicals than there are candidate chemicals for exposures from waste sites (Maugh 1982).

Each waste site is uniquely associated with a physical setting and a profile of waste chemicals. There does not appear to be a generalized approach to estimating

**Table 2**
Summary of Chemical Concentration Data at Hazardous Waste Sites[a]

| Most frequently observed chemical category | Contaminant | Contaminant concentration range | | | | USEPA[b] human health criteria $10^{-6}$ | USEPA[c] primary drinking water standards | USEPA[d] drinking water standards |
|---|---|---|---|---|---|---|---|---|
| | | Groundwater (mg/L) | Surface water (mg/L) | Soil (mg/L) | Air (mg/L) | | | |
| VHOs[e] | 1,1,1-Trichloroethane | Trace–12.0 | Trace–1.8 | Trace–1.4 | 1,062.8 | NS | NS | NS |
| | Trichloroethylene | 0.0–315.0 | Trace–7.50 | Trace–0.10 | ND | 2.7 µg/l | NS | NS |
| | Dichloromethane | 0.132–19.0 | Trace–250 | 0.034 | ND | NS | NS | NS |
| | Tetrachloroethylene | 0.0–4.6 | 0.425 | Trace–20.5 | ND | 0.8 µg/l | NS | NS |
| | Chlorobenzene | 0.177 | 0.02 | ND | ND | NS | NS | NS |
| | Ditromoethane | ND | ND | 1.6 | ND | NS | NS | NS |
| VNHOs[f] | Benzene | 0.001–80 | Trace–22.0 | Trace–43.0 | ND | 0.66 µg/l | NS | NS |
| | Toluene | 0.0009–64.8 | Trace–6.572 | Trace–64.0 | 719 | NS | NS | NS |
| | Xylene | 0.001–18.8 | Trace–1.70 | 2.0–3.8 | ND | NS | NS | NS |
| Metals | Lead | 0.001–810 | Trace–175 | Trace–5,750 | ND | NS | 0.05 mg/l | NS |
| | Manganese | 0.012–120 | Trace–8,900 | ND | ND | NS | NS | 0.05 mg/l |
| | Chromium | Trace–65.5 | 0.001–10 | 0.110–31,765 | ND | NS | 0.05 mg/l | NS |
| | Cadmium | 0.02–0.1 | 0.1–1.0 | 4.1 | ND | NS | NS | NS |
| | Nickel | 0.029–5.50 | ND | 0.076–0.49 | ND | NS | NS | NS |
| | Arsenic | 0.001–2.4 | 0.0–16 | Trace–510 | ND | 2.2 ng/l | 0.05 mg/l | NS |
| | Mercury | ND | 0.0–0.001 | 0.0–734 | ND | NS | 0.002 mg/l | NS |
| Acid compounds | Pentachlorophenol | 0.0003 | ND | 0.9–46 | ND | NS | NS | NS |
| | Phenol | 0.0001–2.3 | 0.011–6.920 | Trace–22.5 | ND | NS | NS | NS |

[a] Fred C. Hart Associates (1982)
[b] U.S. Environmental Protection Agency (1980)
[c] U.S. Environmental Protection Agency (1975)
[d] U.S. Environmental Protection Agency (1979)
[e] VHOs, volatile halogenated organics
[f] VNHOs, volatile nonhalogenated organics
ND, no data available; NS, no standard

the possible contamination from a site without focusing, very specifically, on the characteristics of that site. In the presence of dozens or even hundreds of potentially toxic chemicals in leachate or core samples, a surrogate group of chemicals could be selected as the indicator of the behavior of the reservoir of chemicals in the site. In this way, the positive biological indicator of lead or mercury in those exposed could, as a first approximation, be considered confirmation of exposure to other site chemicals. This approach does not offer a link to quantitative estimation of other exposures; it represents only validation of exposure, in general.

Finally, in the absence of exposure data or biological indices of exposure, one can assume a more remote surrogate of exposure. Distance of residence from the site proper has been used in the design of epidemiological studies of the population exposed. In this case, groups of residents in proximity to the site would be investigated, together with comparison groups distant from the site, for any possible effects on health.

## SUMMARY AND CONCLUSIONS

The insurmountable difficulties associated with retrospective reconstruction of exposure profiles in the vicinity of waste sites clearly points to the need for prospective monitoring of the pathways for exposure. Only in this way will it be possible, at a later date, to estimate risk from dose-response data or to correlate untoward, unexpected effects in the exposed population with dosage. Estimates of risk from retrospective exposures can be made, but they must be recognized as potentially highly inaccurate estimates of maximum risk.

## REFERENCE

Bonazountas, M. and J. Fiksel. 1982. *Environmental mathematical pollutant fate modeling handbook catalogue.* A.D. Little, Cambridge, Massachusetts. EPA Contract No. 68-01-5 146. Oct. 1982.

Fred C. Hart Associates, Inc. 1982. Assessment of hazardous waste mismanagement: Damage case histories. Prepared for the Environmental Protection Agency, Office of Solid Waste under Contract No. 68-01-6474. Draft.

Heath, C.W., Jr. 1983. Field epidemiological studies of populations exposed to waste dumps. *Environ. Health. Perspec.* **48:** 3.

Janerich, D.T., W.S. Burnett, G. Feck, M. Hoff, P. Nasca, A.P. Polednak, P. Greenwald, and N. Vianna. 1981. Cancer incidence in the love canal area. *Science* 212(**4501**): 1404.

JRB Associates. 1980. Methodology for rating the hazard potential of waste disposal sites. McLean, Virginia.

Lowrance, W. (ed.). 1981. *Assessment of health effects at chemical disposal sites,* Proceedings of a Symposium. W. Kauffman. Los Altos, California.

Maugh, T.H. 1982. Biological markers for chemical exposure. *Science* **215:** 643.

Mitre Corporation. 1983. Computer printouts of national priorities list data summaries for the 54B final and proposed sites and 881 sites currently on the data base as of September

7, 1983. Prepared by Mitre Corp. for the U.S. Environmental Protection Agency. Mitre Corp., Metrek Division, McLean, Virginia.

U.S. Environmental Protection Agency, December 24, 1975. National Interim Primary Drinking Water Regulations. 40 CFR 141; 40 FR 59565, as amended.

———. 1979. National Secondary Drinking Water Regulations. 40 CFR 143; 44 FR 42198. Effective January 19, 1981.

———. 1980. Water Quality Criteria Documents; Availability. Federal Register, Vol. 45, No. 231.

## COMMENTS

**J. WILSON:** It seems to me that people living in the vicinity of the site are only going to be exposed in two ways: to pollutants in their well water if they're taking drinking water out of contaminated aquifer or to contaminants in the vapor phase. You can model these exposures. You could probably use tetrachloroethylene or chlorobenzene as a surrogate for the rest of the organics. We've had a pretty fair success in modeling release from soil and transport for those kinds of compounds. The air dispersion modeling is also pretty straightforward. That would leave you with the problem of exposure to the heavy metal, which is going to be a matter of dust, soil, and drinking water exposures.

**CORN:** I didn't discuss modification during transport, which does occur. The compounds change and react. They react in the site, during transport, and you end up with compounds you didn't have at the beginning. Modeling these processes is the next step, and investigators are starting to do just that. There is also another route. In Memphis, people were eating the fish from the rivers near where they lived. In fact, fishing in the Wolf River had occurred for years. We documented that through interviews. The fish were quite contaminated. One of the results of our activity in the early months was that fishing in the river was banned. Also on this site (which is an old site, closed 20 years ago), there was a man who became a private entrepreneur, raised pigs on that site and sold them. The site looked grassy and there were rodents; it didn't look like a Valley of the Drums. He was selling hogs to the neighborhood and residents were eating them. I suspect ingestion was a major route of entry for the hog purchasers.

**PIKE:** You didn't give us any calculations as to what you would have expected to find based on other data and information. If you had made such a calculation, you probably would have realized that doing an epidemiological investigation would be a waste of time; you simply would not find anything.

**ALBERT:** I'm not sure exactly what your approach is. Do you go to a site and get a list of chemicals in it, look at the worst exposure that has ever been encountered anywhere, and assign that exposure to the individual chemicals?

**CORN:** That is correct. We adopt these exposures as worst case estimators.

**LAVE:** We have to clarify the purpose for which you're doing the environmental exposure assessment. If you are worried about what the maximum possible exposure is, you would proceed differently than if you were estimating dose for an epidemiological study. If you gave the former to epidemiologists, they would conclude that doses had been higher than they actually had been and they would underestimate potency. Now, even if you were going in prospectively to see, as Malcolm [Pike] suggested, whether the epidemiology will find anything, you want a best estimate of previous dose. I am not sure what good a worst case estimate of previous dose would do an epidemiologist.

**CORN:** I'm not sure how to obtain a "best estimate." Another useful output of this approach is to rank other exposures with your worst case estimate of total dose. In this way, the waste site case can be placed in perspective with other exposure situations.

**ALBERT:** You're not going to bother drilling wells and doing any sampling around a given waste site?

**CORN:** That would give you data only for that point in time when drilling occurs. It costs a great deal of money to find out how far the pollutants spread. On the other hand, if you tell me the site and tell me what's there, I'll give you the worst possible population exposures. That should place that site in perspective vis-a-vis other sites and other environmental hazards. That's the first step. Millions of dollars are needed for core and well samples, and their value is limited.

**NEEL:** Is part of your protocol some of these somatic cell indicators we've been discussing?

**CORN:** The study group indicated in the protocol they would not use methods yielding results for which they didn't have a clear understanding of their meaning for the volunteer population. These decisions were made by clinical toxicologists and physicians.

# Risk Assessment and Risk Management of Benzene by the Environmental Protection Agency

**BERNARD D. GOLDSTEIN**
Assistant Administrator for Research and Development
Environmental Protection Agency
Washington, D.C. 20460

## OVERVIEW

The Environmental Protection Agency under William Ruckelshaus has actively pursued the use of risk assessment and risk management in the fulfillment of the Agency's mission to protect human health and the environment. Risk assessment of various chemical pollutants have been assigned to EPA's scientists whose duty it is to evaluate the available information. Wherever possible, the assessment of risks is performed independently of the risk manager, i.e., the program managers overseeing regulation of a given pollutant. The assessment contains not only the best estimate of the risk but a full description of the crucial uncertainties. As a corollary, it is necessary for the risk assessor not to bias the estimate towards his own interests or the perceived interests of the risk manager.

Benzene offers an illustrative example of the decisionmaking process in which the management of risk is predicated to a large extent on the assessment of risk. In this paper, I will discuss the basic concepts of benzene toxicity and the formal risk assessment for benzene performed by the Carcinogen Assessment Group of the Office of Research and Development of EPA. In addition, the risk management decisions based upon this information will be outlined.

## BENZENE TOXICOLOGY

Benzene has been a known hematological poison since the 19th century. It is unequivocally causally related to two major hematological disorders: aplastic anemia and acute myelogenous leukemia (Laskin and Goldstein 1979). Aplastic anemia results from a toxic effect of benzene upon bone marrow precursor cells resulting in a decrement in all of the formed elements of the blood: red blood cells, white blood cells, and platelets (Snyder and Kocsis 1975). Lesser forms of the disease, in which the decrements in blood counts may not produce symptoms, are generally kown as pancytopenia. This effect of benzene follows a standard dose-response curve in animals including, as is expected for a noncarcinogenic effect, an apparent threshold. Judging from the literature concerning occupational exposures, a similar dose-response effect with an apparent threshold appears to occur in humans for significant pancytopenia (Laskin and Goldstein 1979).

**293**

The evidence supporting the causal relationship of benzene to human acute myelogenous leukemia, and the variants of this disease, is overwhelming. It includes a large series of case studies from around the world in which frequently a benzene-induced aplastic anemia is observed to gradually change into preleukemia and then into frank acute myelogenous leukemia. More recently, epidemiological evidence has accumulated which again unquestionably implicates benzene as a cause of acute myelogenous leukemia. Of particular note is an epidemic of benzene-induced hematological toxicity in Turkey reported by Aksoy and colleagues (Aksoy and Erdem 1978; Aksoy 1980a,b). The introduction of a benzene-containing glue in the handicraft leather industry led to cases of aplastic anemia and then of acute myelogenous leukemia in Istanbul. Replacement of this glue was associated with a decrement in the incidence of these disorders in the population, consistent with a classic epidemic.

Other evidence supporting the biomedical plausibility of a causal association between benzene and acute myelogenous leukemia is the finding of chromosomal abnormalities in circulating blood and bone marrow of humans and laboratory animals exposed to benzene (Forni et al. 1971; Wolman 1979). It is of note that despite this clear evidence that benzene is genotoxic, the compound has been consistently negative in all short-term bacterial and most short-term mammalian tests for genetic effects. The only notable exception is the finding that benzene promotes sister chromatid exchange both in vitro and in vivo (Tice et al. 1980).

Hematologists have also long noted that individuals with aplastic anemia due to a variety of causes have an increased risk for the eventual development of myelogenous leukemia (Damashek 1967). This occurs following radiation and following treatment with chemical agents capable of damaging the bone marrow. The relationship between aplastic anemia and acute myelogenous leukemia is central to the major argument concerning the shape of the dose-response curve relating benzene to acute myelogenous leukemia. Simply put, it has been argued that benzene by itself cannot produce acute myelogenous leukemia but rather that this disease is an unfortunate outcome of benzene-induced bone marrow damage (i.e., aplastic anemia).

The argument that benzene is only responsible for bone marrow damage implies that some threshold exists for benzene toxicity and this threshold is presumably above levels currently present in general ambient air. Conversely, it can be argued that any one molecule of benzene presents a risk of producing the unique somatic mutation resulting in acute myelogenous leukemia. The latter implies the lack of a threshold and would justify controlling general ambient levels of benzene to prevent acute myelogenous leukemia. In my judgment it is unlikely that this question can be resolved either through further epidemiological studies or through long-term studies in animals. What will be necessary is to achieve an understanding of the mechanism by which benzene produces acute myelogenous leukemia.

## RISK ASSESSMENT

The hazard evaluation process pioneered by the Carcinogen Assessment Group of the EPA Office of Research and Development has been presented on a number of occasions (Anderson and Carcinogen Assessment Group 1983). Some of the salient features include a focus on what is called the plausible upper bound in the approach to models and the reliance on human data when it is available.

Using this approach, the Carcinogen Assessment Group has performed a risk assessment on more than 214 chemicals to date. This is perhaps the largest body of data evaluated in a consistent fashion by any regulatory organization.

The Carcinogen Assessment Group (1979) originally performed a partial assessment of the risk of benzene-induced leukemia in man in 1979. This assessment primarily depended upon three epidemiological studies. The findings of Aksoy and colleagues in Turkey (Aksoy and Erdem 1978; Aksoy 1980a,b) have been described above. The methodological shortcomings of these studies include lack of information as to the size of the population at risk; unavailability of data concerning the expected leukemia rate in Istanbul; and, of greatest importance, only scanty exposure data, consisting of a few samples with no information as to how these samples may have typified the average benzene exposure in the workplace.

The second study used by the Carcinogen Assessment Group was that of Ott et al. (1978) of Dow Chemical Company. Although much more information was available about the benzene dose to workers, the cohort was small and only a few cases of leukemia were observed. It is notable that in one of these cases, leukemia was listed as a secondary diagnosis with the primary diagnosis being pneumonia, a not infrequent cause of death in patients with leukemia. This raises questions about the proper comparison since the expected leukemia incidence usually is based on the primary diagnosis. It also points out a drawback of cohort studies that depend upon death certificates for their diagnosis. In contrast, a more clinically oriented study, such as that of Aksoy in Turkey, while not having the sophistication of a cohort study, does have the advantage in that each of the cases has been seen and diagnosed by the investigator.

The third study utilized by the Carcinogen Assessment Group was that of Infante et al. (1977). This study, which found a markedly increased incidence of leukemia as a cause of death in a cohort of male workers in a rubber industry in Ohio, was a major precipitating factor in the unsuccessful attempt by OSHA to decrease the workplace standard from 10 ppm benzene to 1 ppm benzene (8-hour time-weighted average). This is an excellent study of its type; it clearly demonstrates the increased risk for leukemia among workers exposed to high levels of benzene. As in similar studies, its usefulness for risk assessment is somewhat limited by imperfect knowledge of past exposure. This shortcoming persists despite an excellent follow-up by Rinsky et al. (1981) which gathered all the available industrial hygiene measurements of benzene performed at the workplace. Benzene exposure levels were found to have ranged up to 300 ppm. Evaluation of this data suggested that the exposure of the individuals who developed leukemia was at least somewhat if not substantially higher than that for the average worker. However, it must be emphasized that in dealing with a low incidence phenomenon, it is difficult to utilize general industrial hygiene measurements as a means of typifying individual exposure. In both the Infante et al. (1977) and Ott et al. (1978) cohorts, less than 1% of the total work force at risk developed leukemia. Accordingly, it is questionable whether the reported exposure levels are meaningful in estimating dose to the relatively few workers who developed the leukemia.

As shown in Table 1, individual hazard assessment for the three epidemiological studies revealed reasonably good agreement in the findings. The lifetime risk for nonlymphatic leukemia per $\mu g/m^3$ of benzene ranged from $4.09 \times 10^{-6}$ to $1.43 \times 10^{-5}$. The geometric mean of the three resulted in the unit risk number for lifetime exposure of $7.08 \times 10^{-6}$ per $\mu g/m^3$ (equivalent to $2.23 \times 10^{-2}$ per ppm), which was recently used by EPA in reassessing the impact of the benzene emission control strategies proposed in 1980.

When the original Carcinogen Assessment Group analysis was performed in 1979, benzene was one of only two compounds (the other being arsenic) for which there was ample evidence that it was a human carcinogen without any evidence of carcinogenicity in animals. Since that time, benzene has been shown to be an animal carcinogen by three different groups of investigators. Maltoni and Scarnato (1979) first noted zymbal gland tumors in the ears of rats. These tumors have no known counterpart in man. Since that time a more extensive study by Maltoni has shown that lifetime exposure of rats or mice by inhalation or by gavage produces a variety of tumors (Maltoni 1984). It is of note that a number of different organ sites are involved, with zymbal gland tumors remaining the most impressive in terms of total number. A lifetime gavage study by the National Toxicology Program (1984) has confirmed these observations of Maltoni et al. (1982). Hematological neoplasia was first observed by Snyder et al. (1980; 1984) at New York University. This group noted a statistically significant increase in inducible lymphomas in C57 black mice. They also reported acute and chronic myelogenous leukemia for the very first time in benzene-exposed mice and rats, although the numbers were not statistically significant (Goldstein et al. 1982).

Recently, the Carcinogen Assessment Group has performed an assessment based on the available carcinogenesis data for benzene using their standard techniques. As shown in Table 2, the findings again demonstrate reasonably good agreement among the assessments done on these data sets. Even more remarkable, perhaps even approaching witchcraft, is that the mean of the lifetime risk estimations derived from these four animal studies, $7.3 \times 10^{-6}$ per $\mu g/m^3$, is almost identical to that determined in 1979 from the three epidemiological studies (Table 1). However, it should be pointed out that using different assumptions and methods of extrapolation, one can obviously come up with different numbers. Other investigators have verbally reported benzene risk assessments for the epidemiological studies and the animal studies that are close to one order of magnitude apart.

## RISK MANAGEMENT

The following is a brief discussion of the type of information used by the Office of Air and Radiation and by the Administrator of EPA in decisionmaking concerning

**Table 1**
Carcinogenic Potency of Benzene Calculated on the Basis of Nonlymphatic Leukemia Mortality Rates Observed in Three Epidemiologic Studies

| Database | Estimated relative risk | Estimated continuous exposure | Lifetime risk per ppm | Lifetime risk per $\mu g/m^3$ |
|---|---|---|---|---|
| Infante et al. (1977) | 6.4 | 2.73 | $1.33 \times 10^{-2}$/ppm | $4.09 \times 10^{-6}$ $\mu g/m^3$ |
| Aksoy (1974; 1976; 1977) | 9.96 | 2.22 | $1.82 \times 10^{-2}$/ppm | $5.60 \times 10^{-6}$ $\mu g/m^3$ |
| Ott et al. (1977) | 3.75 | 0.17 | $4.64 \times 10^{-2}$/ppm | $1.43 \times 10^{-5}$ $\mu g/m^3$ |
| | | Geometric mean $= 2.23 \times 10^{-2}$/ppm | | $7.08 \times 10^{-6}$/$\mu g/m^3$ |

**Table 2**
Carcinogenic Potency of Benzene Calculated on the Basis
of Animal Data

| Database | Lifetime risk per ppm | Lifetime risk per μg/m³ |
|---|---|---|
| Female rats (Maltoni et. al. 1982)[a] | $3.4 \times 10^{-2}$ | $1.1 \times 10^{-5}$ |
| Male rats (NTP 1984)[a] | $2.0 \times 10^{-2}$ | $6.0 \times 10^{-6}$ |
| Female rats (NTP 1984)[a] | $3.3 \times 10^{-2}$ | $1.0 \times 10^{-5}$ |
| Male mice (Snyder et al. 1980)[b] | $1.4 \times 10^{-2}$ | $4.3 \times 10^{-6}$ |
| Geometric mean | $2.4 \times 10^{-2}$ | $7.3 \times 10^{-6}$ |

[a] Zymbal gland carcinomas (gavage study)
[b] Hematopoietic neoplasms (inhalation study)

the regulation of benzene emissions under the Clean Air Act. The Office of Research and Development does not participate in the EPA risk management process.

Section 112 of the Clean Air Act directs EPA to evaluate the potential adverse effects of chemicals present in the air, the so-called hazardous air pollutants. Based upon a consideration of such effects, the Administrator can promulgate emission control regulations for specific industries and, as EPA's lawyers interpret the law, take into account the feasibility and costs of the corrective measures as well. This differs from the approach used for control of the so-called criteria air pollutants (ozone, sulfur dioxide, lead, particulate matter, carbon monoxide, and nitrogen dioxide) in which the initial focus is on setting a national ambient standard, not on controlling specific sources of emissions, and for which costs are not considered.

The Administrator of EPA was faced with making a decision on four sets of emission standards for benzene sources. These had been proposed in 1980 but no further action had been taken. Following review of the data shown in Table 3, the Administrator has promulgated national emission standards for benzene fugitive sources. In addition, national emission standards for coke by-product recovery plants were proposed. Three other previously proposed national emission standards were proposed to be withdrawn. These were for maleic anhydride plants, ethyl benzene and styrene plants, and benzene storage vessels.

The rationale for each of these decisions was based on a variety of considerations. A major one concerned the extent to which each of these contributed to ambient exposure and public risk. The importance of the exposure data to the decisionmaking process is evident. It should be emphasized that a risk assessment requires data both on the intrinsic hazard, which has been discussed above, and the exposure. No matter how hazardous a compound, if there is no exposure, there is no risk. The major categories of exposure that are not covered by these five emission standards are the release of benzene to the atmosphere associated with gasoline marketing and with motor vehicle use. Other control methods, including use of

**Table 3**
Summary of Five Source Categories: Intent to Regulate Under Section 112

| Source category | Number of existing facilities | Emissions (megagrams/year) | | Total stationary source emissions | Maximum lifetime individual risk | | Annual cancer cases | | | Cost (millions) | |
|---|---|---|---|---|---|---|---|---|---|---|---|
| | | before | after | | before | after | before | after | difference | capital | annual |
| Benzene fugitive | 229 | 7,900 | 2500 | 18% | 15/10,000 | 4.5/10,000 | 0.45 | 0.14 | 0.31 | $5.5 | 0.4 |
| Coke by-product | 55 | 29,000 | 3500 | 53% | 83/10,000 | 3.5/10,000 | 2.60 | 0.23 | 2.37 | 30.9 | (1.3) |
| Intent to propose withdrawal of proposed standards | | | | | | | | | | | |
| Maleic anhydride | 3 | 960 | 120 | 2% | 76/million | 5.3/million | 0.029 | 0.016 | 0.013 | 6.4 | 2.8 |
| Ethylbenzene/ styrene | 13 | 210 | 68 | 0.4% | 140/million | 9.0/million | 0.0057 | 0.0006 | 0.0051 | 2.7 | 0.97 |
| Benzene storage | 126 | 620 | 400 | 1% | 3.6/100,000 | 2.3/100,000 | 0.043 | 0.028 | 0.015 | 7.3 | 1.3 |

catalytic converters, will control the emissions from motor vehicles independent of the present decisionmaking process. The Agency has recently requested comment on strategies for reducing emissions from gasoline marketing, including options for controlling auto refueling (e.g., auto-equipped versus service station controls).

The crucial aspect of a control strategy is the extent to which it will produce a decrement in the targeted emission. For each of these proposed emission approaches, an estimate was made of its success in decreasing exposure. To convert this into statistics estimating the number of lives that might be saved by the control strategy, it is necessary to know not only the exposure decrement and the unit risk number for benzene leukemogenesis, but also the number of people at risk in the given geographic area where the exposure reduction will occur. These data are also presented in Table 3.

As can be seen, benzene fugitive emissions are believed to produce 0.45 leukemia cases a year at present. The proposed control measures would decrease that to 0.14 estimated cases per year, 0.31 less than with no control. The numbers are higher for control of coke by-product emissions where a total of 2.37 fewer annual cancer cases are predicted due to the control strategies. For the three source categories where EPA proposed to withdraw emission standards, the estimated leukemia cases saved range from 0.0051 to 0.015 per year (i.e., from one case per 200 years to one case of leukemia per 66 years).

Table 3 also provides information as to the maximum lifetime individual risk both before and after the proposed emission control measures for each of the categories. Note that when one expresses the data in terms of the maximum risk to an individual, the numbers all range well above one per million. Obviously, in many of these cases, very few individuals are bearing these maximum lifetime individual risks. It has been argued that the primary concern of an environmental regulatory agency ought to be the maximum lifetime individual risk rather than the number of actual cases. The rationale is that the focus should be on the individual rather than on the population base. However, it is and has been standard public health practice to take into account the population base when managing risk. For example, the frequency of bacterial testing of drinking water has long been based on the number of individuals using the system. Obviously, one must act to prevent unreasonable risk to a single individual. In the case of benzene, none of the residual risks or uncontrolled risks are in the range at which individuals commonly act to prevent risk. Also included in Table 3 is a description of the cost for each of the five proposals for controlling benzene emissions. The most expensive is the control of coke by-product plants, which will cost $30.9 million in capital. Note, however, that there is an annual saving due to this capital investment of $1.3 million. Benzene fugitive emission control has an estimated capital cost of $5.5 million and further annual costs of $0.4 million.

Benzene provides an excellent example of the use of risk assessment for risk management purposes. At this juncture, two points need emphasis. First, the risk estimate for benzene is clearly an estimate. Despite the excellent agreement between the assessments based upon epidemiological data and those based upon animal studies, we must be careful to avoid placing undue credence on this single number. Second, thus far, the risk management process has only resulted in a series of proposals. There are many regulatory and legal steps before these proposals will have the force of law. It will be interesting to see whether actions based so strongly and explicitly on science are more readily sustained in the inevitable legal battles to come than such decisions have been in the past.

## REFERENCES

Aksoy, M. 1980a. Different types of malignancies due to occupational exposure to benzene: A review of recent observations in Turkey. *Environ. Res.* **23:** 181.

_____. 1980b. Malignancies due to occupational exposure to benzene. *Haematologica* **65:** 370.

Aksoy, M. and S. Erdem. 1978. Follow-up study on the mortality and the development of leukemia in 44 pancytopenic patients with chronic exposure to benzene. *Blood* **52:** 285.

Anderson, E.L. and the Carcinogen Assessment Group of the U.S. Environmental Protection Agency. 1983. Quantitative approaches in use to assess cancer risk. *Risk Analysis* **3:** 277.

Carcinogen Assessment Group's Final Report on Population Risk to Ambient Benzene Exposures. 1979. *NTIS* PB82-227372.

Damashek, W. 1967. What do aplastic anemia, PNH, and hypoplastic leukemia have in common? *Blood* **30:** 251.

Forni, A.M., A. Cappellini, E. Pacifico, and E.C. Vigliani. 1971. Chromosome changes and their evolution in subjects with past exposure to benzene. *Arch. Environ. Health* **23:** 385.

Goldstein, B.D., C.A. Snyder, S. Laskin, I. Bromberg, R.E. Albert, and N. Nelson. 1982. Myelogenous leukemia in rodents inhaling benzene. *Toxicol. Lett.* **13:** 169.

Infante, P.F., R.A. Rinsky, J.K. Wagoner, and R.J. Young. 1977. Leukemia in benzene workers. *Lancet* **ii:** 76.

Laskin, S. and B.D. Goldstein. 1979. Benzene toxicity, a critical evaluation. *Toxicol. Environ. Health Suppl.* **2:** 1.

Maltoni, C. 1984. *Am. J. Ind. Med.* (in press).

Maltoni, C. and C. Scarnato. 1979. First experimental demonstration of the carcinogenic effects of benzene. *Med. Lav.* **5:** 352.

Maltoni, C., G. Cotti, L. Valgimigli, and A. Mondriole. 1982. Zymbal gland carcinomas in rats following exposure to benzene by inhalation. *Am. J. Ind. Med.* **3:** 11.

National Toxicology Program. 1984. NTP Technical Report on the Toxicology and Carcinogenesis Studies of Benzene (CAS #71-43-2) NF344/N Rats and B6C3F₁, Mice (Gavage Studies) NTP TF 289. U.S. Department of Health, Education and Welfare. (In press).

Ott, M.G., J.C. Townsend, W.A. Fishbeck, and R.A. Langner. 1978. Mortality among individuals occupational exposed to benzene. *Arch. Environ. Health* **33:** 3.

Rinsky, R.A., R.J. Young, and A.B. Smith. 1981. Leukemia in benzene workers. *Am. J. Ind. Med.* **2:** 217.

Snyder, R., and J.J. Kocsis. 1975. Current concepts of chronic benzene toxicity. *CRC Crit. Rev. Toxicol.* 265.

Snyder, C., B.D. Goldstein, and R. Albert. 1984. Evidence for hematotoxicity and tumorigenesis in rats exposed to 100 ppm benzene. *Am. J. Ind. Med.* **5:** 429.

Snyder, C.A., B.D. Goldstein, A.R. Sellakumar, I. Bromberg, S. Laskin, and R.E. Albert. 1980. The inhalation toxicology of benzene: Incidence of hematopoietic neoplasms and hematotoxicity in AKR/J and C57BL/6J Mice. *Toxicol. Appl. Pharmacol.* **53:** 323.

Tice, R.R., D.C. Costa, and R.T. Drew. 1980. Cytogenetic effects of inhaled benzene in murine bone marrow: Induction of sister chromatid exchanges, chromosomal aberrations, and cellular proliferation inhibition in DBA/2 mice. *Proc. Natl. Acad. Sci.* **77:** 2148.

Wolman, S.R. 1979. Cytologic and Cytogenetic effect of benzene. *J. Toxicol. Environ. Health Suppl.* **2:** 63.

Wood, A.W., W. Levin, and R.L. Chang. 1980. Mutagenicity and tumor-initiating activity of cyclopenta (c,d) pyrene and structurally related compounds. *Cancer Res.* **40:** 642.

## COMMENTS

**PETO:** What data are there on pancytopenia preceding leukemia?

**GOLDSTEIN:** In animals, the only data on hematological neoplasms were for lymphoma, not leukemia. In humans, most of the cases reported in the literature are like this: Someone in a workforce comes to the hospital with bleeding because he or she has severe aplastic anemia; the physician goes into the plant which is, let us say, a rubber raincoat factory where benzene exposure is expected. He finds 40 people with some degree of pancytopenia, follows them, and observes that one severely affected patient will then go from an aplastic phase into what hematologists call preleukemia, and will later, over a period of time, progress into a complete leukemia.

**PETO:** Has there been an unusual number of infective deaths in any of these cohorts?

**GOLDSTEIN:** If the argument you are making is that you should see some infections in these populations, you have to realize that we all have a tremendous ability to withstand infections. The normal white count is between 5000 and 10,000. As a hematologist, I don't worry about someone getting an infection until his or her white count gets below about 1500 or 1200. You could well have had somebody whose white count was 2500, or even half of that, who has no infection whatsoever.

**J. WILSON:** Has anybody done a proper morbidity study?

**GOLDSTEIN:** If you consider a proper morbidity study one in which we have a dose, no.

**SWENBERG:** Did all of the leukemias have an aplastic anemia preceding them?

**GOLDSTEIN:** No. But we don't have any case of a person who was followed after having had a normal white count, and who subsequently came down with leukemia, in a situation in which we could definitely blame benzene.

**PERERA:** Didn't Aksoy report pancytopenia or "preleukemia" in a high percentage of his leukemia cases?

**GOLDSTEIN:** Yes.

**R. WILSON:** Yes, he did. But there were one or two cases where he did not find pancytopenia beforehand. However, Bernie [Goldstein] said that he did not know of any case where he was certain that leukemia started without a precursor; and there were some cases where he did not know whether there was pancytopenia beforehand. There are four or five cases such cases in Aksoy's group of 40.

**GOLDSTEIN:** The problem is that where there are groups whose white counts have been carefully followed, they are generally in the places which have superb industrial hygiene and there haven't been hematological problems in those places. If there are problems, they're the kind of thing where there are two cases of leukemia expected and three observed, and even if we say that one of those people got leukemia due to the benzene, which one of the three would it be? That's why I said that I don't think epidemiology could ever give us the answer.

**PURCHASE:** I just wanted some clarification on the risk figure you gave, which was roughly $2.5 \times 10^{-2}$/ppm. Does that mean 2.5%, or does it mean 0.002%?

**GOLDSTEIN:** It's 2.5% lifetime per part per million of benzene.

**ALBERT:** $2 \times 10^{-2}$ is the lifetime risk for continuous exposure to 1 ppm.

**NEEL:** Could we talk about EPA's use of the "most exposed" person? This has come up recently in the radionuclide regulations. There can be a prevailing wind pattern to the west, and there may be one individual living within a couple of hundred yards downwind of the source with nobody for three more miles; it's going to cost the plant $30 million to protect this one person. As a population geneticist I find that almost ridiculous.

**R. WILSON:** One real instance of this is the maleic anhydride regulation. There was one plant, the Monsanto plant, which was right in the middle of the city in St. Louis. The first proposal was to control all plants to the same level of emissions from the chimney stack. But there were some plants which had been located in the middle of nowhere so that no one was within two or three miles and maybe 50 people were between three and five miles. Yet, they were going to be controlled to the same degree so that there would be no incentive for anyone to follow the sensible siting approach. I'm glad that particular part of the proposed regulation has been dropped.

**GOLDSTEIN:** It has not been dropped completely. You've got to realize that there is a strong push in the environmental law in this country against significant deterioration or degradation.

**R. WILSON:** But that's different. Benzene does not degrade the environment. In that respect it's more like $CO_2$.

**GOLDSTEIN:** What you're saying, though, is you're for pushing industry out of urban areas into rural areas, and that is a social issue which Congress has to decide.

**R. WILSON:** If you believed benzene persisted for a long time in the environment, like $CO_2$, it wouldn't matter where you emit it. But it is believed to break down under exposure to light.

**J. WILSON:** The benzene emission reduction at one plant was caused by a change in feedstock because it was less expensive and only secondarily because air pollution controls were added.

**ALBERT:** You mean you would have done it anyhow?

**J. WILSON:** Yes.

**SWENBERG:** Did you say that by this regulation you estimated how large a decrease in cancer was achieved?

**GOLDSTEIN:** In one of the regulations it was a decrease of two-some-odd cases per year and in the other it was a third of a case.

**SWENBERG:** So we're talking roughly about spending $35 million to prevent two and one-half cases, is that right?

**GOLDSTEIN:** $35 million for the capital cost and an annual cost in one case of $0.4 million; in the other case it's actually a $1.3 million-a-year saving.

**PETO:** This is during a decade in which the asbestos regulations haven't been changed at all.

**R. WILSON:** In your proposals you omit the benzene emitted from gas stations, which, it seems to me, swamps those other exposure numbers.

**GOLDSTEIN:** Other approaches are going to be taken to control benzene as part of all volatile organic compounds. The motor vehicle emissions are large, but they're not really swamping this. You're talking about the same order of magnitude.

# Session 7:
# Risk Quantitation and the Dynamics of Policy Formulation

# U.S. Environmental Protection Agency Revised Interim Guideline for the Health Assessment of Suspect Carcinogens

ROY E. ALBERT
Chairman, Carcinogen Guideline Committee
U.S. Environmental Protection Agency and
Institute of Environmental Medicine
New York University Medical Center
New York, New York 10016

## OVERVIEW

The Environmental Protection Agency (EPA) first adopted Interim Carcinogen Assessment Guidelines in May, 1976. These 1976 Guidelines, which are still in effect, are very brief and broad in character: They use a weight-of-evidence approach for the evaluation of carcinogens and they sanction the use of the high-dose animal biossay, the supportive nature of short-term tests, and the appropriateness of extrapolating cancer risk with several mathematical models, including the linear nonthreshold model. Since 1976, the EPA has gained a great deal of experience in carcinogen risk assessment. It, therefore, seemed appropriate to bring the 1976 Guidelines up-to-date. As before, the central problem has been to choose assessment positions that are appropriate to a regulatory agency in the face of scientific uncertainties. The following is the final draft revision of the EPA carcinogen guidelines which have been distributed for comment to a group of scientific experts outside the EPA. The draft was the work of the Carcinogen Guidelines Committee at the U.S. Environmental Protection Agency including Drs. Roy Albert (Chairman), Mary Argus, Don Barnes, Judith Bellin, Margaret Chu, Bernard Haberman, Richard Hill, Arnold Kuzmack, Bertram Litt, Elizabeth Margosches, Robert McGaughy (Secretary), Paul Milvy, Neal Nelson, Jean Parker, David Patrick, Thomas Purcell, and Todd Thorslund.

## 1.0   INTRODUCTION

This is the first revision of the 1976 Interim Procedures and Guidelines for Health Risk Assessments of Suspected Carcinogens (U.S. EPA 1976; Albert et al. 1977). The impetus for this revision is the need to incorporate into these guidelines the concepts and approaches to carcinogen risk assessment that have been developed in the last 8 years. The purpose of these guidelines is to promote quality and consistency of carcinogen risk assessments within the EPA and to inform those outside the EPA about its approach to carcinogen risk assessment. These guidelines emphasize the broad but essential aspects of risk assessment that are needed by the experts in the various disciplines (e.g., toxicology, pathology, pharmacology, and statistics) required for carcinogen assessment. Guidance is given in general terms since the science of carcinogenesis is in a state of rapid advancement, and overly specific approaches may rapidly become obsolete.

These guidelines describe the general framework to be followed in developing an analysis of carcinogenic risk and some salient principles to be used in evaluating the quality of data and in formulating judgments concerning the nature and magnitude of the cancer hazard from suspect carcinogens.

A summary of the current state of knowledge in the field of carcinogenesis and a statement of broad scientific principles of carcinogen risk assessment, developed by the Office of Science and Technology Policy (OSTP 1984), forms an important basis for these guidelines; the format of these guidelines is similar to that proposed in the National Academy of Sciences report *Risk Assessment in the Federal Government* (NRC 1983).

These guidelines are to be used within the policy framework already provided by applicable EPA statutes and do not alter such policies. The guidelines provide general directions for analyzing and organizing available data. They do not imply that one kind of data or another is prerequisite for regulatory action to control, prohibit, or allow the use of a carcinogen. The analysis of carcinogenic risks will be carried out independently from considerations of the socio-economic consequences of regulatory action.

Regulatory decisionmaking involves two components: risk assessment and risk management. Risk assessment defines the adverse health consequences of exposure to toxic agents; risk management combines the risk assessment with the directives of the enabling regulatory legislation together with socio-economical, technical, political, and other considerations to reach a decision as to whether or how much to control future exposure to the suspected toxic agents.

Risk assessment is comprised of one or more of the following components: hazard identification, dose-response assessment, exposure assessment, and risk characterization (NRC 1983).

Hazard identification is a qualitative risk assessment, dealing with the process of determining whether exposure to an agent has the potential to increase the incidence of cancer. For purposes of these guidelines, malignant and benign tumors are used in the evaluation of the carcinogenic hazard. The hazard identification component qualitatively answers the question of how likely an agent is to be a human carcinogen.

Traditionally, quantitative risk assessment has been used as an inclusive term which describes all or parts of dose-response assessment, exposure assessment, and risk characterization. Quantitative risk assessment can be a useful general term in some circumstances, but the more explicit terminology is usually preferred. The dose-response assessment defines the relationship between the dose of an agent and the probability of induction of a carcinogenic effect. This component usually entails an extrapolation from the generally high doses administered to experimental animals, or exposures noted in epidemiological studies, to the exposure levels expected from human contact with the agent in the environment; it also includes considerations of the validity of these extrapolations.

The exposure assessment identifies populations exposed to the agent, describes their composition and size, and presents the types, magnitudes, frequencies, and durations of exposure to the agent.

In risk characterization the outputs of the exposure assessment and the dose-response assessment are combined to estimate quantitatively some measure of the carcinogenic risk. As part of risk characterization, a summary of the strengths and weaknesses in the hazard identification, dose-response assessment, exposure assessment, and the public health risk estimates are presented. Major assumptions, scientific judgments, and, to the extent possible, estimates of the uncertainties embodied in the assessment are also presented, distinguishing clearly between fact, assumption, and science policy.

## 2.0 HAZARD IDENTIFICATION (QUALITATIVE RISK ASSESSMENT)

### 2.1 Overview

The qualitative assessment or hazard identification part of risk assessment contains a review of the relevant biological and chemical information bearing on whether or not an agent may pose a carcinogenic hazard. Since chemical agents seldom occur in a pure state and are often transformed in the body, the review should include information on contaminants, degradation products, and metabolites. *and human B.*

Studies are evaluated according to sound biological and statistical considerations and procedures. These have been described in several publications (Mantel and Haenszel 1959; IRLG 1979; Mantel 1980; Peto et al. 1980; NCTR 1981; U.S. EPA 1983a,b,c; Interdisciplinary Panel on Carcinogenicity 1984; NTP 1984; OSTP 1984). Results and conclusions concerning the agent, derived from different types of information, whether indicating positive or negative responses, are melded together into a weight-of-evidence determination. The strength of the evidence supporting a potential human carcinogenicity judgment is developed in a weight-of-evidence stratification scheme.

### 2.2 Elements of Hazard Identification

### 2.2.1 Physical-Chemical Properties and Routes and Patterns of Exposure

Parameters relevant to carcinogenesis, including physical state, physical-chemical properties, and exposure pathways in the environment should be described.

### 2.2.2 Structure-Activity Relationships

This section should summarize relevant structure-activity correlations that support the prediction of potential carcinogenicity.

### 2.2.3 Metabolic and Pharmacokinetic Properties

This section should summarize relevant metabolic information. Information such as whether the agent is direct-acting or requires conversion to a reactive carcinogenic (e.g., an electrophilic) species, metabolic pathways for such conversions, macromolecular interactions, and transport in, fate in, and excretion from the body as well as species differences in metabolism should be discussed.

### 2.2.4 Toxicologic Effects

Toxicologic effects other than carcinogenicity (e.g., immunological suppression, endocrine disturbances, organ damage) which are relevant to the evaluation of carcinogenicity should be summarized. Prechronic and chronic toxicity evaluations, as well as other testing results, may yield information on target organ effects, pathophysiological reactions, and preneoplastic lesions that bear on the evaluation of carcinogenicity. Dose-response and time-to-response analyses of these reactions may also be helpful.

### 2.2.5 Short-term Tests

Tests for point mutations, numerical and structural chromosome aberrations, DNA damage/repair, and in vitro transformation provide supportive evidence of carcinogenicity and may give information on potential carcinogenic mechanisms. A range of tests from each of the above endpoints helps to characterize an agent's response spectrum.

Short-term in vivo and in vitro tests that can give indication of initiation and promotion activity may also provide supportive evidence for carcinogenicity.

### 2.2.6 Long-term Animal Studies

Criteria for the technical adequacy of animal carcinogenicity studies have been published (IRLG 1979; Feron et al. 1980; Mantel 1980; U.S. FDA 1982; U.S. EPA 1983a,b,c; NTP 1984; OSTP 1984) and should be used to judge the acceptability of individual studies.

The strength of the evidence that an agent is carcinogenic increases with increasing number of tissue sites affected by the agent; increasing number of animal species, strains, and sexes showing a carcinogenic response; the occurrence of clear-cut dose-response relationships as well as a high level of statistical significance of the increased tumor incidence in treated with respect to control groups; dose-related shortening of the time-to-tumor occurrence or time to death with tumor and a dose-related increase in the proportion of tumors that are malignant.

Long-term animal studies at or near the maximum tolerated dose level (MTD) are used to ensure an adequate power for the detection of carcinogenic activity. Negative bioassays at exposure levels above the MTD or partial lifetime exposures at the MTD may not be acceptable because of toxicity or if animal survival is so impaired that the sensitivity of the study is significantly reduced below that of a conventional chronic animal study at the MTD. Positive studies at levels above the MTD should be carefully reviewed to ensure that the responses are not due to factors which do not operate at exposure levels below the MTD. Evidence indicating that high-dose testing produces tumor responses by indirect mechanisms that may be unrelated to effects at lower doses should be dealt with on an individual basis.

The mechanism of the carcinogenic responses under conditions of the experiment should be reviewed carefully as it relates to the relevance of the evidence to human carcinogenic risks (e.g., the occurrence of bladder tumors in the presence of bladder stones and injection site sarcomas). Interpretation of animal studies is aided by the review of target organ toxicity and other effects (e.g., changes in the immune and endocrine systems) that may be noted in prechronic or other toxicological studies. Time and dose-related changes in the incidence of preneoplastic lesions may also be helpful in interpreting animal studies.

Historical control data are often valuable and could be used along with concurrent control data in the evaluation of carcinogenic responses.For the evaluation of rare tumors, even small tumor responses may be significant compared to historical data. In the case of tumors with relatively high spontaneous rates, a response that is significant with respect to the experimental control group becomes questionable if the historical control data indicates that the experimental control group had an unusually low background incidence.

Agents which are positive in long-term animal experiments and also show evidence of promoting or cocarcingenic activity in specialized tests should be considered as complete carcinogens unless there is evidence to the contrary. Agents which show positive results in special tests for initiation, promotion, or cocarcinogenicity and no indication of tumor response in well-conducted and well-designed long-term animal studies should be dealt with on an individual basis.

There are widely diverging scientific views (Tomatis 1977; Ward et al. 1979a,b; Nutrition Foundation 1983; OSTP 1984) about the validity of mouse liver tumors when such tumors occur in strains with high spontaneous background incidence and they are the only tumor response to an agent. These guidelines take the position that the mouse-liver-only tumor response, when other conditions for a classification of "sufficient" evidence in animal studies are met, should be considered as "sufficient" evidence of carcinogenicity with the understanding that this classification could be changed to "limited" if warranted when a number of factors such as the following are observed: occurrence of tumors only in the highest dose group and/ or only at the end of the study; no substantial dose-related increase in the proportion of tumors that are malignant; the tumors are predominately benign, showing no evidence of metastases or invasion; no dose-related shortening of the time to the appearance of tumors; negative or inconclusive results from a spectrum of short-term tests for mutagenic activity; the occurrence of excess tumors only in a single sex.

Positive carcinogenic responses in one species/strain/sex are not generally negated by negative results in other species/strain/sex. Replicate negative studies which are essentially identical in all other respects to a positive study may indicate that the positive results are spurious.

Evidence for carcinogenic action should be based on the observation of statistically significant tumor responses in specific organs or tissues. Appropriate statistical analysis should be performed on data from long-term studies to help determine whether the effects are treatment related or possibly due to chance. These should at least include a statistical test for trend, including appropriate correction for differences in survival. The weight to be given to the level of statistical significance (the *p*-value) and to other available pieces of information is a matter of overall scientific judgment. A statistically significant excess of tumors of all types in the aggregate, in the absence of a statistically significant increase of any individual tumor type, should be regarded as minimal evidence of carcinogenic action unless there are persuasive reasons to the contrary.

## 2.2.7.  Human Studies

Epidemiological studies provide unique information about the response of humans who have been exposed to suspect carcinogens. Descriptive epidemiological studies are useful in generating hypotheses and providing supporting data, but can rarely be used to make a causal inference. Analytical epidemiological studies of the case-control or cohort variety, on the other hand, are especially useful in assessing risks to exposed humans.

Criteria for the adequacy of epidemiological studies are well recognized and include factors such as the proper selection and characterization of exposed and control groups, the adequacy of duration and quality of follow-up, the proper identification and characterization of confounding factors and bias, appropriate consideration of latency effects, and the valid ascertainment of the causes of morbidity and death.

The strength of the epidemiological evidence for carcinogenicity depends on the magnitude, specificity, and statistical significance of the response and increases rapidly with the number of adequate studies which show the same results on populations exposed to the same agent under different conditions.

It should be recognized that epidemiological studies are inherently capable of detecting only relatively large increases in the relative risk of cancer. Negative results from such studies cannot prove the absence of carcinogenic action; however, negative results from a well-designed and conducted epidemiology study which contains usable exposure data can serve to define upper limits of risk which are useful if animal evidence indicates that the agent is potentially carcinogenic.

## 2.3  Weight-of-Evidence

Evidence of possible carcinogenicity in humans comes primarily from two sources: long-term animal tests and epidemiologic investigations. Results from these studies are supplemented with information from short-term tests, pharmacokinetic studies, comparative metabolism studies, structure-activity relationships, and other relevant toxicological studies. The question of how likely an agent is to be a human carcinogen should be answered in the framework of a weight-of-evidence judgment. Judgments about the weight-of-evidence involve considerations of the quality and adequacy of the data and the kinds of responses induced by a suspect carcinogen. There are three major steps to characterizing the weight-of-evidence for carcinogenicity: (1)

characterization of the evidence from human studies and from animal studies individually, (2) combination of the characterizations of these two types of data into a final indication of the overall weight-of-evidence for human carcinogenicity, and (3) evaluation of all supportive information to determine if the overall weight-of-evidence should be modified.

A system for stratifying the weight-of-evidence is recommended, and EPA has developed a scheme (cf. Appendix 1). The EPA scheme is modeled after the classification system developed by the International Agency for Research on Cancer (IARC 1982). In the IARC classification method, the evidence that an agent produces cancer in humans is divided into three categories: sufficient, limited, and inadequate. A similar characterization of evidence is provided for animal data.

EPA has in general adapted the IARC approach for classifying the weight-of-evidence for human data and animal data. The classification system for the characterization of the overall weight-of-evidence for carcinogenicity (animal, human, and other supportive data) includes: Group A—Carcinogenic to Humans; Group B—Probably Carcinogenic for Humans; Group C—Possibly Carcinogenic to Humans; Group D—Not Classifiable as to Human Carcinogenicity; and Group E— No Evidence of Carcinogenicity for Humans.

The following modifications have been made for classifying human and animal studies. For human studies: (1) The observation of a statistically significant association between an agent and life-threatening benign tumors in humans is included in the evaluation of risks to humans. (2) A *no evidence* category is added. This category indicates that no association was found between exposure and increased risk of cancer in well-conducted, well-designed independent analytical epidemiology studies. For animal studies: (1) An increased incidence of combined benign and malignant tumors will be considered to provide sufficient evidence of carcinogenicity if the other criteria defining the "sufficient" category of evidence are met. Benign and malignant tumors will be combined unless the benign tumors are not considered to have the potential to progress to the associated malignancies of the same morphological type. (2) An increased incidence of benign tumors alone as "limited" evidence of carcinogenicity is added. (3) Under specific circumstance, such as the production of neoplasms which occur with high spontaneous background incidence, the evidence may be decreased to "limited" if warranted (e.g., there are widely diverging scientific views regarding the validity of the mouse liver tumor as an indicator of potential human carcinogenicity when this is the only response observed, even in replicated experiments, in the absence of other short-term evidence). (4) *No evidence* of carcinogenicity is also added. This operational category would include substances for which there is no increased incidence of neoplasms in at least two well-designed and well-conducted animal studies of adequate power and dose in different species.

## 2.4 Guidance for Quantitative Assessment

The qualitative evidence for carcinogenesis should be discussed for purposes of guiding the dose-response assessment. The guidance should be given in terms of the appropriateness and limitations of specific studies as well as pharmacokinetic considerations that should be factored into the dose-response assessment. The appropriate method of extrapolation should be factored in when the experimental route of exposure differs from that which occurs in humans.

Agents which are judged to be in the EPA weight-of-evidence stratification Groups A and B would be regarded as suitable for quantitative risk assessments. The appropriateness of quantifying the risks from agents in Group C, specifically those agents which are at the boundary of Groups C and D would be judged on a case-by-case basis. Agents which are judged to be in Groups D and E would generally not have quantitative risk assessments.

## 2.5 Summary and Conclusions

The summary should present all of the key findings in all of the sections of the qualitative assessment and the interpretive rationale which forms the basis for the conclusion. Uncertainties in the evidence as well as factors which may affect the relevance of the chronic animal study to humans should be discussed. The conclusion should present both the weight-of-evidence ranking as well as a description that brings out the more subtle aspects of the evidence that may not be evident from the ranking alone.

## 3.0 DOSE-RESPONSE ASSESSMENT, EXPOSURE ASSESSMENT, AND RISK CHARACTERIZATION

After data concerning the carcinogenic properties of a substance have been collected, evaluated, and categorized, it is frequently desirable to estimate the likely range of excess cancer risk associated with given levels and conditions of human exposure. The first step of the analysis needed to make such estimates is the development of the likely relationship between dose and response (cancer incidence) in the region of human exposure. This information on dose-response relations is coupled with information on the nature and magnitude of human exposure to yield an estimate of human risk. The risk-characterization step also includes an interpretation of these estimates in light of the biological, statistical, and exposure assumptions and uncertainties that have arisen throughout the process of assessing risks.

The elements of dose-response assessment are described in Section 3.1. Guidance on human exposure assessment is provided in another EPA document (U.S. EPA, 1984); however, Section 3.2 of these guidelines include a brief description of the specific type of exposure information that is necessary for use in carcinogenic risk assessment. Finally, in Section 3.3 there is a description of the type of information and its interpretation necessary for accurately characterizing risk and the degree to which it can be known.

It should be emphasized that calculation of quantitative estimates of cancer risk does not require that an agent be a human carcinogen. The likelihood that an agent is a human carcinogen is a function of the weight-of-evidence, as this has been described in the hazard identification section of these guidelines. It is nevertheless important to present quantitative estimates, appropriately qualified and interpreted, in those circumstances in which there is likelihood that the agent is a human carcinogen. Appropriately qualified quantitative estimates of risk, together with estimates of their uncertainty, are useful in cost-benefit analyses, setting regulatory priorities, and for evaluating residual risks associated with the application of regulatory controls.

It should be emphasized in every quantitative risk estimation that the results are uncertain. The uncertainties due to experimental and epidemiological variability, as well as uncertainty in the exposure assessment, can be important. There are major uncertainties in extrapolating both from animals to humans and from high to low doses. There are important species differences in uptake, metabolism, and organ distribution of carcinogens, as well as species and strain differences in target site susceptibility. Human populations are variable with respect to genetic constitution, diet, occupational and home environment, activity patterns, and other cultural factors. Risk estimates should be presented together with the associated hazard assessment (cf. Section 3.3.3) to ensure that there is an appreciation of the weight-of-evidence for carcinogenicity that underlies the quantitative risk estimates.

## 3.1 DOSE-RESPONSE ASSESSMENT

### 3.1.1 Selection of Data

As indicated in Section 2.4, guidance needs to be given by the individuals doing the qualitative assessment (toxicologists, pathologists, and pharmacologists) to the statisticians doing the quantitative assessment as to the appropriate data to be used in the dose-response assessment. This is determined by the quality of the data, its relevance to human modes of exposure, and other technical details.

If available, estimates based upon human epidemiological data are preferred. If adequate exposure data exist in a well-designed and conducted negative epidemiologic study, an upper-bound estimate of risk should be used in preference to higher risks estimated from animal data. In the absence of human data, data from a species that responds most like humans should be used, if information to this effect exists. Where, for a given agent, several studies are available which may involve different animal species, strains, and sexes, at several doses and by different routes of exposure, the following approach to selecting the data sets is used. The tumor incidence data are separated according to organ site and tumor type. All biologically and statistically acceptable data sets are presented. The range of the risk estimates is identified with due regard to biological relevance (particularly in the case of animal studies) and appropriateness of route of exposure. Because it is possible that human sensitivity is as high as the most sensitive responding animal species, in the absence of evidence to the contrary the biologically acceptable data set from long-term animal studies showing the greatest sensitivity should generally be given the greatest emphasis, again with due regard to biological and statistical considerations.

When the exposure route in the species from which the dose-response information is obtained differs from the route occurring in environmental exposures, uncertainties about the dose delivered to the target organs from different exposure media should be explicitly considered and the assumptions should be carefully stated.

Where two or more significantly elevated tumor sites or types are observed in the same study, extrapolations may be conducted on selected sites or types. These selections will be made on biological grounds. To obtain a total estimate of carcinogenic risk, animals with one or more tumor sites or types showing significantly elevated incidence should be pooled and used for extrapolation. If the tumor sites or types are occurring independently, this is the same as summing the risks from the several kinds of statistically significant tumors. The pooled estimates will generally be used in preference to risk estimates based on single sites or types.

Benign tumors should generally be combined with malignancies for risk estimates unless the benign tumors are not considered to have the potential to progress to the associated malignancies of the same morphologic type. However, the contribution of the benign tumors to the total risk should be indicated.

### 3.1.2 Choice of Mathematical Extrapolation Model

Since risks at low exposure levels cannot be measured directly either by animal experiments or by epidemiological studies, a number of mathematical models have been developed to extrapolate from high to low dose. However, different extrapolation models may fit the observed data reasonably well but lead to large differences in the projected risk at low doses.

No single mathematical procedure is recognized as the most appropriate for low-dose extrapolation in carcinogenesis. When relevant biological evidence on mechanism of action exists, the models or procedures employed should be consistent with the evidence. However, when data and information are limited, as is the usual case given the high degree of uncertainty associated with the selection of a low-dose extrapolation model, specific guidance on model selection is necessary to provide a desirable degree of consistency in risk assessments. The choice of low-dose extrapolation models should be consistent with current understanding of the mechanisms of carcinogenesis and not solely on goodness of fit to the observed tumor data. Although mechanisms of the carcinogenesis process are largely unknown, at least some elements of the process have been elucidated, e.g., linearity of tumor initiation. In further support of a linear model, it has been shown that, if a carcinogenic agent acts by accelerating the same stages of the carcinogenic process that lead to the background occurrence of cancer, the added effect of the carcinogen at low dose is virtually linear. Thus, a model which is linear at low dose is plausible.

The linearized multistage model procedure for low-dose extrapolation (U.S. EPA, 1980) is therefore recommended in most cases unless there is evidence on carcinogenesis mechanisms or other biological evidence that indicates the greater suitability of an alternative extrapolation model, or there is statistical or biological evidence that excludes the use of the linearized multistage model.

It should be emphasized that the linearized multistage model leads to a plausible upper limit to the risk which is consistent with some mechanisms of carcinogenesis. However, such an estimate does not necessarily give a realistic prediction of the risk. In certain cases, the linearized multistage model cannot be used successfully with the observed data as, for example, when the data is nonmonotonic or flattens out at high doses. In these cases it may be necessary to make adjustments to the procedure to achieve low-dose linearity.

When pharmacokinetic or metabolism data are available or when other substantial evidence on the mechanistic aspects of the carcinogenesis process exists, a different low-dose extrapolation model might be considered more appropriate on biological grounds. When a different model is chosen, the risk assessment should clearly discuss the nature and strength of the evidence that lead to the choice. In most cases, considerable uncertainty will remain concerning response at low doses; therefore, an upper-limit risk estimate using the linearized multistage model should also be presented.

### 3.1.3 Equivalent Exposure Units Among Species

Low-dose risk estimates derived from laboratory animal data extrapolated to humans are complicated by a variety of factors that differ among species and potentially affect the response to carcinogens. Included among these factors are differences between humans and experimental test animals with respect to life span, body size, genetic variability, population homogeneity, existence of concurrent disease, pharmacokinetic effects such as metabolism and excretion patterns, and the exposure regimen.

The usual approach for making interspecies comparisons has been to use standardized scaling factors. Commonly employed standardized dosage scales include mg per kg body weight per day, ppm in the diet of water, mg per $m^2$ body surface area per day, and mg per kg body weight per lifetime. In the absence of comparative toxicological, physiological, metabolic and pharmacokinetic data for a given suspect carcinogen, the extrapolation of body weight 0.67 is considered to be appropriate.

### 3.2 Exposure Assessment

In order to obtain a quantitative estimate of the risk, the results of the dose-response assessment must be combined with an estimate of the exposure to which the populations of interest are likely to be subject. While the reader is referred to a separate set of Exposure Assessment Guidelines for specific details, it is important that the cancer risk assessor and the decision maker have an appreciation of the impact of the strengths and weaknesses of exposure assessment on the overall cancer risk assessment process.

At present there is no single approach to exposure assessment that is appropriate for all cases. On a case-by-case basis appropriate methods are selected to match the data on hand and the level of sophistication required, e.g., preliminary assessment using crude data and worst case assumptions versus a final assessment using extensive monitoring data. The assumptions, approximations, and uncertainties need to be clearly stated since, in some instances, these will have a major effect on the risk assessment.

In general, the magnitude, duration, and frequency of exposure provide fundamental information for estimating the concentration of the carcinogen to which the organism is exposed. These data are generated from monitoring information, modeling results, and/or reasoned estimates. An appropriate treatment of exposure should consider the potential for exposure via ingestion, inhalation, and dermal penetration from relevant sources of exposures. Where feasible, an attempt should be made to assess the dose to the target organ, either through experimental evidence or reasonable assumptions and modeling.

Special problems arise when the human exposure situation of concern suggests exposure regimens, e.g., route and dosing schedule, which are substantially different from those used in the relevant animal studies. Unless there is evidence to the contrary in a particular case, the cumulative dose received over a lifetime, expressed as average daily exposure pro-rated over a lifetime, is recommended as the appropriate measure of exposure to a carcinogen. That is, the assumption is made that a high dose of a carcinogen received over a short period of time is equivalent to a corresponding low dose spread over a lifetime. This approach becomes more problematical as the exposures in question become more intense but less frequent, especially when there is evidence that the agent has shown dose-rate effects.

An attempt should be made to assess the level of uncertainty associated with the exposure assessment which is to be used in a cancer risk assessment. This measure of uncertainty should be included in the risk characterization (see below) in order to provide the decision maker with a clear understanding of the impact of this uncertainty on any final quantitative risk estimate.

## 3.3   RISK CHARACTERIZATION

### 3.3.1   Options for Numerical Risk Esimates

Depending on the needs of the individual program offices, numerical estimates can be presented in one or more of the following three ways.

### a.   Unit Risk

Under an assumption of low-dose linearity, the unit cancer risk is the excess lifetime risk due to a continuous constant lifetime exposure of one unit of carcinogen concentration. Typical exposure units include ppm or ppb in food or water, mg/kg·day by ingestion, or ppm, or $\mu g/m^3$ in air.

### b.   The Dose Corresponding to a Given Level of Risk

This approach can be useful, particularly when using nonlinear extrapolation models where the unit risk would differ at different dose levels.

## c. Individual and Population Risks

Risks may be characterized either in terms of the excess individual lifetime risks or the excess number of cancers produced per year in the exposed population or both.

Irrespective of the options chosen, the degree of precision and accuracy in the numerical risk estimates currently do not permit more than one significant figure to be presented.

### 3.3.2 Concurrent Exposure

In characterizing the risk due to concurrent exposure to several carcinogens, the risks are combined on the basis of additivity unless there is specific information to the contrary. Interactions of cocarcinogens, promoters, and initiators with known carcinogens should be considered on a case-by-case basis.

### 3.3.3 Summary of Risk Characterization

Whichever method of presentation is chosen, it is critical that the numerical estimates not be allowed to stand alone, separated from the various assumptions and uncertainties upon which they are based. The risk characterization should contain a discussion and interpretation of the numerical estimates that afford the risk manager some insight into the degree to which the quantitative estimates are likely to reflect the true magnitude of human risk, which generally cannot be known with the degree of quantitative accuracy reflected in the numerical estimates. The final risk estimate will be generally rounded to one significant figure and will be coupled with the EPA classification of the qualitative weight-of-evidence. For example a lifetime individual risk of $2 \times 10^{-4}$ resulting from exposure to a "possible human carcinogen" (Group C) should be designated as $2 \times 10^{-4}$[C]. This bracketed designation of the qualitative evidence should be included with all numerical risk estimates (i.e., unit risks which are risks at a specified concentration or concentrations corresponding to a given risk). Agency statements, such as Federal Register Notices, briefings, and action memoranda, frequently include numerical estimates of carcinogenic risk. It is recommended that whenever these numerical estimates are used, the qualitative weight-of-evidence should also be included.

## REFERENCES

Albert, R.E., R.E. Train, and E. Anderson. 1977. Rationale developed by the Environmental Protection Agency for the assessment of carcinogenic risks. *J. Natl. Cancer Inst.* **58:** 1537.

Feron, V.J., H.C. Grice, R. Griesemer, R. Peto, C. Agthe, J. Althoff, D.L. Arnold, H. Blumenthal, J.R.P. Cabral, G. Della Porta, N. Ito, G. Kimmerle, R. Kroes, U. Mohr, N.P. Napalkov, S. Odashima, N.P. Page, T. Schramm, D. Steinhoff, J. Sugar, L. Tomatis, H. Uehleke, and V. Vouk. 1980. Basic requirements for long-term assays for carcinogenicity. In *Long-term and short-term screening assays for carcinogens:*

*A critical appraisal,* p. 21. IARC Monographs (Suppl. 2). International Agency for Research on Cancer, Lyon, France.

Interagency Regulatory Liaison Group (IRLG). 1979. Scientific Basis for Identification of Potential Carcinogens and Estimation of Risks. *J. Natl. Cancer Inst.* **63:** 245.

Interdisciplinary Panel on Carcinogenicity. 1984. Criteria for evidence of chemical carcinogenicity. *Science* **225:** 682.

International Agency for Research on Cancer (IARC). 1982. *Monographs on the evaluation of the carcinogenic risk of chemicals to humans* (Suppl. 4). International Agency for Cancer Research, Lyon, France.

Mantel, N. 1980. Assessing laboratory evidence for neoplastic activity. *Biometrics* **36:** 381.

Mantel, N. and W. Haenszel. 1959. Statistical aspects of the analysis of data from retrospective studies of disease. *J. Natl. Cancer Inst.* **22:** 719.

National Center for Toxicology Research (NCTR). 1981. *Guidelines for statistical tests for carcinogenicity in chronic bioassays.* NCTR Biometry Technical Report 81-100.

National Research Council (NRC). 1983. *Risk assessment in the federal government: Managing the process.* National Academy Press, Washington, D.C.

National Toxicology Program. 1984. Report of the ad hoc panel on chemical carcinogenesis testing and evaluation of the national toxicology program board of scientific counselors.

Nutrition Foundation. 1983. The relevance of mouse liver hepatoma to human carcinogenic risk: A report of the International Advisory Committee to the Nutrition Foundation.

Office of Science and Technology Policy (OSTP). 1984. Chemical carcinogens: Review of the science and its associated principles. *Federal Register* **48:** 21595.

Peto, R., M. Pike, N. Day, R. Gray, P. Lee, S. Parish, J. Peto, S. Richard, and J. Wahrendorf. 1980. Guidelines for simple, sensitive, significant tests for carcinogenic effects in long-term animal experiments. In *Monographs on the long-term and short-term screening assays for carcinogens: A critical appraisal,* p. 311. International Agency for Research on Cancer (Suppl. 2). Lyon, France.

Tomatis, L. 1977. The value of long-term testing for the implementation of primary prevention. In *Origins of human cancer* (ed. H.H. Hiatt, J.D. Watson, and J.A. Winstein). Cold Spring Harbor Laboratory, Cold Spring Harbor, New York.

U.S. Environmental Protection Agency (U.S. EPA). 1976. Interim procedures and guidelines for health risk economic impact assessments of suspected carcinogens. *Federal Register* **41:** 21402.

――――. 1980. Water quality criterial documents; availability. *Federal Register* **45:** 79318.

――――. 1983a. Good laboratory practices standards—Toxicology testing. *Federal Register* **48:** 53922.

――――. 1983b. Hazard evaluations: Humans and domestic animals. Subdivision F. PB 83-153916.

――――. 1983c. Health effects test guidelines. PB83-232984.

――――. 1984. Draft Exposure Assessment Guidelines.

U.S. Food and Drug Administration (U.S. FDA). 1982. Toxicological principles for the safety assessment of direct food additives and color additives used in food.

Ward, J.M., R.A. Griesemer and E.K. Weisburger. 1979a. The mouse liver tumor as an endpoint in carcinogenesis tests. *Toxicol. Appl. Pharmacol.* **51:** 389.

Ward, J.M., D.G. Goodman, R.A. Squire, K.C. Chu, and M.S. Linhart. 1979b. Neoplastic and nonneoplastic lesions in aging (C57BL/6N × C3H/HeN)F$_1$ (B6C3F$_1$) mice. *J. Natl. Cancer Inst.* **63:** 849.

# APPENDIX 1

# EPA CLASSIFICATION SYSTEM FOR EVIDENCE OF CARCINOGENICITY FROM HUMAN STUDIES AND FROM ANIMAL STUDIES (adapted from IARC)

## 1.0 ASSESSMENT OF EVIDENCE FOR CARCINOGENICITY FROM STUDIES IN HUMANS

Evidence of carcinogenicity from human studies comes from three main sources:

1. Case reports of individual cancer patients who were exposed to the agent(s).
2. Descriptive epidemiological studies in which the incidence of cancer in human populations was found to vary in space or time with exposure to the agent(s).
3. Analytical epidemiological (case-control and cohort) studies in which individual exposure to the agent(s) was found to be associated with an increased risk of cancer.

Three criteria must be met before a causal association can be inferred between exposure and cancer in humans:

1. There is no identified bias which could explain the association.
2. The possibility of confounding has been considered and ruled out as explaining the association.
3. The association is unlikely to be due to chance.

In general, although a single study may be indicative of a cause-effect relationship, confidence in inferring a causal association is increased when several independent studies are concordant in showing the association, when the association is strong, when there is a dose-response relationship, or when a reduction in exposure is followed by a reduction in the incidence of cancer.

The degrees of evidence for carcinogenicity[1] from studies in humans are categorized as:

i.    Sufficient evidence of carcinogenicity, which indicates that there is a causal relationship between the agent and human cancer.
ii.   Limited evidence of carcinogenicity, which indicates that a causal interpretation is credible, but that alternative explanations, such as chance, bias or confounding, could not adequately be excluded.
iii.  Inadequate evidence, which indicates that one of two conditions prevailed:

---

[1] For purpose of public health protection, agents associated with life-threatening benign tumors in humans are included in the evaluation.

(a) There were few pertinent data or (b) the available studies, while showing evidence of association, did not exclude chance, bias, or confounding.
iv. No evidence, which indicates that no association was found between exposure and an increased risk of cancer in well-designed and well-conducted independent analytical epidemiology studies.


## 2.0 ASSESSMENT OF EVIDENCE FOR CARCINOGENICITY FROM STUDIES IN EXPERIMENTAL ANIMALS

These assessments are classified into five groups:

i. Sufficient evidence[2] of carcinogenicity which indicates that there is an increased incidence of malignant tumors or combined malignant and benign tumors:[3] (a) in multiple species or strains; or (b) in multiple experiments (preferably with different routes of administration or using different dose levels); or (c) to an unusual degree with regard to incidence, site or type of tumor, or age at onset. Additional evidence may be provided by data on dose-response effects, as well as information from short-term tests or on chemical structure.

ii. Limited evidence of carcinogenicity, which means that the data suggest a carcinogenic effect but are limited because: (a) the studies involve a single species, strain, or experiment; or (b) the experiments are restricted by inadequate dosage levels, inadequate duration of exposure to the agent, inadequate period of follow-up, poor survival, too few animals, or inadequate reporting; or (c) an increase in the incidence of benign tumors only.

iii. Inadequate evidence, which indicates that because of major qualitative or quantitative limitations, the studies cannot be interpreted as showing either the presence or absence of a carcinogenic effect.

iv. No evidence, which indicates that there is no increased incidence of neoplasms in at least two well-designed and well-conducted animal studies in different species.

v. No data, which indicates that data were not available.

The categories sufficient evidence and limited evidence refer only to the strength of the experimental evidence that these agent(s) are carcinogenic and not to the power of their carcinogenic action.

---

[2] Under specific circumstances, such as the production of neoplasms which occur with high spontaneous background incidence, the evidence may be decreased to "limited" if warranted (e.g., there are widely diverging scientific views regarding the validity of the mouse liver tumor as an indicator of potential human carcinogenicity when this is the only response observed, even in replicated experiments in the absence of short-term or other evidence).

[3] Benign and malignant tumors will be combined unless the benign tumors are not considered to have the potential to progress to the associated malignancies of the same morphologic type.

## 3.0 CATEGORIZATION OF OVERALL EVIDENCE

### Group A—Human Carcinogen

This category is used only when there is sufficient evidence from epidemiological studies to support a causal association between exposure to the agent(s) and cancer.

### Group B—Probable Human Carcinogen

This category includes agents for which the evidence of human carcinogenicity from epidemiological studies ranges from almost "sufficient," to "inadequate." To reflect this range, the category is divided into higher (Group B1) and lower (Group B2) degrees of evidence. Usually, category B1 is reserved for agents for which there is at least limited evidence of carcinogenicity to humans from epidemiological studies. In the absence of adequate data in humans it is reasonable, for practical purposes, to regard agents for which there is sufficient evidence of carcinogenicity in animals as if they presented a carcinogenic risk to humans. Therefore, agents for which there is inadequate evidence from human studies *and* sufficient evidence from animal studies would usually result in a classification of B2.

In some cases, the known chemical or physical properties of an agent and the results from short-term tests allow its transfer from Group B2 to B1.

### Group C—Possible Human Carcinogen

This category is used for agents with limited evidence of carcinogenicity in animals in the absence of human data. It includes a wide variety of evidence: (a) definitive malignant tumor response in a single well-conducted experiment, (b) marginal tumor response in studies having inadequate design or reporting, (c) benign but not malignant tumors with an agent showing no response in a variety of short-term tests for mutagenicity, and (d) marginal responses in a tissue known to have a high and variable background rate.

In some cases, the known physical or chemical properties of an agent and results from short-term tests allow a transfer from Group C to B2 or from Group D to C.

### Group D—Not Classified

This category is used for agent(s) with inadequate animal evidence of carcinogenicity.

### Group E—No evidence of Carcinogenicity for Humans

This category is used for agent(s) that show no evidence for carcinogenicity in at least two adequate animal tests in different species or in both epidemiological and animal studies.

## COMMENTS

**PURCHASE:** What evidence do you think there will ever be to suggest that benign tumors are not relevant? You say you're going to include them unless there's evidence to suggest they shouldn't be included. What type of evidence?

**ALBERT:** I doubt if there is any persuasive rationale to exclude benign tumors. Benign tumors may represent the weak action of a carcinogen or be a signal that the agent is a promoter.

**WEINSTEIN:** We know that in rats acetyl aminofluorene can produce bladder, liver, and zymbal gland tumors. Why is it scientifically less valid to pool all of these tumors in assessing the carcinogenicity of the compound? We know that in humans cigarette smoking can cause bladder and lung cancer.

**ALBERT:** A statistically insignificant excess tumor response at any given site may only reflect a level of dose that is insufficiently high. This may be true for multiple sites which in the aggregate are statistically significant. That's the reason for calling such a response "weak evidence."

**WEINSTEIN:** What if the agent is just not very organ-specific?

**SWENBERG:** How many of you have looked at the tables of the NTP bioassays that give the number of total tumors in a typical bioassay and what their variation is? Virtually 100% of the animals have tumors. We're not dealing with a situation where 10% or 20% of these animals have tumors. We're talking about multiple tumors at different sites—multiple endocrine tumors, testicular tumors, mammary tumors.

**PURCHASE:** One of the problems is that sometimes you can see an apparent dose-related increase in total tumor incidence, but at the low dose it's a different set of tumors from the high dose.

**SWENBERG:** If you have multiple-site carcinogenicity, usually you can find a dose-response for those multiple sites on an individual basis. What Roy [Albert] is saying is that we don't have that. All we've got is this total number of tumors that we're looking at. I suggest that that is a very weak endpoint. Before you recommend this approach, what you ought to do is go back and take the last hundred bioassays and see what that data is and what the variation is, just in the control groups.

**PREUSS:** No. What he's saying is that you need a statistically significant increase in the treated groups versus the control groups.

**ALBERT:** The point is that you have to make a judgment on the basis of available information.

**WEINSTEIN:** I can see that for neatness of experimental design and maybe for statistical reasons you might want to do that. I don't think you can justify it from a mechanism of action point of view because many carcinogens are not absolutely organ-specific. But the denominator could become troublesome because then you would also have to pool various types of spontaneous tumors.

**ALBERT:** As I said before, this is a draft of the EPA Cancer Guidelines and represents an attempt at a middle-of-the-road position. It is perfectly clear that here, in this meeting, we have views that range from describing this sort of evidence as "poor" to others as "not so bad."

**J. WILSON:** The point is that it is very unreliable information on which to base any decision.

**NEEL:** It sounded as if you were saying that one positive experiment would outweigh dozens of negative ones. Did you say that?

**ALBERT:** Yes, when they're not done under the same conditions. If you have a series of tests, say with a positive result in a C3H mouse and all the other tests were on other strains of mice, the negative responses in the other strains of mice would not negate the positive response in the C3H mouse.

**NEEL:** So then you shop around until you find the most sensitive mouse strain there is, and that sets the guidelines?

**ALBERT:** No, you don't shop around. Risk assessment is a passive operation which accepts the data that comes in.

**J. WILSON:** In effect, you're shopping around.

**ALBERT:** No. We essentially get all the available information.

**NEEL:** You recall our discussion of the biases in using the most sensitive indicator the other day. It strikes me this approach does just that.

**ALBERT:** That's right. There is no denying the fact that this is the approach that's taken in these guidelines.

**NEEL:** It absolutely maximizes the risk estimate.

**ALBERT:** Not absolutely, but it certainly does tilt toward the conservative side, in the sense of being protective. Dr. Gillette said that virtually every animal strain represents some facet of human response. There have been departures from the use of the most sensitive strain, for example, in the National Academy of Sciences' drinking water document which, for instance, used the average animal response.

**PURCHASE:** It certainly doesn't apply for other toxic phenomena. If you take the most sensitive strain, for example in an $LD_{50}$, and ignore the less sensitive data, then when there is lethality data from man you find that it's wrong. Take fluoroacetate, for example, or dioxin. You need to make some judgment about the most relevant data, rather than just taking the most sensitive strain, unless what you're trying to do is to make the most conservative estimate.

**PERERA:** That may be so for some effects other than carcinogenicity, but with carcinogenicity you don't know about the sensitivity of humans relative to that of the animal strain being tested. So, what Dr. Albert is saying is that use of the most sensitive species is consistent with a conservative policy.

**SWENBERG:** Are you sure that that is the case?

**PERERA:** Actually, there are some examples where humans appear to be more, rather than less, sensitive, such as β-naphthylamines and benzene.

**WEINSTEIN:** Often a criterion in evaluating carcinogenicity data is the spontaneous incidence of tumors in the particular animal strain used. For example, the high spontaneous incidence of liver tumors in certain strains of mice is often a source of contention.

**REITZ:** Isn't it true, too, that the Sencar mouse has been proposed as the bioassay system of the future and was selected exactly for that purpose?

**ALBERT:** I had not heard that proposal. That strain is certainly used for studies on mechanism.

**PURCHASE:** One of the long-term consequences of such a policy will be a search for resistant mice or rats.

**ALBERT:** Let me emphasize one point: There is nothing new in what is being proposed here. These guidelines are just a statement of what the Carcinogen Assessment Group has been doing for 8 years. But the question is, what is the alternative. Suppose there are seven bioassays, one of which is positive. Are they going to be averaged?

**PURCHASE:** You could make a risk assessment on the basis of each one, which then gives you a range.

**PERERA:** Zero to whatever.

**J. WILSON:** No, it's never zero because there is always an upper confidence line. You always have a positive number you can start with.

**SWENBERG:** You said that the evidence was going to be based on statistics basically. I'm wondering where the biology comes in. I personally believe very strongly that the statistician's role is to point out those issues that need to be closely examined for a biological effect, but cancer is a biological issue, not a statistical issue. We just reviewed a series of FD&C color studies with paired controls. While it's disputed exactly how many of those paired controls would be called positive versus negative, it's running somewhere in the neighborhood of 50%. That is because we don't know how to apply statistics to the extrabinomial variability that we're seeing in bioassays. The NTP is considering engaging in a series of studies using dual controls. But it's not a moot point.

**ALBERT:** What kinds of controls are you talking about?

**SWENBERG:** Studies that have had two identical controls. If you call control group B treated and control group A control, 50% of the control group B in the FD&C color studies came out being called "statistically positive."

**PERERA:** At a recent NTP meeting, Dr. Haseman of NIEHS reported that he considers that the estimate of 50% is way off and that 10% is probably more likely.

**SWENBERG:** That 10% is based on his historic controls. He himself gave me a range of 45–63% false-positives on data from those studies. The problem is that the FD&C color studies have not gone through the same kind of quality control from a pathology standpoint that the NTP studies do, and therefore he is uncomfortable, as everyone is, just accepting the data. Nevertheless, there is an issue here that needs to be examined.

**PURCHASE:** The International Commission for Protection Against Environmental Mutagens and Carcinogens (ICPEMC) has recently published an extensive study of dose-response relationships in mutagenesis in *Mutation Research*. They studied 20–50 chemicals and found no evidence of thresholds in three-quarters of them; in the remaining quarter there is either evidence or it is uncertain.

**CORN:** Roy [Albert], the fact you institutionally established the unit risk discourages those who would use other models to express the risk; you force them into the unit risk mode. You can't have a unit risk with a nonlinear model, which seems to be usurping that very powerful tool.

**ALBERT:** You could use several benchmarks for a nonlinear response.

**CORN:** This draft says to express it as unit risk, not to express it at several benchmarks using different models with a range of variation. The unit risk approach is very restrictive. Regardless of the argument over which model is best, the use of different models to express the range of uncertainty is ruled out if you restrict the assessor to a unit risk expression.

**ALBERT:** To use the various models to convey the range of estimates is really not appropriate when such models have no biological basis. For example, the log-probit model represents the interaction of multiple factors. It is useful in the observable response range, but it is not known which factors dominate at the very low levels of exposure; there is no biological rationale for extrapolation by the use of the probit model. Conveying a range of estimates on the basis of models which lack mechanistic justification is of questionable use.

**SWENBERG:** Does linearity have it?

**ALBERT:**   To the extent that one can justify it on the basis of single-hit processes interacting with DNA, and also the possibility that the agent has the same mechanism of action as whatever is causing background cancer.

**SWENBERG:**   Yes. But the evidence right now, just from oncogenes alone, is that it requires more than one hit for transformation. The database for the one-hit hypothesis is poor at present and appears to be diminishing. You ought to be thinking of the future instead of the past.

**ALBERT:**   A federal regulatory agency should not swing about like a weathervane in a gusty wind; it is supposed to sense when the trend of scientific evidence becomes sufficiently established to be adopted.

**PETO:**   Is anybody suggesting a specific alternative that should be assumed as a basis for human risk assessment?

**ALBERT:**   Carcinogen risk assessment is an attempt to pull together what there is in the way of scientific evidence and take a position on it. To say, "Let's forget about the science," doesn't serve the purposes of risk assessment.

**TAYLOR:**   No. My point is that when the scientific data do not reveal what is happening at that low level, some policy component has to come into play that says you either take a conservative approach or you make your best guess about what you think truth is. EPA's policy judgment, as I understand it, is not to take a best guess about what the truth is, but to take a conservative approach. I think this is sound public health policy, but don't mistake that for a scientific decision.

**MERRILL:**   Dr. Albert, you indicated the program officers at EPA were insisting on a mathematical expression of risk. Were they insisting on the mathematical integration of those qualifiers?

**ALBERT:**   They didn't really know. It is evident that if there is weak qualitative evidence for carcinogenicity, it ought to be factored into the quantitative assessment. If one regards the public health impact of cancer in terms of the excess estimated numbers of cancer cases, then that estimated impact should be clearly reduced by weak qualitative evidence.

**PREUSS:**   If you could present them separately and discuss them and give the person making the decision some idea of the strengths and the weaknesses on both sides.

**ALBERT:**   All they seem to want to know is "Is it a carcinogen or isn't it a carcinogen?"

**PREUSS:**   And you're going to tell them it's 0.03 of a carcinogen?

**ALBERT:**   No. The bottom line here is the estimate of the number of cancer cases, and that is reduced in proportion to some arbitrary scaling of the probability that the agent really is a human carcinogen.

**NEEL:** Is it possible to get into this document some treatment of the risk of extrapolating four orders of magnitude beyond the data? That's a point on which I think we can agree. It takes just a little shift in the slope of the curve over the range of the data points, and by the time one has extrapolated four orders of magnitude down, the possibilities for error are horrendous. I can swallow the linear model because we can't do much else. But even with the linear model, it doesn't take much of a change in the slope to introduce a factor of ten, or even 100, when you're extrapolating.

**PETO:** You change the slope by changing the data, but you're still going to draw a straight line through the data to the origin. If your data are right within a factor of two, your risk estimate will only vary by a factor of two.

**KALDOR:** We can estimate the slope of a line through the observed data. The slope has a certain associated error and the low-dose estimate is then the risk for which the dose is to be estimated, divided by that slope. The ratio of the standard error to the resulting dose estimate does not change with the risk.

**NEEL:** So you are saying that the requirement that the regression should intersect the origin offsets much of the uncertainty of the data.

**KALDOR:** But not in the relative size of that error.

**PETO:** The risk goes from between one in two to one in one million to two in one million.

**KALDOR:** As a fraction of the thing you're trying to estimate, it doesn't change.

**ALBERT:** If what you were saying were true, things would be in a pickle. The linear extrapolation is billed as an upper limit. Looking at the benzene estimates that Bernie Goldstein showed, an increase of four orders of magnitude would be a national disaster. I can't believe that this could possibly be true.

**J. WILSON:** How can you tolerate using bad experiments if they give positive data and not if they give negative data? That is not only absurd, it is terrible.

**ALBERT:** I don't think that we ever waxed wroth over the data input. We use balanced judgment. We don't get indignant over these things.

# The Changing Role of Risk Assessment in Federal Regulation

**PETER W. PREUSS\*† and PAUL D. WHITE\*†**
Directorate for Health Sciences
U.S. Consumer Product Safety Commission
Washington, D.C. 20207

## OVERVIEW

The converging consequences of a series of events discussed in this paper have resulted in a new and central role for quantitative risk assessment in the decision-making process. Apparent advances in the way in which such assessments are performed and presented, including the use of complex computer models, have moved risk and economic assessments onto a perceived plane of equal precision and reliability. Improved modeling has not appreciably reduced the large uncertainties inherent in risk assessment. The uncertainties in extrapolation from experimental animals to humans and extrapolation from high-dose observations to low-dose human exposures are not removed by precise fitting of curves to high-dose data. However, sophisticated modeling techniques do tend to give a risk assessment the appearance of accuracy and thus contribute to increased emphasis on risk predictions.

Decisionmakers should therefore exercise great caution in understanding the uncertainties associated with the risk assessment process. In spite of recent court decisions and Congressional activities, quantitative risk assessment has not advanced to the stage where it can serve as the sole or prime basis for a regulatory decision.

## INTRODUCTION

The role of quantitative risk assessment in the regulatory process has changed dramatically during the past 5–10 years. From a status in which it was often an ornamental adjunct to decision documents, quantitative risk assessment has become the anchor to which much of the other information in a regulatory decision document is tied. This evolution has come about, we believe, as a result of a number of different factors, including (1) Court decisions which have found that quantitative assessments are integral to the regulatory process; (2) congressional attention which has encouraged quantitation and the concept of comparative risk; (3) efforts by

---

\* The authors were employed by the Consumer Product Safety Commission. Since this paper was written in their official capacity, it is in the public domain and may be freely copied or reprinted. The opinions expressed by the authors do not necessarily represent the views of the Commission.

† Present address: Office of Health and Environmental Assessment, U.S. Environmental Protection Agency, Washington, D.C. 20460

agencies of the Federal government and interagency groups to grapple with the issue and define and describe how quantitative risk assessment is done; (4) increasing accent by recent administrations on the quantitation of economic costs; and, (5) apparent advances in the art of risk assessment, such that today, complex and difficult scientific issues appear to be resolvable through the assessment process.

## RESULTS AND DISCUSSION

During the early to mid-1970s, risk assessment was viewed with suspicion by many because of a lack of confidence that the derived risk predictions were in any way realistic. This was reflected, in part in a report by the National Academy of Sciences in 1975 (NAS 1975) which said:

". . . There is strong reason to believe that a high proportion of cancers in humans is due to environmental factors. . . . The first line of defense against cancer is to identify carcinogens in the environment and, by appropriate measures, to eliminate or reduce their presence to minimum levels."

The point was made explicitly by the Commissioners of the Consumer Product Safety Commission (CPSC) who, in their review of a proposal to ban the use of benzene as an intentional additive in consumer products (CPSC 1978), said:

". . . The Commission's Health Sciences staff has calculated an assessment of the leukemia risk from consumer exposure to benzene-containing paint strippers. . . . While the Commission is not relying upon a specified percentage of increased risk in issuing this ban, the Commission believes that in view of the seriousness of the risks of injury from benzene exposure, any increased risk is unacceptable."

The Commission in essence denied the utility of the risk assessment and stated that no exposure was acceptable. In addition, they stated that:

". . . once the carcinogenicity of a substance has been established qualitatively, any exposure must be considered to be attended by risk when considering any given population, because individual susceptibility to a carcinogen varies widely."

In contrast, a number of years later, when this proposed regulation was finally acted upon, a quantitative risk assessment was an integral part of the decision made by the Consumer Product Safety Commission. The agency based its conclusion on an in-depth exposure assessment, a market survey, and laboratory analysis of benzene levels in products, which were combined with hazard and toxicological information into a quantitative risk assessment (CPSC 1981).

In a very similar fashion, the recent proposal by the Occupational Safety and Health Administration (OSHA) to reduce occupational exposure to asbestos was based in large measure on a quantitative assessment of the reduced numbers of cancers that would result from a reduced exposure level. The Federal Register notice (OSHA 1983) stated:

> "OSHA's determination that a grave danger currently exists is predicated upon quantitative risk estimates in this record which point to a large number of excess deaths from cancer and asbestos among currently exposed workers . . ."

This is in contrast with earlier OSHA regulatory actions which rejected the application of quantitative risk assessment as a basis for regulation (OSHA 1974, 1978).

So, too, the Consumer Product Safety Commission's efforts to deal with the off-gassing of formaldehyde from products such as particle board, plywood, and urea-formaldehyde foam insulation have included quantitative assessments of the increased risk of cancer as integral components (Cohn, this volume; CPSC 1982, 1984).

The five factors mentioned previously have, in one way or another, been major contributors to the evolution of the now central role of quantitative risk assessment.

## The Courts

Probably the greatest impact on the evolutionary process that we have observed was the decision by the Supreme Court overturning OSHA's permanent standard for benzene on the ground that OSHA had failed to show that worker exposure to 10 ppm posed a "significant" risk (USSC 1980). Although no formal policy was published by the regulatory agencies in response to this decision, it has generally been taken to mean that quantitation is required for the regulation of carcinogens. More recently, the Fifth Circuit Court of Appeals vacated a rule promulgated by the Consumer Product Safety Commission banning urea-formaldehyde foam insulation; the Court's decision was based, in part, on their rejection of the CPSC risk assessment. This Court explicitly accepted the need for quantitative assessment and balancing; and, based on their understanding of the science, demanded greater precision in the assessment. The decision by the Court, in part, rejected the input data used in the assessment (which reflected the current state of the art) and seems to have endorsed the concept of a "precise assessment" (Ricci 1984).

## Congressional Attention

Over the past several years, a number of bills have been introduced that have sought to provide more and better risk assessments in the governmental process. Most recently, Congressman D. Ritter and more than a dozen other members of the House of Representatives introduced H.R. 4192. The purposes of this bill are

> "to establish coordinated interagency research and demonstration projects for improving knowledge and use of risk assessment by those Federal agencies concerned with the protection of human life, health and the environment, and to provide for the establishment of a Central Board of Scientific Risk Analysis

as a means of improving the scientific review and evaluation of risk analyses made by Federal agencies . . ."

This bill and its predecessors assume that quantitative risk assessments are desirable and meaningful, that properly done assessments can be used to compare the risks associated with different activities, and that improvements in the process will lead to better social decisions. As Congressman D. Ritter said in 1980 (Ritter 1980):

"These hearings . . . are . . . the first attempt in Congress to use risk comparison in a broad and comprehensive way as a means of making Federal regulation work better."

## Agency and Interagency Activities

Federal agencies have been groping with the issue of quantitative risk assessment for many years, and in so doing have published many statements and guidelines to describe what they were doing and define how they were doing it (NAS 1969; USPHS 1970; FDA 1971; Food Safety Council 1978; IRLG 1979; OSTP 1979; Regulatory Council 1979). The publication of the report of the Interagency Regulatory Liaison Group (IRLG 1979) sparked a great deal of controversy. This report discussed the use of quantitative risk assessments in regulatory decisions and expressed concern about over-reliance on the results obtained:

"With the present state of knowledge, the quantitative assessment of cancer risks provides only a rough estimate of the magnitude of the cancer risks; this estimate may be useful in setting priorities for control of carcinogens and in obtaining a very rough idea of the magnitude of the public health problem posed by a given carcinogen."

Similarly a very recent draft report by the Office of Science and Technology Policy (now published in final form) (OSTP 1985) went to great lengths to describe the many assumptions, judgments, and uncertainties that are still a part of the risk assessment process. This draft report describes a consensus viewpoint of the state-of-the-art by a number of Federal regulatory and research agencies.

The OSTP draft report has, in turn, been used as the basis for the formation of a workgroup set up by the newly formed Interagency Risk Management Council to prepare cancer risk assessment guidelines for the federal regulatory agencies.

## Economic Assessments

During the past three administrations, increasing accent has been placed on the quantification of the costs of agency actions. At the present time, a series of Executive Orders have resulted in extensive analyses by the Federal agencies of the costs and burdens of any action they propose. In addition, proposed actions by agencies of the Executive Branch are subject to review by the Office of Management and Budget, and subjected to futher quantitative analysis. This process, too, has evolved during the past decade and has played an increasingly large role in regulatory decisions.

## Advances in the Art

The published literature on risk assessment has expanded notably over the past decade, and has included the development of technically sophisticated mathematical tools for risk assessment (Crump et al. 1977; Krewski and Van Ryzin 1980). Until recently, risk assessments by Federal agencies generally utilized simple linear models which predicted that cancer risks were in direct proportion to the dose of carcinogen received; this uncomplicated methodology underscored the imprecise nature of risk calculations. Today, Federal agencies generally use complicated model-fitting computer programs in most risk calculations. The statistical techniques in these calculations are sophisticated and can be so involved that risk assessors themselves do not fully understand the details. The use of computerized models has led to some improvements in risk predictions, particularly in situations where the linear model does not fit experimental tumor data well. However, the fundamental uncertainties arising from extrapolations between experimental animals and humans and from high doses to low have not significantly decreased.

## AN EXAMPLE: EPA REGULATION OF HAZARDOUS AIR POLLUTANTS

In contrast to the marked changes in the application of risk assessment by OSHA and CPSC, the process utilized by EPA for evaluating hazardous air pollutants under Section 112 of the Clear Air Act over the past decade has remained constant in many of its formal features. EPA has utilized and given weight to risk assessment throughout this period; however, an examination of the rules and proposed rules issued by EPA show an increasing emphasis on numerical risk calculations as decision tools. The EPA actions discussed here demonstrate relatively subtle but important changes that provide an example of the evolution of risk assessment considerations in decisionmaking.

In 1976, EPA issued a final rule restricting emissions of vinyl chloride from industrial plants (EPA 1976). In issuing this standard the agency determined that: "Reasonable extrapolation from these [cancer] findings cause concern . . . at present ambient levels. The purpose of the standard is to minimize vinyl chloride emissions" from all known sources at the regulated plants "to the level obtainable with best available technology" (BAT). A quantitatative risk assessment was presented; however, the risk assessment was not cited in discussions of the categories of sources that were selected for regulation, or in the decisions not to require emissions reductions beyond BAT. In this rule BAT was strictly defined: "EPA believes that costs may be considered under Section 112, but only to a very limited extent; i.e., to assure that the costs of control are not grossly disproportionate to the amount of emission reduction achieved." In proposing this standard, EPA had predicted that some plant closings would occur.

The EPA proposals to regulate benzene emissions in 1980 provide a second picture of the Agency's approach to the utilization of risk assessment. In proposing to regulate the emission of benzene from maleic anhydride plants (EPA 1980), risk assessment was utilized to rank-order benzene exposures from different categories of stationary sources. Maleic anhydride plants ranked high on this list, but the actual magnitude of the risk estimates was not emphasized. However, the agency's decision not to require control beyond the level of BAT was largely based on risk assessment considerations. Thus, risk assessment was an important, but not the central, consideration in the proposed regulations.

A recent picture of EPA regulations is given by the proposed standards for inorganic arsenic (EPA 1983). This notice proposed regulation of certain source categories and stated the agency's intention not to regulate other sources. In this proposal, quantitative risk assessment was emphasized in decisions on regulation: "whether a source category is estimated to cause significant risk will be decided in light of the estimated risks to individuals, and the estimated cumulative risks to populations affected by that source category." Risk assessment was also used to examine the "results from application of various control options." Risk assessment and economic considerations, formed the basis for decisions not to require more than BAT.

In comparing the 1983 arsenic proposal and the 1976 vinyl chloride regulations, one finds considerations of the risk assessment and economic comparisons in both, but to differing degrees. In adopting the vinyl chloride regulations, these factors played a supporting role that contributed only in a broad manner to the control approaches adopted. However, in the arsenic proposal, risk and economic considerations formed a central basis for the decisions on a variety of specific control measures.

## REFERENCES

CPSC (Consumer Product Safety Commission). 1978. *43 Federal Register 21839.*

CPSC. 1981. *46 Federal Register 27910.*

CPSC. 1982. Ban of urea-formaldehyde foam insulation, withdrawal of proposed information labeling rule, and denial of petition to issue a standard. *47 Federal Register 14336.*

CPSC. 1984. Comments of the U.S. Consumer Product Safety Commission staff to the Department of Housing & Urban Development's proposed revisions of the Manufactured Home Construction and Safety Standards (24 CFR Part 3280).

Crump, K.S., H.A. Guess, and K.L. Deal. 1977. Confidence intervals and tests of hypotheses concerning dose response relations for animal carcinogenicity data. *Biometrics* **33:** 437.

EPA (Environmental Protection Agency). 1976. *41 Federal Register 46560.*

———. 1980. *45 Federal Register 26650.*

———. 1983. *48 Federal Register 33112.*

FDA (Food and Drug Administration). 1971. Advisory Committee on Protocols for Safety Evaluation. *Toxicol. Appl. Pharmacol.* **20:** 419.

Food Safety Council. 1978. Proposed system for food safety assessment. *Food Cosmet. Toxicol.* **16(2):** 97.

IRLG (Interagency Regulatory Liaison Group). 1979. Scientific bases for identifying potential carcinogens and estimating their risks. *J. Natl. Cancer Inst.* **63:** 243.

Krewsky, D. and J. Van Ryzin. 1981. Dose response models for quantal response toxicity data. In *Statistics and related topics* (ed. M. Csorgo et al.), p. 201. Elsevier, Amsterdam, North Holland, The Netherlands.

NAS (Natonal Academy of Sciences). 1969. *Guidelines for estimating toxicologically insignificant levels of chemicals in food.* National Academy of Sciences Press, Washington, D.C.

_____. 1975. *Principles for Evaluating Chemicals in the Environment.* National Academy of Sciences Press, Washington, D.C.

OSHA (Occupational Safety and Health Administration). 1974. *39 Federal Register 35890.*

_____. 1978. *43 Federal Register 5918.*

_____. 1983. *48 Federal Register 51086.*

OSTP (Office of Science and Technology Policy). 1979. *Identification, characterization, and control of potential human carcinogens: A framework for federal decision-making.*

_____. 1985. Chemical carcinogens: A review of the science and its associated principles. *50 Federal Register 10372.*

Regulatory Council. 1979. Regulation of Chemical Carcinogens.

Ricci, P.F. 1984. Human-risk-benefit assessment in public policy. *Public Interest* (In press).

Ritter, Hon. D. 1980. Hearings before the Subcommittee on Science, Research and Technology, May 14–15, 1980.

USPHS (United States Public Health Service). 1970. Ad hoc Committee on the Evaluation of Low Levels of Environmental Chemical Carcinogens.

USSC (United States Supreme Court). 1980. Industrial Union Department, AFL-CIO v. American Petroleum Institute. 448 U.S. 607.

## COMMENTS

**J. WILSON:** There's another aspect of this that you might not think about from where you are sitting. There are assumptions built into the risk assessment process as it's practiced and as Roy [Albert] described it that are properly not the place for scientists making the assessment, but properly belong in the domain of the administrator who's going to make the ultimate decision. One of these is the decision to regulate something as though it were a carcinogen. There are many occasions when the best the (EPA) Carcinogen Assessment Group can say to the administrator is, "The evidence is not sufficient to say whether it's a carcinogen or not. It might be and it might not be. If it is, the risk is 'so-and-so,' or the most conservative risk is 'thus.' " It should then be up to the administrator to decide: "Shall I regulate it as though it were a carcinogen, or shall I not?" But as Roy [Albert] describes it, the administrator says, "Don't tell me about all these troubles. Tell me whether it's a carcinogen or not." That decision itself, given the present state of affairs in the United States, presumes that it shall be regulated that way. I don't think this issue should be part of the process of the risk assessment itself; it should be something taken out of it and presented to the decision maker separately. He or she has to judge whether, given the conditions of exposure and every other consideration, whether he or she is going to regulate it as a carcinogen. That brings me to a situation on which I'd like your comment. Suppose you are in the position of worrying about what to do about formaldehyde, and your agency's data on the background exposure of the general public suggest that all of us who are indoors are exposed to approximately one-tenth of a part per million for most of the day. Obviously it goes up and down, depending on where you are, but nearly everybody is exposed to a background of exposure between 0.01 and 0.1 ppm in the air. That's less than a factor of 100 below what is probably the concentration of formaldehyde that perhaps raises the lung cancer rate by 10%. How are you going to deal with that?

**PREUSS:** Are you asking me how to deal with ambient levels?

**J. WILSON:** You are in a situation where you can't affect the ambient levels very much.

**PREUSS:** That's correct.

**J. WILSON:** It is very close to what Lester [Lave] correctly described as the "acceptable risk level" to which he sees the Agency moving. That must put you in a very uncomfortable position if you're going to rely on quantitative risk assessment.

**PREUSS:** To a very large degree, decisions are made on factors other than the quantitative risk assessment. If you examine the locations of the major exposures to formaldehyde, it's fairly clear that there are three major exposures. The first is in the occupational setting; the second is to people who live in mobile homes; and the third is to people who, because of changes in the U.S. construction industry over the last 5 years, live in new homes, or to people who live in homes that have had urea formaldehyde foam insulation installed. I think the answer is, of course, to reduce those levels significantly. I would certainly agree with Jim [Swenberg] that one of the important places to start is the occupational setting. I don't believe that any of the agencies are going to try to achieve zero risk for the ambient and the background levels. It is understood that there is always going to be some kind of background level. But I think the agencies will probably try and get the formaldehyde levels down below where they are today.

**J. WILSON:** Well, they can't get way below where they are today. You can reduce things by a factor of two or ten. Relatively speaking, that's a lot.

**ALBERT:** I would urge you to rethink your position on the uncertainties of quantitative risk assessment. You talk about quantitative risk assessment as being very uncertain, but that isn't really true. If you look at it from the standpoint of its ability to give an upper limit risk estimate, it isn't very uncertain. I think it probably provides a very good upper limit of risk; namely, it's very unlikely that the risk is higher than predicted by the linear extrapolation model. That's a very important distinction because, as you pointed out, when you get upper limit estimates that are negligible, everybody feels quite reassured. If the risks are negligible, even with a conservative approach to estimating risk, there is a pretty strong signal that no strenuous action is called for. This points to a very practical approach to using risk assessment for regulation. If you can demonstrate by the use of upper limit estimates that the risk is negligible, that's fine, you don't do anything about it; if the risk is not negligible, you do something about it. What you do is essentially what you can do from a practical standpoint, namely, economic and technical feasibility.

**PREUSS:** You can run into a problem. We have previously discussed the CPSC's risk assessment on people who live in homes with urea formaldehyde foam insulation. Let's accept your proposition that this estimate is a reasonable upper bound.

**ALBERT:** You didn't use the benign tumors.

**J. WILSON:** It doesn't change the upper limits, does it?

**ALBERT:** It changes it by a factor of ten.

**PREUSS:** If we use the new computer models that Crump has put out, which are more sensitive, we raise it by a factor of—what is it, Murray [Cohn], two?

**COHN:** Yes, 2–2½.

**ALBERT:** No. We just did it. It's a factor of nine.

**PREUSS:** That's just a change in the model from the way we did it before.

**COHN:** It's the difference between using Global 79 and Global 83.

**PREUSS:** And then, when we add the benign tumors, we get a factor of nine, so that the upper limit can go up to about 500 from our original estimate of about 50 per million. Now, let's assume we had done it that way. I don't know that such an exercise would have been very helpful to the person who's trying to make the decision. You can do the same kind of thing for the risk of people living in mobile homes and that's about what you'd have—a lower limit of about zero, ranging through 500 using malignant tumors only, up to an estimate of about 5000 per million if the benign tumors are added.

**ALBERT:** Where did that zero come from?

**PREUSS:** It's approximately zero and is obtained using the MLE from the multistage rather than the upper confidence limit. It gives you a very low number. Clearly it is not zero, but it is very low.

**ALBERT:** It's a very unstable estimate. A small difference in likelihood can give a large excursion in exposure for a given level of risk.

**PREUSS:** The question still remains: What is it that I'm going to tell the person making the decision, even granting everything that you've said? Am I going to tell him that the range is from some low number up to 500; is it up to 5000; or am I going to say that the chances are that 5000 is a likely upper limit for people living in mobile homes for x number of years?

**ALBERT:**   You tell them: "It's possible that it is as high as 5000. If you don't think that's worth bothering with, fine. But if you do, you'd better do something about it; namely, what's practical."

**MERRILL:**   But whether it is worth doing something hinges, in part, on whether that number is one in which they can have any confidence. If it is a flat prediction, then it's worth doing something about. If it's a hedged number of an upper limit of 5000 but a lower bound of zero and a probable estimate of 15 or 20, the decision maker doesn't know whether it is worth doing anything about.

**PREUSS:**   My concern, Roy [Albert], is that all of the qualifications get lost and we focus on that number. Then we lose the concept of a plausible upper limit. We lose all the rest of it, and the head of the Agency says, "I have a possible risk of 5000 per million here from this kind of situation," without understanding the rest of it.

**J. WILSON:**   I agree with you.

**PERERA:**   I would like to go back to a point that Dr. Pike made earlier. He said you can't necessarily look at that as an upper limit; the real risk might be several orders of magnitude lower or higher. In extrapolating from the animal model, we face the problems that Dr. Gillette and others have discussed— namely that the human population is genetically heterogeneous and likely to be much more variable in response than the animals and that humans have concurrent exposures to other agents. These factors could lead to a greater susceptibility. When Dr. Albert says that is definitely the upper limit, and that's as high as the risk could possibly be, I'm not so sure we can be that certain. It could be off either way by orders of magnitude.

**ALBERT:**   Give us an example.

**J. WILSON:**   I'll give you an example. Suppose you're making a decision on whether or not to license this new drug that's called thalidomide. You have done animal testing on it, and you have calculated, based on the animal tests, an upper limit to the probability that it will cause teratogenic response.

**PETO:**   Surely the tests were done on thalidomide. They looked nasty and the evidence was suppressed. It's interesting that the most egregious example you can find was one where a process of this sort was deliberately bypassed.

**PREUSS:**   But the point is, Frederica [Perera], I was granting Roy's [Albert] point for the purposes of discussion. The fact of the matter is that everybody here is talking about how difficult the risk assessment process is and how uncertain we are about our estimates at various stages of the assessment. What I find disturbing is that the decision makers are focusing only on the number that we give them. When the EPA Administrator announced his actions on EDB, he didn't talk about "possible ranges." The discussion within the Federal government focused on whether EPA's assessment, or FDA's assessment, or USDA's assessment was correct; they differed by a factor of seven, I think. The rest of the science was forgotten, and the uncertainties put aside.

**ALBERT:** I am not trying to play down the uncertainty. I am talking about an approach to dealing with these uncertainties from a practical regulatory standpoint. You use the risk assessment at its maximum strength, to define risks which you are content to regard as negligible.

**J. WILSON:** Do you mean a worst case approach?

**ALBERT:** That's right. If a risk is not negligible, the assessment should trigger some action.

**J. WILSON:** You have too much faith in your data.

**ALBERT:** If you don't want to do it that way, give us another approach.

**J. WILSON:** If you say "This is the best that we can do and we have to do something," I'll agree with you. But that's very different from saying "The number is real; it means something; and we are going to predict the risk accurately," because you're not.

**PREUSS:** But are you willing to go along with the number?

**J. WILSON:** Yes.

**PETO:** Which is the upper limit.

**SWENBERG:** But it is not presented as an upper limit. It's presented as an absolute number.

**ALBERT:** No, it is presented as an upper limit.

**SWENBERG:** Not to the media.

**COHN:** That's a different story.

**NEEL:** It doesn't come through as an upper limit.

**ALBERT:** This may be a failure in communication, but it seems to me the job here is to try to get a handle on what to do about risk assessment. I don't accept the position that if you do good bioassays you are very likely to miss something horrendous.

**J. WILSON:** If you know what to look for.

**ALBERT:** If you take the known human carcinogens and test them properly in animals, you find a very good concordance between animal and human responses. It may not be in the same organ, but there is a correspondence between animals and humans.

**SWENBERG:** Nobody is arguing against that.

**ALBERT:** The counterargument to using the upper limit estimate to define a negligible level of risk from a regulatory standpoint is that you should not ignore levels of risk, which turn out to be negligible, from animal data. That is the point.

**PERERA:** What I said was I don't know whether we can be certain that that is in fact the upper level.

**ALBERT:** Which means that even when the risk is negligible, you're advocating regulatory action.

**PERERA:** No. I was arguing with the terminology that you used—that this is the maximum possible risk. I'm saying that it might or might not be.

**ALBERT:** All I am saying is that you have to take a position; and if it isn't that position, then it's got to be another one.

# Concluding Remarks

**I. BERNARD WEINSTEIN**
Division of Environmental Sciences
School of Public Health and the Cancer Center
Columbia University
New York, New York 10032

The subject of this conference reminds me of the comment made by the biostatistician Marvin Schneiderman that "risk extrapolation is dangerous." I think that we all share considerable concern about the scientific basis for current approaches to risk extrapolation. We might now focus, therefore, on the following questions: How can we improve the state of the science in this field; and what are the scientific needs in laboratory studies, in epidemiology, and in policymaking?

At the same time, I don't think we should be too discouraged by the current state of the field because, as Peter Hutt mentioned at the beginning of our conference, this endeavor is only a few decades old. The subject of chemical toxicity is extremely complicated; and the biology and biochemical mechanisms are just being revealed. The latter advances offer considerable promise for improving the scientific basis for risk assessment.

I am also impressed by the fact that, in the field of chemical toxicity, approaches to risk extrapolation are being attempted with a much greater precision than exists in several other "older" areas of risk extrapolation, such as physical hazards. The problem of predicting chemical hazards to human health is more complicated than that of physical hazards, such as the risks of driving an automobile. Furthermore, we have lived with the problem of assessing physical hazards for a much longer period of time, and a cultural wisdom has developed. The problem of assessing chemical hazards is relatively new to both scientists and the general public. In a sense, it is a consequence of the chemical revolution in industry. Both scientists and the general public must develop experience in this new area of risk assessment. Although I am skeptical that the assessment of chemical hazards can ever be done with great quantitative precision, the problem is an extremely important one with respect to public health and we should make every effort to improve our skills in this area.

How can we improve the sources of data that are used for such purposes? The current sources of data include: rodent bioassays, short-term tests, and epidemiology. Can entirely new methods be developed? The field is relatively new and there are rapid advances in the biomedical sciences and in biotechnology that could provide new concepts and methods. At this conference we have discussed the use of molecular methods and the concept of molecular epidemiology. Hopefully, these and other new approaches will help to solve some of the major problems related to risk extrapolation including: (1) the extrapolation from data obtained at high dose to the predicted risk at low dose; (2) the extrapolation from one species (often rodents) to another (humans); (3) the extrapolation from a subset of the human population to the general population, or from a high-dose human exposure to a low-dose human exposure; (4) the extrapolation from a well-defined experimental condition, usually with only one variable (i.e., exposure to vinyl chloride or formaldehyde), to a human exposure situation where there may be previous or concurrent exposure to other agents that can enhance or inhibit the effect of the agent in question; (5) variations between humans in terms of susceptibility factors (both inherited and acquired); and (6) the problem of extrapolating from a very simple biologic system (i.e., bacterial or somatic cell mutagenesis assays) to the much more complex intact human organism.

An obvious limitation in conventional epidemiologic studies is that the endpoint that is scored is the occurrence of cancer. This limits the number of cases (or "markers"). Because of the long latent period in cancer development and other factors, the epidemiologic approach limits our sensitivity and makes it difficult to establish cause and effect relations. It would be desirable, therefore, to have surrogate endpoints that can be scored in humans and are predictive of an increased cancer risk. The immunoassays for carcinogen-DNA adducts that were discussed at this conference are only one example of the types of biochemical or molecular markers that might be developed for the "on-line" monitoring of humans. I am confident that through imaginative research and collaborative efforts between laboratory scientists and epidemiologists additional methods can be developed that will provide a sound scientific basis for public policies related to risk quantitation.

# Concluding Remarks

**DAVID G. HOEL***
Radiation Effects Research Foundation
5-2 Hijiyama Park
Hiroshima 730, Japan

As has been discussed in this conference, quantitative risk assessment is playing a greater and greater role in public health decisionmaking. Various government agencies have been attempting to reduce this process and its many scientific components into an algorithm that they can apply to most chemical agents. Further, there is now the curious interest in attempting to adopt the same algorithm by all Federal agencies. Some feel that this would reduce, or possibly eliminate, the conflicting results that are sometimes observed. What must be recognized by those in the risk management area is that risk assessments should incorporate as much relevant information as possible. As such, each chemical or group of chemicals will essentially be unique in its risk analysis. Therefore, we should consider risk assessment on a case by case basis.

As Dr. Weinstein has pointed out, molecular techniques hold the real promise of advancing risk estimation beyond its current state of development. It is expected that these techniques will provide the key information on issues such as dose-response functions, population heterogeneity, and species differences. Data gathered at the molecular level which address these points would then be combined with the usual measures of toxicity to produce risk estimates with much greater scientific confidence and precision. Even with the great amount of data, both animal and human, accumulated on the carcinogenic effects of ionizing radiation, we find continuing debates on the shape of dose-response curves, the effects of dosage patterns, and the degree of population heterogeneity.

Molecular techniques will be especially important in the area of human monitoring for exposure to toxic chemicals. There is a pressing need to understand the possible hazards associated with chemical dump sites. Since chemical dumps usually consist of a variety of chemicals, some of which are unknown, ordinary risk analysis techniques are inadequate for describing multiple exposures resulting from these sites. Therefore, we must develop sensitive techniques for studying individuals who have been exposed. Although analyses for chromosomal aberrations are used, we need methods with greater sensitivity which measure both exposure and effects.

The future of risk assessment lies in the development of molecular methods in order to address both population monitoring and the assumptions used in quantitative modeling. In the meantime, public health officials must treat each risk assessment

---

* On leave from the National Institute of Environmental Health Sciences, Research Triangle Park, North Carolina

as an individual case in which all data and theories are incorporated into the analysis. The attempts at arriving at a consensus on a single, detailed quantitative technique are, in my opinion, ill-founded and likely to produce more heat than light. What is needed instead is a greater emphasis on research, so that the quantitative methodologies will advance at an accelerated rate.

# Concluding Remarks

**FREDERICA P. PERERA**
Division of Environmental Sciences
School of Public Health
Columbia University
New York, New York 10032

I agree with Dr. Weinstein's conclusion about the need for caution in carrying out and interpreting quantitative risk assessments. Uncertainties at each step of the process should be clearly recognized by scientists, policymakers, and the public. The magnitude of the uncertainty means that, although their use in setting priorities for regulation is appropriate, certain other applications of quantitative risk assessment, such as formal cost-benefit analysis to set regulatory goals, is not. It also means that the risk estimates could be "off" either way by several orders of magnitude. The greater public health concern is that the assessments not underestimate the risk to humans, since a 10–100-fold error in that direction could have very serious health consequences. Therefore, it seems prudent, as a policy matter, to base priority-setting decisions on the estimated upper limit of risk derived from a linearized extrapolation model.

In regard to the "acceptable" levels of risk for individual carcinogens, several speakers have suggested that we need to see lifetime risks of one in 100 or one in 1000 to be concerned. I believe that this is a myopic attitude deriving from the fact that we always talk about risk assessments for a single substance as if it existed in a void. We forget that humans are exposed to a considerable number of carcinogenic substances or agents with possible additive or interactive effects. For example, if we assume simple additivity of risks on background exposures and ongoing carcinogenic processes, we can calculate that exposure to ten carcinogens, each with estimated lifetime risks of one in 1,000,000, would put us in a one in 100,000 risk category. Nine more risks of that magnitude moves us to the one in 10,000 category and so forth. Therefore, federal cancer policies to date have wisely characterized risks of one in 1,000,000 as "actionable." Agencies then do what is practically possible, given economic and technological considerations, to reduce risks of that magnitude or higher.

Another misconception is that most chemicals cause cancer in animal bioassays and that conservative risk assessment policies will result in regulating almost all chemicals. Given that there are over 40,000 chemicals in commercial use in the U.S., and as many as 500–1000 new ones are introduced each year, this would mean a hopeless regulatory situation. However, such is not the case. If we look at industrial pesticides that have been tested in the rodent bioassay, only an estimated 10–15% have given some evidence of carcinogenicity. These include many chemicals selected for testing because they were already suspected of being carcinogenic.

**347**

Thus, it is not true that "everything out there will give you cancer." Moreover, carcinogens vary widely in potency and in magnitude of estimated risk—hence in terms of needed stringency of regulation.

For these reasons, I am optimistic that the problem is manageable and that we can reduce the burden of human cancer by promptly identifying carcinogens, assessing their risk, and applying preventive risk management policies. That process is greatly facilitated by established cancer policies, such as EPA's, which provide consistent guidelines for risk assessors within and between agencies.

Using such agreed-upon principles, we should do what we can now to set priorities for regulation using risk assessment as one of the tools. At the same time, we should encourage new scientific approaches that can improve the process. The development of molecular markers to detect and quantitate dose and response to carcinogens holds great promise for reducing the uncertainties in risk assessment as currently practiced.

## CORPORATE SPONSORS OF COLD SPRING HARBOR LABORATORY

Agrigenetics Corporation
Biogen, Inc.
CPC International, Inc.
E.I. du Pont de Nemours & Company
Genentech, Inc.
Genetics Institute
Hoffmann-La Roche Inc.
Johnson & Johnson
Eli Lilly & Company
Molecular Genetics, Inc.
Monsanto Company
Pall Corporation
Pfizer, Inc.
Schering Corporation
Upjohn Company

## CORE SUPPORTERS OF THE BANBURY CENTER

The Bristol-Myers Fund, Inc.
The Dow Chemical Company
Exxon Corporation
Grace Foundation Inc.
International Business Machines Corporation
Phillips Chemical Company
Texaco Philanthropic Foundation Inc.

# Name Index

# Subject Index

Biological stochastic models, as dose-response models, 121

Biomonitoring
definition, 212
methods of, 213

Bladder tumors, and high levels of orthophenyl phenate, 244

Boyle, Robert, and development of chemistry to detect food adulteration, 17

Cadmium, duration of exposure to and respiratory cancer, 67

Cancer
age and time dependence of in asbestos exposure, 90–91
annual deaths from in U.S., 10
death rate, risk goal for regarding nuclear power, 6
doubling dose, relationship of to genetic doubling dose, 169
gastrointestinal
epidemiological studies of, 58–59
use of asbestos to estimate risk of, 55–64
incidence, in asbestos workers, 89–93
liver, relationship of to aflatoxin in peanuts, 39–40
lung
and asbestos exposure, 90
and exposure to asbestos, welding, and radiation, 72
model for, 91–92
in nickel refinery workers, 93
and PAH exposure, 59–62
rates of in nonsmokers as comparison, 63
relative risks of in smokers, 85
risk of in British carbonization workers, 62
risk of in U.S. coke oven workers, 62–63
and smoking, choice of risk model to estimate, 83–84
urban-rural comparisons of, 63
use of polyaromatic hydrocarbons to estimate risk of, 55–64
nasal sinus, in nickel refinery workers, 93
respiratory, and duration of exposure to cadmium, 67
risk, use of epidemiological data in assessing, 79–87
stomach
exposure to radiation, choice of risk model for, 82–83
relative risk of in A-bomb survivors, 83
relative risk of in ankylosing spondylitis, 83
relative risk of in irradiated cervical cancer patients, 83

Carbonization workers, study of PAH exposure and lung cancer in, 62

Carcinogen. See also Specific names.
DNA binding, monitoring method for carcinogen exposure, 211–229
early stage, risk estimation for, 11–112
expression of effective dose of, 120
human
categorization of, 322
possible, categorization of, 323
probable, categorization of, 323

Carcinogenesis
multifactor, human, 235–236
multistage, 231
human, 235–236
model of, 93–95
relevance of to risk assessment, 231–240
somatic mutation theory of, 241

Carcinogenic potency
correlation of with toxicity, 146–148
probability distribution for, 141
vs. acute toxicity, 140

Carcinogenic process
equation for model of, 121
model for, 120

Carcinogenic risks, human, estimation of, 275

Carcinogenicity
assessment of evidence for, EPA system, 321–323
correlation of with mutagenicity, 151–152
correlation of with toxicity, 140–141
evaluation of by spontaneous tumor incidence, 326
qualitative evidence for, 309–312
quantitative evidence for, 313–318

Carcinogens. See also Specific names.
complete, 232
determination of acceptable levels of risk for, 347
formulation of risk goals for, 5–6
initiating, 232
late-stage, risk estimation for, 110–113
as mutagens, 168–170
safety factor for, 20–21
secondary, and Delaney Clause, 25–26
suspect, EPA guidelines for health assessment of, 307–329

Carcinoma, zymbal gland, after benzene exposure, 116–117

Cell proliferation, as factor in DNA repair, 131

Cell replication, role of in low-dose risk estimates, 264

CERCLA. See Comprehensive Environmental Response, Compensation, and Liability Act.

Chadwick, and importance of sanitation for public health, 17

Chemical Industry Institute of Toxicology formaldehyde bioassay, 270–271